T0341483

THAT FURTHER SHORE

That
Further Shore

A MEMOIR OF IRISH ROOTS AND AMERICAN PROMISE

John D. Feerick

FORDHAM UNIVERSITY PRESS   NEW YORK   2020

Copyright © 2020 Fordham University Press

All rights reserved. No part of this publication may be reproduced, stored in
a retrieval system, or transmitted in any form or by any means — electronic,
mechanical, photocopy, recording, or any other — except for brief quotations
in printed reviews, without the prior permission of the publisher.

Fordham University Press has no responsibility for the persistence or accuracy
of URLs for external or third-party Internet websites referred to in this
publication and does not guarantee that any content on such websites is, or
will remain, accurate or appropriate.

Fordham University Press also publishes its books in a variety of electronic
formats. Some content that appears in print may not be available in electronic
books.

Visit us online at www.fordhampress.com.

Library of Congress Control Number: 2020901993

Printed in the United States of America

22 21 20   5 4 3 2 1

First edition

This book is dedicated to Emalie, the love of my life, and our family, and in memory of my dear parents.

Contents

Foreword

Thomas J. Shelley

Unlike many egocentric chroniclers of their own life, John Feerick fills this delightful Bronx tale with expressions of gratitude to the many individuals and institutions that enabled this firstborn child of Irish immigrants to attend Fordham College and Fordham Law School. The recollections of his childhood years provide a rare and uniquely evocative social history of the long-vanished world of the Hibernian South Bronx.

Within seven years of graduation from Fordham Law School, John Feerick became a partner in a small New York City law firm that developed into a well-known and prestigious firm in the New York legal world. John was also asked to participate in the drafting of the Twenty-Fifth Amendment to the Constitution of the United States. Fourteen years later, in 1982, he readily sacrificed a lucrative private law practice to become the dean of the Fordham Law School because, as he said, "There was something strong within me saying it was time to give back something to the world." Father James C. Finlay, S.J., the president of Fordham University, was ecstatic at John's acceptance of the deanship.

As dean of Fordham Law School, John established a phenomenal record as a fundraiser. Academically he addressed a long-standing concern by reducing the student-to-faculty ratio and managed to help raise academic standards at the same time that the School was maintaining a high enrollment and diversifying the student body as well as the faculty and administrative staff. In 1984 he began the first expansion of the physical facilities of the Law School in more than two decades, and in 2000 he inaugurated a campaign for a new Law School building that was dedicated in 2014. He demonstrated his commitment to public service by establishing several centers or institutes, most notably the

Stein Institute of Law and Ethics, the Public Interest Resource Center, and the Joseph R. Crowley Program in International Human Rights.

Dean Feerick established a reputation that continues to the present day as a respected constitutional scholar, dedicated public servant, political reformer, and facilitator of peace in the land of his ancestors. He has been called upon to mediate and arbitrate many disputes, and has served as chair of the board of the American Arbitration Association as well as president of the New York City Bar Association and the Citizens Union Foundation.

On three occasions, beginning in 1987, governors of New York State have prevailed upon John to head state commissions on government integrity and ethical standards. The first commission, the Commission on Government Integrity in 1987 (sometimes called the Feerick Commission) developed an ethics reform agenda for the state.

John was told that the success of this commission influenced another governor to select John twenty years later to chair the newly formed State Commission on Public Integrity. In making the announcement of this appointment, the governor explained that he had asked John to chair this commission because "he is pre-eminent among all New Yorkers in standing for the principles of integrity in government." The New York Times concurred, stating in an editorial that the governor could not have made a better choice to head this commission because of John's "sterling reputation" for integrity. When John stepped down as dean in July 2002, he had served in that position for twenty years, setting the second longest record in the history of Fordham Law School.

No matter how famous John has become, he has never forgotten his roots. He is immensely proud that he is the son of Irish immigrants from whom he inherited his deep Catholic faith, his passion for excellence in everything that he does, his commitment to hard work, and dedication to social justice for all of God's children. He is equally generous in expressing his gratitude to Emalie, his wife of fifty-seven years, and to his six children and his grandchildren, and to his siblings.

He has also frequently acknowledged his debt to the Ursuline Sisters and the scandalously underpaid lay teachers who staffed St. Angela Merici parochial school where he received his elementary school education. For many years John has been a zealous supporter of this school, which is now a thriving inner-city Catholic school in the poverty-stricken South Bronx. It is a long-standing example of his commitment "to give back something to the world." Today it enables a new generation of Hispanic, African American, and African children to enjoy the advantages of a Catholic education that New York's first archbishop, John Hughes, made possible 150 years ago for the descendants of Irish immigrants like John Feerick.

A colleague and close friend of John was not surprised to hear mention of John's modesty. He said that no one will ever be able to write a comprehensive biography of John because he did so many admirable things quietly, unobtrusively, out of the public eye, especially for his colleagues, students, and alumni and alumnae.

Robert Caro once asked Robert Moses why he admired Governor Alfred E. Smith so much. Moses replied that Governor Smith (for Moses, Smith was always Governor Smith, never Al Smith) was always loyal to the people with whom he worked. That loyalty has also been abundantly evident both in John's distinguished professional career and throughout his personal life.

Another apposite comparison comes to mind. At the conclave that elected Cardinal Jorge Bergoglio Pope in 2013, as it became evident that Bergoglio would be the next Pope, the Brazilian Cardinal Claudio Hummes, a Franciscan friar, trusted friend, and outspoken advocate of social justice, turned to Bergoglio in the Sistine Chapel and whispered to him affectionately, "Don't forget the poor." No one ever felt the need to whisper those words to John Feerick.

Msgr. Thomas J. Shelley,
July 19, 2019

Preface

We are workers, not master builders; ministers, not messiahs.
We are prophets of a future not our own.
— ARCHBISHOP OSCAR ROMERO PRAYER: A STEP ALONG THE WAY

The writing of this book has been challenging. There is joy in glancing back and reliving happy moments in one's life. But it is by no means easy to review the past and focus on loved ones and friends who no longer are around. To leave behind some accounting, however, is important to me for many reasons. My brother Donald wanted me to write a book about our parents, Mary Jane and John Feerick—a request that influenced me in more ways than can be described. My sister Maureen told me that Mom had in mind recounting her own family history, giving to Maureen for safekeeping a box of photographs of us as children.

In an oral history in 2005, Maureen said:

I like to recall those early years. They remind us where we came from and how we became who we are. I think if we didn't come from this kind of background, maybe things would be different. And there were good days, and there were sad days when we lost members of the family and were confronted with other kinds of challenges. There were hard times for Mom and Pop, difficult times, maybe not having enough money to do things. Going forward I feel a book of memories would be a boon to our children and grandchildren.

I hoped this book would be shorter, but there was so much I wanted to impart. At the end of the day, to borrow from a poem by Kathryn Cahill: "It is my magnum opus / Where patterns from a life / Spread out before you / Slivered fragments of my soul / In every room. / It is my statement, / My wailing at the moon."

In the pages that follow, I tell what my grandson Ian described as a grandfather story. I begin this book with my ancestry and early-life experiences before delving into my career as a practicing attorney and law school dean, my public service involvements, and my role in helping to craft an amendment to the U.S. Constitution. However, it is my family, most especially, and the friends and opportunities that came along that have given me the most joy.

So hope for a great sea-change
On the far side of revenge.
Believe that further shore
Is reachable from here.
Believe in miracle
And cures and healing wells.

— SEAMUS HEANEY, *THE CURE AT TROY:*
A VERSION OF SOPHOCLES' PHILOCTETES

Introduction

The tide recedes, but leaves behind bright seashells on the sand. The sun goes down, but gentle warmth still lingers on the land. The music stops, yet echoes on in sweet, soulful refrains. For every joy that passes, something beautiful remains.

— UNKNOWN AUTHOR

In the summer of 2009, I had the special joy of watching my oldest child, Maureen LeBlanc, and four of my grandchildren, Ryan, Connor, Liam, and Roddy, climb to the top of Croagh Patrick in County Mayo.[1] My youngest daughter, Rosemary, would have climbed along with us, but her son Ian had other ideas after they started up the mountain that windy and rainy July day. Croagh Patrick is one of the holiest of sites in Ireland and has a small chapel on the summit, 2,507 feet up. How far I went is clouded in debate. My claim of halfway was found "excessive" by my grandchildren.

What took me to Ireland was a desire to share with some of my children and grandchildren the beauty and history of Mayo, the county in which Mom and Pop were born. Ireland has thirty-two counties, but Mayo is the one dearest to me.

Mom and Pop lived humble and simple lives. They spent their youth in Ireland, their adult years in the Bronx, and their final years in Lake Carmel, north of New York City. Their remains rest in the St. Lawrence O'Toole Cemetery in Brewster, New York, beneath a double tombstone inscribed with these locations that they called home and a Celtic cross. The tombstone identifies them as Mary Jane Boyle, so that Mom's maiden name is never forgotten, and John Feerick, for whom a middle name was never established. (Pop said

he had no middle name, but when he needed a middle initial, he used "J.")
With their deaths began my quest to tell their story and mine, as their firstborn.

I began by searching genealogical records, visiting websites on the Feerick,
Moran, and Boyle surnames, and speaking to relatives and neighbors in both
Ireland and America. I examined church records, read books and newspapers,
combed through family scrapbooks, spoke extensively with relatives, studied
census reports of Ireland and the United States, and collected whatever notes
or scraps of paper I could find in my old file cabinets of weathered folders.

I found that standing on a dock in Queenstown (Cobh), County Cork,
Ireland, where Mom and Pop, both teenagers, stood as they set off to travel
to America in the 1920s, gave me a sense of their history and the challenge
that had awaited them. Locating the passenger lists of the ships on which they
came to America and their U.S. citizenship applications and supporting documents gave me an enormous lift, and the small but rich library of the Bronx
County Historical Society allowed me to learn more about the borough in
which they settled.

But it was in cemeteries where my quest for origins gained a foothold.

A search for the graves of my grandfathers proved most difficult. On my first
trip to Ireland in 1989, I met for the first time Mom's brother, John Boyle. He
was then 88 and confined to a nursing home in Ballina, Mayo. At my request,
he agreed to take me to the grave of his father and my grandfather, Patrick
Boyle, who had died on September 13, 1915.

The grave was located at an old cemetery in Toomore in Foxford, Mayo,
Mom's place of birth. On arriving, John directed me toward a distant area
surrounded by overgrown weeds where many cracked and tilting headstones
protruded from the ground. "Your grandfather's grave is over there," he said,
pointing.

With difficulty I made my way through the maze of graves, my feet sinking into the ground on occasion. I couldn't tell which stone or wood post
belonged to my grandfather, as most of the names of the headstones were
illegible, having faded over the years. Because of the rocky terrain and John's
age, it was too hard for him to reach the gravesite to show me. Finally, I simply
told him, "I see it," and we left. I would return on other occasions to look for
it, but I never did find it.[2]

Fortunately, in Craggagh, another Mayo cemetery, I had no trouble finding
the tombstone of John and Mom's mother, Maria Moran Boyle. Elsewhere
at Craggagh I found tombstones of other relatives, including my maternal
great-grandparents, Robert and Mary McNulty Moran.

On Pop's side of the family, I encountered similar challenges. Local people who knew his father, David Feerick, said that his grave could be found in an old section of the Ballinrobe Town Cemetery. But that cemetery also was hard to navigate for the same reasons as the one in Toomore. However, the grave-digger there asked if he could help. He was quite elderly, dressed in raggedy clothes, and I was reluctant to rely on his favor, frustrated and hopeless as I was. Still, I gave him my name and number. To my astonishment, the next day he called to tell me where I could find my grandfather's grave.

I rushed over to the cemetery with my cousins Mary and Kevin Boyle and found a headstone bearing his name in a newer section. At the top of the headstone was the name of Mary McDermott, his sister-in-law, followed underneath by the names of David Feerick, Ellen McDermott (Pop's mother), and their son, Martin Feerick. However, Mary had died on June 3, 1950, and the headstone had been erected by Pop's mother, who died in 1964, and Martin died in 1985. My grandfather died in 1944, which seemed to pre-date this newer section. I was left wondering whether my grandfather was actually buried in an older section of the cemetery, his name having been placed in this section as a matter of convenience.

With the help of my daughter Maureen and five of my grandchildren, I checked out this theory in the summer of 2009. Encouraged by a one hundred–dollar reward, my grandchildren quickly set off to locate a gravesite with the name David Feerick. Mary and Kevin joined in the search. But no sight of a David Feerick was to be found there. I still gave my grandchildren the one hundred dollars.

Although the search for my grandparents' graves resulted in some success, finding the location of their parents' graves proved far more difficult. I had no success locating the graves of my great- or great-great-grandparents (except for Robert Moran and Mary McNulty). In 2009, acting on a suggestion from a relative, I visited Teampall Maol, an old cemetery near Foxford dedicated to victims of the famine of the 1840s, the black flu, and the Irish War of Independence. But as hard as I tried, I couldn't identify the precise location of my ancestors, if any of their remains were even there.

Tracing a family history, however, provides unexpected surprises. In 2002, as I was writing a tribute in memory of Fordham Law graduate John M. Moran, a courageous firefighter who died in the September 11th terrorist attack on the World Trade Center, I learned from Uncle Pat that I had a granduncle with the same name and occupation.[3] Uncle Pat said that he had lost his life in a building collapse in Chicago in 1911. With the help of New York City Fire Commissioner Nicholas Scoppetta and his Chicago counterpart, I learned of my great-uncle's heroic death in a theater at the age of 35, which had been prominently covered in the local newspapers of May 14, 1911. John's name continues to be honored in that fire department's history, just as John Moran's name is remembered for his heroism on September 11th.

The members of Chicago's fire department expressed to me regret that John's daughter's name had not been listed on his tombstone, though her remains are buried there with her parents and brother. When her father died, she was just a few months old. She lived a long life but had no family of her own. Her brother, John, who was a young child in 1911, didn't live beyond age 21, and their mother died many years later. When she died, no one was left from the immediate family to inscribe her name.

Deeply affected by this, I decided to do something about it. First I had to find her given name and gather more details. A person associated with the fire department suggested that I go to the Cook County Clerk's Office. Upon arriving, I mistakenly identified Cook County as the place of death of a "Margaret Moran." The person on duty said the computer system showed no one with that name buried in Cook County but offered to check the records for a suburb called Lombard.

There she found the following information: A Marguerite Moran, born in 1911, had died in 1995 and was buried at Mount Carmel Cemetery in Lombard. I immediately headed to the cemetery and arranged to have her name placed on John Moran's tombstone.

I passed along to the Morans of County Mayo a picture of the tombstone with Marguerite's name alongside the names of her parents and brother. We shared tears of joy, knowing a long-forgotten member of our extended family was now reclaimed for posterity.

But not all of my searches brought me to distant graveyards. One search occurred a short distance from home. In 2012, encouraged by my daughter Jean, I began searching for the grave of my great-aunt and godmother, Honora "Nora" Feerick Pire, a sister of Pop's father. I recall visits she'd made to our apartment in the Bronx when I was young to help Pop out when Mom was ill and hospitalized.

Nora had been born in the Parish of Neale in Mayo in the early 1880s. She came to America as a teenager, passing through Ellis Island in 1902 and heading upstate to Schenectady, New York, to stay with a cousin and find a job, working, at different times, as a waitress, a servant, and a maid. She married Arthur Pire, who had come to America from Belgium. They had a child, John Julius Pire (nicknamed "Jackie"), who was born on Christmas of 1915.

Jackie died at just one month of age on January 24, 1916, apparently from the flu. A High Mass was celebrated for him at St. John the Baptist Church in Schenectady. He was temporarily buried in a potter's field along with other children, perhaps for economic reasons. On June 18, 1918, his parents bought a burial site, one large enough to accommodate six graves, where he now rests. At some point Nora and Arthur divorced, after which she lived alone in Schenectady. During those years Pop appears to have been her closest friend.

When Nora died on September 8, 1963, she was buried next to her son after a funeral Mass at St. John the Baptist Church. Aside from Pop, who was the executor of her will, I'm not aware of any relative visiting her gravesite, and I lament the fact that it took me so long to do so. I undertook such a journey in the spring of 2012. Although I couldn't find her grave, I was struck by the beauty of the cemetery and how carefully maintained it was.

I approached a woman who was sprinkling wine on her husband's grave and told her what I was looking for. She said she would speak to the caretaker, who to my surprise called me a few days later to pass on what he had in his file regarding Nora and her child: their graves were located in the cemetery's Section Five.

I returned to the cemetery that July, met the caretaker, and set about my search. I walked back and forth among the plots, hoping the names would appear and be legible. Some graves had only a single identifying letter of the alphabet; other tombstones were very small and marked with faded names.

Then, almost by accident, my eye was caught by two very small headstones sitting side by side, one marble-like and the other granite, and each protruding slightly from the ground. On the top of the marble one was the word "Baby" above the words "Jackie Pire" and the year, "1916." The other headstone bore the name "Nora Feerick Pire." I couldn't believe my luck. I said a prayer, took pictures, made notes, and left the cemetery to do research on Nora at the local courthouse.

The luck of the Irish was with me that day. In the courthouse I found that the records of the deceased were well organized and cared for. Within minutes I was given a folder containing details about my Aunt Nora. I discovered that she had died with considerable assets for a woman who had come to this country with barely a penny. Her life savings amounted to $43,455.32, adjusted to $35,042.64 after payment of taxes and expenses. In addition to the $991.87 she had in two savings accounts, she owned stock in three companies — General Motors (200 shares), General Electric (150 shares), and New York Telephone and Telegraph (120 shares) — valued in 1965 at $42,463.45.

Nora's will stipulated that her life's savings were to be distributed to six nephews (including Pop), three nieces, and one grandnephew — me. Her unexpected gift proved life-changing. Most of the beneficiaries, myself and Pop excluded, lived in England or Ireland, where the gift was announced by an Irish newspaper under the headline "Windfall for Irish Cousins." The accompanying article described Nora Pire as a woman with "no children of her own" and noted that she had once, in 1914, returned to her birthplace, Ballinrobe.[4]

Her gift bestowed upon each beneficiary a sum of $3,494, an amount that would have covered my entire tuition at Fordham College several years earlier. Instead, the money became a big part of the down payment for the first house I purchased, at 41 Highridge Road, Mount Kisco, New York.

The trip back home to Larchmont, New York, was emotion-filled. I thought of one of Aunt Nora's visits to my family when she emptied my soft drink into the kitchen sink and threw away my chocolate-filled cupcakes. I recalled responding cheekily and then feeling badly about my conduct, which I still do. Aunt Nora had high standards and expected me to toe the line. The years she toiled in her jobs undoubtedly shaped her approach toward us.

Who would have guessed that she would be the source of a "windfall" that would ripple through and change the lives of so many distant relatives, myself included? Her story encapsulates the profound but sometimes imperceptible web of connections that spanned oceans and continents that have defined and will continue to define my family.

PART I
My Family and Its Irish History

So we beat on, boats against the current, borne back ceaselessly into the past.

— F. SCOTT FITZGERALD

1
What's in a Name?

What's in a name? That which we call a rose
By any other word would smell as sweet.

— WILLIAM SHAKESPEARE

I inherited three of the most popular surnames of Ireland — Boyle, Moran, and McDermott. The surname Feerick, however, is nowhere to be found in the lists of such names, so I decided to devote my greatest effort to pinning down its history.

Growing up, I heard of the surname only once, when Tom Ferrick joined the New York Yankees in 1950 as a relief pitcher. I later met lawyers at American Bar Association (ABA) meetings who said that I reminded them of a Professor Martin Feerick of Tennessee Law School. I also recall Mom telling me of visits made to her apartment in the 1970s by James Feerick, a lawyer in Pennsylvania, and John Feerick, a travel agent from Ballinrobe, both seeking to learn more about us. Unfortunately, I was so busy in those years that I wasn't able to follow up on those visits.

But Pop's death and Mom's declining health dramatically changed the focus of my life. An inner voice told me I should drop everything and go to Ireland to learn more about my family's history and, though I didn't realize it at the time, my own identity. What was it like for Mom and Pop to be children in the West of Ireland? What were their parents and siblings like? These and similar questions began to consume my thoughts.

As my journey into my family's past began, Maureen surprised me with information from the 1930 U.S. Census. She said that the name "John Feerick" appeared 13 times, with nine Feericks living in New York, two in South

Dakota, and two in Missouri. Unfortunately, Pop was not listed at all. According to Maureen, the name "Feerick" appeared 144 times in the census, with most of the Feericks having arrived in the United States after the 1880s. The name "Ferrick/Feerick," along with other spellings, also appeared more than 1,000 times in the 1930 and 1940 Censuses, with many of its owners listing their birthplace as Ireland, England, Hungary, Czechoslovakia, Poland, Germany, and Russia. Of the Ferricks, there were 45 John Ferricks living in the United States.

I would discover that, in Ireland, the name "Feerick" had a longer history than I'd realized, although the various spellings presented special challenges. According to a 1960 National Library of Ireland survey of surnames, "Feerick" appears as "Fearick," "Ferick," "Ferricks," and "Ferrick." Other variations included "Ferack," "Feerack," and "Fyricke." As to the origin of "Feerick," various theories shared with me by John Feerick of Ballinrobe, slightly abridged, said:

(a) According to a local Ballinrobe source, the Feericks were a family of Welsh cotton pickers who immigrated to the Mayo area in the mid-eighteenth century;

(b) They were a Catholic family who emigrated from Northern Ireland after the Battle of the Boyne in the late 1690s. This theory was put forth by Cardinal O'Fee, the late Prelate of All Ireland and a noted Gaelic scholar and historian;

(c) They were originally of Scandinavian origin with "Feerick" being translated from "Fear Ucht," which in Gaelic could be translated to "Man of the North";

(d) They are a subset of the Bermingham family, one of the premier Norman families who came to Ireland in 1171. This was stated by MacLysaght in his history of Irish names; and

(e) They were Scottish in origin.

The genealogist Aiden Feerick, whom I met in the genealogy section of the National Library of Ireland in Dublin, sent me an unexpected letter dated November 15, 2012, which noted the following:

With regard to a), as far as I know, Ireland is not a cotton growing area. I wonder what Welsh cotton pickers were doing there! I can find no documentary evidence to back up that statement.

With regard to b), I went through the list of people who came from Northern Ireland to Connacht and there are traces of surnames

in north, central and east Mayo but none in the Ballinrobe area. A
Michael Feerick from the Neale was among the flax growers who
received financial help in 1796.

With regard to c), it is interesting but I would not go so far as
Sweden to find "a man from the north." The DNA test that I had
done some years ago excludes the typical markers characteristic of the
Scandinavian countries. Could "north" here mean the northern part
of Mayo, around the Ceide Fields, where there had been a farming
population three thousand years before the Christian era?

Regarding d), I have found no documentary evidence linking the
Feerick families with the Berminghams. It is true that in the 1590s
there were Feerick families living in and around Dunmore but in the
Chancery documents from the reign of Queen Elizabeth I, there is no
confusion between Feyrick/Ferrick and Bermingham. The Berminghams took the Gaelic patronymic Mac Feorais just as the other great
Norman families did. The Feerick name in the Gaelic language is
probably Mac Phiaraic/Mac Phiaruic. In another document from the
17th century, there is mention of Walter Bermingham's sept [a clan or
family] without any further elaboration. I do not think you can go from
that to say that the sept took the Bermingham patronymic and moved
from around Dunmore to the area around Ballinrobe. In addition, the
location of that sept was in Dunmore, Co. Galway in "Bermingham
County." Again, going back to the DNA test I did, the typical Norman
markers do not show up. At best, the Feericks were followers of the
Berminghams as distinct from descendants. And even today there is a
cluster of Feerick families in and around Dunmore, Co. Galway.

With regard to e), there is no proof that the Feerick family is of
Scottish origin. Had the family hailed from Scotland there would be
a Feerick clan in that country. To the best of my knowledge, there
is not.[1]

Aiden offered his own conclusions, based on his remarkable scholarship
regarding the surname in Mayo and Galway, as follows:

Evidence of the existence of families called Feerick (or variants) goes
back to the reign of Elizabeth 1; they are mentioned in the Fiants of
that Sovereign in the years 1590 to 1595;[2] the families mentioned were
living in the very north of County Galway in the parishes of Dunmore and Addergoole. In 1783, Father Francis Xavier Blake compiled
a list of parishioners in the Parish of Ballinrobe when he was parish

priest there; 11 Feerick families appear in various townlands in the parish. Evidence for Feerick families in Co. Mayo outside the Parish of Ballinrobe begins when the Tithe Books were compiled between 1823–1834.

Unfortunately, the even longer history of the name remains a mystery to me. Using DNA, Aiden Feerick traced the name back to the Stone Age. Once, Mary Pat Kelly, an Irish author and filmmaker, pointed to a module on my palm that's been associated with a Viking background. But as my law school professor John Calamari would say, "Who knows?"

The surnames associated with Mom and Pop's parents, Boyle, Moran, and McDermott,[3] according to Aiden Feerick, "have a greater presence in Ireland than our surname and the link between your ancestors and the people who bore their names centuries ago will be tenuous." Indeed, the 1890 Census of Ireland shows that Boyle was ranked as the 47th most popular Irish surname, Moran as 56th, and McDermott as 96th.[4] The 1930 U.S. Census also contained thousands of listings of Boyle, with 125 "Mary Boyles" in New York City alone. Mom's name was listed among them, along with the information that she was working for a family in Yonkers, New York, which coincided with what she had told us.

Coat of arms and crest identifications provide further insight into the history behind a surname. Unlike coats of arms, which had to bear the imprimatur of the monarch, crests were easily obtainable. Crests, which date back to Roman times, have uniqueness to them for a family. The Moran coat of arms, for example, uses the colors yellow and gold, which signify generosity, and sable and black, which signify constancy and sometimes grief. The five-pointed star on the coat of arms denotes virtue, learning, and piety. The Boyle coat of arms also includes the colors yellow and gold but adds the color green, signifying hope, joy, and sometimes loyalty in love, along with an oak tree, acorns, and oak leaves, traditional symbols of antiquity and strength.

The McDermott crest includes a motto, "honor probataque virtus" ("honor and approved valor"), and includes the colors gold and yellow but also blue, representing loyalty and truth, and red, the martyr's color, signifying military fortitude and magnanimity. The chevron symbolizes protection, often granted as a reward. The annulet is a symbol of fidelity, and the boar represents the bearing of a warrior. The crosses often represent faith or Christian beliefs, possibly relating to the Crusades.

There was no coat of arms for the surname Feerick, but there are two Feerick crests. One has the colors blue and gold with a shield and helmet. It also has the head of an eagle holding a key in its mouth, along with the motto "fidelitas et veritas," meaning fidelity and truth. The other crest contains lions, which symbolize strength and royalty.

But crests, coats of arms, and traces of royalty were not part of the vocabulary that Mom and Pop passed along to us. They spoke only of their farming history in the West of Ireland.

2
Mom's and Pop's Origins

Those we love will never die as long as we keep their memory alive.
— JEAN AND OLLIE BOYLE

Mom's and Pop's history began in the County of Mayo, in the province of Connacht in the West of Ireland. Mom was born on December 14, 1908, in north Mayo and Pop was born July 12, 1909, in south Mayo. When traveling in Mayo, one glimpses the county's past in fields, cottages, religious sites, and museums. The Céide Fields, the National Museum of Country Life, and Ashford Castle add to the specialness of a Mayo visit. The history of the county involves religious persecution, suppression of the language and culture, land evictions, ravaging famines, and extreme poverty.

Mayo's citizens, arguably, include some of the greatest in Ireland's history, among them the incomparable athlete Martin Sheridan, whose bronze and three gold Olympic medals brought fame to his beloved Mayo in the early twentieth century.

Another was Michael Davitt, the founder and chief organizer of the Land League, which helped to carry out a revolution that would enable tenant-farmers to own their own land.[1] He died in 1906 and is now buried in a cemetery at Straide,[2] five miles from Foxford. My Uncle Pat was proud that his father and grandfather had marched in Davitt's funeral procession: "As long a procession as anyone had ever seen in Ireland," Pat said. As the Irish writer Seumas MacManus noted: "English aggression drove [Davitt] in support of the landlordism whose power it was his manhood's task to break. He succeeded; and dear to Irish hearts is that grave in Mayo which encloses the mortal remains of a man whose spirit could not be broken."[3]

Foxford

Mom's Foxford has a history of music and iron works and is the bridgehead between Castlebar and Ballina. One of the earliest mentions of the village was in a survey of 1682; Foxford was referred to as a plantation of the English and the Scots. According to Aiden Feerick, "Foxford is the anglicized version of the name of the town on the River Moy. The Gaelic name for Foxford is Beal Easa, which means the 'mouth of the waterfall.'" The River Moy, which attracts fishermen from other parts of Ireland, meanders through the village on its way to the sea at Enniscrone, Sligo.

In *Foxford: Through the Arches of Time*, the author tells of the village's strategic importance for the British government, the decline of its music tradition under Cromwell, and the impact of famines on its rustic lifestyle.[4] The author also notes that the poorest of the poor could be found in Foxford and, quoting the *Topographical Dictionary of Ireland*, records that Foxford was a "'place of great antiquity' with 209 houses indifferently built."[5]

The famines of 1845–1849 and of the 1870s left their impact. In an 1880 inspection of Foxford by the British government, an official recorded that he had witnessed "scenes of wretchedness and misery that were wholly indescribable."[6] Of the area where Mom's ancestors lived, the official wrote that "in no Christian country of the world . . . would so barbarous a spectacle be tolerated, except in Ireland."[7]

The townland of Culmore lies outside of Foxford and is divided into an upper and lower area. Upper Culmore, where Mom was born, consisted of twelve to fifteen houses clustered on a hillside and occupied by families who were related by blood or marriage.

The poverty in Foxford led the Irish Sisters of Charity (Mother Agnes Morrogh-Bernard in particular) to take an interest in the village in the 1890s and establish a woolen mill that brought jobs, vibrancy, and attractiveness to the area. Locals became skilled in crafts, creating tweeds, blankets, and rugs that brought some prosperity to the community. The woolen mill continues to produce blankets, sweaters, and other items that are sold worldwide.

Whenever Mom returned to Foxford, she would bring us back gifts from the local area, including material for a tweed suit for me, which I subsequently had made but have never worn. Its country style didn't seem to work for me in New York City! Her favorite shop was Carabine's, across from the woolen mill. The Carabines were special to my family, as members of their family participated in the Irish War of Independence (1919–1921) alongside my uncles.

Ballinrobe

Pop's Ballinrobe is one of several towns that circle two lakes, Lough Carra and Lough Mask. The town was built on the River Robe and developed around a seventh-century church. Ballinrobe became an important economic center when it received permission in 1606 from King James to obtain a market charter. The market brought about an exchange of goods and money, thereby improving the local economy. Each commodity was displayed and sold on a particular street. Even into the 1900s, peat, hay, potatoes, turnips, and cabbage were sold on Abbey Street, poultry on Glebe Street, calves on Bridge Street, and cloth, flannel, woolen goods, and oats inside the Market House.[8] Pop grew up a few miles outside the town on the Kilmaine Road, which was lined with clusters of dwellings.

The locals suffered greatly during the Great Famine of the 1840s. Pestilence spread through the workhouses, which offered accommodations and employment to paupers and those evicted from their homes. In one week of April 1849, ninety-six people died in a workhouse and were buried in shallow, unmarked graves at the town's edges.

According to a history of St. Mary's Catholic Church, the town, as of 1930, evolved along these lines:

> [I]n 1840 the population of the Town was 2,700, and it had then a
> flour-mill, a brewery and malting establishment and a tanyard, all in
> prosperous condition. Since then its population has declined almost
> by half. The waters of the Robe (which run through the town) still
> turn the wheels of the flour-mill, and though the buildings of the
> old brewery and tanyard remain, both the brewery and tanyard have
> disappeared.[9]

St. Mary's Catholic Church opened in 1853, while the Sisters of Mercy, who arrived earlier, attended to the needs of the poor and sick and the education of children. Their educational efforts were supported by the Irish Christian Brothers upon their arrival in 1876.

In the late nineteenth century, local shops in parts of Mayo refused to serve land agent Charles Cunningham Boycott, who worked for John Crichton, the 3rd Earl Erne. The event gave rise to the word "boycott." Another land agent, David Feerick, was killed in the 1880s, but the murderer was never found. His connection to my ancestry is unclear.

Pop's Ancestors

While the limited number of households with the surname Feerick enabled me to conduct a focused search of several generations of my family, I was left with questions as to the exact identity of my great-grandfather, John Feerick, because others with the same name were alive at the time in Mayo, even living on the same townland as Pop's family. After examining death certificates in Dublin, I began to focus on a certain John Feerick who died in 1905.

According to the Irish census of 1901, my great-grandfather lived at 1 Carrowkeel, Neale, in a thatched stone cottage, with his wife, Ellen Hyland, and their son David, and daughter, Mary. By the time of the 1911 census, both of my great-grandparents had died, and the land was occupied by my grandparents, David Feerick and his wife, Ellen McDermott, and their children, Pop, the oldest, and his father's brother Patrick. Despite residing in the townland of Carrowkeel, Pop would say he was born in Ballytrasna, an adjacent townland where his family had been given property by the Land Commission.

To my amazement, Aiden Feerick was able to identify my great-grandfather in his genealogy search, locating his will in court records. His death was reported by his daughter Mary in 1905. The will directed his son David to support and maintain his mother in the house, and if she wanted to live elsewhere, to provide her with one pound a month. David was left ninety pounds — one pound appeared to be the average weekly earnings of an Irish worker at the time. The will also stated that David was to support Mary, his sister, until she reached 27 or married, with the further provision that he was to pay her fifty pounds upon her marriage or at age 27. John's son Patrick was left five pounds in the will but only if he demanded it. Ellen Hyland died a year later.

I was also unclear as to the identity of my great-great-grandfather, specifically whether he was David or Patrick Feerick. As for my great-great-great-grandfather, I had little hope. Yet, various sources of information helped me create a clearer picture of all three ancestors, among them *The Tithe Applotment Book of 1834*, which showed David and Patrick Feerick to be young tenants living on small land holdings, with a James Feerick having a larger holding, suggesting that James may have been their father and had subdivided part of his holding to his sons.[10] "Land sub-division was very common at the time," said Patsy Walsh, a distant cousin, and was "one of the causes of the subsequent Great Famine of 1845–1849."

By the time of Richard Griffiths's 1856–1857 valuation of land tenements, David was recorded as leasing his house from Patrick Feerick which, according to Gerald Delaney, a genealogist in Ballinrobe, was likely "an informal relationship between close family members." James Feerick, no longer listed as the occupant of land, had likely died. Aiden Feerick, the genealogist, noted that David Feerick (c. 1813–1894) called his eldest son James "which, if in accordance with the traditional Irish naming patterns whereby the first male child was called after his grandfather, would make James, David's father."[11]

This continued with David's eldest being named John, in turn his oldest son was named David, and Pop named me John, although everyone called me David, his father's first name, thereby respecting the tradition. Possibly my first name, John, was in memory of my godmother Nora Pire's only child, John.

My great- and great-great grandparents lived through turbulent times. Walsh observed that, by the 1840s, the population of Ireland was over 8 million, but when late blight struck the potato crops from 1845 to the end of that decade, a million people are thought to have died of starvation, while a million more emigrated. By the time of the 1911 Census of Ireland, the population declined to 4.4 million.[12] Between 1841 and 1851, the population in the townland of Carrowkeel, Mayo, where Pop's family lived, fell from 107 to 73. Similarly, the population in County Mayo fell by 30 percent during the same period.[13] This occurred, Walsh noted, "despite the fact that Ireland had some of the best agricultural land in the world and, at the time of the famine, 30–50 ships per day of corn and meat that would easily feed the entire population were exported to Britain to maintain the great landlord estates."[14]

In the nineteenth century in Carrowkeel, landlords controlled much of the land, and land titles were passed along from father to son, one generation to the next. But according to Walsh, the Great Famine set in motion many changes in Irish society, "undermining the unjust system of land ownership" and altering "the Irish landscape from an intensively tilled one to a much more pastoral one." Land reforms originating in Mayo in the late nineteenth century made it possible for Irish tenants to buy and own their own land. When my great-great-grandfather, David Feerick, died in 1894, Aiden Feerick noted, his son, John, inherited the farm at Carrowkeel "without much formality."

Pop's mother, Ellen McDermott, the youngest of eight children, married David Feerick in Ballinrobe's Roman Catholic Church on August 27, 1908. She was the daughter of Patrick McDermott (of Cloonagashel) and Margaret Ruane, his wife, both of farming families. According to records assembled for me by Gerald Delaney, Pop's maternal great-grandfather, Michael McDermott, "held a house and land in the townland of Cloonagashel as a tenant of the Earl of Lucan."[15] The Oxford Dictionary of National Biography states that George Bingham, 3rd Earl of Lucan, lived from April of 1800 to November of 1888. He was an Anglo-Irish aristocrat and landowner who became an Irish Representative Peer in June 1840 and Lord Lieutenant of Mayo in 1845.

Mom's Ancestors

Tracing the roots of Mom's father, Patrick Boyle, was easier. He was the first-born of James Boyle, a Mayo farmer and stonemason. He married Jane Pryle, whose roots trace to a member of the French General Humbert's 1798 ill-fated invasion of Ireland, one of many efforts to gain freedom and independence for the Irish. The general landed in Killala Bay, Mayo, in 1798, with a small force,[16] which was joined by native Irishmen. His invading force met with initial success all the way to Castlebar but was ultimately defeated by the English. The resulting peace settlement allowed the French to stay in Ireland, but many of the native Irish who fought alongside them were executed.

Two of the French soldiers who remained behind, it appears, were brothers named Pryal. One of them, Michael, married a woman named Bridget Maloney, who lived in the Foxford area and settled there. Their son James was the father of my great-grandmother, Jane Pryle.

Pryle family members living in Ireland and England informed me that Jane Pryle's family survived the famine by growing turnips and other vegetables, likely made possible because of their large tract of land. Jane Pryle appears to have died sometime between the Irish censuses of 1901 and 1911, as she was listed in the 1901 census but not in 1911's.

Her husband, my great-grandfather, James Boyle, was born in Culmore. An old, unused granary there bears his handiwork. The two-story building, buttressed by huge stones, was used to store corn in the winter. When empty, and until the parish hall was built in Foxford, its wooden floors made for a popular dance hall. According to Uncle Pat, James Boyle lived into the 1920s, reaching the age of 96, a record Pat would surpass (97), as would Pat's first cousin James Boyle (98).

The marriage of my grandfather, Patrick Boyle, appears this way in the records: "Maria Moran, a spinster of full age, the daughter of Robert Moran, a farmer, married on the first of February 1898, Patrick Boyle, Culmore, a bachelor farmer of full age, the son of James Boyle a farmer." The land on which Mom's parents raised their family is believed to at one point have been part of the Pryle's acreage, explaining in part the affection Mom and Uncle Pat had for their cousins in America, Michael, Beatrice, and James Pryle.[17] In addition to Patrick, my Boyle great-grandparents had four other children: Michael, Mary, Jane, and Catherine, who immigrated to Illinois.[18]

Turning to the Moran part of my story, I'm indebted to the pathbreaking work overseen by Mary and Robert Moran of Currinara, Foxford, tracing the history of the Moran family of Cashel, Mayo. It states Mom's grandfather, Robert, a "tenant bachelor farmer of full age in Callow, the son of John

Moran, a tenant farmer," married "on the 1st of February 1864, Mary McNulty, Callow, a spinster of full age, the daughter of Owen McNulty, a tenant farmer. The couple was married in the parish of Killasser Catholic Church, by Reverend Father John Finn, Parish Priest."[19] The history further records that "Mary McNulty could not write." Robert Moran was born around 1830 and died on March 17, 1911, and Mary died on April 15, 1919.

My great-great-grandfather, John Moran, according to the Moran family history, was born around 1798 in Callow and lived to 80.

My great-grandparents, Robert and Mary Moran, had five children: Mom's mother, Maria, her brothers Robert, John, and Richard (who lived only seven days), and her sister, Elizabeth. Robert remained in Ireland while his siblings, John and Elizabeth (married name Sheridan), immigrated to Chicago around the turn of the twentieth century.

Of My Grandparents

My grandmothers, Maria Moran and Ellen McDermott, were exceptional women. Maria Moran, born in 1869, spent her entire life in and around the townlands of Callow and Culmore. One relative remembers her as an elegant and hardworking woman who was passionate about Irish independence. In 1878, Maria's parents were forced to leave land they occupied in Callow as tenant-farmers, a traumatic experience for them.[20] According to one account, the landlord wanted to develop a sheep farm on the property. According to the Moran family history, "the Moran family originated in Callow but was given property in Cashel by the landlord who needed the property in Callow for his own purpose."

My sister Maureen offered this description of Maria's brother, Robert, and his wife, Ellen, from her first visit to Ireland in December of 1963, when she was a student at the Sorbonne in Paris. On that visit she stayed in the cottage where Mom was born, then occupied by Mom's bachelor brothers, John and James Boyle. According to Maureen:

> On one occasion I was sent "up the hill" to visit my grand-uncle
> Robert and his wife, Ellen. When I arrived at their cottage, I felt as if I
> were viewing a painting by Norman Rockwell. The four people inside
> were either sitting or standing in various spots, still as can be. I felt
> they were expecting me, although I don't know how since telephone
> was non-existent. I concluded that there had to be a vast subterranean
> network of leprechauns.

Directly ahead of me I could see my grand-uncle, Robert, who had tears in his eyes, knowing that he finally met one of Mom's children, and commented that I was the spitting image of Mom, whom he was anxious to see again. He was over 90 years of age and passed away several months before Mom's first arrival. An abundance of gray hair surrounded his face, and since he was chair-bound, I couldn't determine his height, but he was very alert and witty. He wanted to know all about Mom and Pop and was interested in learning about our life in America. Near him was his wife, who was quiet but listened to everything that was said. Directly opposite the front door was the fireplace and an oven in the fireplace from which drifted the scent of fresh bread.

Maureen added, "When I left, a loaf of bread accompanied me. It was the last time I saw them."

When Maria Moran married Patrick Boyle, they chose to live in a cottage close to the Morans, the Boyles, and the Pryles. It was there that my grandparents raised Mom, Uncle Pat, and their siblings and later cared for my great-grandfather, James Boyle. From atop a hill behind the cottage, you can see the Shrine of the Blessed Mother at Knock. Nearby were the remnants of an underground tunnel used by the local Irish during the War of Independence to escape from Culmore to Cashel. On one of Mom's last trips to Ireland, in a letter to Catherine and Uncle Pat, dated August 20, 1972, she wrote of being back home: "It's so nice and quiet here. I don't know how I'll take the mad city again." On my visits to Ireland, I find myself inevitably drawn to Mom's home. Maria Moran lived there until she died on August 27, 1950, predeceased by her husband, Patrick Boyle, in 1915. Although a new family now lives there, the cottage remains sacred to me.

My paternal grandmother, Ellen McDermott, was born in February of 1879,[21] and died on January 21, 1964, just as Pop was planning to return to Ireland for the first time since leaving in 1929. By several accounts, she was tall, attractive, had a strong personality, and was well spoken and energetic, with an appreciation of America from having spent some time in Philadelphia with cousins. (It was said that they brought the Philadelphia style of rolling one's hair to Ballinrobe.) When Pop's father died, his mother took over the management of the farm with the help of her son Martin.

Breege Rowe of Galway, as noted, the daughter of Pop's sister, Margaret, said of our grandmother: "My grandmother was a strict Irish mother. She and her family survived with a certain amount of hardship, minding cattle, etc., winter feeding, with little or no production of income." Breege added that "the land produced hay, which was the mainstay for their cattle during the winter, corn/wheat for animal feed and for food for the family. Some vegetables were produced; this was mainly for the consumption of the family, i.e., potatoes, carrots, onions, and fruit — apples, raspberries, and strawberries in season." My sister Maureen, based on her 1963 visit, described our grandmother as financially shrewd, very sociable, and a great cook, though at times, Maureen said, "it appears, she could be temperamental."

My grandfathers were by all descriptions quiet and hardworking. David Feerick was short, very strong, and dedicated to life on the farm, though at times he worked on roads to earn extra money. He died at a hospital in Castlebar because of exhaustion, according to medical records, on October 14, 1944, at the age of 71. Pop was then serving overseas and was greatly saddened when he learned of his death, as he had not seen him again after leaving for America in 1929.

Mom's father, Patrick Boyle, traveled annually to England to help farmers collect the harvest, according to Uncle Pat. "He'd tend to the hay and he set to planting the turnips, whatever the farmers really grew," Uncle Pat said. "He made extra money for doing that. He used to work piecework for the farmers and he was a good, hardworking man and a good farmer."[22] On returning from England after the summer, he resumed work on the family farm, cared for the thatched cottage and the barn, and made creels (wicker baskets) to be carried by donkeys.

Mom's father's death was particularly hard on her mother. Uncle Pat recalled, "I tell you, it wasn't easy for her. She was left with many children. She was a hardworking woman." Mom was only 6 and Pat was 10 when their father died. Their mother did all of the cooking and made their sweaters, shirts, socks, pants, shawls, and dresses. Some of her talent rubbed off on Mom.

3

Mom's and Pop's Childhood

Nobody takes care of a child like a mother, and children need a mother.

— MARY JANE FEERICK

My grandparents' families were large. Mom was the sixth of eight children and the first daughter, and Pop was the oldest of seven children.

The thatched cottage where Mom grew up consisted of an upper and a lower room, with a main room separating the two. The main room had a fireplace near a curtained alcove shielding a cot and a kitchen table. When Maureen visited Pop's house in 1963, the bedrooms were cold, and to keep warm, a heated brick wrapped in wool was placed at the foot of the bed. May Mannion, Pop's cousin, who stayed at the house under the care of Pop's mother after her mother died during childbirth, described one bedroom used by the boys as a "closet" and the one occupied by my paternal grandparents as distinguishable by its feather bed.

These houses had no plumbing, electricity, or running water. Open fields and a barn were more than sufficient for bodily necessities. An outhouse adjacent to the home of his birth was added by Uncle Pat, with help from his brother, Jim, on his first return to Ireland in 1947.

Water for cooking, bathing, cleaning, and heating on the fireplace hearth had to be hauled back from an outside well in a bucket. In both homes, the main fireplace was a dominant feature, a place for conversation, storytelling, fiddle playing, dancing, reading, and resting. Its burning peat helped light the room, as did oil lamps and candles.

Both houses were surrounded by beautiful gardens. Pop's garden was particularly noticeable for people traveling on the Kilmaine Road. Flower boxes in the windows made the house especially attractive. In later years, with the arrival of the automobile, drivers would stop to admire the house's beauty and take pictures, sometimes leaving a gratuity. But neither house remains as it was. Pop's has been replaced by an attractive contemporary home. Mom's has been modernized, although much of the original remains intact.[1]

Mom and Pop spent most of their childhood engaged in farm chores, indoor and outdoor play, and schoolwork. The farms belonging to Mom and Pop's families required that everyone in the family work. Tasks ran the gamut from bringing in the hay and stacking it in the barn, caring for the animals, milking cows, and planting oats and vegetables, to fetching well water, watering the garden, and cultivating the turf, to name just a few. Mom's family had several cows but no sheep because, according to Uncle Pat, "they would go over the fence and keep going." In the winter, he said, "dry hay was not sufficient for the cattle, turnips and cabbage being important food items for them." He added, "You had to work, otherwise you had no food. There was always something to be done. You had to do everything so you got used to everything. No one bothered much about age. There were very few rich families."[2]

The bogs that produced the peat for heating Mom's home were located two and half miles away. Men were responsible for cutting, drying, and stacking the turf, as well as transporting it to their homes by donkey. This was an annual communal ritual, as enough had to be stored to last through each winter. Women generally provided the men working on the bog with sustenance. Typically, even children had to help with the collection of the turf, even if they had to miss long periods of school to do so. This was true for Pop and his siblings, as Pat recalled: "You couldn't go to school and work. So you went to work and you didn't go to school."

Mom and Pop both attended primary school for a few years; how many is not entirely clear. There they learned the basics of reading, writing, history (English and Irish), geography, math, and the Catholic religion. Pop never forgot these lessons as he would quiz my children as to the counties and provinces of Ireland and other pertinent data to be sure they knew about his place of origin. He and Mom studied these subjects in Gaelic. I have no recollection of their speaking Gaelic to us when we were young, although Maureen remembers Mom saying her prayers — the Our Father, the Apostles' Creed, and the Sign of the Cross — in Gaelic.

Mom attended the Cloongee National School outside of Foxford, reaching it by making her way down a mountain trail. My cousin Breege Rowe recalled of Pop's family:

My mother, Pop's sister, went to the Convent of Mercy School in Ballinrobe. Your Dad went to the Christian Brothers School in Ballinrobe
Town. They would have traveled to school by walking in fine weather.
They may not always have worn shoes and may sometimes have traveled by horse and cart, or with neighbors. The distance was about two
miles; both schools are a short distance apart. When they got older,
they probably borrowed their parents' bicycles. An older sibling would
have taken a younger one on the crossbar of a bike.

Beyond chores and schoolwork, Mom and Pop appeared to have enjoyed
many activities, especially those involving music. As a young girl Mom picked
berries in the hills of Ireland, sold them, and used the proceeds to pay neighbors for dancing lessons. And did she ever learn to dance, as I observed watching her perform jigs, reels, waltzes, stack of barley, hornpipes, and Irish dancing sets. Pop's talent was with the concertina, or the "squeeze box," as he'd
call it.

Both developed their musical abilities in families with musical talents, including singing and dancing. The concertina, tin whistle, fiddle, ukulele, gui-
tar, and *bodhrán* were particular family favorites. Mom's nephew Desmond
"Des" Boyle, influenced by his father and uncles, spent much of his life enter-
taining audiences with the tin whistle and concertina. On his sole visit to the
United States, it was a joy for me to accompany him to Irish pubs in New York
City and Yonkers and listen to him play.[3] Pop's brother Martin, whom I never
met, was renowned for his ability to play the violin and for his knowledge of
operas, thanks to a Ballinrobe opera society.

Mom's and Pop's homes were always open to visitors and neighbors. Music,
singing, and dancing were constants in Irish homes in Foxford and Ballinrobe,
along with tea, soda bread, and brown bread. Reflecting the musical flavor of
Foxford during Mom's youth was a highly popular pipe band of fourteen flute
players who performed on special occasions.

In addition, there lived within each village poets and storytellers, also
known as seanchaí, who would weave stories of Irish myths, legends, and local
history. My sister Maureen recalls listening to the stories of a distant relative,
Martin Boyle, who spent hours telling tales and making her laugh, sometimes
with a glass of homemade liquor called Poitín in his hand. "He spoke often
of a Paddy and Mike," Maureen recalled, "and their adventures in meeting
up with ghosts in the hills of Foxford on nights when there was a full moon."

Thanks to her mother, Mom was familiar with stories of leprechauns —
fairies usually depicted as little bearded men in red or green coats who work
as shoemakers and have a pot of gold at the end of the rainbow — and with

stories of banshees, "spirits" whose wailing warned of the impending death of a loved one. Mom passed along these stories to us and told Maureen that she had heard the cry of a banshee shortly before she learned of the death of her mother in 1951.

Music and storytelling weren't the only activities that engaged Mom and Pop. Hide and seek, card playing, pitch and toss, and roll a stone were popular activities among the children of their time. But as Mom and Pop grew into adulthood and looked to the future, the effects of the conflict between England and Ireland remained a constant, and there were no jobs for young people when they came of age other than working on the family farm.

As a result, both Mom and Pop decided as teenagers to do something profoundly different. They set their sight on a land three thousand miles away, one they envisioned as a place of opportunity and promise. Mom left Ireland in 1928, then 19 years old, and journeyed to America, as did Pop and Uncle Pat the following year, when they were 19 and 24 years old, respectively. As Pat said of his decision, "I went to America to do something new . . . to get work." In deciding to make this journey, they joined millions of their countrymen and countrywomen who, during a time of economic turmoil in their native Ireland, made the brave decision to emigrate to a distant land in hopes of making a better life for themselves.

PART II
A New Home in America

I am an immigrant on the sea,
Looking at the huge Lady Liberty.
I am an immigrant escaping poverty;
I was so poor I lived under a tree.
I am an immigrant filled with glee,
However, I miss my family.

— BY MY GRANDSON, DYLAN SNOW (AGE 10)

4

An American Odyssey

Mayo's soul has emigrated and has contributed in a mighty way to the
best and most progressive Irish image in the world.

— CORMAC MACCONNELL

Mom, Pop, and Pat, each traveling alone, crossed the Atlantic with only a few
pounds and a few possessions, comforted by the anticipated presence of some
family and friends already in America. Mom joined her oldest sibling, Michael Boyle, who had made the journey the year before and had encouraged
her to follow. But of her siblings, only Uncle Pat would settle permanently
in America, with Michael returning to Ireland to live and find work. None
of Pop's siblings would join him in America, with only his sister, Margaret,
coming for a short visit decades later, though two of his brothers would leave
Ireland to settle in England for employment.

With a family to raise and a lack of savings for travel, Mom never saw her
mother again and Pop never saw either of his parents again. The heartbreak of
this was brought home to me when I asked Uncle Pat to describe his mother's
response when he returned to Ireland for the first time in 1947. He said that she
came running from the house, threw her arms around him, and exclaimed,
"You came back to see me!" I cried when he described this moment for me.
I couldn't imagine never again seeing my children or Mom and Pop. After I
graduated from law school, and with the help of my siblings, we made sure
that Mom and Pop were able to return to Ireland as often as they could. Each
trip was filled with emotion for them and for us. Mom made a final trip to
Ireland in 1980 to visit family members who were still alive. It would be her
last visit, as her health would permit no further trips to the land of her birth.[1]

Mom and Pop each traveled alone to Queenstown by train, where they found accommodation, before boarding the ship to America. When they boarded the ship, no family members were present to say goodbye. But neighbors of Mom told me that on the day before she left, there was a party for her, described as an American wake, where music, poetry reading, singing, and dancing took place until the wee hours of the morning, with many tears shed throughout the evening. A similar event occurred in honor of Pop.

The site from which they departed in Queenstown was unique because of the millions of Irish who emigrated from there in the late eighteenth and early nineteenth centuries to find opportunity in other parts of the world. Queenstown was also the place where the *Titanic* made its last stop as it headed westward in April of 1912, taking on additional passengers before hitting an iceberg and sinking in the Atlantic, an event that brought the death of 1,517 passengers and crew members — well over half of those on board.

Mom and Pop arrived in America at the Port of New York City, rather than at Ellis Island, as its facilities for processing immigrants had closed in 1924. Mom arrived on April 20, 1928, on the *S.S. George Washington*. Pop arrived on May 5, 1929, on the Cunard's *S.S. Carmania*.[2] He said he was seasick during part of the trip and had only five pounds in his pocket when he arrived. He was listed as passenger No. 25 on the ship's manifest and gave as his next of kin his father, David Feerick. Uncle Pat arrived on the *S.S. President Harding* in June of 1929.

Each had relatives in America. Pop's Aunt Nora lived in Schenectady, New York. He also had cousins in New York City, and for a while he stayed with one of them, Mary Lynaugh, whose hospitality he never forgot. Mom had cousins in Chicago whom she visited in 1932, and they in turn visited her when we were growing up in the Bronx.[3]

Michael, Mom's brother, came to America in 1927 and lived for a short while in a boarding house in New York City, later finding work in Plattsburgh, New York, near the Canadian border. He sponsored both Mom and Uncle Pat and arranged a room in Manhattan for each of them to stay in after their arrival. But Michael left America after losing his savings during the Depression and didn't return until the late 1940s. At some point, he chose to live a block from 2305 Grand Avenue, where Mom and Pop lived after 1961. My sister Anne said that in her preteen years, he would visit Mom from time to time, always with a candy bar for her.

Mom and Pop met in New York City in the early 1930s. After dating for a while, Mom traveled to Chicago to visit aunts and other relatives who lived there. The year was 1932, the year her sister Elizabeth died, which likely was the reason for the trip. Mom returned within a year and resumed dating Pop. In an oral history of Pop shortly before he died, Maureen inquired as to how they got back together again. He responded with a twinkle in his eye, "I wouldn't know, Maureen."

Mom and Pop were married on April 25, 1935, at St. Angela Merici Church, located between 162nd and 163rd Streets on Morris Avenue, in the Bronx. I came along, their first child, on July 12, 1936. Donald was born two years later on April 10, 1938, and Maureen followed on April 28, 1941. After World War II, two more children joined the family, Kevin on July 29, 1946, and Anne on July 4, 1953.

While dealing with the challenges of raising five of us, Mom and Pop regularly sent cash, clothes, and other items to their families in Ireland. My first cousins, Breege Rowe, Eileen Condon, and Mary Allen, recalled for me how poor they were growing up in a family of nine children and how grateful their mother, Margaret Whelan (Pop's sister), was in receiving these packages. "Your mother was our mother's angel in heaven," said Breege, "sending us clothes when we had none to speak of. Her extraordinarily generous spirit and how she touched our mother are memories we all took from our youth and continue to deeply cherish."

As with many immigrants, becoming an American citizen was important. On December 17, 1934, Pop was sworn in as a citizen in the U.S. District Court for the Southern District of New York (Certificate Number 3827117). His petition for naturalization listed his occupation as a laborer and described his complexion as ruddy, his eyes as blue, his hair as brown, his height as five foot eight, his weight as 145 pounds, and his address as 747 Melrose Avenue. Mom did not become a citizen until June 16, 1943 (Certificate Number 383897). (Pop's decision to work abroad might have been a factor for her petition.) Her petition, dated July 8, 1941, listed her occupation as housewife. She described herself as five foot five, 145 pounds, and of fair complexion, with gray eyes and light brown hair. Pop, one of her two witnesses, described his occupation as an assistant steamfitter. Her second witness, Uncle Pat, listed his occupation as an elevator operator.

Pop had a wide-ranging employment history. Before the war, he worked in the change booths of the New York City subway; for the Sheffield milk company, doing office work and lifting crates; in the shipbuilding industry in Kearney, New Jersey; as a sandhog, or tunnel worker, in the city's subway and water tunnels; and as an assistant steamfitter.

Pop's work as a sandhog was difficult and dangerous. Rocks could fall and tunnels could cave in or flood. The drills that bore into the bedrock were deafening, and the air was thick with mist and dust. Pop told Maureen that going so deep underground gave him anxiety, but that it was "a job where you could make some money." Sandhogs sometimes worked up to sixty stories down. The job could be dangerous for other reasons. Pockets of compressed air, used in underwater tunnel building to prevent the river bottom from caving in, could blast out of a chamber, creating a vacuum that sucked workers through the break. Workers could drown or be buried under the debris and never be found again. In one case, a sandhog was blown twelve feet through a muddy riverbed, through the river itself, and hurled into the air by a geyser four stories high.[4] He lived and became a legend among his peers.

But Pop was always ready to meet a challenge, as was evident in World War II, during which time he worked for government contractors on military installations in strategically important locations, first as a carpenter in Bermuda, then in Trinidad, Newfoundland, Greenland,[5] Iceland, and the Aleutian Islands in Alaska. He helped build barracks and air facilities. In an oral history interview with Donald, Uncle Pat recalled that, at the equivalent of a "shape up"[6] for overseas work during the war, Pop would raise his hand whenever a group was asked who had carpentry skills or who could drive a large vehicle. According to Pat, Pop possessed neither skill, but he was hired for these jobs abroad, given the dire need for volunteers.

In all, Pop spent almost four years abroad on military projects, often in places where enemy submarines were present. His best friend and neighbor, James "Jim" Doyle, died when the *Dorchester*, the ship he was traveling on, was sunk by a torpedo off the coast of Greenland. Pop had been scheduled to take the next ship to that location. Jim's death was devastating for Pop. My family carried with us the sadness of him having died in such dreadful circumstances.

Nearly seven hundred men lost their lives that fateful night in February 1943. Survivors described the utter chaos and terror.[7] Reading these accounts was incredibly difficult, especially picturing Jim jumping into the frigid Artic waters despite the fact that he was unable to swim.

Pop returned from the war with a skill at carpentry and the ability to operate large vehicles. His newly acquired carpentry skills would be a priceless asset for the rest of his life, particularly when it came to the construction of Uncle Pat's home in Lake Carmel and, time and time again, for work needed in my home in Mount Kisco, since I wasn't to be trusted when it came to fixing things. Thanks to his wartime service, Pop also became adept at operating trolleys and buses, and this employment formed the core of his working years until his retirement in 1974. He was hired by a private transportation company, the Third Avenue Railway Company, as a trolley car operator. In 1948, he began driving buses, sometimes following routes that took him near Fordham University in the Bronx, George Washington Bridge, and upper and lower Manhattan.

Pop's diligence led to promotions to bus dispatcher and to jobs in the money room of the bus company at West 129th Street in Manhattan. Since he earned less than one hundred dollars a week, he sometimes moonlighted, working part-time in a liquor store on 240th Street and Decatur Avenue in the Bronx. According to Edward Sheran, a friend who assisted him, Pop "was a great salesman." He added, "He knew every liquor bottle in the place, and when a patron sought a brand not in stock, he had no difficulty persuading the customer to purchase an alternative." Sheran also said that Pop "was smart and charming and possessed a good sense of humor. It was hard to turn him down when he made a suggestion."

Because of his heavy workload, Pop was not around a lot when I was growing up, but we had our special moments together, one of them being when he bought me my first two-wheel bicycle at Davega's on Third Avenue. I also remember watching him play handball with friends at the courts outside the old Yankee Stadium and sometimes joining him to watch an Irish football or hurling game in Gaelic Park in the Bronx, where he met, chatted with, and drank socially with friends from Ireland. At the time I found all the talk boring; now I wish I had paid more attention.

While Pop was working hard to support our growing family, Mom worked behind the scenes to care for us. Before Mom married, her employment record was as wide-ranging as Pop's, but she worked much less outside the home after she married and I was born. After she arrived in the United States, she worked as a maid, a waitress, and a nanny, among other jobs. According to Maureen, her job with a family in Yonkers, noted in the 1930 census, was hardly pleasant; it entailed scrubbing floors and washing walls, windows, and bathrooms.

Sometime later, Mom was happy to find a job with the family of a Dr. Peters in New York City, whom she told us was very kind to her. She took care of his daughter and apparently traveled with him and his wife to Canada and elsewhere. Once, when Mom broke her nose, the doctor repaired the injury, a kindness she never forgot.

As children, we were oblivious to the challenges Mom faced when Pop was away during World War II. But our neighbors were caring and supportive, none more so than the Doyles and the Vaughans. Delia Doyle, who lived next door, had to bear the loss of Jim, her husband, on the *Dorchester*. His death left her alone to raise their four children. They became our closest friends. The oldest of the Doyle children, James, who became a religious brother, once wrote me:

> My mom had a very difficult life — raising four young children, with no father present, and with almost all of her own and my father's relatives living thousands of miles away in Ireland. But my mom coped wonderfully well, and was always very upbeat and positive, due to two factors: one was the presence of so many dedicated nuns and priests who saw to our very fine intellectual and spiritual formation. (Later on as the number of religious declined — my mom would say: I'm glad I lived when I did, and raised you kids back then.)
>
> And the second factor was the wonderful charity and compassion and friendliness of so many of our neighbors — many of whom were immigrants themselves — and in particular, in a super special way, was the great bond and love between my mom and yours! They were kindred souls, and each was involved, heart and soul, in one another's life and family.
>
> My mom never spoke too much of my dad — lest she should get too sad and overwhelmed. She always encouraged us to get a little job — so as to become more self-reliant and also help out the family.

Delia's son Joseph remembers sharing many meals with us. There was always plenty of food on the "Feerick kitchen table," he recalled. Mom's soda bread and muffins were particular favorites.

The Vaughans were also the dearest of friends. I remember as a child communicating with their son John by walkie-talkie across apartments. We also found it exciting to listen to the radio over the walkie-talkie.

And of course Mom had no greater friend than Uncle Pat. "What struck me as a youngster growing up in the Bronx," Maureen said, "was the very caring and loving relationship Pat had with Mom. From my early years I would remember his visits. I'd watch them in the living room talking softly out of earshot and at other times would listen to their laughter. They depended on each other, and when it was difficult to make ends meet, Pat was there to help out. He would also listen to Mom's advice. Together, so far away from their mother in Ireland, they knew they could count on each other for whatever was needed."

Mom and Pop experienced the collapse of the American economy, a world war, the rebirth of the United States after the war, the emergence of the Cold War, the assassinations of an American president, his brother, and the Rev. Martin Luther King Jr., the resignations of a president and a vice president, recessions, and the landing of the first man on the moon. They felt it was their civic duty to vote, to be responsible and caring citizens, and to participate in the life of America by contributing to religious and Irish-American causes. To us, as their children, they were exemplars of honesty and hard work, and the ones from whom we received our deep Catholic faith.

Pop, sociable, proud of his family, and generous with his time, wore hats, drove Volkswagens in the 1960s and 1970s, loved dogs, and enjoyed playing music. His social side was expressed at functions with wartime friends, surnames Stewart, Trainor, and Morrisson, with Uncle Pat or family friends like the Conroys, McCarvills, Costellos, Duffys, Pryles, or Dalys, and others of Irish background, or at a local pub where he often found pleasurable moments on a Sunday afternoon with neighborhood friends.

Pop was quite taciturn with all of us and ruled with firmness. "Spare the rod and spoil the child" was part of his philosophy. Kevin recalled, on one occasion, returning late one night to Mom and Pop's house in Lake Carmel, where he was staying at the time, to find the front door locked and no response from within. To get in the house, Kevin decided to jimmy open the back door, only to be startled to find Pop pointing a shotgun at his head.

Initially, Pop probably felt challenged by the possibility of an unwelcome visitor but, upon learning it was Kevin, decided to scare him to make a point on how he felt about his late hour and possible drinking. He obviously didn't pull the trigger. Upon learning of the incident, Donald removed the gun. I never knew Pop had a firearm and never thought he needed one, given the size and strength of his dogs, usually German Shepherds. According to Kevin, Pop enjoyed the fact that they were so intimidating. Sometimes he would bring a dog to the local pub to make a point of sorts.

Pop was multifaceted and tender-hearted behind his bark if you probed. He was a big tipper, not because he had money to give away but because he understood how important tips were for waiters and waitresses. He also had a sense of humor, as when Maureen was in high school and told Pop that she wanted to go to college and become an engineer. His response was, "What? You're only going to be breaking dishes in the kitchen." She responded, "Ha! I'm going to use unbreakable dishes." He turned away grinning and speechless. She had one-upped him.

Mom made singing, dancing, cooking, and knitting part of her repertoire. She knew all the Irish songs, especially songs of separated lovers and sons who went off to war. We became quite emotional when she sang "Kevin Barry,"[8] but delighted in her rendition of "When Irish Eyes Are Smiling," "Peg O' My Heart," "Galway Bay," "Danny Boy" and "The Wild Colonial Boy." But "The Snowy Breasted Pearl" was at the top of her list:

There's a colleen fair as May
For a year and for a day
I have sought by every way
Her heart to gain . . .

Oh, thou blooming milk-white dove
To whom I've given true love
Do not ever thus reprove my constancy.

Mom and Pop, and Uncle Pat on his visits, often discussed politics and current events. President Franklin D. Roosevelt, and later the Kennedys, were particular favorites of theirs. They appreciated what President Roosevelt had done in responding to the Great Depression, and not surprisingly they found Kennedy's Irish heritage appealing. In his oral history, Pat spoke of Roosevelt closing the nation's banks and freezing what money people had on deposit. But there was no question, said Pat, that "Your money was going to be returned to you. Roosevelt made sure that everybody that had money in the bank would get their money out, one way or the other." As Pat himself did in time.

Pop spoke of union meetings he attended, of collective bargaining negotiations involving transit workers, and of transit union leaders such as Michael Quill and peacemakers such as Theodore Kheel.[9] Quill's Irish brogue and booming voice was effective. Pop admired him greatly, impressed by the pressure Quill put on New York City mayors such as William O'Dwyer, Robert Wagner, and John Lindsay when it came to issues important to the working man. Wages, pensions, and employee benefits were always a major part of those negotiations, with my family among the many beneficiaries. It was Pop's union pension that provided a lifeline for him and Mom when he retired and their health declined.

Of the many memories I have of Pop, one stands taller than all the others. On October 3, 1951, in the last of a three-game playoff series with the Brooklyn Dodgers for the National League Championship at the Polo Grounds, Bobby Thomson of the New York Giants hit a three-run homer in the bottom of the ninth. "The Shot Heard Round the World," the most famous in baseball history, was a stunning moment for me, but for other reasons. I'd heard the game on radio along with Pop in our apartment. I left as the top of the ninth ended, with the Giants coming to bat, declaring, disappointedly, to Pop that the game was finished, that the dreaded Dodgers had won the pennant by two runs.

Pop asked if I wanted to bet what was then my life's savings — a jar of pennies, nickels, and dimes — on the game. I said yes, placed the jar on a living room table, and left the apartment. As I walked up to the corner of 161st Street and Morris Avenue, I peered into a window of a bar and saw Thomson's ball sail over the left field fence for a home run. I ran home with tears in my eyes, realizing that the Giants had won the game and Pop had won the bet. As I entered the apartment, I saw him with the jar in his hand and a smile on his face. He looked at me sheepishly and handed me back the jar, stating, "This belongs to you." I was never so happy in all of my childhood.

After the deaths of Donald and Uncle Pat, I learned of a written portrait of Pop, which they had quietly drafted and submitted over Pat's signature to the *Irish Echo*, an Irish American weekly newspaper, in 1996, nominating him for its unsung hero series. It concluded:

> The support of his family has allowed one son to become the Dean of Fordham University Law School. This son recently accompanied President Clinton to Ireland. This was a great honor for a first generation son and Bronx Boy. The other sons are acknowledged professionals in the legal and business communities while one daughter became a language specialist in the field of Education and the other daughter excelled in the health care industry. Jack left 19 grandchildren who also have been given the mantle of education. Some are lawyers, some are teachers, some are business people and some are pursuing their education. Jack's support has enabled this family to touch the lives of many people. This is my Unsung Hero.

The nomination of Pop was not successful, although the family was pleased by the tributes to Uncle Pat that appeared in the *Irish Echo* in 2002.[10] Years later when I was acknowledged by the *Irish Echo* and *Irish Voice*, I made sure to mention the role that Pop and Mom played in my life.

5

Settling in the Bronx

New York is to the nation . . . the visible symbol of aspiration and faith.
— E. B. WHITE

After Mom and Pop married, they decided to settle in the Bronx. When I was born in 1936, they occupied a small apartment on the top floor of a five-story walk-up at 972 Sherman Avenue, at 164th Street. The many working-class Irish immigrant families in the neighborhood, as well as the nearby Catholic church and school, made the area an inviting place to live. Mom and Pop also had friends there, and housing was affordable.

Later, they moved within the neighborhood to other apartments, including to Sheridan Avenue at 225 East 163rd Street and then to an apartment building across from the St. Angela Merici School on Grant Avenue at 410 East 162nd Street. In late 1941 or early 1942, with three children on the scene, they moved to No. 305 East 161st Street, a six-story red brick tenement on the north side of the street between Park and Morris Avenues.[1] They lived the prime of their lives in apartment 1-D of this building. Kevin estimates that their rent couldn't have been more than fifty dollars a month.

What we know of today as the Bronx was originally part of Westchester County, a place where governors lived, and included a proposed site for the first capital of the United States. Among its famous residents were Lewis Morris, a signer of the Declaration of Independence, and his brother Gouverneur, whose pen drafted the final version of the U.S. Constitution. I don't remember hearing their names when I was growing up or even understanding the historical significance of the name "Morris Avenue." Nor did I focus on the nearby streets bearing the names of Civil War generals.

In the late nineteenth and early twentieth centuries, the Bronx became a magnet for people of different socioeconomic groups, some of whom left their homes in Manhattan, attracted to the promise of life to the north. The migration to the Bronx was facilitated by the expanded Third Avenue Elevated line ("the El") and the New York Grand Central Railroad (now Metro-North). The El made its appearance in the 1890s; the railroad came earlier. Indeed, Webster, one of the earliest railroad stops built in the Bronx, is right next to where I grew up.

Living in the Bronx also made perfect sense for other reasons: rents were low; the stores on Third Avenue and farther up on Fordham Road were not far away and easily accessible by trolley or bus; parks and movie theaters were within walking distance, as were our church and our school; and subway trains with connections to all parts of New York City were a few blocks away. Also looming not far in the distance was Yankee Stadium, "The House That Ruth Built."[2]

The Bronx: It Was Only Yesterday, a book published by the Bronx County Historical Society covering the years 1935–1965, is filled with pictures and illustrations of places we knew. The years this publication spans coincided with Mom and Pop's marriage and my earliest years as a lawyer.

"It is difficult to believe that the swirl of events changing our world between the middle of the Great Depression and the onset of the Great Society occurred such a short time ago," the book begins. "Yet, in the midst of this change, which had a great impact on each of us, the Bronx remained the center of our lives and the reference point from which we viewed and measured the life beyond the neighborhood in the rest of the world."[3]

We grew up in a working-class neighborhood with families of many different ethnic backgrounds, although there was limited racial diversity. African Americans mostly lived in the tenement buildings in the Morrisania area of the Bronx. We were oblivious to the fact that the Cross Bronx Expressway was being built just a mile to the north of us to connect New Jersey with Long Island and New England. The construction of this highway from 1948 to 1972 would destroy neighborhoods and displace thousands of residents and local businesses, contributing to the social and economic devastation of communities to the north and south of it. By the 1970s the devastation was so great that the "South Bronx," the name by which that area was by then known, had become a synonym for the worst sort of urban destruction.

My youth centered on the few blocks surrounding our apartment on 161st Street. Just to the west was another apartment building (No. 301), owned by the same landlord, and on the corner of 161st Street and Park Avenue, just east of No. 305, another building complex. Stretching west from No. 305 to the corner at Morris Avenue were several private homes, an empty lot with billboards, a supermarket, and a bar. Across the street from us were a few apartment buildings, some private homes, and an empty lot at the corner of Park.

Those empty lots became the setting for many activities, memories, and dreams, not to mention pranks and mischievous behavior. On the lot near Morris Avenue was a billboard advertising cigarettes and beer. At age 10, however, I was more interested in the network of beams crisscrossing the back of the billboard challenging me and my friends to achieve Tarzan status. We would swing back and forth on them before jumping onto the roof of the adjacent Safeway supermarket. Needless to say, we didn't think too much about our return trip to earth.

After my first jump to the Safeway roof, I came to the realization that I wouldn't be able to make it back to the billboard. In my attempt to get down, I clung to the edge of the rooftop and draped my body flat against the side of the Safeway building. I hung like that, frozen in fear. Pop's friend Frank Doyle, the brother of James Doyle, saw me splayed against the wall and gently encouraged me to release my fingers and take the fall. Trusting him, I made the nine- to ten-foot fall, safely landing on the rocky terrain of the lot below. After that I no longer feared making the drop.

The lot was also the place where we'd warm up for our stickball games on 162nd Street, throw around a football, and dig trenches to hide in and play war games. We even lined our underground "fortress" with linoleum, which we found elsewhere in the lot, and did the same for the platforms and huts we built on the billboard.

But there was more to 161st Street than empty lots. Running east and west was a busy two-lane thoroughfare that accommodated cars, trolleys, buses, milk trucks, and other vehicles. At times we hitched a ride for several blocks on the back of a trolley, keeping our heads low so as not to distract the operator. Traveling further west took you past a majestic apartment house, rail yards, an ice house, and then the Grand Concourse, with its larger-than-life courthouse, hotel, parks, and impressive apartment buildings.

West of the Concourse was the Earl Theatre. Across the street was the famous Addie Vallins ice cream parlor, a luxury we seldom took advantage of, either because of cost or because we lived on the other side of the Concourse. The more affordable Nedick's, a juice and hot dog place, was our preferred choice. A few yards west, on 161st and River Avenue, were stops for the elevated Interborough Rapid Transit Company (IRT), the old Yankee Stadium, Macombs Dam Park, and, on the north side of the street, on what is now the site of the new Yankee Stadium, there was a track, a football field, and playground with a pool for young children.

Heading east on 161st Street were less pretentious places. There was Melrose Park and its adjacent train station; Courtlandt Avenue and its famous eating places (among them Alex and Henry's); Webster Avenue and the buses I'd later take to and from Fordham College; the Third Avenue El; a Bronx County courthouse, and a police station. Third Avenue itself, stretching south to 149th Street and lined with stores, evokes memories of Mom shopping for clothes, furniture, and other items. It was on Third Avenue that Pop bought my first two-wheel bicycle and Mom opened my first savings account at the Dollar Savings Bank, although I don't think the account ever held much more than ten dollars. On special occasions, Mom would bring us to Hearn's Department Store, where a photographer took small, black-and-white pictures of us for a few pennies. Otherwise, she'd use her own small camera to take our pictures on the asphalt surface of the roof of our apartment building.

On the east side of Morris Avenue there was a bar at the corner of 161st Street, as noted, and a drugstore at 162nd Street. In between was a real estate office, Moe's Candy Store, a Chinese laundromat, a tailor shop, another candy store, and Cherico's butcher shop. Moe's was the best place for penny candy, licorice, and cherry Coke. The candy store next to Cherico's advertised ice cream, but when you entered, you were hard-pressed to find any. However, my friend John Vaughan said that when he asked for an ice cream cone, the proprietor went into the back room and came out with the biggest cone he had ever seen. "I think the store was really used as a bookmakers/numbers hangout," John explained, although, he added, this didn't discourage him from returning "pretty often for ice cream."

Also on the east side of Morris Avenue, between 162nd and 163rd Streets, were apartment houses, a public library, a bakery, and a grocery store that sold delicious cold cuts. Across the street between 162nd and 163rd Streets was St. Angela Merici Church and School. On the west side of Morris at 163rd was a public school, P.S. 35, and on the east side at 163rd and Bonner Place an A&P supermarket and a funeral home. One block or so beyond the A&P was the Fleetwood Movie Theatre, which had leather seats and featured two programs of double features, cartoons, and the news, all for fourteen cents. The Earl Theatre, near Yankee Stadium, charged twenty-five cents and had plush seating.

A block further north on Morris Avenue was a playground Mom sometimes took us to. I don't recall traveling beyond that point, but I do remember traveling south a few blocks from 161st and Morris to play basketball in the auditorium of a Baptist church, whose minister was very welcoming. On the west side of Morris Avenue, between 161st and 162nd Streets, were Sal's Italian Deli and Sam's butcher, where I worked part-time jobs.

The narrow strip of 162nd Street between Morris and Park Avenues was lined with apartment buildings, fronted with trees, and busy with traffic heading east. It was there that we played most of our stickball games and stoop and curb ball, rode our bikes and handmade scooters, and roller-skated. I like to go back there from time to time, walk around, and reminisce about my childhood, although when I took my grandson Liam on a tour of the Bronx in 2010, he said he would get claustrophobic living in such tight quarters, accustomed as he was to the spaciousness of the suburbs.

Like the vast majority of our neighbors, we had no car, nor did we have a need for one (although ten years later, after I'd left home, Pop would put his meager savings on the line to buy a second-hand Volkswagen). Virtually everything was within reach by bicycle, by public transportation, or by foot. As for news from the outside world, the radio was more than sufficient. The roar of the crowd at Yankee Stadium served as our signal to rush home and turn on the radio. Not until the early 1950s would a small black-and-white television set arrive in our apartment. Until then, the radio captured for us the magic of Yankee Stadium. Donald, Pop, and I watched baseball games on that TV and would roar when the Yankees were winning. Donald and I had trouble watching the Yankees lose. Pop was more stoic, watching games to the end.

In the late 1940s, Mom and Pop got a telephone. It had a party line, a connection shared by two or more customers with separate phones, and you had to give the operator the number you wanted to call. To discourage our using such a luxury, Mom and Pop had a lock placed on the telephone, which was hardly necessary as we had no need for such a "foreign object." None of us, besides Maureen, were important enough to receive phone calls, and we had little interest in calling others. In fact, we hardly knew anyone else who owned or even used a telephone.

The interconnected system of streetcars and subways in the Bronx provided transportation to Orchard Beach, the Rockaways, the amusement parks and the beaches at Coney Island, and to the movies at Times Square. Usually we watched Westerns and thrillers, not the forbidden movies as decreed by the Catholic Legion of Decency. Not infrequently, we walked for miles without relying on transportation.

Our apartment, 1-D, was in the rear of the building's ground floor. It was small and consisted of a long hallway, two bedrooms, a kitchen, a living room, and a bathroom. Kevin described it as "a real cocoon." He added, "You didn't have a lot, but you had what you needed." The building itself was, as Maureen remembers, "very beautiful." There was a wide stoop on the front with two columns and wrought-iron railings on each side. The entranceway inside was shiny and marble-like.

When you opened the door to 1-D you would come upon a hallway where there would often be a baby carriage or bicycle. To the left was a bedroom with a double bed and sometimes a crib or a cot. Mom and Pop would sleep there, and my younger siblings at different points occupied the crib. Around the corner, you'd come to a vestibule, from which other rooms could be reached — a tiny bathroom with a tub, and a small kitchen with a window that opened onto the fire escape. A drying rack with eight to ten lines for hanging clothes was suspended from the kitchen ceiling. A pulley helped with the lines. There was also a refrigerator, a wash basin, a small kitchen table, and two pictures hanging on the wall, one of an Irish donkey cart.

"Our kitchen was small with a Formica and chrome table," Maureen remembered. "Chairs had chrome legs with vinyl-covered cushions on the seat and back. When cuts appeared on the cushions, Mom would replace the vinyl. It was a tight squeeze to fit all of us around it. On special occasions such as Christmas, Thanksgiving, or Easter, or when there was company for dinner, a folding table would be set up in the living room, with a pretty Irish linen tablecloth placed on top."

Beyond the kitchen was a bedroom with three beds side by side. With the dressers immediately opposite, you had barely enough room to reach your bed. Two windows opened to the backyard, facing an apartment building and a grassy lot. The lot was a haven for stray cats that Kevin liked to feed and play with. We used a clothesline outside the bedroom window to hang our clothes to dry. Next to the bedroom was the living room, with two windows framing a bookcase. A couch converted into a bed for visitors.

In the vestibule, between the bathroom and kitchen, was a mahogany veneer secretary where bills and knickknacks were kept by Mom and Pop. We did our homework mostly around the kitchen table while Mom cooked, washed dishes, and did the laundry. The kitchen was the most heavily used room in the apartment.

Kevin recalls riding the dumbwaiter down the garbage chute next to the bathroom. The dumbwaiter, a two-tiered open box attached to a rope pulley, was there to slide garbage down to the basement. A particular challenge within the apartment involved the radiators. In winter, water rattled through the pipes, and tenants, hoping that the landlord would keep the furnace going through the evening, would bang on the pipes.

Outside the kitchen window was a fire escape that hung twenty feet above the cement courtyard below. If we forgot the keys to the apartment or if Mom and Pop were out, we could go to Ann and Paddy Vaughan, the sweet couple who lived above us, and they would let us go down their fire escape to enter through our kitchen or bathroom window. I regret having to admit that Donald and I had, at times, locked each other out of the apartment, forcing the other to use the fire escape to get in, sometimes "accidentally" breaking a window to do so.

Mom liked to keep a neat apartment. She loved flowers and made them the basis of her decor, with patterns on the carpet, furniture, and wallpaper. "We walked on them, sat on them, and sometimes could pick up an imaginary scent as we looked at them on the wall," Maureen recalled. "In later years," Maureen said, "I would make her dresses, and they all had floral designs." (In 1962, after Mom and Pop had moved to Grand Avenue and 183rd Street in the Bronx, Pop wallpapered the bedroom that Maureen shared with Anne with a floral pattern.)

The apartment at No. 305 was also inundated by plants. Mom's cousin Della Clark worked in a hotel and would bring Mom plants left by guests that needed doctoring. "They were cared for and blossomed under Mom's loving care," Maureen recalled. We sometimes felt as if we lived in the Bronx botanical gardens. "Della would come for a visit frequently," Maureen added, "and, I believe, she was somewhat lonely and loved to spend time with Mom, who was always very pleasant and kind-hearted. They were kindred spirits from the 'old country of Eire.'" As the evening progressed, Pop would announce that he had to work the next day and was going to bed in the hope that Della would take the hint and leave, although she rarely did. Once she bought us a cage with two singing yellow canaries, which raised Pop's stress level, though Anne was assiduous in caring for them. One morning we woke up to silence and noticed that the top window was open.

Mom was in perpetual motion. The rite of passage from winter to spring was something to behold: Windows were cleaned, heavy drapes were removed, washed and boxed, and mattresses flipped, leaving a cloud of dust in their wake. We knew what was in store when Mom pulled out a curtain stretcher to ready the summer lace curtains for draping on the window. Although they were washed before storing them for the winter, Mom always rewashed them.

The stretcher was a contraption that resembled an easel, only it was ten times larger and took up the entire living room. After the curtains were washed and starched, they would be stretched over the frame and held tight to dry by two-inch pins protruding from the frame's sides. This would prevent the curtain from shrinking or from losing its original shape. Maureen was the unlucky person designated to help Mom place the curtains and would often prick herself on the pins. Several curtains were layered on top of each other. They remained on the stretcher until they were thoroughly dry, usually overnight, and the following day Mom would check them to ensure they looked just right for hanging. Linen tablecloths were also subjected to this stretcher.

While I was serving in the U.S. Army in 1962, Mom and Pop left the home of our youth for what they described as a "better neighborhood." The area surrounding No. 305 had become more dangerous, with increasing gang violence. Kevin recalled getting into a fight with a group of kids who stole his fire crackers. When he and his friends confronted the group, they pulled knives out and jabbed at Kevin and his friends. Luckily, no one got hurt. Maureen, too, noticed the neighborhood change. "I think my parents worried about me," she recalled. "In the summers of my high school and college years, I worked long hours in Yonkers and didn't get home until after ten at night. My mother was always waiting on the front stoop for me."

It was jolting to return in July of 1962 to a new apartment on the fourth floor of a five-story building on Grand Avenue, about two miles northwest of our old apartment. Mom and Pop relished now having three bedrooms, but the building had no elevator, which eventually became an issue as their health declined. However, they were buoyed considerably by the arrival of former neighbors. The Vaughans moved to the same building, and not far away were Delia Doyle and her family, who had moved to 2284 Grand Avenue.

A month after my return home, Emalie and I married and began our own family journey. We moved to the Riverdale section of the Bronx, a location that allowed us to remain close to Mom and Pop. Whenever Emalie and I visited their new apartment we found it accommodating, and we often left our children with them for babysitting.

As Mom and Pop aged and the neighborhood changed, they considered moving out of the Bronx. At the time, Pop was helping Pat build his own house in Lake Carmel, north of New York City. An early dream of ours was to build a house for them on a small plot of land Pop had purchased in the area. Encouraged by Uncle Pat, and thanks to my partnership at Skadden, that dream became a reality. In 1975, they moved to their new home. Still, whenever I see the numbers "305," I think of the grand palace we occupied on 161st Street.

6

Growing Up in an Irish Immigrant Family

Bliss was it in that dawn to be alive, But to be young was very heaven!

— WILLIAM WORDSWORTH

When all the others were away at Mass
I was all hers as we peeled potatoes . . .
I remembered her head bent towards my head,
Her breath in mine, our fluent dipping knives —
Never closer the whole rest of our lives

— SEAMUS HEANEY

My sister Maureen offered a vivid description of what it was like to grow up in an Irish Catholic neighborhood in the middle of the twentieth century. "We had a very limited experience," she recalled:

> We didn't think there was another world out there because it was just a very narrow environment in which we lived, but at the same time the neighborhood was very nurturing. Neighbors such as the Vaughans and Doyles watched out for us and gave us a sense of security and stability. While growing up and going to school and coming home, we did venture out from 161st Street, but it was all in the immediate area, and really, for me, it probably wasn't until high school that I really ventured out, since I had to go to Manhattan.

So, too, in my case.

Pop's paycheck had to cover the cost of food and clothes, medical expenses, rent, and our tuition at parochial high schools. Mom ran the household, feed-

ing us, pushing our baby carriages, buying clothes for us, dressing us, celebrating our birthdays, attending to our cuts, bruises, and fevers, bringing over
the doctor when we were very sick, taking us to dentists, and making sure that
we attended school and church, went to bed on time, did our homework, and
said our prayers.

While Mom was gentle and soft in her dealings with us, Pop was firm and
demanding. Praise was not a part of his vocabulary; he worried that it would
go to our heads. My sister Anne put it this way: "My father left the running
of the household to Mom. It seems he came from the school of hard knocks.
He would tell us we'd better use our brains, or else we'd be using our backs."
There was a reserve about him when it came to sharing his feelings, but there
was no ambiguity about his feelings when it came to our conduct at home,
toward Mom, in the neighborhood, or at school. Mom showed her love in
abundance, and it flowed everywhere in our home throughout every day, but
Pop's was different — understated although always present.

Food and Meals

Mom was insistent on healthy diets, and breakfast with oatmeal was an especially important meal. Winter would herald farina and cream of wheat ce-
reals, which we'd refuse to eat if there were any lumps. High on Mom's list
was nutrition, with eggnog topped with Bosco, a chocolate syrup containing
vitamins, reigning supreme. To make the eggnog, a raw egg would be added
to a glass of milk and mixed thoroughly with an eggbeater. Mom considered
this drink a powerhouse, and we never refused it. She also made sure we took
cod liver oil by the teaspoon in the morning.

Anne recalls buttered toast, and Kevin didn't know what a sunny-side up
egg looked like until Aunt Catherine, Uncle Pat's wife, made one for him
when he was 12. We often ate cereal or boiled eggs out of an egg cup. A
container of orange juice could always be found in the refrigerator. Sunday
breakfast was special as after Mass one of us would pick up jelly doughnuts
and fresh-baked rolls from a nearby bakery or a grocery store. We would lather
the rolls with butter at home to make them delectable; my favorite was a roll
with bacon inside.

Mom liked to have everybody together to eat when Pop woke up. He
worked varying hours, so our meals took place around his schedule, but we
always had to be home for dinner. And dinner would be a big meal, with potatoes, meat, and vegetables. We'd have roast beef or roast leg of lamb along
with potatoes and vegetables, or roast chicken or meatloaf with onions. On
Sunday afternoon there were usually at least two chickens roasting in the oven

with the most delicious stuffing. We'd hover nearby in anticipation of eating the necks, gizzards, or livers, each of us preferring a different part.

A big pot of mashed potatoes would sit on the stove, and Mom would make gravy in the black cast-iron frying pan. When served, a hole was created for the gravy. Peas, corn, beets, green beans, and carrots were frequently on the table, along with parsnips, radishes (which I loved), turnips, creamed white onions, and creamed cauliflower on holidays. We knew spring was upon us when Mom prepared rhubarb, boiling it with sugar.

We took peanut butter and jelly sandwiches to school. Chocolate pudding and Jell-O, especially strawberry- or cherry-flavored, were favorite desserts, along with ice cream and rice or tapioca pudding. If we were lucky and happened to be in the kitchen when Mom made pudding, we'd fight over who'd be first to clean the pot with a spoon.

For snacks, we'd dunk graham crackers with butter in hot tea or milk. Social tea biscuits and vanilla wafers would be hidden throughout the apartment and brought out of hiding for us to enjoy. When Pop's cousin Ann McCarvill came for a visit, we knew a chocolate cake was in the offing and would peek into the kitchen patiently waiting for the white bakery box to be opened.

We always seemed to have apples, bananas, oranges, grapes, and plums on hand. We didn't like apples because of the skin, but they were delicious when Mom peeled them for us. "Frequently Mom would come into the living room, sit on the chair while we were watching television, a bunch of apples in her lap, and would proceed to peel the apples, cut them up and start eating them," Maureen recalled. "We would then jump up and grab the cut-up apples and eat them. That's how we were made to eat apples — with a smile on Mom's face."

Often sitting on our kitchen table was Mom's soda bread. Its creation was quite a production. The table was covered with flour, baking soda, baking powder, raisins, buttermilk, and the cast-iron frying pan. After she mixed the dry ingredients together, the liquids were added, and a thorough stirring took place before the batter was placed on the table, there to be kneaded into a soft ball. She then scored the dough, cutting a cross on the top of the ball with a knife, and placed it in the frying pan before baking it in the oven for an hour. The aroma filled our apartment.

When done, the bread was wrapped in a towel to prevent it from drying out and placed on the windowsill to cool. I remember sneaking into the kitchen and cutting off the crust, covering it with butter. Donald and Maureen also liked the crust and would cut off the remaining edges, transforming the round soda bread into a crustless square. Although Mom made a fuss about our torturing the bread, she was secretly delighted that we enjoyed her baking.

Maureen said, "My own attempts at making soda bread were a disaster. The bread was so hard that my brothers tossed it around the kitchen like a football."

Complementing the soda bread at times were Mom's Irish muffins filled with raisins. It was heavenly to come home from school and find freshly baked muffins on the kitchen table. There were meals, however, we didn't like, especially those featuring fish, tongue, carrots, or liver. We would have no part of the blood pudding and pig knuckles enjoyed by Pop. My favorite meal was spaghetti, which, when smothered with onions, was stupendous.

Christmas Day dinner included turkey, creamed onions, fabulous turkey stuffing, cauliflower with cream (the only way we'd eat it), sweet potatoes, mashed potatoes, corn, green beans, peas (my favorite), carrots, turnip, apple pie with ice cream, Mom's Irish soda bread, and her delicious gravy made from the turkey drippings.

Soft drinks weren't a popular item in our home. A bottle of ginger ale could usually be found in the fridge, but its use was restricted by Mom and Pop for mixing highballs for guests. We weren't allowed to drink it, although sometimes my siblings and I would find a way to sneak out some for ourselves.

Medical Needs

Mom was especially attentive to our medical needs. We'd only visit our family doctors for vaccinations or when it seemed that we were close to death's door. Our doctors were Dr. Gersh and Dr. Manfredi. Both had offices near our home. Once, when Kevin developed croup, Dr. Gersh came to our apartment to check his vital signs and dispense medicine. As it turned out, Kevin needed to be taken to the hospital by ambulance, where he was monitored for a few days; he still recalls the sirens blaring en route.

Every spring, while Donald suffered from allergies and asthma, my eyes would swell shut from hay fever. I would also often come down with bronchitis in the winter. My sister Anne remembers being tricked into going to Dr. Manfredi for immunizations. She also recalls Dr. Manfredi administering a shot in her behind when she had the measles. She never did like him after that! Without credit cards or checking accounts, Mom and Pop paid our doctor's bills in cash or on "time" through an installment plan.

Many natural remedies were used to avoid a doctor's visit. Mom's favorite remedies were wine or whiskey, although she stopped this treatment when she found me sitting up in bed eagerly waiting for the curative elixir. Coca Cola syrup from Moe's candy store provided intestinal relief, while gargling warm salt water helped ease a sore throat. When we were home sick from school we were allowed to drink the ginger ale in the refrigerator. Vicks VapoRub on the chest helped when we were congested, and we had no problem taking Cheracol cherry syrup for our coughs, often asking for more. When we saw Mom approaching with the enema bag, we knew we were in for an unpleasant experience.

During the winter of 1953 my mother, then 44, complained frequently of intestinal pains and thought she had gas, only to discover upon her visit to Dr. Manfredi that she was pregnant. She came home shocked by the news. On the Fourth of July, she gave birth to Anne, leaving for us on our kitchen table a cooked leg of lamb for dinner before taking off for the hospital. All of us children were born in the Bronx Maternity and Woman's Hospital, located on the Grand Concourse.

Healthy teeth were another concern. We had two dentists, Dr. Pressmen and Dr. Kunkel, both of whom we bobbed and weaved to avoid. Novocain didn't alleviate the pain felt when the dentist's drill struck a nerve, if it was used at all. Gloves or masks weren't in use, and the smell of tobacco was strong on the fingers of one of our dentists. Perhaps telling of the experience, Kevin recalls thinking his dentist's large teeth looked like fangs.

Religion

From the earliest age it was understood that attendance at Sunday Mass was compulsory. We also attended Mass on holy days and went to confession frequently. The confessional style of the priests varied. Some were formal with the penance, requesting the reciting of a few prayers, for example, while others were informal, requesting an extra good deed for the day. Baptisms, First Communions, and Confirmations were major family celebrations, and friends and relatives were invited to take part in the festivities, which included socializing, music, and food. By the time we were eight, we had received four of the seven possible sacraments.

Being a good Catholic in the pre-Vatican era required strict adherence to many rules. Food couldn't be eaten after midnight on Saturday if we wanted to receive Communion (the Eucharist) on Sunday. Confessing our sins to a priest was stressed, and meat couldn't be eaten on Fridays. As a result, we became accustomed to eating tuna fish, fried flounder, or trout with spaghetti. During the seasons of Lent and Advent, we participated in the Stations of the Cross, Missions, and Novenas. Recitation of the Rosary took place at home, usually in the living room. Lent was forty days of partial fasting along with prayer, starting with Ash Wednesday and culminating in the Resurrection celebrated on Easter Sunday. We were encouraged to give up candy for the duration, and we tried to convince Mom that Sunday was a free day, although to no avail.

And as Maureen remembered:

> Easter Sunday found us dressed to the nines: Hat, bonnet, dress, black patent leather shoes, pocketbook, and gloves. David wore a suit.[1]
> After Mass, we feasted on chocolate Easter bunnies. During Advent, a period of preparation before Christmas, the birth of Christ was emphasized at home, and we faithfully put together the nativity set each year, purchased a Christmas tree on Christmas Eve, decorated it and placed a star on the top. The majority of Christmas ornaments were religious in nature, and we basked in the beauty of our church and its decorations.

Pictures of the Sacred Heart, the Blessed Mother, and the Holy Family graced the walls of our home, expressing Irish spirituality, along with several crucifixes. We wore miraculous medals and scapulars as visible signs of our faith and as protection against evil. One of Mom's favorite nighttime prayer was "Lovely Lady Dressed in Blue":

> Lovely Lady dressed in Blue, teach me how to pray!
> God was just your little boy, tell me what to say!
> Did you lift Him up, sometimes, gently on your knee?
> Did you sing to Him the way Mother does to me?
> Did you hold His hand at night?
> Did you ever try telling stories of the world?
> O! And did He cry!
> Do you really think He cares if I tell Him things, little things that
>   happen?
> And do the Angels' wings make a noise?
> And can He hear me if I speak low?
> Does He understand me now?
> Tell me, for you know. Lovely Lady dressed in blue, teach me how
>   to pray!
> God was just your little boy, and you know the way.

We also learned the prayer to our guardian angel, and books of the saints were read to us. Mom encouraged us to kneel by our bed to say our nighttime prayers. Our homegrown faith was nurtured at school and reinforced by friends and neighbors, almost all of whom were Roman Catholics. Not until we were teenagers did we begin to socialize more actively with non-

Catholics. If we played outside and misbehaved, neighbors would reprimand us, reinforcing the values impressed on us at home. It was a very innocent time, with Mom and Pop passing on the virtues of faith, hope, and charity, in addition to the values of honesty, integrity, service, and justice.

Our Play

I start with an early memory of the "horsing around" and "fighting" Donald and I would engage in as children in our apartment. As Maureen put it politely: "You and Donald weren't exactly saints growing up. You had your share of battles." Some, she recalled, had to do with which program we were to listen to on the radio or watch on television. She mentioned that, while we were out, one might think we wore halos. To quote Mom, we were "home devils and outside angels."

Fortunately, because our apartment was so small, many of our activities took place outdoors. When we were young, Mom's coping strategy was to keep us outside as much as possible and then, after we were in bed, to do housework. We rode bikes and scooters, played games in the streets and parks (at times at Melrose Park, just down the street), roller-skated, and swam.

Of Melrose Park, now surrounded by a large apartment complex, Maureen remembers: "It was right next to the Grand Central stop "Melrose," and we used to go down, dangerously so, to cross the tracks. There were swings in the park and seesaws and slides to play on." We also used to play what we'd called "Johnny ride a pony." A group of "Johnies" would pile on the designated "pony" until the child collapsed under their weight. The child who could carry the most children won the game. "I also remember playing jacks in that park where there was an attendant by the name of Charlie," Maureen recalled. "He was the kindest person you would ever know."

Stickball was my favorite game; in fact, I fantasized having a career as a stickball player. This sport required a broomstick, a Spaldeen (a special rubber ball made by Spalding), and chalk to mark the bases. Having no organized sports in the neighborhood, we organized our own games on 162nd Street. As the oldest in the group, I gained leadership training. We discussed where the bases should be, what constituted a home run and a foul ball, and who'd be on each team. Sometimes, we used manhole covers to mark the bases. A home run usually sent the ball flying toward the Melrose train station, causing those in the outfield to zigzag among the cars heading south.

In the winter we loved to go sleigh riding in Franz Sigel Park[2] on the Grand Concourse, where, at its southern end, there was a steep slope followed by a long stretch of land. On snow days, I'd grab my American Flyer sled and, along with Donald and neighborhood friends, head for the park. With our pants tucked into our galoshes and wearing earmuffs, a warm jacket, mittens, and a knitted hat, we'd make the seven-block trip.

I'd make a running jump with the sled onto the snow, trying to build up speed as I raced downhill. Sometimes Donald would jump on top of me and try to hang on to both me and the sled. We'd spend hours sledding or having snowball fights. Arriving home cold, wet, and famished, we'd be marched by Mom into the bathroom to remove our wet clothes and change into something warm and dry. Often awaiting us was cocoa and graham crackers, vanilla cream cookies, or muffins.

Mom also took us to the Jerome Avenue Park, where the new Yankee Stadium is now located, because it had swings, seesaws, wading pools, and a large children's pool. It also had a track that I used for exercise. An adjacent grassy area was perfect for throwing around a football, and I remember watching older kids play organized football games there.

The open lot across the street from us on the southwest corner of 161st and Park Avenue provided a place to play baseball. Our "field of dreams," however, was dangerously close to a small private home. On a few occasions, our home run hits, including my own, broke through the glass window of that home. Frightened, we'd immediately disperse before the occupant could emerge and see us. Each time, as the day wore on and our guilt grew, we'd take up a collection to cover the estimated cost of a new window, place the proceeds in an envelope with a note of apology, and, in the evening, I'd slip the envelope under their front door.

One summer a year later, when I was working as a cashier in the A&P supermarket on Morris Avenue, a woman I was ringing up asked pleasantly if I was that young boy who had broken her window. I don't recall my response, but I was no doubt in a state of shock. (She did thank me for bagging her groceries.)

In high school I played basketball, football, and baseball in the parks around Yankee Stadium. At six feet, one inch tall, I fancied myself a basketball star with a "deadly" one-hand shot, but that glory proved fleeting when I had to face the six-foot, seven-inch James "Red" Davis, who went on to stardom at St. John's. For hours we played pick-up basketball games on the courts in Macombs Dam Park. I had "potential" in the sport, but I never developed it.

As with the holy sacraments, graduations were occasions to invite cousins and friends over to celebrate. We had a record player on which we could play Irish music, and sometimes we'd all do the eight-hand reel. As Anne remembers, Irish friends of our parents "would sit around and talk, laugh, and drink highballs. My father would play the concertina. When asked, Mom would demonstrate an Irish jig, and she frequently sang Irish songs. In those days,

I didn't care for the Irish songs as I thought they were old-fashioned. Now I love to hear Irish music. It brings back memories of Mom and Pop." I, too, get quite nostalgic when I listen to Irish music and often cry recalling those warm memories.

Holidays and Vacations

School would close in observance of religious holy days and civic holidays. Our usual play activities resumed on such days, unless the holy day required attendance at Mass. Mom and Pop and our teachers made certain that we never missed Mass. They might only relent if we were suffering from a 104-degree fever.

Thanksgiving, Christmas, and Easter were the most special days. Our meals were delicious on these occasions, and often friends of Mom and Pop and cousins would join us for the celebration. It was a long time before I stopped believing in Santa Claus and the Easter Bunny. The presents that came down the "chimney" (actually from the fire escape) at Christmas and those found in Easter baskets were eagerly awaited and excitedly received. Even on the Christmas Day that Mom was dealing with a serious health problem at Morrisania Hospital, she made sure beforehand that Santa Claus would still make his visit.

As Maureen recalled, when we were teenagers our family went searching for a Christmas tree every Christmas Eve, when prices were the lowest. After Christmas dinner, distant relatives of Pop arrived with a present for each of us. Uncle Pat, who came with his wife, Catherine, would give each of us a dollar bill when Catherine wasn't looking. Catherine had a gift for each of us too, usually a shirt, socks, or underwear, but the dollar bill made the biggest impression. It was a lot of money back then. We never had to surrender it to Mom and Pop, nor did they ask.

For vacation we'd often go to Orchard Beach in the northeast Bronx. There we learned to swim, built castles in the sand, buried each other in the sand with only a face protruding, and threw footballs, Spaldeens, and baseballs. Being fair-skinned, we'd often come home badly sunburned. Since sunscreen wasn't available, apple cider vinegar was poured over our backs while we stood in the bathtub; the aroma of salad dressing would drift through our apartment.

On a few summer occasions, Mom and Pop took us to Rockaway Beach, where we rented a room for a few days. Although the accommodations were exceedingly tight, we loved swimming in the ocean, plunging into the breaking waves, and inching out as far into the water as we dared go. At the end of the day, we usually enjoyed the rides at the nearby amusement park.

In 1944 and 1945, when Pop was overseas, we spent summers with Mom on Maple Farm, a family farm in Port Murray, New Jersey. Mom didn't drive so we traveled there by public transportation. We'd enjoy meals with other guests around a long dining room table in the farmhouse. Everything on the table matched, whereas at our home, we didn't have dishes or cups that were all the same. I remember going out to the barn to watch the cows being milked and the pigs being fed, and going on hayrides. And I especially recall pots and pans being banged together in celebration when World War II ended.

Most enjoyable of all was swimming in a nearby creek with a huge rock you could dive off of. Donald and I would meet locals there. I was told that one girl, Joyce, had a crush on me, while I had a crush on another girl named Barbara. Years later, when I began writing this book, I went back to Port Murray to say hello to them and to the farmer and his wife (Willard and Elsie Sauck), who had been so kind to us, but they were no longer around. The farm had changed hands, but I did learn, however, that Joyce was happily married and Barbara and her family had moved to Florida.

Discipline

My brothers and I gave Mom and Pop sufficient reason to resort to discipline at times. Maureen noted that, with seven people living in such close quarters, there would inevitably be some kind of conflict, so Pop had to be strict. "Pop was the disciplinarian," she recalled to me. "He would take the belt out if any of us were really bad. But he would never do the belt on me. I think he would give you and Donald the belt if you got into trouble for anything or came in late." On the other hand, Maureen said, "Mom was very gentle, very encouraging. She would get angry at times, however. Being in charge of a bunch of rambunctious kids in the house was not an easy chore, so she was a certain type of disciplinarian, trying to keep us going and trying to keep everybody calm."

Kevin recalled, when he was 12, how he was disciplined by Pop after being rude to Mom:

> I think I just told her to shut up and it became apparent I should get out of that apartment very quickly. I recall running down the hall and Pop was running after me. I passed my bicycle on the left, tipping it over so he would fall over the bicycle. Unfortunately, he did not fall over the bicycle; he managed to get around it very quickly and caught me before I could get out of the front door. He just pushed me quickly up against a wall and whacked me in the stomach. It wasn't a very

big whack, but it did imprint on me not to speak nastily to Mom in any way.

Pop's bark was menacing at times, but, in my experience, there was usually little follow-up. I more remember Mom's efforts to restrain him as he threatened me with the belt. She was often successful, but not always. Despite her interventions, Pop had a way of keeping me in line.

Kevin also recalls Mom chasing him with the broom and whacking him on the legs. "She was more physical than Pop," he said, "but Pop was more intimidating. Mom you could play with the discipline. But she would hit you with the broom. It was like fun. Almost." What bothered him most was when Maureen roamed the neighborhood to find him when it was time to come home: "It was an embarrassment having your sister grab you by the ear and drag you home for dinner."

Education

Mom and Pop stressed the importance of getting an education and making something of ourselves. Pop was taught by Irish Christian brothers in Ballinrobe, but, like Mom, his education didn't go beyond the primary grades. Nevertheless, they both could write and express themselves with clarity, and they had a great interest in learning from the world around them. They read newspapers, especially the *New York Daily News* and the *Journal-American*, listened to news on the radio and later on the television, and chatted with friends about current events.

Pop had a sharp mind for mathematics, largely developed through work experience. In his later years, he loved doing crossword puzzles to keep his mind alert, often calling Emalie or Maureen for help when he came upon something that stumped him.

Mom and Pop's approach to each of us differed, as Maureen recalled in describing an incident during her high school years:

> Toward the end of my senior year at St. Jean Baptiste High School, Father Dahm, the administrator of the school, called me into his office. I was very nervous because I had no idea what the issue was. He asked me how I would feel if I received a four-year tuition scholarship to the Catholic college of my choice. I was stunned at the suggestion and speechless. He told me that a parishioner at St. Jean's donated four scholarships to the top graduating seniors, and I was one of the recipients due to my high school record.

Feeling on top of the world for the rest of the school day, I couldn't wait to get home to tell Mom and Pop. I ran into the house and told my mother the good news. She was elated and thrilled and called Pop into the kitchen. When he came in, I said, "Guess what? I received a four-year full tuition scholarship to college!" With a look of astonishment, he said, "Why would they do that?" and then, "How did you get it?" I responded, "Brains, Pop, brains." He then left the room without saying anything else.

Kevin, five years Maureen's junior, had a different kind of experience with Pop. As Kevin recalls, "At the time of consideration of college in my high school junior year, I approached Pop as to what he would do to help me. After all, he had helped put my older brothers and sister through college. The response was more than I could imagine. 'I have done my job with those three. You should join the Navy!' And then he walked off. I was shocked, angry, and all around pissed off. What unfairness! Whether it was intentional or not he certainly got my attention and started me on a study routine that led to my attaining a Regent's scholarship."

As the years went by, each of us would hear stories from others about the pride Pop took in our educational achievements, but we never heard that at home. Perhaps he wanted to make sure that our feet remained firmly planted on the ground. Mom, on the other hand, never failed to express her joy and delight in our accomplishments. Thanks to both of them, all five of us earned college degrees, a tradition that continues in our family in a major way.

7

Uncle Pat, Our Life-Long Companion

May you not die until a dead mule kicks you to death.

— PATRICK BOYLE

Uncle Pat, my godfather, was a confidante with whom I shared my inner thoughts. I benefited tremendously from his example, stories, and wisdom. My good fortune was due to frequent, if not weekly, visits with Pat over the last thirteen years of his life. An unexpected blessing was the opportunity to spend the last week of March of 2002 visiting with him daily, just before he died on April 2 of that year. On these visits, as we sampled Jameson Irish Whiskey and enjoyed food, tea, and his favorite vanilla ice cream, I made detailed notes of his life's history.

The one evening when I didn't visit him, because of a work conflict, was, as chance would have it, the night before his death. Fortunately, our son John was able to visit Pat that evening and was joined by Kevin, who lived nearby. It was an evening of stories, Jameson, and spaghetti, Kevin recalls. They spent time in Pat's living room and kitchen, then Kevin helped him change into his pajamas and put him to bed. There was no expectation that this would be their last visit. I was stunned to receive the news of his death the next day and broke down crying during a hearing I was conducting at the time.

Pat was born in 1904 and lived in every decade of the twentieth century. As a youngster, he had a reputation for his strong work ethic. He not only worked the family farm, he also helped a man named Tunney who had a farm nearby with eleven cows. Tunney was "not very friendly," Pat recalled, but his wife, Pat's aunt, was a "very nice person." Pat gave the ten shillings he earned each week to his mother. He said that he dug clay for many hours each day, planted oats and cabbage, and sorted cabbage into hundred-pound bags. A single bag, Pat said, covered what Tunney paid him for the entire week, suggesting that Tunney's profit margin was huge indeed.

Pat recalled "drawing the turf" for his own family home, making many trips each day up and down the mountain for that purpose.[1] "There was nothing for nothing, meaning no reward for no work," he remarked, noting that he cleaned out manure and fed the cows and other animals, and adding that he "was glad for Sundays when no one worked."

Pat greatly admired his older brother James ("Jim") and was eager to join him in fighting for the cause of a free Ireland, but he was underage (15) when he tried to volunteer, and thus was turned away by the local authorities. Pat said that he had attended a political rally in Foxford where Maud Gonne MacBride, an Irish activist, was speaking, apparently seeking support for the independence movement in Mayo. Upon seeing Pat, she gave him a warm smile and asked him his age, remarking how young he was and noting that she had a son of the same age.

Maud Gonne was then regarded as one of the most beautiful women in Europe, a fact Pat was quick to confirm to his mother on returning home that evening. That son of Maud Gonne, Sean MacBride, went on to win the Nobel Peace Prize, acclaimed for "mobilizing the conscience of the world in the fight against injustice." Upon coming to America, Pat also fought against injustice through his involvement with groups dedicated to serving others, especially through the Emerald Society, of which he was a co-founder.[2]

Notwithstanding his age, Pat ultimately did participate in the Irish War of Independence, as did his older brother Jim, working as a decoy and courier in Mayo. He knew where all the safe places were for soldiers fighting the black and tan on his home turf — "every inch of the ground," he said.

An oral history account of Pat's life in 2001 by Enda Brogan, my second cousin, reveals the brutality of the war in western and northern Mayo and the roles that Pat and especially Jim played in the cause of freedom and independence.[3] Upon the signing of the Anglo-Irish Treaty in 1921, neither brother agreed with its provisions requiring continued allegiance to the crown and the division of the country into northern and southern sections. This led to Jim leaving the country for England because of these differences.

In the 1920s, Pat traveled to England to join his brothers Jim and Michael. They worked on construction sites and in coal mines, and they never failed to send money home to their mother. "No one talked about what we did," Pat noted. "You just did it." He worked in the mines, ten hours a day, five or six days a week, earning four pounds a week. "It was not easy," he said. "The air was not good." Though not very tall, Pat had great physical strength and became a foreman. He was also a talented wrestler, with an eye for the holds necessary to deck a much larger person, although I found this hard to believe because, like Mom, he was so gentle and soft-spoken.

Pat returned to Ireland briefly in the late 1920s and then decided to emigrate to America. "There was nothing," he said. "There were no jobs in Ireland. There was a factory in my town. They had about two hundred people working there. I [didn't] know if I could get it."

"I was living in the country a few miles away on a farm," he added. "To live in Ireland, you can't live anywhere unless you have money and a job, and I didn't have either. I had no money. Oh, yes, you get jobs and work for neighbors for a day, for a couple of days here and a couple of days there. Maybe cut turf and you dig — plant potatoes and dig fields for oats. But all in all, you didn't get much money."

As for his decision to come to America, "I wanted to better myself. I was working in the coal mines and I had a good job and was a foreman. But I was working long hours. And I figured there must be an easier way. I was working ten hours a shift, and that's a lot of hours underground. So I figured out that I could better myself by coming to the United States."

Uncle Pat's experience with concrete and the mixing of all "kinds of stuff" gave him an expertise that initially led to a job laying bricks in America. "You asked no questions," he said. "You were happy if you got a job. If you wanted to make a dollar in those days, you had to work. So, when I come here, I'm working days. So I'm living like a human being. I can sleep nights. But I was sleeping days in England. I enjoyed it much better here." Though he made "big money" working in a coal mine in England, he said that the job was unhealthy, adding, "New York was much better for me. I am glad I made the change." From every paycheck he received in America, Pat sent part home to his mother.

In the 1930s, Pat lived a bachelor's life, occupying rooming houses in Manhattan and at some point moving in with Mom and Pop. He lived with us for a short period when I was a young child. When Pat married Catherine Maxwell on April 17, 1940, they lived on Dyckman Street in Manhattan until they moved to Lake Carmel upon their retirements. While they had no children, they treated the children of their extended families as their own. They had more than two hundred nephews, nieces, grandnephews, and grandnieces, including a significant number in Ireland and England.

Dating Women in America

Not until I read Enda Brogan's oral history did I learn about Uncle Pat's dating history and philosophy. He often "ran by" Mom a number of his dates, but her response was always, "She was not for you." But Catherine, Mom said, "was different."

In the oral history, Pat described the dating challenges confronted by Irish immigrants in America and the strategies they used to meet one another:

> When I came to the United States, there were Irish dance halls. You had to be very careful. There were a lot of girls around there and you'd get acquainted with them, you might make a date with them. If you made a date with them before you asked them questions, that's when you were making a mistake. Some of these girls lived ten to fifteen miles outside of New York City, and to get them home, you had to take the railroad. Then you had to find a way to get back home and then, say two to three o'clock in the morning, you got back to where you were living in the city.

Such long trips on a Saturday night, Pat said, "would ruin you because the next day was Sunday and you didn't have enough sleep and you got up and you went to church and then you went to see the football game in Gaelic Park." It was important, Pat added, that you try to find somebody who lived in the city. "If you made a date and backed out upon finding where she lived, you would be known as a mean guy, and you didn't want to get that title."

In lieu of going to dance halls, Pat found that meeting women at house parties was far more successful and less expensive. "You were meeting different types of girls," he said. "Girls that lived in the city, some of them lived only a block or two from where the party was, some of them a mile or two away. But that was different. Transportation in the city was terrific."

It was possible that Pat met Catherine at such a party or at a charity event. They enjoyed forty-nine years together until Catherine's death on January 23, 1989, at the age of 82. "I think it was a very, very successful thing," Pat said of his marriage.

Pat and Catherine threw themselves into all kinds of causes, financially and otherwise, and were cherished participants in all our family events. Catherine spent her work life at the New York Telephone Company. She drove their car and managed their savings, and the two of them were present, with gifts, at every important occasion of my childhood and those of my siblings.

Work History in America

As for his work history in America, Pat said he was laid off shortly after the death of his sister Elizabeth in 1932. How to find work and learn a trade, he said, "was my biggest job then." He added, "Jobs would come up and I learned pretty fast." Sealing in a building was one job he secured. Another involved gutting out a building. Of that job, Pat said, "Bricks and everything had to be cleaned out, everything scrubbed and cleaned. The stairs and windows, floors swept, whatever had to be done." Foremen made sure you "put in a day's work," adding that there was no time to "fool around or loaf." But, Pat said, "you didn't mind that as long as you had the job."

Pat then started training to be an elevator operator in an office building. "The operator would give me the controls when nobody was ringing the bells," he said. "If there were passengers ringing, you rode up and down with him, but you didn't touch the controls." But this job didn't last long, he said, because he got a job in another building operating an elevator.

"The controls you'd have to reach all the way, one hundred percent around," he said, "and you had to bring them back the same way to stop the elevator — there was a big lever one had to pull back. So I didn't like that. But I worked at that, and the people that tested me, for one reason or another, they wanted me on the job." Pat thought he might have gotten the job because he was, as he put it, "clean cut and dressed fairly good." He came to like this job, and he kept it until World War II, when he went into war work.

When Rockefeller Center was being built in the 1930s, Pat said he sought jobs there as a laborer and bricklayer, but he wasn't successful. He thought it had something to do with not belonging to a union. "I knew all about the work, but I didn't know the gimmicks, as they called them then," he said. "Who to see who could get you in there. There was those kind of people around, but I didn't know them."[4] He felt that some kind of clique was at work and regretted not being able to get these jobs since few skyscrapers were being built at the time, given the Depression. He continued to do repair work and work in private homes, but very few jobs lasted for long.

The surprise attack on Pearl Harbor by the Japanese on December 7, 1941, changed everything overnight. "The country, the people that had money and had factories started manufacturing around the clock," Pat said. "Then, the addition — trained men into shipyards and building ships and building planes. But the next thing you know, the country is turning around. Everybody had a job. Nobody was out of work."

During the war, Pat worked in shipyards in Brooklyn in the sheet metal section, where he became an expert measurer. After the war, he got a job with someone who owned fifty apartment buildings, saying that he "did a little of everything for the owner, but you had to know what you were doing." In handling cement, he said, "it was important how you laid it out and to know how much stuff you needed."

Of the postwar years Pat said, "They started building the houses, more repair work and putting up different kinds of buildings, skyscrapers." Immigration restrictions were relaxed, but the results were not entirely pleasing to him. He lamented the fact that many Irish were not permitted entry and felt that too many people with money, "radical" ideas, and less interest in working were allowed in. "The country was run by immigrants that worked really hard that came from various countries," he concluded. "And there was nothing handed to them. They had to work for it, which they did. The Irish did just that."

Pat's Education

After his father died, Pat dropped out of school, either in the third or fourth grade, to help his mom by working on the farm. He fondly recalled his first-grade teacher, a cousin named Brigid Boyle, and another teacher named James Boyle. In the 1920s, when he worked in England, Pat found time to attend night school, go to the library, and read books. "I took advantage," he said. "I knew I had to learn. So I did."

He continued his own course of studies in America. He said he "read a lot of papers," adding, "I got the meaning of words. I improved. Went from good to better. I was able to educate myself to a certain extent, where I could understand everything."

That's how Pat learned how to sketch and build a house. In fact, once, from reading a sketch, Pat saw that the foreman was placing a wall in the wrong place. He mentioned the fact to co-workers but hesitated telling the boss that he'd made a mistake. The wall went up, and apparently after a co-worker called the matter to the boss's attention, the wall came down and was placed where Pat saw it belonged. Of his silence, Pat said, "When he's a boss, he's a boss. You take an order from him." The co-worker often referred to Pat as the "greenhorn" because he was the most junior person on the job. "The general foreman over the job said," as Pat remembered, "the greenhorn knows what he is doing, but you don't." The co-worker who had pointed out the mistake was apparently let go.

Reflecting on his life in Brogan's oral history, Pat said: "I had experts coming in here [his Lake Carmel home] who could read what they couldn't build.

They were handicapped. They could draw the sketch, read it, but that was the limit. I could draw the sketch and build from that sketch. That's what I did with my own house."

After his retirement, Pat read books and newspapers, listened to news on the radio, and watched television two hours a day, especially enjoying game shows like *Jeopardy* and *Wheel of Fortune*. He could speak on almost any subject to people of many different backgrounds, from Cardinals and judges, to craftsmen, workers, and those struggling to find a job. I recall one occasion when Pat complimented John Cardinal O'Connor, then Archbishop of New York, on a speech he had given about justice delayed being equivalent to justice denied, to which the Cardinal replied, "He knows my speech better than I do."

Building His Own House in Lake Carmel

In 1950, Pat bought property in Lake Carmel to build a home to retire in. He said he had first visited the area when he was newly married and liked it very much. He didn't have the money to buy a house, and he didn't like the idea of having a mortgage. "So," Pat said, "I'll build a house myself and I won't need any mortgage."

Pat sketched the house out and then began building, using weekends and free time. He built the garage first, installing in it gas and a stove and adding a bed and a convertible couch, plus two beds "so that if we had anybody visiting, they could sleep also in the garage." He added an outside pump for water along with an outhouse and a storage room.

On the Fourth of July weekend in 1956, when I was turning 20, he had the foundation poured. Not long after that he added walls and a cellar, covering the walls with tar paper for insulation. The next spring, he put in a ground floor, an attic, a roof, windows, and doors, and then finished the floors and added carpeting. "So I get everything in it I need," he said, "and what I can't do is the plumbing. I have that done. The electric, I have that done. Everything else, I did myself."

Pat said that Pop knew more about carpentry work, noting:

I was on the cement side of the business and the brick. He used to
come every Saturday to help me, so we got along very good. I was
happy he'd come on Friday night and go back on Saturday night. He
helped me till I completed my house. So I couldn't ask for more.

In appreciation for what Pop had done, Pat told me that he wanted to leave the house to him after he and Catherine died. Instead, Pop told him to leave

it to me (his oldest son, an Irish tradition). Upon learning this, I told Pat that
Kevin needed a house more than I did and that Kevin should get it when he
and Catherine died.

Pat's retirement lasted more than a quarter of a century. In this time, he
became famous among neighbors and family members for building walkways,
patios, and basements for others, all free of charge, although he would not
refuse a cup of tea or a shot of Jameson as an expression of gratitude. Whatever
he did was done the right way, and his own house was built like a fortress. "It
never had a leak," Pat said. "And it never will."

One story told by Kevin at Pat's wake in April of 2002 provided another
glimpse of this rare human being. When a post in a split-rail fence around
Mom and Pop's Lake Carmel house had to be replaced, Pat supervised the
project and Kevin did the labor. At eight on the appointed morning, when
Kevin opened the front door, there was Pat, then in his nineties, sitting next to
the fence with a coffee cup in his hand, ready to begin work. Pat said that the
post had to be planted in cement and positioned thirty inches into the ground.
The first task was to dig a hole for the post. It seemed that the old one had not
gone down the necessary depth. According to Pat, that was why it had rotted.

Kevin took the shovel and had dug fifteen inches into the ground when
he came upon a large rock, so massive that a bulldozer would be needed to
remove it. "Not to worry," Pat said. "I have the tools you need — star drills. Go
get them from my garage as well as the two-pound and eight-pound sledge
hammers."

Kevin was already sweating and could see the enormity of the task. Surely
there was a way around the problem. But Pat was not moved by Kevin's presentation. The post had to go into the ground right there, Pat said. Kevin, one
of those smart New York lawyers, argued that a few inches to the right or left
would make things easier. Then it wouldn't be uniform, Pat replied. It had to
go where it had to go. There was no basis for negotiation.

Hours later, after Kevin had attacked the rock with drills and sledges, it
cracked. The cement was mixed and the post inserted. Pat took a drink and
Kevin an aspirin. To this day, if you pass that house on Echo Road, you'll see
a fence with a sturdy, perfectly centered post as straight as an arrow. Such was
Pat Boyle's way, persistent and determined, doing things just so.

Catherine and Pat spent many happy years in that house, and when Catherine died Pat lived there by himself until his death. He was never alone
because of regular visits from relatives and daily visits from neighbors. The
curtain on the window of Pat's kitchen door, the entry point for visitors, was
always pushed aside whenever he expected someone, like on weekends when
I came to take him to Mass.

Saying Goodbye

Uncle Pat, as the oldest, was the undisputed head of the family in America. Although he didn't drive, he managed to get around after Catherine's death, either by bus or as a passenger in the car of a friend or relative. He did his own laundry and his own cooking. In the last two weeks of his life, with a Jameson in his hand, he regaled visitors with stories of his beloved Ireland, thanking everyone for even the smallest things that they had ever done for him. He appeared to have his mortality very much on his mind.

When Pat died at age 97, leaders of the Irish community and many friends in Carmel paid tribute to him. His friend Owen Farrell described him as a "rebel with a cause that he never dishonored and probably the last person I would ever know who helped found a new nation." Sean Hamilton, another friend, said that speaking to him was like "living Irish history." Eddie Burke called him an "outstanding patriot" of Ireland and "a loyal citizen of the United States." And John Mulvihill said, "There was something about this man. Everyone listened and respected him, and even my eleven-year-old grandson loved to meet and talk with him." As for me and my siblings, he was simply Uncle Pat, Mom's beloved brother.[5]

Enda Brogan captured Uncle Pat in a profile written for the Mayo Society of New York:

> He is one of life's unsung heroes, a person who has never sought
> public acclaim for his actions. He is a person unbittered by age, a man
> who has retained a positive outlook throughout his long and eventful
> life. He possesses great lucidity and vitality for his years (then 93) and
> it is always a pleasure to visit him and listen to his stories told with
> sincerity, humour, and accuracy.[6]

Uncle Pat had a genial spirit, a happy disposition, and was always helping others. He had wise counsel for all who sought his assistance. Shortly before he died, he celebrated St. Patrick's Day at home with family, watching the St. Patrick's Day Parade on TV around the dining room table. Emalie, who cared for him that day, said that he embodied the spirit of the day — in his loving, caring, and joyful ways.

When Kevin and I visited Pat's home after his death, we found church offertory envelopes that he had collected during his illness but hadn't been able to return. As his surrogates, we took the envelopes and made all of the donations that Pat had wanted to make. We also found an unopened bottle of Bushmills Malt Irish Whiskey that I had given him but that he refused to drink out of protest that no Catholics were allowed to work in the company's plant in Ireland. Kevin, as his executor, gave me the bottle, which I considered my inheritance. I thought I would pass it on to one of my family members, but after holding onto it for many years, I decided to give it to William Treanor after he participated in a class I was teaching at Fordham. He had just become dean of Georgetown Law School. Dean Robert Reilly, who witnessed the moment, described it for me:

> When you presented the bottle to Bill, explaining that it was one of the few possessions of Uncle Pat's that was passed along to you, I was watching Bill's face as he did all he could to maintain his composure. I knew that he understood the immense personal attachment you felt to Uncle Pat, what he had meant in your life, and that you would not part with this treasure lightly. . . . Even the students understood that this was a gift beyond price.

Uncle Pat seemed to have an encyclopedic knowledge of every important event of the twentieth century. But he lived totally in the present, absorbing and storing away everything for future telling and retelling. He loved to have an audience. His stories ran one into another, and as you were about to leave, he'd have just one more for the road. He was always positive about life, never complaining or criticizing, and always anxious to give you a cup of tea or a shot of Jameson, of which two shots each day, he proclaimed, were the key to a long life.

In a 1995 radio interview given during his last trip to Ireland, Pat regaled his audience with the story of a Texan who had lived to 105. When asked what habits he had that accounted for his longevity, the Texan said he couldn't recall any, but noted that he had one bad habit — he could never refuse a drink. Pat roared in the telling of this story, which he did many times.

Pat fell short of the Texan's longevity by seven years, but not for want of trying. Pat's name will not be found in any history book, but it will endure in the hearts and memories of all who knew him and, often invisibly, on the stoops, patios, stairs, basements, and walkways that he built for his neighbors and family. This was part of his legacy.

8

Memories of the Nearby House That Ruth Built

I may have been given a bad break, but I have an awful lot to live for. With all of this, I consider myself the luckiest man on the face of this Earth.

— LOU GEHRIG

The original Yankee Stadium opened in April of 1923. When it closed in 2008, I wrote a personal account of its presence in my life, beginning with the last game I attended, on September 19, 2008. That night my grandson Ryan and I watched the Yankees beat the Baltimore Orioles 3 to 2 in a thriller, with two home runs, great fielding, and wonderful pitching. We had tears in our eyes, and as we left the stadium, Ryan said, "That was the best game I ever saw." We took pictures of each other with the field in the background. Neither of us wanted to go home.

As a child I attended many baseball games at Yankee Stadium. I had no trouble getting tickets, either buying them at a discounted price through my participation in the local YMCA, or receiving them from people who had an extra ticket or ticket stub from having left the game early. Donald was particularly adept at acquiring these tickets.

I loved to watch players such as Joe DiMaggio (the "Yankee Clipper"), Mickey Mantle, Yogi Berra, Phil Rizzuto, Tommy Henrich ("Old Reliable"), Whitey Ford, Allie Reynolds ("Superchief"), and reliever Joe Paige. Mantle was an amazing runner and home run hitter; DiMaggio was graceful in how he moved around in center field; Rizzuto was a fielder and bunter extraordinaire, and Berra was unbelievable in his ability to hit every kind of pitch, high, low, or outside. Not surprisingly, almost all of these players are now in the Baseball Hall of Fame.

I also saw games at the stadium played by the football Giants. Of those games, I'll never forget the pain I felt when the Giants lost the NFL championship to the Baltimore Colts on December 28, 1958. I was sitting with Donald in the mezzanine, on its metal frame. We absorbed every play in what has come to be called the greatest NFL game ever played, although I don't think either of us saw it that way because of the outcome.

I recall many other great NFL games at the stadium, including two in the 1950s between the Giants and Cleveland Browns, in one of which Pat Summerall kicked a forty-nine-yard winning field goal in blinding, blizzard-like conditions. On that occasion, Donald and I huddled together near a fire in the bleachers to keep warm. I remember another year when the Giants beat the Bears for a championship, with Giants players wearing sneakers for better footing on the frozen field.

I also watched the Giants lose an NFL championship to the Green Bay Packers, whose three linebackers were the fiercest I ever saw. Still vivid to me is the incredible running of Jim Brown of the Cleveland Browns, the ferocious line-backing of Dick Butkus of the Chicago Bears, and the precision-nature quarterbacking of Otto Graham of the Browns and Johnny Unitas of the Baltimore Colts. My heroes, however, were to be found on the New York Giants. Frank Gifford, Kyle Rote, Charlie Conerly, Jimmy Patton, Roosevelt Grier, Roosevelt Taylor, and Andy Robustelli were my particular favorites.

I saw many other great baseball and football games at the stadium. Among the most memorable was Game 6 of the 1977 World Series, in which Reggie Jackson hit three home runs and the Yankees won their twenty-first World Series championship. I recall Steve Garvey of the Dodgers coming out of the dugout and joining in the ovation. "Why not?" he essentially said. "This was an historic moment." It was bittersweet for me to see the old stadium close, but the new stadium, which opened in 2009, was built, as I previously noted, on a site where I had played when I was young, so I still connected it with many important parts of my life.

Just west of Yankee Stadium is Macombs Dam Park. It was there that I observed the intense football rivalry of a "gang" from Highbridge known as the Ikes, associated with Sacred Heart Parish, and one from Morris Avenue called the Dukes, associated with St. Angela Merici Parish, many of whose members I had grown up with.

The so-called gangs never seemed to finish a game. At some point fisticuffs would break out, sometimes including the use of chains, clubs, and other implements of warfare. Whether you were in the game or not, when these fights started you ran for daylight because New York's finest would be arriving on the scene and rounding up everyone in sight. I was a Duke in spirit but became an adjunct member of the Ikes in high school, after finding some of the Ikes as classmates.

Although I moved away from 161st Street, I was always close enough that I could easily return to the stadium with my wife, children, and grandchildren. I've attended exciting games at the new Yankee Stadium, including the Yankees' second playoff game in 2009 against the Minnesota Twins. I saw this game with my grandson Ryan, and the Yankees came from behind to win in 11 innings, although not without clutch home runs by Alex "A-Rod" Rodriguez and Mark Teixeira. It was a thrilling experience.

We saw this game, and others, from twenty-dollar grandstand seats (Section 410, Row 8, Seats 12 and 13). We also saw the Yankees win their twenty-seventh world championship, beating the Philadelphia Phillies by a score of 7 to 3. On the day of the game (November 4, 2009), I was offered two tickets by a family member stranded abroad. When I left that game with Ryan, I wondered if I'd ever see the Yankees win another world championship. I was happy, however, that one of my grandchildren attended the game with me, believing that he would likely see another such championship and perhaps recall that he had seen the first one with his grandfather.

On September 7, 2014, I traveled to Yankee Stadium for "Derek Jeter Day." Many Hall of Fame athletes and celebrities were present for the occasion, and, on a huge stadium screen, players and coaches from other teams could be seen bidding Jeter goodbye, offering best wishes for his future, and thanking him for the class and grace with which he performed both on and off the field.

It was a busy day for me, but I put everything aside to attend with my brother, Kevin. "With all his greatness as a player," Kevin said, "his humility stood out." There were many tears in the stadium as Jeter spoke to the fans. "I want to thank you for helping me feel like a kid for the last 20 years," Jeter said. "In my opinion, I've had the greatest job in the world. I got a chance to be the shortstop for the New York Yankees—and there's only one of those."[1] As a *New York Times Magazine* contributor wrote, "He led the Yankees to 16 post-season tournaments and five World Series titles. He has hit better than .400 in 10 different playoff series and is the all-time playoff leader in singles and doubles and tied for the lead in triples and is third in home runs and fourth in RBI's . . . he never won an MVP award. He was almost certainly the best shortstop of his generation."[2]

Postscript

I thought of my experiences at Yankee Stadium when I traveled to Arizona in 2008 to watch Super Bowl XLII at the University of Phoenix stadium in Glendale. Because of my service as an NFL arbitrator, I'd received from the NFL Management Council and Players Association two tickets to the Super Bowl. I attended the game with my grandson Roddy, then 8 years old. Little did I realize that Roddy and I would witness what Giants co-owner John Mara would later describe to me as the greatest game in the team's history.

The Patriots had been undefeated that season and were predicted to win the Super Bowl. The Giants had played well in the earlier playoff games and were not pushovers. The game was well played by both teams, and with slightly more than two minutes to go, the Patriots gained a four-point lead.

Roddy became hysterical, believing that the game was over. He was trembling and was so devastated, and he asked me to take him out of the stadium. I told him that life was filled with difficult moments and it was important to work through them. I said that if Tom Brady could get a touchdown in two minutes, so could Eli Manning. I pulled Roddy close and he buried his head in my chest, afraid to watch. Then, in the final two minutes of the game, Manning escaped the grasp of three New England Patriots defensive players, throwing the forward pass that wide receiver David Tyree famously caught on his helmet. As the Giants raced down the field and the crowd roared, Roddy peeked out at the field to see what was happening. Before we knew it, the Giants had scored a touchdown and were ahead by three points, 17 to 14, with only seconds left in the game. When the Giants won, Roddy, stunned, had a smile on his face the likes of which I'd never seen before.

Jeter Broke Gehrig's All-Time Hitting Record

On Friday, September 11, 2009, America commemorated the eighth anniversary of the terrorist attack at the World Trade Center. A tribute to those who had lost their lives was held at Yankee Stadium before the game between the Yankees and the Baltimore Orioles. In that game Derek Jeter broke Lou Gehrig's all-time hitting record as a Yankee. The record of 2,721 hits had stood for seventy years.

I attended alone, with an unused ticket in my pocket, hoping a family member would come. On my arrival, however, the rain was so heavy that it seemed the game would be suspended. I walked around the stadium for a while to kill time and then went to my seat in the grandstand, Section 410,

Row 8, Seats 12 and 13. Although there was a covering overhead, the rain came in anyway. The section was practically deserted, with no one in my row or the rows in front of or behind me. It was an eerie feeling to be so alone.

No players could be seen on the field as the rain poured down, and a tarpaulin covered the infield. At about 7 p.m., it was announced that the game would be delayed until 8:20 p.m. Between 7 and 8 p.m. the rain became lighter, almost like what the Irish call a "soft rain." I sensed that there would be a game after all.

Sometime around 8 p.m. cheering began as groundskeepers came out on the field to remove the tarp and fasten the bases. The game began around 8:30 p.m., after the ceremonial first pitch by Secretary of the Department of Homeland Security Janet Napolitano. The Yankee players took the field to a great roar, and "The Star-Spangled Banner" was sung by an officer in the U.S. Navy.

The Orioles batted at the top of the inning, and when Jeter caught a pop fly for the third out, the fans roared. You could feel the growing excitement as Jeter went first to bat at the bottom of the first. Fans were on their feet chanting his name. When he struck out, we knew he'd be back again to hit. He returned to bat at the bottom of the third inning, and once again it seemed that everyone in the stadium was standing.

The Yankee relief pitchers and coaches in the centerfield bullpen had left their seats to watch from the front railing. No one wanted to miss history in the making. It felt like all of the nearly forty-seven thousand fans at the stadium were yelling, chanting, screaming, and roaring for Jeter to break the record at this very moment. The noise was deafening.

With the count 2 to 0, he hit the ball solidly. It went down the first base side of the field and into the outfield for a single. Jeter rounded first base, clapped his hands, and returned to the base. Lou Gehrig's record was broken, and this moment in history could not have been more dramatic. Yankee players rushed out of the dugout to embrace Jeter. The ovation in the stadium was thunderous. Jeter pointed to his family and friends in the stands and tipped and waved his batter's helmet to express his gratitude to the fans. Even players for the Orioles stood at the top of their dugout applauding. Tears trickled down my cheeks for reasons I cannot explain.

As I left the stadium, officials announced another rain delay. On the way out, I bought a red baseball cap to honor the day. The players of both teams had worn red caps throughout the game to pay tribute to the lives lost on September 11, and I wanted to join in solidarity. I learned later that the Yankees did not win, but it hardly mattered. Their triumph ran much deeper than a single game. They were the heroes of my childhood, my community, and my family.

PART III
My Salad Days

Education is the most powerful weapon which you can use to change the world.

— NELSON MANDELA

PART III

My Salad Day

9

St. Angela Merici Grammar School, 1942–1950

See how important is this union and concord. So long for it, pursue it, embrace it, hold on to it with all your strength; for I tell you, living all together thus united in heart, you will be like a mighty fortress, a tower of strength.

— ST. ANGELA MERICI, *LAST COUNSEL*

Although Mom and Pop had a limited formal education, they made sure that was not the case for me and my siblings. My formal education began when I was 6 and ended when I was about to turn 25. Those nineteen years gave me a foundation that would serve me for the rest of my life. Until I reached college, my teachers were almost all members of religious orders or priests of the Archdiocese of New York. Their only real compensation was the joy that accompanies a religious ministry. I owe them an unpayable debt for what followed in my life.

My first day of school was in September of 1942 at St. Angela Merici grammar school, named for the first woman to establish a Catholic religious order for women. The school was a magnet for children of immigrant families, largely Irish and Italian, with some students of German and Polish heritage. Its history was beautifully described by Graceann McKeon, a graduate of the school who also pursued a career in law. She noted that at the turn of the nineteenth century, the Bronx was made up of "farms and villages," noting that residents of what was then the village of Melrose were mostly of German and Irish descent.[1]

The founding priest of St. Angela Merici, Father Thomas Wallace of the Archdiocese of New York, celebrated the first parish Mass in 1899 in a private house near Morris Avenue and 158th Street. On June 24, 1900, in the same location as the present church, a first Mass was again celebrated in the newly built church, a small wooden building. The first parishioners had the satisfaction of having built that church "with their own hands," McKeon said. Then a small country parish, St. Angela Merici was located, she added, near "large empty meadows, a place called Dandelion Farm, and the Fleetwood Race Track."[2]

Under the leadership of Father Wallace, a kindergarten was opened in the parish school in 1907, followed a few years later by primary grades. According to McKeon, the "small parish hall, on the Grant Avenue side of the church, housed the first school." Father Wallace chose the Ursuline Sisters to run the school, with Mother Alphonsus as the first principal. Soon the Ursuline Sisters began a Provincialate for the Ursuline Order and opened a school and academy for girls and convent school for sisters on 165th Street and the Grand Concourse, which remained there until 1959.

In 1909 the parish school was moved to the site of the Morrisania Clubhouse on nearby Bonner Place. In the early 1920s the present church and school building was constructed, and it was dedicated by Cardinal Hayes on October 26, 1924. As McKeon noted: "The building is a unique design, the church in the center with wide corridors on the right and left sides, off which are the spacious, high ceilinged classrooms, each with a wall of windows."[3] A plaque at the side of the main altar lists Mr. and Mrs. "Babe" Ruth among the donors of the three marble altars.[4]

Emerging from such humble beginnings, St. Angela Merici has educated thousands of students. I attended its grammar school from 1942 to 1950. Donald, Maureen, Kevin, and Anne followed me, although Anne left after a few years to finish elementary school at St. Nicholas Tolentine after Mom and Pop had moved to that parish in the Bronx. As parishioners, we didn't pay any tuition at St. Angela. Our classes were taught by the Ursuline Sisters, who took vows of poverty, chastity, and obedience. Of the habit they wore, Maureen said:

> It consisted of a floor-length garment with a large, crisp white bib, and when they wanted to know the time, a watch would be brought out from under the bib. A black veil was draped from their coif, and rosary beads extended down the side of their robe. The coif had a white interior, and it was impossible to discover if they had hair.
>
> When Mother Immaculata, my second-grade teacher (who served the school from 1924 to 1975), passed down the row, I would put my head down on the desk in an effort to peek under the bib to locate the

hook for the watch. I never found it. Their bibs were always white and crisp, and it was inconceivable that they ate spaghetti and meatballs, since no stains were ever detected. The garments had deep pockets, and when something had to be extracted from the interior, their hands would travel a serpentine path until they retrieved the object of their search.

Attendance at Sunday Mass was obligatory and began precisely at 9 a.m. Students proceeded down the main aisle of the church, waiting for the cricket (an object like a castanet) to make its appearance, and after hearing the click, we'd genuflect in unison, wait for the second click, rise from our knees, and, on the third click, file into the pews. The girls would sit on one side of the church, the boys on the other. "The perils of association with the opposite sex were ingrained in us," Maureen said, "but it did not prevent the furtive glances."

We were encouraged to go to confession often. The confessional was a little cabin protruding from the wall of the church interior, and in the center was a door with two side entrances covered with drapes. The priest sat on a chair in the middle of the confessional, separated on each side by a partition with a screen. A penitent would kneel on either side of either partition, and the screen would be slipped back when it was the penitent's turn to speak. As Maureen remembered:

> I had to make my way in the dark behind the curtain and find the kneeler, wait patiently until the priest in the center slid open the screen, and then utter those words forever ingrained in me, "Bless me, Father, for I have sinned," gushed forth in a torrent, reciting my sins as quickly as possible. Receiving a decade of the rosary as penance meant I was quite a sinner and that I wasn't lucky to find the priest who gave the shortest penance.

My experience with confession was similar. I usually chose the priest with a reputation for giving soft discipline. We didn't want to commit sins because of fear of a black mark being placed on our souls, but we thought an act of charity could win us points in heaven. Indulgences were received for reciting certain prayers or attending novenas. "I can't wait to see how I'll fare at the pearly gates," Maureen said, "when I show up with a record number of indulgences. Between points and indulgences, I should be a shoo-in." I agreed with her, although unsure about myself.

I received my first Holy Communion on June 3, 1943. I was encouraged to become an altar boy, and I became one under the tutelage of Monsignor

Joseph Foley, who served as the pastor from 1936 to 1959. I was an altar boy until I graduated from St. Angela Merici in 1950. I had trouble understanding and speaking the Latin part of the Mass, but I became skilled at ringing the altar bells at the appropriate time during the consecration. Service as an altar boy at a wedding was pleasant, since it usually meant a generous tip. Doing so at a funeral was less inviting.

I recall at one point accompanying a priest very early in the morning to the Ursuline Convent on the Grand Concourse, where Mass was celebrated for the sisters who taught us and for the nuns and novices at the convent in attendance. When the academy closed in 1959, Monsignor Edward Martin, Foley's successor as pastor, built a convent for them on Morris Avenue at 162nd Street, allowing these devoted sisters to continue to teach there until 1987. The Ursuline Sisters remained at their academy on the Grand Concourse in the Bronx until 1959.

At St. Angela, the boys attended classes on one side of the school and the girls on the other. Uniforms were worn by all — a navy jumper and a white blouse for the girls and navy pants and a white shirt for the boys. For special occasions the boys wore gray military jackets with white belts. It wasn't unusual to have thirty to forty students in one classroom. I'm not aware of having paid much attention to the girls, since we weren't encouraged to mingle and were separated from each other by the church proper. The parish today is as beautiful as it was in the 1940s, despite being surrounded by tall new buildings, including courthouses.

My religious education consisted of the Socratic method of questioning as found in the Baltimore Catechism, a book used to counter the Protestant Reformation of the sixteenth century. This manual of Catholic teaching was first introduced in the United States in 1891, and the second edition, which was used in the 1950s, had 421 questions and answers, all of which Maureen memorized. She said of her experience: "If I didn't know the answers, Mother Annunciata, my eighth grade teacher, would narrow her eyes and purse her lips. It didn't take me long to learn the answers. We knew God made us to know Him, love Him, and serve Him in this world, and to be happy with Him in the next."

If we didn't behave, Mom and Pop would be asked to come in for a meeting. We learned the basics: reading, writing, math, history, religion, and geography. Recess was spent outdoors on a concrete lot.

I wasn't a particularly good student. This was confirmed by a visit I made to St. Angela Merici during Christmas week of 2009 to review my record. It was pleasant to return, this time at age 73, but it tested my memory of past accomplishments at the school. I didn't expect the experience to be as humbling as it was. I discovered that, in my family, my sister Maureen had the best record, with Donald a close second. Kevin was a close third, and my record was terrible. I was "on trial" by the third grade, with a C average for the year.

This visit confirmed a memory passed on to me by Maureen of a time when Mom was called over to the school to receive a sobering report about my performance. Maureen recalls Mom crying on that occasion. But I challenged myself to improve, earning a C+ in the fifth grade, and converting a 54 in math (a failing grade) to a 95 by the sixth grade. The math successes were because of Pop, who kept me home all summer to work on math exercises. He showed me little mercy, insisting that I keep working on my exercises at the kitchen table, but in doing so he made a difference in my life. I graduated with a B average overall, hardly enough to seek admission to Regis High School in Manhattan, the Jesuit favorite. Top honors went to my classmate, Thomas Shelley, later Monsignor Shelley. I did however receive, I believe, a prize at graduation for deportment. Mom expressed astonishment, noting that my space at home was always a mess. Frankly, I was glad to graduate and move on to Bishop Dubois High School, where I would eventually hit my stride.[5]

I left grammar school with a sense of community that would serve as the foundation of my personal and professional life.

Postscript

In 2010 I rejoined half of my classmates from St. Angela to celebrate the 60th anniversary of our graduation. Several members of the class had died, and others were unable to attend because of distance, health, or scheduling conflicts. Of the class, two of us became lawyers, several pursued business careers, and three pursued religious vocations. Most chose careers in public service, serving as teachers, in fire and police departments, or in the military. A remarkable number have stayed in touch with one another over the years through annual get-togethers at Rory Dolan's popular Irish restaurant in Yonkers, a tradition I take part in.

When I was dean of Fordham Law School, I was invited to serve at St. Angela as the school's volunteer principal for a day. I used this position to briefly talk to each class about a career in the law. The experience was as joy-filled as any in my life, as the students asked me questions, some telling me they wanted to be a prosecutor and others a defense lawyer. When asked by students to suspend classes at noon, I sadly had to tell them that my authority did not extend that far. Perhaps that's why I've never been invited back to be an acting principal.

10

Bishop Dubois High School, 1950–1954

Bishop Dubois High School is proud to be one of the sanctuaries of scholarship dedicated by His Eminence Francis Cardinal Spellman to the noble task of building citizens who will reflect credit on their Church and on their country. Here the student's mind is developed, and his body strengthened. The end result is the Catholic Gentleman — prepared to take his place in society, to choose his career for the future, and to work out his salvation for eternity.

— DUBOIS 1951 YEARBOOK

My decision to attend Bishop Dubois High School in Harlem was a practical one. I took its test and passed, but I had to decide whether to accept the offer before taking the test for Cardinal Hayes High School, located on the Grand Concourse. Hayes was my first choice, but I used "lawyer reasoning" to conclude that if I turned down Dubois and didn't pass the test for Hayes, I'd have no Catholic high school to attend. In as devout a family as ours, the idea of attending a non-Catholic school was out of the question. Neither my family nor I could accept this risk, so the bus trip across 161st from Morris Avenue to Amsterdam Avenue in Manhattan to attend Dubois became my daily ritual for the next four years.[1]

I arrived at Bishop Dubois in September 1950 and graduated on June 26, 1954. The school bore the name of Bishop John Dubois, who had served as Bishop of New York from 1826 to 1842. Bishop Dubois never had an easy time in New York. Because he was a French Bishop, it was a challenge for him to gain the acceptance of his Irish constituency who were relentlessly hard on him.[2]

At the time of my admission, Francis Cardinal Spellman, a graduate of Fordham College, was Archbishop of New York. Monsignor Michael Buckley was the school's principal. The Monsignor was a very kind and gentle person. To my everlasting gratitude, he responded to Pop's admission that he couldn't afford to pay the monthly ten-dollar tuition. Monsignor Buckley asked if he could manage five dollars, to which Pop said yes. For my entire high school career, that's what he paid. Years later I reimbursed the Archdiocese of New York for this tuition advance, with interest, by making an appropriate gift to John Cardinal O'Connor. When I gave him the money at an Inner-City Scholarship Fund luncheon, he seemed momentarily speechless.

My freshman class consisted of about a hundred male students, many of whom came from the Catholic parishes of Manhattan. The school's teachers included nine priests, six Marist religious brothers, and two laypersons. The curriculum consisted of classes in English, Latin, religion, social studies, French, math, and science. One of the brothers was the dean of discipline, who intimidated us and kept me in line. I have a recollection of ending up in Jug (detention) at least once, for a reason that escapes me.

During the first half of my Dubois career, I wasn't a strong student. In fact, I was apparently at risk of not gaining admission to a good college as I began my third year. I struggled in courses involving foreign languages, science, and math. Fortunately, a concerned Diocesan priest at Dubois came to my rescue. That priest was Father Matthew Cox, the head of the Department of Social Studies. He asked whether I planned to attend college, and upon hearing that I did, he urged me to improve my marks. In response, I turned more intensively to my studies, improved my grades, and, to the surprise of my family, received at graduation the general excellence medal for my last year, along with a prize for French.

As to the French medal, Uncle Pat recalled me saying I didn't understand a word said by the person who presented the medal because he spoke in French. I was good at memorizing, but I was otherwise very limited in my ability to speak the language, as was brought home to me in college when I received my lowest grade in conversational French.

Without Father Cox's intervention, I'm not sure what direction my life would have taken. Surely I wouldn't have been admitted to Fordham. Many years later, when I chaired the New York State Commission on Government Integrity, I received a letter from Father Cox asking if I was the same person he knew at Dubois. I was astonished that he remembered me and called him on the phone to catch up and tell him how important he had been to me when I needed focus in my life. Sadly, he died about two weeks after our call, before we could meet again, as we had planned.

My Dubois classmates were diverse, with minority students throughout the school. *Brown v. Board of Education,* the landmark case in which the justices of the U.S. Supreme Court would rule unanimously that racial segregation of children in America's public schools was illegal, was being argued at this time. But we paid little attention to the issue of desegregation. I didn't experience a separation based on color during high school, although in grammar school there were no students of color.

At Dubois I enjoyed watching classmates compete in baseball and basketball games against other schools and recall fondly attending a dance in junior year with the sister of a classmate. This was my first date with a girl, and no other dates followed until I was well along at Fordham College.

The opportunities to speak at a student assembly of the entire student body and to serve as editor of the yearbook in my senior year stood as singular experiences. I had never spoken to a large group before and was afraid that I might forget my words. I spoke on the subject of courage and told the story of a Howie Hansen, a UCLA football player whose wife had died a few days before his last collegiate game. Hansen played in that game because he thought his wife would have wanted him to do so. In doing so he became a hero, leading UCLA to a 39–0 victory. I concluded my speech with the words, "Maybe his final words in the Bruins' dressing room after that memorable game can leave us all with one moral lesson. 'There is a merciful God.'" In many ways this speech marked a turning point for me in high school, building my confidence.

On November 2, 2017, at St. Patrick's Cathedral, I thought of my talk of more than sixty years earlier as I climbed the pulpit to deliver my dear friend James "Jim" Gill's eulogy and reflect on his life of courage.[3]

High school ended joyously. Mom and Pop celebrated my graduation in our apartment. Classmates dropped by, and friends and relatives came over, including Uncle Pat and Aunt Catherine. They all enjoyed Mom's cooking and watching her dance Irish jigs and reels as Pop played the concertina. I didn't realize at the time the specialness of the moment — becoming the first member of the family to graduate from high school.

11

Fordham College, 1954–1958

What is a Jesuit education all about? It is about nothing less than empowerment and transformation. [Students become] men and women of competence, conscience, compassion, and commitment to the cause of the human family. They become men and women with a difference — and men and women who make a difference in the world.
— JOSEPH M. MCSHANE, S.J., PRESIDENT, FORDHAM UNIVERSITY

Mom and Pop drilled into us the importance of education beyond the high school level. I applied to all of the Catholic colleges in the area, hoping to be admitted to a school like Fordham, Iona, Manhattan, or St. John's. I was accepted by Fordham, a relatively short subway ride from my home, and began my studies there on September 14, 1954.

Until 1907 Fordham College was known as St. John's College. Bishop John Hughes, then Coadjutor Bishop of New York, bought the Rose Hill Property in 1839, on which the school's Bronx campus is located. The college formally opened on June 24, 1841.[1] In purchasing the property, Bishop Hughes said, "I had not, when I purchased the site of this new college . . . so much as a penny to commence the payment of it."[2]

In 1846, the New York State Legislature elevated Fordham College to the rank of a university. The same year, the Society of Jesus bought the school from the Archdiocese of New York for $40,500, and when the seminary was removed and its land became available, the Society purchased that for an additional $45,000. The first Fordham Jesuits came from a very rural setting — St. Mary's College in Kentucky.[3]

Bishop Hughes, who was born in 1797 in Ireland's County Tyrone, Province of Ulster, grew up in a world in which Presbyterians and Catholics had neither civil nor religious rights, and the flags of England, Scotland, and Wales flew prominently throughout the country. In 1817, at the age of 20, he came to America, where he would leave behind, as a legacy, the establishment of not only Fordham College but also of St. Patrick's Cathedral and Mary-mount College for Women.

The Fordham College catalogue of 1954–55, my first year, described the school as a "Liberal Arts College for Men" and read, "If it were possible to summarize in two words the educational system at Fordham one might advert to the motto on the official seal of the University, *Sapientia et Doctrina*, wisdom and information." The curriculum placed a heavy emphasis on theology, a required course in each of my four years, and on scholastic philosophy, a major subject in my last two years. A Fordham education is structured on the principle the Jesuits call *cura personalis*, which means care of the whole person. In my experience as a student, Fordham fostered not only my education, but my moral, emotional, and spiritual growth.

Students had three programs to choose from: a Bachelor of Arts program, with an emphasis on Greek, Latin, and English classics; a Bachelor of Science program, with an emphasis on physics, chemistry, and biology; and a Bachelor of Science in social sciences. I pursued the latter program, remembering my earlier difficulties with subjects in the other programs.

The yearbook for 1955 described my first-year class in these terms:

> September, 1954 . . . the beginning of an adventure, an experience, a new life. We were "college men" . . . all four hundred and fifty-eight of us. We had come to Fordham from Bogota, Colombia and the Flatbush section of Brooklyn; from Hood River, Oregon, and lower Manhattan; from Santurce, Puerto Rico and . . . the Bronx. We were awkward and new as we entered on the Rose Hill scene.

I was one of those "college men" from the Bronx, but by no means alone. At Fordham I grew in knowledge, understanding, and confidence, and developed friendships that have lasted a lifetime, especially with Joseph T. C. Hart and Louis Viola, both lawyers. The years from 1954 to 1958 were the most peaceful in my life, if not my happiest school years. For the first time in my life I was free to choose my courses, to explore new areas, and to participate where I might in the life of the school.

It was a great time to be at Fordham, with athletes in track and basketball winning acclaim. I remember watching Tom Courtney run on the campus in my freshmen year and rejoiced, as did all of Fordham, when he won two gold medals in the 1956 Olympics. The legendary Jack Coffey described his performance as the greatest of any Fordham athlete in history.[4] I also remember sneaking a look in the gym from time to time to watch Ed Conlin throw basketballs into the hoop from mid-court. Conlin would later play in the NBA and coach men's basketball at Fordham.

I traveled to Fordham by either bus, the Third Avenue El, or the Grand Central train, which stopped at Melrose. The latter cost a few pennies more than the others, so I rarely traveled that way, although it was the fastest and most luxurious of the three.

My annual Fordham tuition of $600 was modest by current standards, but it wasn't easy for my family to amass the necessary funds. Mom and Pop had others in school for whom they were paying tuitions. I worked weekends in college at a supermarket on 116th Street and Lexington Avenue and full-time during some of my college summers. Donald did the same, and my sister Maureen had a job as a waitress.

Toward the end of my college years, I received an unexpected prize of $25 for an essay I wrote on civil rights from the Institute of Social Order of the Society of Jesus. Then I was awarded a scholarship grant of $350, the first in my life, enabling me to enter the spring semester of 1958 as a United States Rubber Company Foundation Scholar. The grant covered the entire tuition for my last semester and was a godsend for Mom and Pop. They were also appreciative of a communication from the college's Dean Leo McLaughlin, S.J., in December of 1957, congratulating them for my appearance on the Dean's list. I had come a long way from my rocky years at St. Angela Merici and my early goings at Bishop Dubois.

I enjoyed my college teachers and especially my political science, history, English, theology, and philosophy professors. From the outset I threw myself into my studies and decided to major in political science. Dr. William Frasca, chairman of the department, was a prime influence in my choice. His first-year course on government stirred within me an interest in the Constitution that would grow over the years (and would prove profoundly important by the time I reached my late twenties, when I became involved in the crafting of the Twenty-Fifth Amendment). Part of his magic was his knowledge of and enthusiasm for conveying the subject to young students like me who were wet behind the ears. In appearance, he reminded me of Theodore Roosevelt.

Another memorable teacher was Dr. Francis Connolly, vice chairman of the English department. Dr. Connolly, whose class in English literature I took, was elegant in both style and speech. I've often thought that Dr. Frasca and Dr. Connolly were my two best teachers. Both encouraged me when I needed encouragement and made me feel important, perhaps helping me compensate for the insecurities which grew out of my earlier academic performance.

I did well in other classes, taught by both religious and lay teachers. I had many favorite teachers: Father John Bush, S.J., who taught a history course in my first year; Father Lawrence McKenna, S.J., whose political science courses provided the foundations of my understanding of government and international relations; and Dr. Mary Clark, one of the few women who taught at the school at the time, whose course on constitutional law was magnificent. The opportunity she gave me to deliver a class lecture on the landmark case of *Marbury v. Madison* is one I still treasure.

I also loved my Jesuit teachers: Father David Cronin, S.J., who stressed repeatedly the fact that success was about perseverance; Father Joseph Doncell, S.J., whose philosophical insights pushed me to my analytical limits; Father Edward McNally, S.J., whose philosophy course and teaching manner made being a student a delightful experience; Father Thomas Hennessy, S.J., a theology teacher whose personal qualities were of saintly proportions; and my theology teacher, Father Robert Gleason, S.J., whose brilliant teachings have served as helpful guides throughout my life.

Father Gleason's explanation of mortal sin has remained with me to this day. In one class, he spoke about a person who realized that if he had another drink, he would be drunk and out of control. Father Gleason used the example to highlight the importance of reflection and deliberation in moral reasoning. Because alcohol would impair one's capacity for moral reasoning, to take another drink under such circumstances would be a sin.

Father Cronin's junior philosophy class was unforgettable. He used to talk about his walks to and from Yankee Stadium, a six-mile distance, which impressed me greatly, given that he wasn't that young, judged by my then age. I remember once having to give a speech in his class on St. Augustine and being told by him that I had to aspire to the speaking level of Bishop Fulton J. Sheen, then renowned for his talks on television. I began my speech seven or eight times. Each time I was cut off by Father Cronin and told to start again. I eventually completed the talk only because Father Cronin took pity on me.

Vaughan Deering, an instructor in communication arts, taught a class on voice and diction and required me to take extra sessions on speed-reading because I read so slowly. I don't think he ever felt that I read quickly enough, though I had improved. He was Shakespearean in appearance and speech and a perfect gentleman, but persistent in the classroom. There was a charm about him that I found endearing.

As for other Jesuits, three remain luminaries in my memories: the dean of the college, Leo McLaughlin, S.J., who was revered by us all; the president of the university, Laurence McGinley, S.J., who was both imposing and inspiring as he walked through the campus reading from his prayer book; and Timothy Healy, S.J., director of alumni relations, who was a popular presence at athletic and academic events.

My classmates at Fordham College (all boys at the time; the school did not admit women until 1974) were, like my teachers, an extraordinary group. Many were, like me, sons of immigrants and the first in their families to go to college. The vast majority of them were graduates of Catholic high schools.

In my first year I joined the Booster Club, founded by an admired classmate, Robert Bradley, and rooted for the school's basketball, football, and track teams. I participated in intramural sports, especially softball, where I pitched, and touch football, where I played in the secondary. We played these games with great determination on Fordham's Edwards Parade Grounds. When at one point I ended up on the same team as my classmate Tommy Giordano, I knew that my pitching career was over (or so I thought until I played on my law firm Skadden's softball team). Giordano was an outstanding participant in intramural sports at Fordham, and his windmill pitching was phenomenal.[5] He would be recognized by Fordham University as athlete of the year.

Giordano later pursued a career in the field of education. He served as the dean of discipline at Middle School 45, which now bears his name, and was the founding principal of Fiorello H. LaGuardia School in the Bronx. He became affectionately known as "Mr. G" by the schoolchildren of district 10 and the Belmont community where he served.[6]

Over time I found myself becoming more involved in government. Beginning in my second year and continuing throughout the rest of college, I served in a representative capacity, first of my sophomore section, and then as vice president of my junior class under the leadership of class president Joseph Doyle, who later became a Jesuit priest. In my last year, I served as vice president of the student body under the leadership of Joseph Simone, whose death at an early age greatly affected me. The plaque my sophomore section classmates gave me, which reads, "Thanks for a Job Well Done," is among my most valued possessions.

My service as a representative of the sophomore class had a transformative impact on me, as the position challenged me to be a spokesperson and to organize events. Perhaps based on a suggestion, I organized several "beer" parties — though I did not drink alcohol — at a tavern in the neighborhood known as Germantown on East 86th Street, called the Rhineland. The parties became popular among Fordham students and among women who were studying at nursing schools in Manhattan. When I ran for student vice president, my classmate Lou Boccardi, later president of the Associated Press, coined the theme expressed in my campaign literature of "best noted for his sellout beer parties." I attribute my electoral success to those parties.

Boccardi also said that I was "one of the best possible men to have on any ticket" and noted that I had a brother, Donald, in the first-year class. I needed that lift inasmuch as the election for vice president was quite competitive. I won by a vote of 559 to 376. My running mate, Joe Carrieri, had a larger margin of victory—208 votes—defeating the incomparable Tom Giordano. Another running mate, John Macisco, went on to become a distinguished professor at Fordham University. Carrieri became a great lawyer, representing foster care homes while writing several books about sports, including my favorite, *Searching for Heroes: The Quest of a Yankee Batboy*.

Calling ourselves the Fordham Party, we ran on a platform of "practicality," which included increasing career services for students, developing a student book exchange, organizing a college-wide Communion breakfast, restoring the magazine rack to Keating cafeteria, arranging for intramural championships in football and basketball, publishing a student government handbook, establishing suggestion boxes throughout the campus, and setting up a ticket discount for Broadway shows.

We succeeded in implementing some of these ideas. We arranged for the Communion breakfast to be held at the Glen Island Casino on November 10, 1957, with the distinguished author and publisher Frank Sheed as the guest speaker. We were later pleased to receive from Dean McLaughlin the following note: "I have frequently resolved never to attend 'Communion Breakfasts.' It's like smoking. The fact that I am going to be present at the student government Communion Breakfast is a sign not only of my weakness—I never thought I'd see the day!—of a new folly. I'm even happy at the thought of being there."

As student body officers, we encouraged financial support for the new McGinley Center, then in the planning stages, and helped make a 1958 class gift under the leadership of class president Robert Bradley, although none of us could contribute much more than a few dollars. In response to an inquiring photographer's question as to what I'd like to see in the building, I said, "A modern beautiful dance hall for on-campus dances, an increase in the number of offices for all student activities . . . and perhaps most important of all, a chapel." (My ideas did not quite make it into the new building.)

Another contribution I made was writing a student government publication describing the different offices of government and the responsibilities of each, entitled "Government . . . at Rose Hill: The workings of the Fordham College Student Government." It was a smashing success, although no copy can be found at Rose Hill today. I also helped publish a student directory, was a member of the Fordham Club, and helped edit a class newspaper called *Dateline '58*. One editorial I wrote took issue with criticism in the school newspaper, the *Ram*, of a student in the year after me who, shortly after becoming president-elect of the student body, resigned, apparently for medical reasons.

The article in the *Ram* contended that the student should not have run in the first place. After making an investigation, I defended the student's withdrawal. My article, titled "Speculation vs. Fact," concluded that the student "showed a rare degree of foresight and character in resigning when he did." As the incumbent vice president, with election authority, I rejected the idea of a new election, believing that succession in such circumstances fell, constitutionally, to the newly elected vice president-elect under the student government constitution.

The ruling stood. The resulting vacancy in the vice presidency, however, was filled by the unsuccessful candidate for the presidency, a happy conclusion under the circumstances. This experience influenced my future interest in presidential succession and inability.

I graduated on June 11, 1958. I have few memories of the day, unfortunately, other than experiencing joy because of the accomplishment, gratitude for the opportunities that had come my way, and sadness in saying goodbye to my classmates.

Mom, Pop, and my siblings were present at the commencement, as were Uncle Pat and Aunt Catherine. It was a happy moment for all of us to have a college graduate in the family, but it wouldn't be long before I was joined by my siblings, Donald of the Fordham Class of 1960 and then Maureen of the College of Mount St. Vincent Class of 1963. In 1968 Kevin graduated from Fordham with a Bachelor of Arts and in 1971 received a Master of Science in counseling and psychology from Fordham's School of Education, followed by a law degree from Fordham in 1982. Anne received an associate degree from Bronx Community College and later a Bachelor of Science in nursing and a Master of Arts in health care administration from California State University.

12

Fordham Law School, 1958–1961

When you come to a fork in the road, take it.

— YOGI BERRA

As college graduation approached, I began to consider what was next. I had no job offers dangling before me other than an opportunity to work in Fordham's alumni office, thanks to Father Healy, its director. Since high school, I'd often thought of a vocation as a priest or religious brother, but I never acted on the idea. Thanks to my previous part-time jobs, I also considered a career in supermarket management. I learned about an executive recruitment program I might apply to, but I didn't pursue the idea.

Something within me, however, said that I should go to law school. I knew no lawyers except for James Dolan, who had helped Pop find a nursing home for Aunt Nora Pire, my godmother. Aside from chatting with Dolan about life as a lawyer, the only other influence that pointed me toward law school was the Perry Mason TV series, which showed lawyers in action in the courtroom.

Mom and Pop supported my decision to go to law school. I applied to several schools, was accepted by Fordham and St. John's, and chose Fordham. The dean, William Hughes Mulligan, couldn't have been impressed by my low (an understatement) LSAT score, but fortunately I'd been on the Dean's List each of my four college years, placing seventh in the class in my senior year with an academic average of 89.99. Later I'd learn that Mulligan had only recently introduced the LSAT as part of the school's admissions criteria but paid more attention to what he described as "qualities of heart and mind," as might be discerned from an admissions application. My essay, a source of comment later by a Fordham University president,[1] described my intellectual qualities as adequate but not great, my ability to work hard as strong, and my character as my best asset. I wouldn't have made the cut, however, under twenty-first century standards at either of these schools, given their emphasis on high LSAT scores.

Our Dean

In accepting admission to Fordham, I was influenced by my love for Fordham College along with the school's closeness to where I lived, a thirty- or forty-minute subway or bus ride away. I didn't know much about the school or what a career in the law involved. However, I'd heard of the dean, William Hughes Mulligan, in one of Dr. Frasca's government classes, and Father Healy invited me to attend the annual luncheon of the Law School's alumni association, held in March of 1958. The Waldorf Astoria's grand ballroom was overflowing on that occasion. The principal speaker was then Senator John F. Kennedy, who two years later would be elected president of the United States.

Forty-four years later, on March 2, 2002, I would stand where Kennedy stood and say goodbye as dean of the school, a point which I noted in my remarks on that occasion. Standing near me was Thomas Moore, a lawyer extraordinaire, to whom I was honored to be presenting the alumni association's highest award. He modestly accepted the award, saying simply, "Thank you," then turned to me and said, "This is your day, not mine."

Dean Mulligan, who had become dean of the Law School in 1958, became a central part of my life. He was renowned for his wit and humor. His humor was never at the expense of others, although he occasionally poked fun at people who were overly preoccupied with themselves. I'll never forget his witty speech to judges and lawyers of the Second Circuit during the Watergate years when he introduced James Reston of the *New York Times*. Upon taking the podium, Reston said, essentially, "Thank heavens there is a lawyer around who can make people laugh during this terrible period."

The wit of some of Dean Mulligan's famous speeches can be found in a wonderful book edited by his son, Bill, that was published after his father's death.[2] At his funeral Mass, presided over by John Cardinal O'Connor, I had the privilege of delivering remarks, along with Bill, who gave a moving eulogy.[3] I concluded my reflections by reciting a beautiful poem, "Remembering Bill Mulligan," that was composed by Emalie, which followed the cadence of William Butler Yeats's "The Fiddler of Dooney":

When I smile and my eyes start to twinkle
You know there's a thought in my mind.

'Tis a thought that will make you all chuckle
For it's one of the Mulligan kind.

It's a thought where the parts fit together
In a sort of preposterous way.
When I say it aloud it will make you
Feel jolly and happy and gay.

For life is a mixture of blessings
With sorrows and joys large and small
And when I put on my ROSE glasses
I just want to laugh at it all.

For when life is a vision of color,
A garden is made of this earth;
And when people can laugh at their troubles,
They find they're united in mirth.

So remember me telling my stories
That lifted your spirits like leaven
And if you can find solace in laughter,
I'm sure you'll have one foot in Heaven.

Our Building

The Law School, which had opened in 1905, was located at 302 Broadway
in Lower Manhattan. It was part of a building owned by Fordham University
and was described as housing the university's City Hall Division. Known as
the Vincent Building, it was situated on the corner of Broadway and Duane
Street, and in addition to the Law School, it housed the university's schools of
education and business. The once beautiful Romanesque revival style structure was built in 1899 as the American headquarters of the Astor family at a
cost of $900,000.[4] Its assessed value had fallen by the time Fordham bought
the building in 1943 at $122,000. Fordham moved into the building in Sep-
tember of 1943.[5]

A distinctive feature of the building was its elevators. They were hand-
driven, with steel panels on the sides, ceiling, and hand rails. On a stone
plaque on the front of the building were words in Latin that translated: "Bernard loved the valleys, Benedict the hills, Francis the towns, Ignatius the large
cities. The 11th Day of October 1943 A.D." There was a chapel on the first
floor, named in memory of Private James V. Meade of Fordham College,
who had died heroically in action in World War II. On occasion I attended

Mass there, and I visited it in times of stress and worry, such as exam time. When President Kennedy was later assassinated, students gathered there for a candlelight service. Also on the first floor was a large room for first-year orientations.

There was a lounge in the basement of the building, of which a Fordham Law School oral history said:

> There were no locker rooms anywhere in the building: Fordham could not afford them at the time, and further there was no place for them. Students would leave their coats over a chair in the lounge . . . and come back six hours later — no one ever seem[ed] to suffer from theft in the days of 302. This same . . . lounge, with the old stuffed couches that adorned it pushed to the side, used to house student dances as well. There was a small kitchen in the hall which served well at these and other occasions.[6]

"There were few amenities on premises," my classmate Jim McGough recalled. "The cafeteria was three tired vending machines in a corner of the basement. There was a black-and-white TV set but control of the channels was usually determined by students from the business and education schools."[7] Of the sparse office space, he said: "Faculty luxury was also limited. In the main office, Dean Mulligan had a small office. The rest of the faculty (some 15 or 16) shared a single office, a Y-shaped area. One entered at the front of the Y, then squeezed ahead to left or right to barely make it around a desk to an uncomfortable swivel chair. Whichever professor arrived earliest in the day claimed the chair — and kept it until surrendered for class or lunch." Professor Leonard Manning was the only one who had his own office (as moderator of the *Law Review*), which was a large closet. I'd sometimes take naps there after long nights working at the *Law Review*.

Despite its limitations, this building became my home away from home. As I'd discover, the school enjoyed a proud history of producing outstanding trial lawyers, public servants, judges, teachers, and general practitioners of law.[8] Most of Fordham's graduates practiced in New York, New Jersey, and Connecticut. With a few exceptions, the large Wall Street law firms had not yet swung their doors fully open to Fordham's graduates.

Around the time I arrived, Fordham University was engaged in litigation to establish its right to build a Lincoln Center campus, starting with a new law school building.[9] In my second year, Dean Mulligan asked me to be present when its cornerstone was laid on May 3, 1960, with remarks by U.S. Chief Justice Earl Warren. Twenty-two years later I'd be placed in charge of a campaign to renovate and expand that facility.

The Faculty and Students

The faculty consisted of only thirty professors, many of them part-time. As James McGough said, we were provided "terrific practical education by superb teachers." There were morning and afternoon sessions and an evening program that made a career in the law possible for students who had to work full- and part-time. Many of us worked before or after class.

I began law school on September 2, 1958, as a member of the morning section, joined by eighty-nine other students, a number of whom had been my classmates at Fordham College. An additional seventy-eight students were in the afternoon session and one hundred in the evening program. Dean Mulligan made clear to all of us that many "would fall by the wayside" for failing to work hard enough in our studies.

The tuition for the first year was $700, the second and third year it was $600 for the day division. For the evening division, the first year tuition was $525, $430 for the second year, $470 for the third year, and $415 for the fourth year. I was fortunate that by working part-time I could cover my tuition cost, partly because I lived at home and traveled to and from school by subway.

I remember some extraordinary teachers, and years later I paid tribute to some of them. In a memorial tribute to Professor Leonard Manning, I said:

> No person ever loved the students of Fordham Law School more
> than he did. I can see him now sitting on the classroom desk at 302
> Broadway without any notes and with his arms folded across his chest
> speaking at a relaxed tone about the cases assigned the previous week.
> He stretched our minds by asking, but never answering, what the cases
> meant, and when we were about to reach a conclusion, he would
> introduce another element which made the conclusion less clear.[10]

Of Professor John Calamari, I recalled the thoroughness of his lectures on contract law. When we asked him which view to go with on examinations, the majority or minority view, he simply replied, "Who knows?" and moved on. Because he was so masterful in contracts, I decided to take his elective course in suretyship law and pass up a course in basic labor law, the field in which I'd spend most of my years as a practicing lawyer.[11]

Another remarkable professor was Raymond O'Keefe, later the recipient of Fordham Law School's 1999 Humanitarian Award.[12] In a letter to his wife, Stephanie, after his death, I said of Ray:

> He was an extraordinary teacher, with a talent for conveying a sub-
> ject through humor and his knowledge and brilliance in the areas he

taught. I still remember the . . . examples he gave to illustrate. The crowded subway, with people pushing and shoving, was the laboratory of learning the essentials of assault and battery. The pebble in Russia which started a series of events resulting in an injury in New York was grist for understanding the concept of proximate cause. A few of us were up on our feet quite a bit to discuss cases but more than that to confront Ray's grimaces, asides, and snarls when we stumbled.

Joseph Crowley's course on legal remedies became the grist for my early life as a lawyer practicing in the lower courts of New York. The courses of Professors Robert Kessler and Martin Fogelman introduced me to the world of business. My adjunct teachers were also extraordinary. Joseph Doran was methodical in teaching the law of sales, sometimes sprinkling the subject with Latin phrases and promising that he'd stop teaching if the Uniform Commercial Code was adopted in New York State. He was true to his word. When the Commercial Code was adopted, he left academia to become a judge. John McAniff was magical in his way of conveying information on the subject of wills, waving his hands and speaking in a deep raspy voice. He taught at the school for almost sixty years, leaving when his eyesight failed.

I did well as a student thanks to a study group of several classmates. We supported one another in many ways. A classmate recalled me sharing cookies and a thermos of tea with them, while I remember sessions at his home where we enjoyed his mother's cooking. I gained admission to the *Law Review* where I learned to research and write well enough to be published.

But success in this area didn't come immediately. My first draft of a case note was thrown back at me by the editor at the time, who exclaimed, "This is like an editorial in the *New York Post*." I didn't know what he meant because I didn't read the *Post*. I thought my draft was pretty good, but the problem was that it was too opinionated. I soon learned how to write law review style. Another time I was chided for a minor punctuation error on a fifty-page comment. The time spent on research, case citation checking, footnoting, editing, and writing would greatly influence me throughout my career, and the opportunity to serve as editor-in-chief of Volume 29 of the *Review*, published in the 1960–1961 school year, remains my most important and meaningful experience at law school. My co-editors and I, along with our able staff, approached the work on the *Review* as if we were writing the Constitution of the United States.

I began my last year at law school with an offer to join Skadden as a first-year associate after I graduated. I received offers from a few other law firms as well, but turned those down. Before accepting the offer, I decided to try my luck at a federal clerkship. I didn't appreciate how high I was reaching, nor did I realize that graduates of schools more prestigious than Fordham were far more likely to land such positions, as was clear from the rejection letters I received. Judge Harold Medina wrote, "I am sorry to say that because I taught at Columbia Law School for twenty-five years, I have . . . adopted the policy of leaving it to the faculty of Columbia Law School . . . to select my law clerk for me." The legendary Judge Billings Learned Hand wrote, "I have always left the selection of my law clerk with the Harvard Law School." A gracious letter from Judge Charles Clark said, "At the moment I am interviewing applicants particularly from the Yale Law School, which in some ways is the most convenient source of supply, since I live and do most of my work here in New Haven."

Dean Mulligan, ever anxious to open doors for students, arranged for several of us to travel to Washington, D.C., for an interview with Supreme Court Justice Potter Stewart.[13] It was an engaging experience, but it was clear from the start of the interview that the justice chose his clerks from schools other than Fordham. In 1961, a fellow student named Malachy Mahon secured a clerkship with Justice Tom Clark, becoming the first graduate in the Law School's history to clerk a full term for a sitting Supreme Court justice.[14]

Not winning a clerkship allowed me to begin my career at Skadden. But there were preliminary matters I had to deal with, such as putting the last issue of Volume 29 of the *Law Review* to bed. An article written by a distinguished lawyer, Eugene Morris, needed substantial rewriting. The task fell to me, and each day, before and after my bar review course, I would work on the article, barely finishing it before the bar exam. The article then appeared as part of a first-ever symposium issue of the *Review* on the subject of land-use planning.[15] Morris was grateful for my assistance and later offered me a partnership at his firm.

I also had to pass the New York bar exam. At the time, an applicant could pass one part and fail another, requiring a test on the part you failed. To guard against that, I took a six-hour-a-day bar review course with Professor Charles Sparacio of St. John's Law School. I remember waiting with a group of my classmates outside of the *Herald Tribune* building in Midtown Manhattan late one night, as the next day's paper would contain the bar exam results. Happily, I passed both parts, cleared the character and fitness requirements, and was admitted to the Bar in the First Judicial Department on December 11, 1961. The world was now my oyster. I proposed to Emalie, the love of my life, that December, and she said yes. I eagerly anticipated our marriage, I had a job as a lawyer, and I awaited beginning and completing my active duty in the U.S. Army.

13

Meeting the Love of My Life: Emalie

May the road rise to meet you,
May the wind be always at your back,
May the sun shine warm upon your face,
The rain fall soft upon your fields.
And, until we meet again,
May God hold you in the palm of His hand.

— AN IRISH BLESSING

As a child, Mom and Pop and my siblings were at the center of my life. This all changed in August of 1962 when I married Emalie Maureen Grace Platt of Southampton, Long Island, New York.

302 Broadway, March 26, 1960

On Saturday, March 26, after a day of participating in Fordham Law School's trial moot court program, I met Emalie, then a senior at Manhattanville College. She was 21 and I was 23. She served as a juror on one of the competitions, but we only met afterward at a social in the basement of 302 Broadway.

I had originally planned to meet one of the other jurors at the social. She brought along several of her friends, including Emalie. At first, I was not thrilled to have a crowd, but when Emalie spoke, my attention was immediately drawn to her. She was polite and down to earth, without any pretensions. She expressed an inner beauty and a softness and gentleness when she spoke that deeply appealed to me. She was exceedingly attractive and nicely attired, wearing a white blouse and charcoal gray suit. Her eyes were blue, her hair brown, and her smile lovely.

As I was speaking to Emalie, Dean Mulligan interrupted. He took her aside, stating, as I learned years later, "If you are interested in that fellow, hold onto him. He just became editor of the *Law Review*." When our children celebrated Emalie's sixtieth birthday in 1998, they disclosed the contents of a letter she'd written to her parents at the time, mentioning our meeting and describing me as a rather "unsophisticated" boy — without airs, she said she meant — "of whom the dean had spoken well." I didn't realize then that this was the consummate praise from Emalie. I'll forever be grateful to Dean Mulligan for the boost he gave me.

Meeting Emalie, however, complicated my life as I was then dating a classmate of mine. In time, however, everything worked out. Emalie and I went on several dates during the remaining months of the 1959–1960 school year. We went bowling (she won big), to the circus, to a dance at Manhattanville, to the Broadway production of *Camelot*, and to a dinner dance for her graduating class of 1960 at which I met her parents. Her father was quite imposing and her mother very sweet and gentle.[1]

On later dates, Emalie and I rowed boats in Central Park, strolled around the park holding hands, and attended an outdoor concert at City College's Lewisohn Stadium. One memory stands out more than the others — the 1960 Fourth of July weekend in Southampton, when I had the opportunity to meet her siblings and Aunt Teresa and Uncle Harold. Teresa and Harold were exceedingly kind, taking me to Ridgely's Restaurant, where I had one of the finest steak dinners I've ever had. I was struck by the happiness I found in her home, as her mother played the piano, her father cooked dinner, and Emalie mothered younger siblings and washed and dried dishes. There was a lot of happy noise going on, which reminded me of my own upbringing. We also went to the beach, where I gave Emalie my first kiss. I was a late bloomer by any standards, and the kiss was a quick one and on her cheek. She later told me that she'd wondered why I'd taken so long.

Another highlight of that weekend was attending the local Independence Day Parade. The parade took no more than an hour, with the distance from beginning to end only a few city blocks, with everyone crowded along the parade route. The lineup included a progression of fire engines, police vehicles, ambulances, attractively decorated automobiles (past and present), war veterans, volunteer firefighters and police officers, floats with children, singers and dancers, marching bands, representatives of religious groups and lodges like the Masons and the Elks, and delegations of local officials and businesses. The noise was deafening, with sirens, horns, whistles, and music expressing the spirit of this rural community. The American flag flew from storefronts and was carried by both marchers and the spectators. Volunteers handed out candy and flags, and some, dressed in festive red, white, and blue, posed for pictures with children and parade-goers.

What I enjoyed most was sitting with Emalie's many relatives on folding chairs under the trees along Main Street, chatting as we watched the marchers pass by. It was a Platt/Guldi family tradition to do this each Independence Day outside of Guldi's Electric Shop, owned by Emalie's maternal grandfather, Adolph Guldi, across the street from the law office of Emalie's father. Her father owned the two-story building in which his office was located, and from time to time he would glance quickly at the parade from his upper-story window.

The occasion was unlike anything I had experienced growing up in the Bronx. There were patriotic parades on the Grand Concourse, but I seldom had a chance to watch them. The Southampton Parade would later become part of our own family tradition after we married. The stores along Southampton's Main Street, particularly the candy, fudge, and ice cream stores, have since become a favorite destination of mine to take my children and grandchildren on Fourth of July celebrations. The older generation who started it all have passed on.

Sometime that weekend, Emalie and I had dinner at Herbert McCarthy's highly popular Bowden Square, a restaurant in Southampton Village. The food was delicious, the dancing was delightful, and the music by Lester Lanin was heavenly. We were having such a great time that I was inspired to write on a table card, "What would you say if I told you I love you?" and hand it to Emalie. She glanced at the note for an interminably long period but didn't say anything. I didn't know what to say either.

I took her silence as a negative to my marriage proposal (though I didn't mention the word "marriage"), but I was nevertheless polite about her silence. Later, Emalie would tell me that on that evening she had been speechless and dumbfounded because, she said, "we really did not know each other very well." I took Emalie home and said goodnight, as I was staying with her Uncle Harold and Aunt Teresa, across the street from her house, and then headed back to the Bronx the next day.

As I was leaving Southampton, I remember meeting Emalie's brother Harold and offering him advice as he prepared to go to Georgetown College. He would later become an honored graduate of Fordham Law School (class of 1971), a successful lawyer, and, for me, a wonderful brother-in-law. Harold was followed at Fordham by his brothers Jonathan and Bill, who died in 2011. Over the years, Bill transitioned from electrician to attorney. He later established a successful career for himself in his father's law office, with a special talent for tracing land titles. They all became dear friends of mine.

During that summer of 1960, Emalie took me up on an invitation to meet Mom and Pop and, in time, told me that the visit was memorable, most notably because she found that none of us pronounced "th" in a word with those letters, such as "theater," making such words sound Irish, as if spelled with only a "t." She noticed differences among us as to how we pronounced our own family name, some with an emphasis on the two e's and some making it sound as if the name had two r's.

She found distinctive our Sunday morning breakfast ritual, never having seen anything like it in Southampton. She commented on the contrast between the spaciousness of her Southampton home and the smallness of our two-bedroom Bronx apartment. At the time I slept on a couch in the living room, with Mom and my two sisters in one bedroom and Pop and my two brothers in the other.

Emalie and I separated at the end of summer because of what I took to be a lack of interest on her part, but which we later both understood to be a misunderstanding. She continued to remain deeply on my mind as I worked away day and night on the *Law Review*. During the year, she sent me notes from time to time concerning her life, which led me to believe that she might be interested in resuming our relationship. During the second semester of my final year of law school, I decided to act on an impulse and visit her. I knew she was teaching in Sayville on Long Island, and one day I took the train to her school to ask her if she had an interest in reviving our dating. Emalie, happily surprised by my appearance, agreed to do so.

Over the summer, as I was studying for the bar, Emalie toured Europe. I received no communications from her and I concluded that her interest in me had waned. I later learned that she had sent me cards but to the wrong address.

Then in October 1961, I received a note from her congratulating me on passing the bar exam. It became clear how much we loved each other, and we began dating again. Just before Christmas of 1961, I surprised Emalie with a visit to Sayville, this time with a ring, which she happily accepted. When I asked her father that Christmas for her hand in marriage, he replied, "No," startling me, but, after a pause, he added, "It's all or nothing," meaning that I'd have to take all of her and not just her hand. Appreciating his sense of humor, I happily agreed.

Six months on active duty in the Army intervened. Emalie and I stayed in regular touch, and from time to time she would visit the base in Fort Dix, New Jersey. My army diary is filled with references to Emalie — "called

Emalie long distance with overtime charges," "sent Emalie a Valentine card," "received letter and fudge and cookies from Emalie," "anticipating seeing Emalie on Sunday," "letter to and phone conversation with Emalie followed by conversation with bunk mates on 'love,'" "a wonderful day with Emalie," "Emalie enjoyed the movie *Murder, She Said*," "wrote letter to Emalie after receiving a letter," and "day (April 1, 1962) most enjoyable, very much in love with Em — wonderful girl."

My diary doesn't note that she became popular among my Army mates because, whenever she would visit, she would bring an abundance of home-made brownies. Nor was her popularity limited to my Army friends. In a letter of July 25, 1962, Joseph Callahan, a classmate at Dubois and a distant relative, said, "The next time you're speaking with Emalie, please admonish her for the way she was doing the twist at our apartment. She really twists!!!"

Emalie and I were married on August 25, 1962, by Monsignor George Killeen at the Church of the Sacred Hearts of Jesus and Mary in Southampton. I was 26 and she was 23. Even today, I remember quite clearly just how stunning she looked, as she gracefully walked down the aisle. She wore a long gown, with a fitted bodice and full skirt, and she was holding a modest bouquet of flowers. Her blue eyes were shining. Surrounded by the eighteen members of our bridal party, as well as the more than a hundred people that attended the wedding, we had the love and support of all our family and friends. Emalie's sister, Meredith Platt Joyce, stood by her side as matron of honor and my brother, Donald, stood by my side as best man. The younger members of our families also played important roles. Kevin served as an altar boy, while Emalie's brother Rick served as the ring bearer. My sister Anne and Emalie's sister Elin were junior bridesmaids.

The day was glorious — bright, sunny, and crisp. The sky was blue without a cloud in sight. One member of the bridal party said that when he awoke, in a room overlooking the water, he thought he was in heaven.

What went through my mind was how lucky I was to be marrying some-one as beautiful, positive, easygoing, and spiritual as Emalie. I brought to the church that day a bulky old tape recorder to record the ceremony. Emalie's family arranged for a photographer. Many of the details of the Mass celebrating our union have faded into my memory, but our words of commitment to each other remain vivid.

The wedding reception was a glorious affair as my Irish friends and family from the Bronx mixed with the Platts and Guldis of Southampton and their friends. Mom was in her splendor, doing Irish dances, and when I joined her on the dance floor, she carried me along as if I knew what I was doing. A single bar in the corner of the reception hall at the Perkins Hotel in Riverhead tempered the drinking that might have occurred, as Emalie's mother wanted no wine or beer bottles on the table and no heavy drinking of any kind. Donald delivered the toast, using the Irish blessing quoted at the beginning of this chapter. Emalie's sister, Mary Jo, sat next to her on a dais. Emalie and I did our first dance to Irving Berlin's "Always." The song has remained a constant in our love notes to one another throughout the years.

After the reception, we started out from the hotel in Emalie's old Volkswagen, planning to end up in Cape Cod for our honeymoon. I had only a learner's permit, however, so as soon as the crowd behind us disappeared from sight, I stopped the car and Emalie took the wheel.

The first leg of the trip was a ferry ride from Port Jefferson to New London, Connecticut. Eventually Emalie got tired and suggested we abandon our plan to get to the Cape. I thought we could reach our destination and enjoy what I had arranged for our first night married — a bottle of champagne in a room filled with flowers. Despite Emalie's expert driving, we missed by a few minutes the ferry that was scheduled to take us to the Cape. At that point it was close to midnight. We didn't know the area and faced the challenge of finding a place to stay in Rhode Island. Luckily, a taxi driver offered to lead us to a nearby motel. The flowers and champagne I'd arranged for were waiting for us the next day when we arrived at the Terrace Gables Hotel in Falmouth Heights.[2]

From Falmouth, we moved on to a Fordham classmate's place in New Hampshire, then to the Tyler Place in Highgate Springs, Vermont, and then north to Montreal and Quebec City. (Tyler Place was a delightful family resort, but hardly a honeymoon haven because of the lack of privacy; there were too many children around for that. We resolved to return when we had our own children, and we did so for many years, as our children sometimes did with their children.) During our honeymoon, we relished the boat rides on Lake Champagne, the horseback riding, and the general ambience of Tyler Place, established by its incomparable director, Judy Tyler. We did a lot of moving around during our two-week honeymoon, something that would for me be a constant for the rest of our marriage.

On our honeymoon, we also visited the Trapp Family Lodge in Stowe, and by chance met Maria von Trapp, whose story was told in the 1965 film *The Sound of Music*. To this day, our extended family meets there annually to celebrate the holidays and enjoy skiing at Stowe.

Looking back on fifty-seven years of marriage to Emalie, I'll conclude by quoting from a tribute I made to her on our 40th wedding anniversary at a prayer service arranged by our children:

Forty years ago . . . I thought I understood then the meaning of being married to another but I now realize how thin, if not superficial, my understanding really was at that time. I, of course, felt strongly the romance of the moment and accepted the vows to be faithful and to love you in good times and in bad times, for better or worse, for the rest of my life.

I enthusiastically renew these vows today but this time with an understanding of their significance that runs very, very deep — an understanding not blinded by a young person's romantic feelings and urges but informed by forty years of togetherness during which you, Emalie, have been so total in your devotion and commitment . . .

As I renew our vows, I want you to know how greatly I love you, how gratefully I appreciate what you have made possible, and how resolved I am to start the process of trying to balance the scales of our marriage which at this point have been so grossly weighted in my favor.

What I was referring to in those final words was the fact that, over the years, I'd been so preoccupied with my career and with the many various causes I was involved in, a preoccupation that left Emilie to run our household and raise our six children often on her own.

Emalie's contribution to my professional career is indescribable. She accepted the reality that long hours would be part of my work and that there would be endless conversations on the presidential succession system, among other causes in which I became passionate, if not obsessive. Our deep and close collaboration with respect to my research and writing on the subject of presidential inability helped lead to my participation in the crafting of the Twenty-Fifth Amendment to the Constitution. She brought to these collaborations a skill for deep and active listening, a keen intelligence, a beautiful writing style, editing skills, and a total dedication to helping me. None of what followed in my personal and professional life would have been possible without this companionship.

In those early years, since I didn't have a driver's license, Emalie also chauffeured me to the homes of our parents, to weekly army reserve meetings, and sometimes to meetings outside New York City relating to my law practice. All the while, we yearned to have a family of our own, and in time we were rewarded in abundance. In the process, Emalie became my moral compass, the person on whose wisdom and judgment I most depended.

PART IV
Career as a Lawyer

Somewhere ages and ages hence:
Two roads diverged in a wood, and I —
I took the one less traveled by,
And that has made all the difference.

— ROBERT FROST, FROM "THE ROAD NOT TAKEN"

14

Learning in Part-Time Jobs

I'm a great believer in luck, and I find the harder I work the more I
have of it.

— THOMAS JEFFERSON

As the child of immigrant parents with five children and limited resources,
it was hardly surprising that I accepted opportunities to work part-time jobs
during my early years. As a result, I brought to my life as a lawyer a varied
employment history.

I often shoveled snow in front of private homes on 161st Street and was
rewarded with tips. I remember shoveling snow on Morris Avenue during
the blizzard of 1948, along with other young boys. Though the job involved
heavy lifting, I liked being part of a group effort even then. I also delivered
the Sunday editions of the *Daily News* and the *New York Times* to local residents at the request of Moe, who ran the candy store around the corner. In
addition, I worked on Saturdays at Sam's butcher, delivering meat to people
who lived nearby on my bicycle, which was equipped with a basket for that
purpose. Sam paid me a few dollars every Saturday, which was more than I'd
ever earned before.

From time to time during the summer I worked making sandwiches at Sal's
Italian hero shop on Morris Avenue. I also helped out for a while on a milk
truck, collecting empty bottles left outside apartments and replacing them
with bottles of fresh milk. One neighbor paid me a few dollars for walking her
young son each day to and from St. Angela Merici grammar school. (Years
later I would meet him again; at that point he was a police officer, assigned to
the Bronx Supreme Court. Small world.)

As I entered high school, I worked part-time after school and on Saturdays at a tailor shop on 162nd Street and Sheridan Avenue, earning a few dollars a week. I delivered freshly laundered clothes to people who lived in apartments on the Concourse, at the Concourse Plaza Hotel, and at Thomas Gardens Apartments between 158th and 159th Streets. The gardens that were part of this complex are described in glowing terms in *Boulevard of Dreams*: "Yet hidden within their embrace and occupying about half the site sat a small jewel, a Japanese garden offering a touch of Zen tranquility in what was fast emerging as one of the city's most densely developed neighborhoods."[1] Unfortunately, I didn't appreciate the architectural history of this and other buildings to which I made deliveries. I was always in a rush.

The people to whom I delivered clothes, some of whom were lawyers and judges, were friendly and generous. I learned a lot by listening to the shop's proprietor, Phil, and to customers who used to hang out in the store. They talked about their families, sports, politics, betting, and women. Phil was very kind to me, and it was with sadness that I never saw him again after I started college. Nor did I again see Moe, Sam, or Sal, all of whom I would list in my application to the New York Bar in describing my employment history. Eleven years later, despite my best efforts, I could not find them to obtain an affidavit of employment for my bar admission application.

And as I mentioned, in college I worked on weekends and during some summers in a supermarket. While working there, I experienced the sense of accomplishment that comes from being part of an enterprise based on teamwork and selling a product you believed in, in this case the store itself. In a strange way, this approach later became a kind of model for me when I became dean of Fordham Law School.

I stocked shelves and operated the cash register, meeting people of all backgrounds and dispositions. The manager, John Meyer, was a role model for me, and my immediate supervisor, an Irish immigrant named Tommy Egan, was my mentor. Egan was in perpetual motion. He saw before anyone else which shelves needed to be refilled and then hustled down to the basement, found the necessary cartons, threw them onto a conveyor belt, rushed upstairs to place them on a dolly, and then rolled it to the proper location. I sometimes worked alongside him but would need a break before this frantic work cycle was completed.

Egan later offered me a job on weekends during my first year of law school. He and Meyer had taken charge of a supermarket on Lenox Avenue at 137th Street in Manhattan. I worked the overnight shift on Friday nights, for which I earned triple-time pay. Alone in the store, I'd blare music through the speakers while stocking shelves.

I never knew his name, but I remember in college a young police officer directing traffic on the corner near the supermarket. On occasion he was invited to take home some meat or other foods, but he always declined. Responsible for maintaining the integrity of his position, he couldn't accept favors that might influence his judgment or the performance of his duties. Egan made mention of that to me, saying, "He was different." I have thought often of this officer. He became a model for me of honestly in the performance of one's duties.

During college, I worked a second job during the summer break at H. W. Wilson, a publishing house near Yankee Stadium, where I shelved books. For a summer or two, I also worked a second job in the evening at Youth House for Boys, on Spofford Avenue in the Bronx.[2] I was a dorm supervisor, which was fatiguing and mentally challenging work. Many of the boys there had committed serious offenses, and in some cases would later serve time in a correctional institution upstate. Since I wasn't very muscular, I had to use my wits to maintain discipline in my unit. I later learned that Lee Harvey Oswald, the man accused of assassinating President Kennedy, had spent time at Youth House.[3] The jobs I had during my college summers kept me busy day and night, but over these years, at one dollar minimum wage, I earned several thousand dollars.

I spent my law school summers working at two law firms. As the managing clerk at the Landis, Feldman, Reilly & Akers firm during my first year, I learned how to search court files and records, serve papers, and process documents. I earned a reputation for my ability to serve subpoenas to evasive parties, and if pressed, I could share interesting war stories concerning that experience, including serving a subpoena to a very surprised doctor in a hospital stairwell and to a famous television producer whose wife was suing him in a matrimonial action. Lawrence Reilly was a particular role model and mentor to me, whose kindnesses I'll never forget. I used to say to myself that, at age 35, I would like to be a lawyer like him, not simply because of his ability but more importantly because of what he was like as a person. He engaged with everyone in a friendly and kind manner. I will always appreciate his interest in mentoring a young law student like me, and for providing me with opportunities that allowed me to learn and grow as a lawyer.

James Landis, former dean of Harvard Law School, was a senior partner of the firm, and Justin Feldman, who had been an administrative assistant to Franklin D. Roosevelt Jr. when he was a member of Congress, was another senior partner. Landis was also a close friend of Joseph Kennedy, succeeding him as chairman of the Securities and Exchange Commission. From time to time, I saw famous political figures pass through the office, among them

Eleanor Roosevelt and Robert Kennedy. George Brenner, another senior partner, was considered a major player in New York politics. But the lawyer who
had the greatest impact on me, aside from Reilly, was Paul Frank, a recent Columbia Law School graduate who was invaluable when it came to explaining
to me at times the confusing legal concepts covered in my law school classes.

I spent the summer of 1960, between my second and third year, as a law
clerk at Skadden at the salary of seventy-five dollars a week. The registrar at
Fordham Law School, Mary Long, had spotted me in the school's library in
the fall of 1959 and suggested that I contact William Meagher, a Skadden partner. I did so and received a job offer, though not without embarrassing myself.
When Meagher asked if I had a resume, I said I was unfamiliar with such a
requirement. He seemed perplexed, asking, "Didn't someone at the school
tell you that?" I said "not really" — at the time Fordham had no placement or
career services office.

Meagher then proceeded to write out my first resume on a sheet of yellow
paper, which I brought to my other interviews at the firm that day. At the end
of the day, Meagher walked me to the elevator and asked that I return the
sheet in typed and expanded form, with any additions needed. I did so, but
years later, upon examining that first resume, I found the content and attention to detail unimpressive. As it turned out, because of his own association
with the school, Meagher wanted a Fordham Law student as part of the firm's
summer program. I became that person.

Skadden was then a very small firm, just 12 years old, with an unclear future. It had opened its doors on April 1, 1948, founded by three men who knew
one another at the Wall Street firm of Root, Clark, Buckner, Howland &
Ballantine. Marshall Skadden, one of the three, who died in January of 1958,
was described by Leslie Arps, another founder, as one of the "best corporate
lawyers in New York," someone who was "blessed with a sunny disposition,
was never rattled, and was an immaculate dresser." Arps had a distinguished
war record with the Operations Analysis Section of the U.S. Air Force and
enjoyed a close relationship with John Harlan, who later served as a Supreme
Court justice.

John Slate joined the two from the legal department of Pan American
World Airways, where he worked closely with Henry Friendly, later chief
judge of the U.S. Court of Appeals for the Second Circuit. In a draft history
of Skadden, Arps said of Slate: "He was a brilliant lawyer, a gifted writer, and
a fine poet." He had articles published in the *Saturday Evening Post*, *Fortune*,
and the *Atlantic Monthly*, and his clients included the Trappist monk Thomas
Merton.

Mr. Meagher, as I called him as a student and young lawyer, had been born in Manhattan in 1903 and, like me, had been raised in the Bronx. He graduated with honors from Fordham College in 1924 and Fordham Law School in 1927. He distinguished himself as a trial and appellate lawyer in both federal and state courts. From 1928 through the mid-1940s, he was also a lecturer at Fordham Law School, teaching over time different courses in the curriculum.

In 1938, Governor Lehman designated Meagher to serve as special assistant attorney general to investigate and prosecute official corruption in Brooklyn and Queens. His reputation in the courts led in the early 1940s to an offer to join the legendary John W. Davis at Davis, Polk & Wardwell, where he stayed until 1958, when he became a named and senior partner at Skadden. Meagher once told me that when he was interviewed, Davis said to him, "I want to be your only student," as a result of which Meagher resigned his part-time teaching position at Fordham. He told me that he cast his first presidential vote for Davis. Upon mentioning that to him, Davis responded, "That's one vote that did not hurt America!" In April of 1974, Meagher was appointed counsel to Skadden, and he died on October 28, 1981, at 78 years of age.

Meagher was a masterful advocate with a flair for brief writing and oral advocacy I never again encountered. Not surprisingly he was drawn into some of the milestone cases of the past century, given the reputation of the Davis Polk firm. Among these cases was *Arizona v. California* and *Brown v. Board of Education*. *Arizona* involved the rights of states and Indian reservations to draw water from the Colorado River and its tributaries. Meagher carried his firm's representation of the state of Arizona to Skadden, and as a summer associate, I became immersed in understanding the rights of the Indian tribes to such waters for irrigation and planting purposes.[4] In *Brown v. Board of Education*, Davis Polk represented the state of South Carolina, defending racial segregation in public schools. Meagher assisted in writing the state's brief and recalled for me that, after the Supreme Court arguments, John Davis "expressed confidence in the result," saying the law uniformly supported the state's position. He hardly expected the Court's eventual unanimous decision dismantling public school segregation in the United States.

I recall being in Arps's office as a summer associate and listening to a conversation he was having with a client. Thinking he was mistaken on an aspect of New York Criminal Law, I left his office and found the relevant volume on New York's Criminal Law. Realizing that I was correct, I promptly returned to his office and placed before him the relevant section of the law while he was still on the phone. Upon hurriedly reading the section, Arps changed his view on the matter. At the end of the telephone conversation, he turned to me and said, "You have learned a key ingredient to being successful. Always make the partner look good."

The opportunity to work with Arps and Meagher led to my decision to accept their offer to join the firm upon graduation rather than accept offers from larger firms, such as Cleary Gottlieb and Dewey Ballantine, or to return to the Landis firm, from which I received an offer. I sensed that my decision to join Skadden may have disappointed Dean Mulligan as the firm was quite small. He wanted as many Fordham graduates as possible to join the large Wall Street firms as a way of underscoring the quality of the school's students, but partially because of its small size, Skadden seemed like the right fit for me. Little did I expect that Skadden would grow astronomically in the 1970s and that Dean Mulligan himself would join the firm and become a cherished and beloved partner when he left the federal bench in 1981.

15

Joining a Small Law Firm — Skadden, Arps, Slate, Meagher & Flom

Doing good is the only certainly happy action of a man's life.
— SIR PHILIP SIDNEY

When I graduated from Law School in the spring of 1961, men my age were subject to the draft, which meant, if drafted, a two-year commitment in the U.S. Armed Forces, or you had the option to serve six months on active duty by joining an Army Reserve Program or the National Guard. I decided to enter the Reserve program of the Army's 77th Liberty Division, encouraged by my brother Donald, who had done such service and was then in the Army Reserves. I later learned that Arps had joined this division when it was formed in 1942.

I was on active duty from January to July of 1962. It was demanding, but I made a number of good friends, including Ronald Harrigan of St. Peter's College in New Jersey and New Hampshire attorney Charles De Gramphire, who talked me out of an additional military commitment. I contemplated making a larger commitment as the war in Indochina was heating up, but I decided not to change course at that point, with my job at Skadden waiting for me and my plans to marry Emalie set for August 25, 1962. I was never completely sure that I had made the right decision, wondering if I had a moral obligation to serve longer. Except for those six months of active duty leave, I spent twenty-one years at Skadden.

I started with the rank E-1 — an enlisted rank of private, reflecting my training status. I achieved the rank of E-3, private first class, and came to admire and respect those who served as sergeants, first sergeants, lieutenants, and higher.

My Fort Dix diary describes my ups and downs as an infantry soldier in training. My grandson Dylan was most impressed by my entry for April 2, 1962: "PT test—6 pull ups, 12 pushups, 39 squat jumps, 42 other, and 300 yards run at 57 seconds," with the additional note, "first in my competition and very happy." Other items note the early hour of waking up, formations, marches, and parades, KP duty (washing and cleaning in kitchens after food service — "not a desirable duty"), preparation for inspections, learning to shoot a rifle and use a bayonet ("learning to kill killers"), proficiency tests, night duty, lectures on military subjects (such as atomic warfare, squad tactics, assault line attacks, night fighting, and battle formations), and, as mentioned, visits from Emalie. On those occasions, we usually walked around the base, holding hands and chatting about our planned life together.

At the end of this service I received a Certificate of Training stating that "Pvt. John D. Feerick BR 12 634 033 has successfully completed six (6) months active duty training under Reserves Forces Act of 1955 and is awarded Primary MOS [Military Occupational Specialty] of 112.00 Heavy Weapons Infantryman." I spent the next five-and-a-half years in the Army Reserve program, the first few years as an infantryman in the 77th Division and the rest in the Army's Fourth JAG Detachment, achieving the rank of captain. Although I didn't pursue a career in the military, I was proud to be associated at Fordham with a number of graduates who served on active duty.

During my years at Skadden, the firm grew from twelve lawyers (in 1961) to almost three hundred lawyers when I left on June 30, 1982, and then to more than two thousand lawyers. Many people contributed greatly to this growth. Arps, Meagher, Joseph Flom, Barry Garfinkel, and Peter Mullen were always in my pantheon, but everyone would point to the remarkable success of the firm's first associate, Joseph Flom, in the field of corporate takeovers and mergers. The story of his life, as told in Malcolm Gladwell's *Outliers: The Story of Success*, is required reading for anyone who wants to understand Flom's impact, not simply on Skadden but on the entire American legal profession and business world. I was fortunate to be a colleague of these men and to enjoy the success that accompanied the firm's growth, which made it possible for me to leave at age 45 to become a law school dean.[1]

At Skadden, I helped develop the firm's labor and employment practice and contributed to the creation, design, and operation of its system for hiring lawyers. Its hiring premise was that good lawyers could be found in every ABA-approved law school and of diverse backgrounds. Like the other senior partners, Flom made it clear that the firm was a meritocracy, making it an honor to chair the firm's hiring committee for a number of years and to help recruit lawyers from law schools around the country. I eventually gravitated toward the

field of labor because of Meagher, who asked me to help him on several collective bargaining and litigation matters involving labor unions in the 1960s,
and because of other partners who sought my help with aviation clients with
collective bargaining relationships that involved labor and employment issues.

Skadden from 1961 to 1982

My work in the beginning of my career was quite extensive. It included litigation, real estate closings, corporate, taxation, matrimonial, estate and trust
law, and labor and employment matters. The assigning partners had only a few
associates to turn to, hence the variety. I became familiar with matters in state
courts of limited jurisdiction, notably the New York City Municipal Court
and City Court, which later merged into the New York Civil Court. I drafted
pleadings, made and argued motions, dealt with bills of particulars, took depo-
sitions, and handled document review and other discovery matters. But I rarely
tried cases because clients preferred settlements to the cost of going to trial.

The first case I tried was in the New York State Supreme Court before
Justice Joseph Martinis. I represented an actuarial firm that hadn't been paid
what I recall was a less than $50,000 bill. I put in an enormous amount of
time preparing for that non-jury case. I became a nervous wreck, but my
father-in-law came to the rescue with sage advice that served me well. "Forget
what happens if you lose and simply focus on doing your best in court," he
said. "You can't control the outcome, but you can control your effort to establish the client's side." The client ended up winning the case.

I also handled personal injury matters and real estate closings for relatives
of clients and staff of the firm. The latter experience made me briefly the
firm's real estate "expert." That expertise had its limitations, however, as I discovered when I was asked to draft a party wall agreement for a client — a party
wall being a shared structure between two buildings or units. Because no one
at the firm could help, I turned again to my father-in-law, who had done just
about everything in the area of real estate. I sketched out information to him
over the phone and then he dictated a draft of the document to my secretary.
With a few changes and careful review, the draft became the firm's agreement
in that matter.

Another time Peter Mullen asked me to represent a woman with two children who'd been abandoned by her husband. I pursued the husband in the
Family Court in New York City, secured orders requiring child support, and
when he left New York State to escape these obligations, I found ways to follow him, so to speak, across state lines under the Uniform Interstate Family
Support Act. This matter dragged on for years, with no compensation to the

firm, but the recommending party, the general counsel of a major company, appreciated the representation of his friend. My diligence made a favorable impression on both the general counsel and Mullen. Mullen, an incredible lawyer, had joined the firm in 1961 and became a partner on January 1, 1962, along with Barry Garfinkel and Maurice Roche. As Skadden grew, the four of us enjoyed a special collegiality.

Thanks to Flom, Mullen, and Roche, my early corporate experience was wide-ranging, consisting, among other things, of drafting, reading, and analyzing corporate indentures and other transaction documents. I found some of this work tedious but, in hindsight, important in helping me to focus on detail. I enjoyed the chance to set up a corporation and develop its bylaws and other governance documents. My most significant experience in this regard was for Orin Tovrov's Easterly Productions, which later produced the television series *The Doctors*.

My most challenging assignments, however, were in the field of labor relations. My very first was helping Meagher handle an arbitration proceeding brought by the New York Stereotypers' Union against the *New York Times*. On my second day on the job, I met with the newspaper's labor relations director as a replacement for Meagher and almost froze in my chair when he asked me to explain the meaning of the phrase "without prejudice," which I had invoked as the meeting began.

Stereotypers made curved, lead printing plates from forms assembled by typographers.[2] Each form represented a page of the newspaper. The labor contracts at the time addressed processes associated with metallic typecasts and plaster molds. The *Times* insisted on using a new plate-casting machine called the Supermatic that it claimed required practically no manning by its stereotypers.

The *Times*'s position would have resulted in the elimination of many jobs and, if established, would have led other newspapers to adopt the same position. The hot metal plate-casting machine to be replaced required four men for its operation, whereas the new machine, according to the *Times*, required only one. After Meagher spent months presenting the matter before an arbitrator, with the help of Skadden associate Geoffrey Kalmus, while I was away on Army duty, a settlement was reached that called for manning by five men when two machines were operated in tandem and three when operated alone.

Because of that success, the Stereotypers Union and labor-related unions in New York and New Jersey called on the firm to handle other matters involving automation, which was becoming an issue of growing importance in the newspaper industry. As Meagher's associate I became involved in these matters and learned more in that period than ever before or since about representing a client. Meagher was totally immersed in these struggles with newspaper publishers and expected the same of me. We worked together on labor and litigation matters throughout the 1960s and early 1970s until Meagher moved on to become counsel to the firm. I then became the firm's principal lawyer for labor and employment matters.

As an associate, as noted, I also assisted other partners on labor and employment-related matters for airlines and other clients, including New York Airways, Aeronaves de Mexico, Pakistan Airlines, Goya Food Products, and Progresso Foods. These partners included Arps, Robert Ensher, John Slate, and Barry Garfinkel. I gained problem-solving experience in all phases of labor relations — plant closings, collective bargaining negotiations, union organizational campaigns and elections, grievance arbitration hearings, court and administrative proceedings, jurisdictional disputes, and unfair labor practice charges.

I spent time in printing plants when new equipment was introduced in order to learn the operating intricacies of machines. I became proficient in examining and cross-examining witnesses, as if the machines were part of my daily work, and in using my knowledge to persuade publishers in settlement discussions. Unlike the typical labor lawyer at the time, I might represent a company in a proceeding to uphold a disciplinary action and also a union in a proceeding seeking to overturn the suspension or firing of an employee.

In one case, an employer client fired its treasurer, who allegedly embezzled about one hundred dollars. The treasurer was divorced and had seven children. I hated to present that case before an arbitrator and did everything I could to bring about a settlement, a resignation with severance pay, but neither she nor her union representative was willing to compromise. The arbitrator sustained the termination, but I felt no happiness.

In another case, Skadden represented a union whose member allegedly tampered with equipment belonging to the employer. I second-seated Meagher. The evidence against our client was strong, but when I visited the scene and considered the angle from which the supervisor said he saw the tampering, I realized that he couldn't have seen below the employee's elbow and thus he couldn't truthfully testify that he actually saw someone tamper with the equipment.

I reported these facts to Meagher. During his cross-examination, the witness grudgingly admitted that he hadn't actually seen the tampering. Meagher moved to dismiss the employer's case on the ground that it hadn't established its case beyond a reasonable doubt. The arbitrator granted the motion, and the employee was reinstated.

During this period I had to deal with union grievances of all kinds that involved interpretation of collective bargaining agreements, with compensation and job security issues often present. Two involving publishers in New York City remain vivid. One involved an issue of whether a shift change of the hours of employees triggered extra compensation in the absence of sufficient advance notice. The disputed contract provision had two sections on shifts, the last sentence of one requiring a week or more advance notice. The other section, applicable in this situation, contained no provision regarding advance notice.

The union felt strongly that advance notice was still required. This led to a review of the long history of the contract provision and the discovery that in the 1930s the two sections were a single provision, with a paragraph for each shift and with the notice as the last sentence in the section. The two paragraphs were split into two sections when the collective bargaining agreement was rewritten, without any indication that the notice provision was meant to be treated differently. I claimed, based on this history, that the notice provision was supposed to apply to both shifts. At the beginning of the hearing we made a presentation to the counsel for the publisher, and he ultimately conceded that the merits were with the union and that the workers were entitled to the extra compensation.

The second grievance would have had far greater consequences if found meritorious. The issue was whether a certain group of employees, about thirty-five, were entitled to lifetime job guarantees even though they were categorized as "regular substitutes" as opposed to regular situation holders. The language of a jointly executed letter on job guarantees, attached to the recently concluded collective bargaining agreement, was ambiguous.

The publisher appeared to be in the driver's seat in the arbitration until a union member telephoned me and said that he thought the publisher had taken a different position on the status of "regular substitutes" at an unemployment insurance hearing during an earlier newspaper strike. It was claimed in that proceeding, he said, that regular situation holders and regular substitutes were the same, which would affect their entitlement to unemployment benefits. This claim led to both groups being denied unemployment benefits for several weeks of the strike, based on a New York State statute. We located the stenographer at that hearing and asked for a transcript of her notes, which showed that the union member was correct. Based on the evidence, the arbitrator decided in the union's favor.

One case illustrated for me the justice that can be obtained through arbitration. It involved a claim by the Stereotypers Union against the *New York Times*. The union opposed the paper's plans to print a new addition in another state, claiming that it violated the collective bargaining agreement. They were also concerned that it would set a precedent for outsourcing to non-union employees that other papers would follow. The equities were with the publisher, but the contract provision favored the union. I presented the case, arguing that economic justification did not trump a written contract provision. The arbitrator agreed with the union's position. The union was subsequently happy to negotiate an exception as long as the *Times* was willing to guarantee a lifetime job to every stereotyper it employed. The resulting agreement became a precursor to other such agreements by unions, allowing newspapers to automate in return for lifetime job guarantees.

Becoming a Partner

It was a joyful day for me when on November 1, 1968, at the age of 32, I became a Skadden partner, along with my good friends Norman Donald and James Freund, resulting in ten partners and thirteen associates at the end of the firm's first two decades. After I became a partner, one colleague suggested that I might want to pursue a career as a trial lawyer rather than remain involved in the labor field. He believed that I had potential in the courtroom.

But my heart had been won over by my labor and problem-solving experiences. While I felt quite at home representing stereotypers and pressmen, the future of Skadden's labor department was inextricably tied to corporations, which made it difficult to develop a labor practice on the union side. Conflicts were inevitable if any effort was made to do so, though the labor practice was expansive in the printing field. Once a retainer client of the firm, an employer notorious for anti-union practices, asked me to represent it in a matter that involved organizing. I declined because of the firm's representation of printing unions. The firm, initially expressing some reluctance, accepted my views about the inappropriateness of such representation in the face of our printing union practice.

As Skadden grew and became increasingly eminent, I stayed with the practice of labor and employment law, a field that expanded after the passage of civil right statutes in the 1960s. Some of these matters were quite sensitive, but many were resolved through settlement negotiations with the federal Equal Employment Opportunity Commission, and those that went to court usually ended up being settled eventually. Claims ranged from allegations of discrimination based on race, age, and nationality, to issues of unjust dismissal, defamation, and false imprisonment.

As the labor practice grew, the *New York Law Journal* asked me to write its monthly column on labor relations, later broadened to include employment law. I recall a conversation with the *Law Journal's* president, Jimmy

Finkelstein, who worried that the column was moving away from traditional labor subjects like strikes, boycotts, and pickets. I comforted him by describing what was happening in law firms as a result of the civil rights statutes. But out of deference to his wishes, I continued to write columns on these more traditional subjects[3] and to accept invitations from the *Law Journal* to write on other subjects.[4]

At times I received requests from the *Law Journal*, with urgency attached to them.[5] In 1974, for example, I was asked by the publisher to help him write a front-page article involving the confirmation of Nelson Rockefeller as vice president under Gerald Ford, after which Jerry Finkelstein sent me a sentimental note dated October 7, 1974, that said, "I appreciate everything you've done in the past for us and particularly today's piece for me."

I also wrote on labor subjects for other publications and appeared on programs to educate lawyers about civil rights and employment law. There were many invitations and I seldom said no. I was pleased by the opportunity to join forces with Joseph Barbash of Debevoise & Plimpton as co-chair of the first video program offered by the Practicing Lawyers' Institute (PLI). We each separately conceived of a program on unjust dismissal, one that nearly three thousand people watched. Although the program ushered in the technology era for PLI, it did little for my own technology skills!

Finally, in the late 1970s, I was asked by a company called Law and Business Inc. to put together an 800-page treatise on the right of working people to decide whether or not to be represented by a labor union. The National Labor Relations Board (NLRB) administered the elections. The book, entitled *NLRB Representation Elections — Law, Practice and Procedure*, responded to the void in the legal literature on the subject and would eventually become a key resource. Many contributed to it but no one more than co-authors Henry Baer and Jonathan P. Arfa, our devoted legal assistant Joseph DeGiuseppe Jr., and Professor Joseph Crowley.[6]

Of the discrimination cases I handled, one had a strange twist. It involved an employee fired by a corporate client. The employee brought a lawsuit in state court seeking damages, claiming that his poor performance was tied to his alcoholism, a disability within the meaning of the law. Before suing, the employee had sent the company a letter expressing gratitude as to how he had been treated by the company.

I was asked by Meagher to handle the case and make a motion for summary judgment. I did so, only to lose the motion in the New York Supreme Court in a decision by Judge Martin Stecher. I later learned that Jonathan Lerner, a young lawyer working with me on the matter, had gone to Meagher to suggest the summary judgment motion. Upset by Judge Stecher's decision, Meagher instructed me to appeal, which I felt would make matters even worse if the appellate court affirmed the decision, as I thought likely.

I argued the matter and was surprised by how few questions I was asked and by how many were put to opposing counsel regarding the letter his client had sent. A few weeks later, the court unanimously reversed the original decision, granting the motion for summary judgment and stating: "The critical issue is not whether alcoholism is a disease, but whether plaintiff was disabled by that disease. The failure to claim disability and the fact that plaintiff continued to perform his functions until discharged are important factors."[7] I was thrilled and thanked Meagher for his guidance, if not for rescuing me. He and Lerner had seen what I had not.

Another appellate experience, working closely with Skadden's founder, Leslie Arps, went less well. We represented Aeronaves de México in a breach-of-contract claim by Triangle Aviation Services, a company that provided cleaning services. We sought to stay an arbitration of the claim brought by the company, arguing that the claim didn't fall within the scope of the contract's arbitration provision. The federal district court judge disagreed. I argued the appeal in the Second Circuit Court of Appeals before a bench presided over by Chief Judge Irving Kaufman.

The court later affirmed the decision against us unanimously.[8] But what I didn't expect was a call from Arps a few days later, asking me to come to his office. He said he had run into Judge Kaufman at a bar association meeting, and the judge had said to tell "that young lawyer in your office who argued before our Court to pay attention to the time-signal lights the next time." We proceeded with the arbitration and achieved an award that seemed to give something to both parties.

Later, in a tribute to Judge Kaufman, I described my appearance before him:

> The experience was among the most formidable and memorable of
> my entire professional career. I became so engrossed in my argument
> that day that I forgot to pay attention to the lights which signaled
> either the end or near the end of my allotted time. To be sure, Judge
> Kaufman did see the light and was determined, and distracting I might
> say, in pointing to it repeatedly, until I simply gave up and ended my
> argument prematurely, I thought. It was not an auspicious beginning
> to our relationship.[9]

In the 1970s, I was the firm's senior lawyer on legal matters and cases concerning the Economic Stabilization Act, which President Nixon had signed into law in August 1971. Among other things, the program placed a freeze and then a limitation on the nation's wage and price increases. One matter I worked on involved a freeze on wage increases that affected newspapers in New York City. I represented the New York printing unions before the federal Pay Commission to urge that the newly-agreed-upon wage increases be placed into effect, noting that the publishers had implemented advertising price increases in anticipation of the new wages. I thought the argument was a winning one, only to discover that the Pay Commission sent the issue to the Price Commission, which rolled back the price increases. The Pay Commission then denied the unions' application.

For another matter, in July of 1971, I traveled to Savannah, Georgia, to help a corporate client deal with an imminent strike. In reviewing its collective bargaining agreement, we discovered that the union had given insufficient notice that it was terminating the agreement. We discussed the pros and cons of issuing a press release saying that the threatened strike would violate the contract and that the union would be held responsible for damages.

One colleague, Alfred Law, said that no press release should be issued, advising that one should never declare another party's strike. When you position a party publicly, he suggested, you make it harder for that party to back away from its threat without appearing weak. "If you don't want a strike," he said, "you need to leave that party with all of its options open and bring what pressure you can to accomplish a resolution."

Following this advice, we simply sent a letter to the union stating that a strike would violate the contract notice provision. The union hesitated in proceeding with the strike, and I returned home to New York. A month later I flew back to Savannah as the union pushed ahead with its plans to strike, but after I got off the plane I was informed that President Nixon had passed the Economic Stabilization Act, making any strike to secure a wage increase illegal. Happily, I headed back to New York. Months later I learned that the company and the union had concluded a new collective bargaining agreement without a strike.

The unionization of legal offices became an issue in the 1970s, and I found myself providing assistance to a few law firms without labor lawyers. One of these matters resulted in a labor board precedent favorable to law firms that might be faced with a union seeking representation of some of its employees. In that case, the labor board ruled that a bargaining unit of a few employees was not appropriate for bargaining purposes and, hence, the union's petition for representation was not successful.

While I concentrated on labor and employment at Skadden during the 1970s, I also pitched in on the litigation side of some takeovers, taking depo-

sitions and drafting papers and the like. At times, usually at the request of
Joe Flom, I was drawn into sensitive matters because of my problem-solving
background. Some of these matters involved partnership disputes.

As my career as a practicing lawyer came to an end, the labor and employment practice at Skadden continued to grow, with new clients on the horizon.
However, I knew there was a talented team of lawyers in place to handle
them, led by Henry Baer, a great human being who would later become a
dear friend.

A Retrospective Glance

In taking account of my career at Skadden, on the occasion of my 70th birthday, I was deeply touched by gifts from my former colleagues. I reciprocated
by sending to the firm some reflections on my special moments and the special people I came to know. I said in part:

> I remember with great fondness all the wonderful people who backed
> up the lawyers at the firm, especially Tony Arbisi, who helped me with
> just about everything, and Linda Plaza, who gave me so much secre-
> tarial support with my writing on presidential succession, late into the
> night and on weekends.
>
> I remember Les Arps reminding us about achieving the "upper
> margin" in all things and the importance of not turning away potential
> clients . . .
>
> I remember Bill Mulligan coming to the firm and asking him how
> he wanted to be addressed. He said simply: "Your worship."
>
> I remember telling Peter Mullen after one hiring season that a
> majority of our summer associates were women, which took everyone
> by surprise.
>
> I remember Ed Yodowitz in the managing clerk's office wanting a
> chance to be an associate, which I encouraged, and then some years
> later becoming a partner with Joe Flom as his strong advocate.
>
> I remember when I mentioned my leaving to Bill Meagher, he
> was in a state of disbelief, telling me that I was not making the right
> decision, but then the next day he changed his mind. He died a
> month later. Les Arps was also shocked by my decision, causing me
> to tell him I would be back in four or five years. I thought that would
> happen.
>
> And I remember the dinner given for me as I left to go to Fordham.

I cried that night because I was leaving my family in the law for a different journey in areas I was not sure about. So many wonderful memories of Skadden times past fill me at this time (and they still do!).

There are some other moments at Skadden that often come to mind. I recall interviewing Bob Sheehan at Pennsylvania Law School, with few students showing up because of the snow that day. We therefore spent a lot of time together just talking. With so few students to choose from, I invited him to interview at the firm. Little did I realize that he would become the firm's executive partner and one of New York's leading lawyers.

At the urging of Joe Flom, I called Bill Frank while he was on vacation in Brazil, leaving a message for him that he was needed at the firm. Frank later told us that, at the time, he was horseback riding in an isolated region on a mountain. He was startled by the sound of his name being called in the distance, followed by the message: "Mr. Frank, please call your office immediately." Frank returned, commenting on the challenge of getting an uninterrupted vacation, even if located thousands of miles away. Frank would become a firm superstar.

I recall Jim Freund telling me that he interviewed a student at Harvard, Henry Baer, saying he would work well with me in the labor field despite being older than I was. Baer, it turned out, was a gentleman and had a charm about him that made him a client favorite.

Postscript

More thoughts on my colleagues: Tom Schwarz, a Fordham lawyer I introduced to the firm, said of Meagher: "As a lawyer, his attention to detail, his preparation, his facility with language and brevity of expression are unmatched. He spent as much time in the library as the youngest attorney in the firm and his ability to research was unsurpassed and thorough. He viewed it, properly so, as the linchpin of being a good lawyer."

Schwarz added: "As a teacher of lawyers . . . Bill was patient and available. He [was] not afraid to explain his thinking, his energy, his thought process and to subject it to cross-examination. . . . He was willing to be talked out of a position." Schwarz recalled a case in which Meagher's adversary as counsel said at the end of a heated deposition taken by Meagher of his client, "You're the best lawyer I've ever seen." "Certainly the highest compliment that can be paid," noted Schwarz.

To work with Arps was an experience. Your whole being became absorbed in every matter, and you worked around his coffee table at all hours, day and night. You reasoned aloud with him, thought and read with him, and together wrote every sentence of every document relating to the matter at hand. He never allowed a brief or memorandum to leave his office if you disagreed with something in it. On one of the last major cases, a four-month class action in Texas, these characteristics served his client well. The jury became so enamored by him that it spontaneously stood and sang happy birthday to him on the day he turned 73. They were joined by the judge. With millions of dollars at stake, shortly thereafter the suing plaintiff decided instead to work out a reasonable settlement with Arps' client.

It was to Arps that we at Skadden all went when issues involved the canons of ethics. I was honored to be a trustee of his estate, to be invited by his beloved wife, Ruth, to speak at his memorial tribute, and to deliver the Leslie H. Arps Memorial Lecture at the New York City Bar on April 1, 1996, titled "Judicial Independence and the Impartial Administration of Justice."[10]

I consider this my most important speech on a legal subject. I sent a copy of my speech to Justice Ruth Bader Ginsburg. She responded in a letter, "An independent judiciary is our nation's hallmark and pride. Reminders of that from voices like yours will consign current unfair comment to the place such comment has gone in the past." The speech's conclusion became the rallying cry for the New York Bar in responding to attacks on the independence of the judiciary.[11]

Later, in 1976, when my book *The Twenty-Fifth Amendment: Its Complete History and Applications* was published, I gave Arps and Meagher each a copy inscribed with special notes of gratitude. Meagher responded in a handwritten note: "How inexpressibly moved I am by the words you inscribed. . . . I am in the midst of reading it, and all I can say is: If, in fact, I have 'inspired' this great achievement of yours, I shall myself have achieved much indeed. Surely, by this, you must know that I claim you as my 'son in the law,' of whom I am most proud and fond." Arps replied: "I was deeply touched by the inscription and I shall prize both the book and the inscription for the rest of my life. I must in all candor say I do not deserve the inscription but that does not lessen my enjoyment of it."

16

Leaving Skadden

Parting is such sweet sorrow

— WILLIAM SHAKESPEARE

While at Skadden, people with whom I had professional relationships offered me opportunities to join their law firms. One was Lawrence Reilly of the Landis firm; another was Eugene Morris of Demov and Morris, an up-and-coming real estate firm. Both were great lawyers, and saying no to them was not easy. But Skadden had become my home.

Still, I felt a restlessness from almost the beginning of my career as a practicing lawyer about what I should do with my life long-term. After President Kennedy was assassinated, a new sense of purpose manifested from this restlessness, leading me to become immersed in a major constitutional cause. President Kennedy had inspired my generation with his clarion call, "Ask not what your country can do for you — ask what you can do for your country," and I felt a need to do as much public good in the world as I could.

I also began to consider teaching and reached out to Georgetown and Fordham law schools. Georgetown had nothing available, but in 1964, Dean Mulligan of Fordham offered me a full-time teaching position for $9,000 annually. I was then earning $11,000 at Skadden. After consulting with Fordham Professors Joseph McLaughlin and Manning, I declined the offer. McLaughlin was surprised by my interest but helpful in answering my questions. Manning suggested I think further about the idea. He was then recovering from a life-threatening illness and spoke about the economic pinch his family might have experienced had he not survived. I was influenced by Manning's implicit counsel.

I also considered starting a law firm with two Fordham schoolmates, James McGough and James Tolan. We thought that doing our own thing would be exciting, but we hesitated. Tolan reminisced on the idea, saying, "We were captured by emotion and thinking that on our own, we would have a better chance of 'making a difference,' getting involved in civil rights–type cases, legal aid type defenses." Tolan had three children, and I was hoping to follow his lead. We never returned to the question, but as Tolan later remarked, "It was the best law firm that never practiced." In the 1980s, McGough would join me at Fordham Law School to create the school's first financial aid office, and Tolan became a leader of the alumni association while I was dean and, later, a co-chair of the school's strategic plan involving alumni.

I also wrestled with a repeated offer from my father-in-law to join his law practice in Southampton. I considered the idea, but ultimately rejected it as my heart was still with Skadden and with living in the Bronx, close to Mom and Pop.

Another opportunity appeared when I was a young Skadden partner. William T. Gossett, then president of the ABA, asked if I would be interested in becoming associate general counsel of the Ford Motor Company.[1] The position would allow me to be considered for general counsel in a year's time. However, it meant moving to Detroit, uprooting family, and leaving loved ones in New York. Emalie immediately dismissed the idea, so I declined.

In April of 1981 another kind of career appeared as a distinct possibility — that of becoming an academic lawyer by returning to Fordham Law School as its dean. Why such a change at the height of my earning power and as the firm's success was escalating? A history of my activities involving Fordham provides a glimpse of the answer.

Throughout my Skadden career, Fordham was an important part of my life. Shortly after I graduated, I began receiving invitations to school events, such as alumni luncheons, state bar functions, and law review events. Two graduates, James Murphy and Raymond Ryan, subsequently saw to it that I got involved with the Law Review Association, first by asking me to bring trays of hot dogs from Nathan's Restaurant on Broadway to its Christmas party and then by asking me to join them on the association's board of directors.

I attended many functions of both associations in the 1960s and came to greatly admire the leadership of graduates like Caesar Pitassy and Denis McInerney. During this time, I also wrote articles for the *Law Review* and sometimes helped students in their careers.

When Professor McLaughlin became dean in 1971, he asked me to become president of the alumni association, an invitation I declined because of the enormity of my work at Skadden and in the organized bar. I did, however, accept his invitation to become president of the Law Review Alumni Association, a time commitment I could meet, as well as an invitation to join the alumni association's board of directors under the leadership of Harry McCallion, then general counsel of New York Life and a gentleman of the first rank.

In 1972, McCallion asked me to chair an alumni committee with a mission to develop recommendations for a continuing legal education program at the school, something Dean McLaughlin hoped to achieve. The committee recommended that the school revive a program it had between 1958 and 1962, one that dealt with business and trade with Europe. We were encouraged by Professor Joseph Crowley and a young faculty member he brought on board for the project, Barry Hawk, who had a strong academic commitment to this area.[2]

Dean McLaughlin accepted our recommendations but cautioned that if we didn't break even in terms of cost, the program would end. Thanks to the incredible energy of younger graduates of the school,[3] we were able to bring in a profit of $10,000 from an attendance of some 150 people. The alumni team was ecstatic with the outcome, as was the dean. This program would repeat itself annually and eventually became the springboard for the school's LL.M. program in the late 1980s.

In the fall of 1973, Dean McLaughlin reached out again to ask me to reconsider becoming president of the alumni association. He was anxious to have a younger generation at the helm, and I was his candidate. I couldn't turn him down again, although I still wasn't sure I should take on the extra role as my labor practice at Skadden was growing, as well as my family and my activities in the organized bar. However, when the invitation to serve came in from McCallion, I said, "Yes, I would be honored to do so." I didn't know how to say no.

The years from 1974 to 1978 turned out to be joy-filled ones for me. The school was growing under McLaughlin's towering leadership, and he was anxious for new initiatives and open to suggestions from the alumni. We gave him our ideas, one after the other, which he responded to enthusiastically. I relished these opportunities to help him advance the reputation of the school. The "Beyond the Classroom" section of McLaughlin's hilarious but effective annual dean's reports acknowledged and recorded the activities of the alumni. He was also generous in his comments about me, in one report describing me as "a shadow dean." The Corporate Law Institute, the Stein Prize, new alumni chapters, fundraising successes, student career services, and a broad-based alumni directory had all become realities, thanks largely to McLaughlin's inspiring leadership and the work of the school's alumni.

On receiving the Eugene J. Keefe Award from Fordham Law School students at their graduation in June of 1975, I acknowledged my gratitude for my involvement in these undertakings and added, "My feelings go out to the two fair ladies of my life — to my mother for instilling in me the importance of service to people — and to my wife for her inspiration and her acceptance of my spirit rather than my physical presence during the thirteen years of our marriage." I'm not sure that Mom was able to absorb this moment as her memory had begun to decline, but Pop did and was deeply touched.

During the 1976–1977 school year, thanks to Dean McLaughlin, I realized my early dream of teaching at Fordham by creating, as an adjunct professor, an evening course on employment discrimination, a field in which I had become heavily involved at Skadden. After class I'd return to Skadden for additional hours of work, even though I was often exhausted. I was struck by the students' knowledge; as evening students, they held jobs during the day, and from their work experiences they knew the subject as well as I did. They challenged me, asking me questions to which I sometimes didn't have the answers, requiring additional homework on my part.

One of these students was Denny Chin, who in 2010 would be appointed to the Second Circuit, confirmed 98–0 by the U.S. Senate. In my *Fordham Law Review* tribute to him, I wrote: "He was exceedingly smart, spoke softly but with an already keen knowledge of the subject, answered questions clearly and directly, and participated with effectiveness in class discussions."[4] Another gifted student, Eileen Bransten, became an outstanding justice of the New York State Supreme Court, while a third, Benjamin Tucker, became first deputy New York City police commissioner, the second-highest-ranking position in the NYPD, and the highest-ranking position held by an African American in the department.

Following the end of my tenure as alumni president in March of 1978, Father James Finlay asked me to join the university's board of trustees, and as a result the next four years proved to be extremely interesting ones for me. The board's religious and lay members fervently wanted the university to develop a greater residential capacity at the Rose Hill campus, further securing the school's history in the Bronx. I chaired the board's nominating committee which gave me the opportunity to recommend Claire Flom and Barbara Watson to the board — the only two women to serve as trustees in 1981.

The Law School was an important part of the university's future, but there were issues that needed to be addressed involving the school's accreditor, the ABA. Along with Kathryn Wriston and Ted St. Antoine, I was appointed to a board committee to help resolve these issues. Also looming was a capital campaign to help the Law School renovate and expand its physical plant. Some people questioned whether the school could raise the necessary funds.

In early 1981, McLaughlin announced that he was to be nominated by President Reagan for a federal judgeship. I began receiving calls suggesting that I put in my name to be his successor, followed by encouragement from Father Finlay to apply for the position. As I noted at the time for a Fordham publication: "[Father Finlay] said it would be wonderful if I would help the Society of Jesus and the Law School evolve a vision of its future, and as a Fordham graduate and long-time supporter, I found that empowering."

Others who reached out to me included alumni leaders, such as Jack Vaughan, senior faculty, such as Professors Calamari and Manning, and younger faculty. Ten years earlier, Professor Calamari, as chair of the dean's search of 1970, had asked if I wished to be considered. At the time I declined, saying that I was "fully committed to law practice."

Now at age 44, I felt my life rushing along much too quickly. My four daughters were growing up fast, not to speak of my two sons, then ages eight and five. I hardly had any time to spend with my younger children. Moreover, my experiences in areas of legal reform, both with the ABA and the City Bar, had whet my appetite for a full-time position in public service, possibly working for a congressional committee or the Library of Congress. This was not practical, however, because of my concern for Mom and Pop's health and because of a growing family with roots in New York.

As I harbored these thoughts, I reflected on how involved I'd been in Fordham's alumni life. I had come to know thousands of graduates in my service under McLaughlin. At the top of the list was Francis Blake '44, secretary to the alumni association, who possessed an enormous devotion to the school. Others served as judges in moot court competitions and as directors and members of alumni committees dedicated to helping the school grow. Still others lent the prestige of their positions by attending school events. As president of the alumni association, I also observed graduates who toiled quietly behind the scenes to assure the success of every alumni function. They were my alumni heroes.[5] My passion for Fordham grew and grew in working with Dean McLaughlin.

However, I wasn't sure if I was qualified to be a dean, nor was I certain that making such a dramatic change was a smart idea. I reflected on the idea over the summer of 1981, discussing it with family and friends, and mentioning the possibility to Mullen. Finally, in September of 1981, on the day of the application deadline, I put in my application.

"Are you crazy?" Pop yelled, shocked. "Why would you do this?" For Pop, giving up the financial success I'd achieved made no sense. The starting salary as dean was $62,000, while at Skadden I was then earning more than $1 million a year. However, I felt that this financial success made it possible for me to make a career change. For the first time in my life, I had personal savings, and I had put aside money for college tuitions for my six children. My financial success also enabled me to help Mom and Pop return to Ireland often and to build a house for them in Lake Carmel, and it allowed me to be generous to the institutions that had nurtured me, such as Fordham, and to other charitable causes.

Emalie's view also differed from Pop's. She believed the change might lead to more time for family. Money was never high on her list of things that were important, nor were the associated luxuries, a trait I admired greatly. Some years earlier, when I gave her a fur coat for her 40th birthday, she asked me to return it, which I did. Her encouragement prevailed, and once I was invited to serve, I was excited to build on the legacies of my predecessors.

But let me not forget the person who influenced me the most, aside from Emalie — Fordham's president, Father Finlay. I met Father Finlay when he chaired Fordham's political science department. My relationship with him grew from that start. In 1965 he invited me to give a talk to his class on the subject of presidential inability, prior to the ratification of the Twenty-Fifth Amendment (Emalie attended my talk and asked questions that I didn't know how to answer). And he invited me to join the Fordham University board of trustees, as noted, which I served on until becoming dean and a full-time employee of the university.

Colleagues at Skadden and in the organized bar were shocked by my decision. I explained that I would be serving for four or five years to help the school carry out a new building program and that I'd likely return to Skadden. I declined Father Finlay's suggestion that I remain at Skadden as "of counsel," believing that people would view my decision as opportunistic, which it wasn't. I just loved Fordham, and I thought I was ready for a new beginning.

In the early years of my transition, I missed Skadden terribly, especially the many friends I had made and my labor group. But my insecurity eased as I began to feel the support of students, faculty, and alumni and grew confident in the school's potential and how I could help.

17

Becoming a Law School Dean: An Overview

Fordham Law School is seventy-five years old. From 1905 to the present, from Rose Hill to Lincoln Center, from Paul Fuller to Joseph McLaughlin, our Law School has survived the ravages of time, the trauma of uprootings, and the vagaries of our modern society to become a truly great institution of professional learning.

— CAESAR PITASSY

An entirely new phase of my career began on July 1, 1982, when I received the dean's mantle from the school's superb acting dean, Joseph Perillo, as described in Appendix B. I immediately felt how different it was from law practice: the demands of law students, the heightened expectations of faculty, the aspirations of alumni, and the needs of the university for support from its constituent schools, especially its law school.[1] Looming over all of this was a large renovation and expansion of the school's building, which had seen no real change since 1961.

This required a major capital campaign to raise $6.8 million, a campaign I found difficult because capital fundraising was new to both me and the school. For the next twenty-eight months I devoted more than three-fourths of my time to seeking financial support from graduates around the country and from foundations and friends. I was joined in this effort by Father Finlay, whose tenure ended on June 30, 1984.

The Fordham Law School Dedication of October 24, 1984

The background for the dedication began on September 28, 1983, when Dean Mulligan opened the groundbreaking ceremony for the Law School expansion. Hundreds of students and graduates watched the event from the school's second- and third-floor windows and from a corner of Robert Moses Plaza, which separated the Law School from the Lowenstein Building on Fordham's Lincoln Center campus. I was given a shovel, along with E. Carter Corriston '60, Richard Bennett '42, and Father Finlay, to break the ground. Corriston served as president of the New Jersey chapter of the law alumni association. Richard Bennett served as chair of the university's board of trustees.

The Solicitor General of the United States, Rex E. Lee, was the principal speaker. Also on the platform were two presidents of Fordham University, Father Finlay, whose support for the expansion was unwavering, and President Emeritus Laurence McGinley, S.J., who had brought Fordham to Lincoln Center. Alumni president Paul Curran and Mayor Edward Koch participated in the program, but Dean Mulligan stole the show with his infectious humor. He recounted the day of the original groundbreaking of May 3, 1960, when he picked up Chief Justice Earl Warren at LaGuardia Airport. The day, however, did not go as planned, as he explained:

"On arriving at the airport, the chief justice said that he already had breakfast and asked to go immediately to the site of the ceremony, where there was much dirt and rubble but no available place to hang out, and no one had yet arrived," Mulligan said. He decided to "kill time" by taking a walk up Amsterdam Avenue with the chief justice. He saw several faculty members coming in the opposite direction. When he introduced them to the chief justice, one professor took a step back, hit the edge of the curb, and fell, prompting this comment by Mulligan: "This was the first case in history of a Fordham professor rolling in the gutter while sober."

At the lunch afterward, Mulligan was forced to introduce the chief justice to Cardinal Spellman in the men's room at the University Club. "I even removed my homburg to show proper respect at this summit conference," Mulligan said. He added, "I must say that even the sophisticated members of the club were impressed by my homburg."

Fortunately, the ride back to the airport was pleasurable enough as Mulligan and the chief justice discussed their mutual interest in baseball. The chief justice apparently started each day by reading the sports pages.[2] A year later, the expansion program was over.

On October 24, 1984, our facility opened, with a ceremony at Lincoln Center's beautiful Vivian Beaumont Theater. Some fifteen hundred graduates joined faculty, staff, students, trustees, university officials, and friends inside and outside the university for the celebration. Mulligan, who also presided, jokingly claimed credit for the renovation and expansion, stating that it was his planning for the original law school building at Lincoln Center back in 1961 that made the day inevitable. Later in the program I acknowledged warmly four people for their generosity to the school — Leo Kissam '22, Justice James McNally '20, James "Ned" Doyle '31, and William Platt, my father-in-law.

Emalie's father made a gift of almost half a million dollars in memory of his wife, Edith Platt. He made that gift without any expectation of recognition; he was simply responding to a request from Emalie to help the school.[3]

Ned Doyle, whose generosity of a more than $2 million trust made possible a new building as part of the school's expansion, remarked that everyone seated on the stage behind him wondered when he would be leaving the stage of life so that his trust provision could be triggered. Laughter followed. Sitting behind him were U.S. Supreme Court Justice Sandra Day O'Connor, Mayor Edward Koch, Governor Mario Cuomo, Senator Alphonse D'Amato, Father McGinley, Dean McLaughlin, His Eminence Archbishop Iakovas of the Greek Orthodox Church, and Father Joseph A. O'Hare, S.J., Fordham University's new president. Afterward, countless attendees asked Justice O'Connor to autograph their programs. It was a special moment for the school to host the first woman to serve on the U.S. Supreme Court. It was for me a day like no other, as dean.

After a ceremony several days later, I received a letter from Doyle. I had given him a video of the program as a memento. In the letter he ironically said, "Thank you very much for the videocassette. I haven't got anything to play it on but I know a friend of mine who will."

Building Up and Out

I began my tenure to "build up and out," as proclaimed by Caesar Pitassy, the managing partner of Roger and Wells, who served as chair of the Law School's building campaign and earlier as president of the school's alumni association. However, in many ways my tenure as dean started before my official start date of July 1, 1982. In the preceding months I had met with more than two hundred graduates to discuss the building program in the hope they would support it financially. Also, as I wound down my career at Skadden, I visited other law schools, including Stanford, Boston University, Cornell, and Georgetown to get a sense of how they were structured internally.

I found that they had a more robust administrative structure than Fordham, which led to my creation of several new positions when I started my tenure: an associate dean, an assistant dean of students, a financial aid director, and an assistant dean of alumni relations. I also focused on expanding career services, recruiting students nationally and of diverse backgrounds, and opening a chaplain's office, with the assistance of religious leaders of the major faiths.

A few of these initiatives, because of the costs involved, caused consternation among some faculty. I was in a honeymoon period, however, and everyone was willing to give me the benefit of the doubt and support these changes.

Our first associate dean, Joseph Crowley, became my mentor. He knew how to deal with the faculty and university administration — respectfully and effectively — and he taught me the ropes. He counselled me not to set my sights on other law schools but simply to help Fordham be the best it could be, given its own history and resources — advice I tried to follow. He said it was fine to look to other schools for ideas and to see what they were doing but not to judge the school's success on whether or not it had achieved their level of recognition. He stressed that Fordham Law had its own distinctiveness as an integral part of a venerable Jesuit university.

Crowley's leadership set an immediate tone for me and the school, as I recalled on February 27, 2013, the silver anniversary of the establishment of the clinical legal education program at Fordham:

> In my first year as dean the faculty decided to educate me about academia . . . and they also wished to lay out a vision for the school. This began with the planning and launching of a faculty retreat . . . on the future of the law school. It was held on Friday, October 29, 1982. . . This may well have been the first gathering of its kind in the history of the law school. . . . The planning committee was chaired by . . . Crowley. His retreat committee laid out in several reports a vision of the law school twenty years down the line. One report dealt with clinical education. Others with a graduate program, computers, the recruitment of students from every economic strata, and the establishment of continuing legal education programs and annual institutes and centers, all to occur with a renovated and expanded building campaign.

After a second faculty retreat in October of 1983, the school hired law school graduate Catherine Cronin-Harris to develop a live client clinic and enhance the existing internship program for students. Thanks to her work and the efforts of Donna Welensky, her successor, the few interns of 1982–1983 grew by many hundreds over the following years.

As this was happening, Professor Jacqueline Nolan-Haley created a highly popular mediation clinic in the small claims part of the Civil Court in the Bronx. In the clinic, students trained in mediation would help parties in conflict resolve their disputes. Professor Nolan-Haley's work would have a transformative impact on the school in the field of alternative dispute resolution, with the development of many courses on problem-solving.

There was much more. In 1985 Professor Rachel Vorspan joined the school as director of legal writing and began to develop a writing program that came to rival the writing programs of the country's top law schools. The arrival of Professor James Cohen in 1987 signaled another revolution — namely, the start of the in-house, live client clinic on litigation skills, which later evolved into a federal litigation clinic. Students, under faculty supervision, represented clients in court proceedings. The following year, Professor Beth Schwartz started another clinic that involved advocating for children who had disabilities and special educational needs. In 1991, Professor Ian Weinstein joined Cohen and Schwarz, and as a group they became a formidable force for advancing clinical education, eventually placing the school's program on the national map. A foundation skills course was also added in 1997.

The Changing World and Legal Profession

The last decades of the twentieth century were transformative with leaders like Mikhail Gorbachev and Nelson Mandela and the impacts they made in their spheres of action. American presidents were challenged, one by an attempted assassination and another by a Senate impeachment trial. The World Wide Web was invented and online communication became available. Outer space became more reachable because of the launch of a space shuttle and then space platform. Conflict in the world persisted and the bombing of the World Trade Center in 1993 was a warning that the United States was not immune from terrorism. On a brighter side, as discussed in another chapter, the conflict in Northern Ireland was eased by the adoption of the Good Friday Agreement. By century's end the population of the world had reached 6 billion.

As to the legal profession, it grew during these decades in leaps and bounds. Applications to law schools increased, as did the size of their student bodies and the number of law schools. Students reflected a greater diversity and inclusion than ever before. Law firms also grew in size in terms of the number of lawyers and the opening of offices in different parts of the United States and in the world. As I left practice in 1982, Skadden was approaching 300 lawyers, and by the turn of the century it had reached 1,613 lawyers with offices in nine states and ten countries. The Fordham Law School I joined full-time in 1982 was not oblivious of the wider world and the growth of the legal profession.

The doubling of the size of the space of the school in 1984 made it possible to ease the pressure that existed, to increase the size of the student body and faculty, and to accommodate the development of clinical education and, in time, centers and institutes. It also allowed us to broaden the scope of the basic curriculum by adding newer courses such as, by example, space law,

English legal history, law and economics, advanced bankruptcy law, sports law, patents, international economic development, banking law, mediation, finance law, computer law, landlord/tenant law, and international law. New technology emerged as a tool for research and communication. Thanks to administrators and faculty, the school was brought into the technology age. The students, energized and enthusiastic, created new student journals, student groups, and additional moot court activities. Not left behind was the school's commitment to the community and city of New York. This led to the establishment by students of public interest groups and public fellowships, and the creation of an umbrella entity to serve the poor known as the Public Interest Resource Center, the brainchild of assistant dean Tom Schoenherr. Through the Internet, media, and travel, the school reached into the global world by creating LL.M. programs that would become highly attractive to lawyers not only in the United States but in Europe and other countries as well.

As all of this was occurring, the school was ever mindful of the importance of being an inclusive community and of our foundation as a Jesuit law school in the service of others. I felt this specialness as a student and active graduate in its alumni activities and pledged myself as its dean to support in every way I could a continuation of this history of the school. My annual dean's reports became my principal way of communicating to a broader Fordham world the life of the school. Inside the school I made every effort to attend student programs, their annual dinners, their moot court competitions, and their public service auctions. I enjoyed arriving early each day and walking around the school to say hello to those who were in early. My door was never closed to a student who wanted to see me.

My reports, as summarized in Appendix B, recount in some detail the academic accomplishments and activities of the faculty and students and the generosity of alumni during my tenure.[4] Some highlights follow here:

1982–1983: The Stein Institute on Law and Ethics is established.

1983–1984: The Leo Kissam Memorial Library is established, and Mary McKee trained almost three hundred students in the new Westlaw legal research system. Establishment of the Sidney C. Norris '27 Chair is made possible from the generous gift from the Norman and Rosita Winston Foundation.

1984–1985: Expanded Law School building opens, with a dedication speech by Justice Sandra Day O'Connor. New student groups form, including associations for Black, Hispanic, and Asian students. In partnership with Justice Resource Center, the NYC High School MENTOR Moot Court Competition is established.

1985–1986: A Supreme Court Admission ceremony is established.

1986–1987: The Law School's evening division celebrates its 75th anniversary and J.D./M.B.A. program inaugurated in 1985.

1987–1988: A board of visitors is established, and a million-dollar annual fund is achieved under the leadership of James Gill '56.

1988–1989: The school's first two LL.M. degree programs launch.

1989–1990: The Law School celebrates its Sesquicentennial Anniversary and adopts the motto "In the Service of Others."

1991–1992: The school establishes its first technology center within the Leo Kissam library. Student publications appear on intellectual property and environmental law. The Mulligan Scholarship Golf Tournament is established.

1992–1993: The Stein Scholars Program begins, and a Corporate Counsel Association is established.

1993–1994: The George McMahon, S.J., residence hall at Lincoln Center opens, and the Law School celebrates the 75th anniversary of the admission of women to the school. The Brendan Moore Trial Advocacy Program is established. Chief Justice Warren Burger delivers at Fordham the Sonnett Lecture, his last public speech.

1994–1995: Pro bono guidelines for faculty are adopted, a possible first in the country. Three students win the National Moot Court Advocacy Competition the second time in the school's history. The William Hughes Mulligan Chair in International Legal Studies is established. A joint degree program is established that year with Fordham's Graduate School of Social Service.

1995–1996: The school celebrates its 90th anniversary. The Joseph Crowley Program on International Human Rights is established.

1996–1997: The John D. Calamari Distinguished Professorship of Law and the Philip Reed Chair in Civil Justice and Dispute Resolution are established.

1997–1998: The School announces the Joseph M. McLaughlin Professorship in honor of our former dean. James H. Quinn '49 founds a Chair of Legal Ethics.

1998–1999: The Cooper Chair in Urban Legal Ethics is established.

1999–2000: The school celebrates the millennium at Lincoln Center campus, dedicated to faculty past and present, with Justice O'Connor as guest speaker. The student's Journal of Corporate & Financial Law is established.

2000–2001: The school announces an institute on law, religion, and lawyer's practice. A summer law program begins in Ireland with for-

mer Senator George Mitchell as a visiting teacher. The Archibald
Murray '60 Professorship in Law is established in his honor.

2001–2002: The school celebrates the 90th anniversary of the evening
division and inaugurates the Center for Corporate, Securities, and
Financial Law, and creates a professorship on corporate law.

My friend and successor, Dean Treanor, gave his account of my last year,
2001–2002, as dean. The report noted that the school's clinical program was
ranked 17th by *U.S. News and World Report*, which also had placed the
school's international law and intellectual property programs in the top 20
among all law schools. The report mentioned the commissioning of portraits
of Martin Fogelman, reflecting his teaching for forty-five years, and Dean
Vairo, the school's first woman to serve as associate dean.

The report also said that Chief Judge Judith Kaye was chosen during the
year to receive the Fordham Stein Prize and that Thomas Moore '72, was
presented with the alumni medal of achievement, Abner Greene with the
professor of the year award, and Professor Diller with the Eugene J. Keefe
Award for his dedicated service.

Dean Treanor provided the statistics: there were 73 full-time professors
and two hundred courses listed in the curriculum; 206 employers had visited
the school; annual tuition had risen to $28,000; students were given financial
aid totaling $3.4 million; nearly 700 students had given 62,000 hours of pro
bono service; 93 percent of the class of 2001 were meaningfully employed
within nine months of graduation; forty conferences and symposia were held,
with more than 5,000 people attending; and there were now 14,000 graduates
located in all fifty states and thirty-five countries. Dean Treanor also reported
that 3,622 gifts were received from graduates, foundations and friends, totaling
more than $17 million and making it the most successful fundraising year in
the school's history.

An extraordinary group joined the faculty in my last year. Tom Lee, who
clerked for U.S. Supreme Court Justice David Souter; Sheila Foster, a leading
scholar in the area of environmental justice; Sonya Katyal, who clerked for
two federal judges and had experience in law practice; Catherine Powell, a
former professor at Columbia Law School, with a human rights background;
and Caroline Gentile, who served as a lecturer at UCLA Law School. In 2000,
Susan Block-Lieb joined the faculty, bringing a strong academic and teaching
background.

Dean Treanor summed up by noting that the "law school has grown more
in the past 10 years than in all the 85 years preceding it," pointing to the
number of new faculty, especially minority faculty, the extraordinary scholar-

ship of the faculty, the expansive curriculum and co-curricular activities, the proliferation of student public service organizations and pro bono activities, the national and international reach of the school's graduates, the growth in admission applications and job opportunities, and the growing financial support for the school.

What Dean Treanor concluded largely reflected a community working together with many individuals contributing to the evolution of the school. The following sections in this and in other chapters and Appendix B speak to their contributions.

Faculty Contributions

Appendix B tries to capture the depth and richness of the contributions made by faculty in the last decades of the twentieth century in building the school's reputation worldwide. As there noted, the faculty took many steps to place the school in the forefront of legal education, making ethics education a pillar of the school and a national model, and making it part of the school's mission to educate attorneys to work in public interest and service. Thus, for example, Professors Flaherty and Tracy Higgins made human rights an integral part of the curriculum; Professor Kainen developed the Brendan Moore Trial Advocacy Program; Professors Hugh Hansen, Andrew Sims, Joseph Sweeney, and Nicholas Johnson led the way in establishing new student journals, and Hansen propelled the school forward in the field of intellectual property law, developing a conference that became world-renowned in the field. Professor Earl Phillips focused his writing on consumer issues.

Professor Felsenfeld, an authority on writing skills and a pioneer in banking law education, served as director of the LL.M. program while continuing the work of the Institute on Law and Financial Services. He also was exceptional in helping students find jobs in this field. Professor Donald Sharpe helped establish the school's first public interest loan forgiveness program while teaching evening students the complexity of the internal revenue code. Professors Jill Fisch and Thel built a strong corporate presence for the school. They gave exceptional leadership as scholars and teachers and leaders in the field of corporate law. And Professors Flaherty, Fleming, Greene, Kaczorowski, and Treanor pioneered the development of extraordinarily successful annual programs on the U.S. Constitution.

Professor Diller provided great leadership in his commitment to urban America and social justice; Professor Russell Pearce focused on the place of religion in the work of a lawyer;[5] Professor Charles Whelan, S.J., expressed in all his works the Jesuit heritage of Fordham,[6] and Professor Daniel Capra's energy and excellence in the classroom caught the attention of ABA inspection teams.[7]

Other professors who made remarkable contributions to the successes enjoyed by the school included Edward Yorio, who promoted excellence in teaching and scholarship, and Barry Hawk internationally, who encouraged the formation of the LL.M program. Professor Michael Madison broadened the curriculum in areas of real property law. He excelled in helping indigent clients deal with landlord tenant problems on a pro bono basis. Professor Lanzarone excelled beyond the classroom and gave important leadership to the school, including in the overseeing of admissions. Professors Joseph Sweeney[8] and Marcus became faculty giants — Sweeney excelling as a beloved moderator of the students' international journal and Marcus as coach of the moot court teams. Professor McGonagle, humble and dedicated as a teacher, was incredible in his devotion to the broader Fordham University community. So, too, was Donald Magnetti, a teacher of the year whose quiet service to students and colleagues set a benchmark of excellence. Professor Helen Bender carried on the scholarly legacy of Professors Calamari and Perillo in the field of contracts. Later, Professor Bender would carry on his legacy in a tangible way as well, co-authoring the later editions of Calamari's casebook. David Schmudde expressed at a very high level the service values of the school and was recognized for these efforts with the Eugene J. Keefe Award.

Adjunct Faculty

The adjunct faculty grew to almost two hundred members of the legal profession, among them federal and state judges, government lawyers, practicing lawyers from firms of every size, and corporate counsels. Among the adjuncts over my time as dean were Dean McLaughlin, then a federal judge in the Eastern District of New York; George Brooks, former secretary of General Motors who tendered his resignation as he approached age 87, giving me an elegant handwritten letter describing his sixty-plus years on the faculty; Albert DeStefano, a brilliant teacher in areas of corporate law; and Judge Peter McQuillan, an outstanding criminal law teacher who, as a judge, developed the insanity defense; Judge George Bundy Smith of the New York Court of Appeals;[9] Judge Denny Chin of the U.S. Court of Appeals for the Second Circuit, an accomplished jurist with a dedication to teaching students legal writing;[10] William Lifland, a partner at the Cahill firm who excelled in teaching antitrust law;[11] Joseph Garon, a devoted graduate who taught students about copyrights, trademarks, and patents; and Henry ("Pete") Putzel, who taught lawyering skills for more than forty years. Finally, mention needs to be made of Joseph W. McGovern '33, who taught full-time from 1936 to 1943, and then as an adjunct professor until 1966. Thereafter he served as Chancellor of the New York State Board of Regents until 1975, after which he was honored with the title Chancellor Emeritus. He remained active with the school until his death.

Visiting Faculty

My summaries of the school do not do justice to the many visiting professors who taught at the school, in many cases as distinguished chair holders. These professors gave the school an enormous quality lift through their teaching and interactions with colleagues and students. They included Professors Eugene Gressman of North Carolina Law School; Whitmore Gray of Michigan; Valentine Korah of the University College, London; Victor Brudney and Lloyd Weinreb of Harvard Law School; Henry McGee of UCLA School of Law; and George J. Mitchell, former Senate Majority Leader. Several annual visiting professors made significant contributions to the school, including Margaret Kniffin of St. John's Law School in the teaching of contracts and Mark Davies of St. John's in the area of New York civil practice law and procedure. We knew summer had arrived when George Cochran of Mississippi Law School arrived to teach his constitutional law course and regale us with his stories of civil rights and criminal defense litigation.

Administering the Law School

My greatest support as dean came from the faculty who served as associate deans — Professors Crowley, Robert Byrn, Vairo, Michael M. Martin, Hollister, and Zipursky — as well as Professor Perillo as acting dean. These individuals made it possible for me to travel all over the country to build alumni groups, fundraise for the building expansion, make presentations to alumni, represent the school at ABA meetings, expand course offerings, cope with the school's growing budget, and manage a community that grew from 1,224 students in 1982 to 1,543 in 2002, with students present from every state and many countries.

Behind the associate deans was an incredible staff of assistant deans, directors, and other administrators. Staff members who were central to the administration of the school during my tenure included: Judith McNatt, assistant dean of finance and administration, who worked on just about everything and at all hours of the day; Dean Moore,[12] who ably guided the school in selecting students for admission from thousands of applicants (keep an eye on the athletes,

Mom and Pop on their wedding day, April 25, 1935

Mom posing for a picture as a young woman

Pop and the trolley car he operated, c. 1948

Pop holding me on his knee

Mom holding me in her arms in the Bronx in 1936

Pop playing the squeeze box

Donald and me in the park

Mom and Pop in the kitchen with a rack on a pulley for drying clothes. *From right to left*: Kevin, Anne, Maureen, and me

Mom and Pop in the kitchen with their children (*right to left*: Donald, Anne, Kevin, and Maureen) at 305 East 161st Street, the Bronx

My sister Anne on a swing in Melrose Park

Donald, Maureen, and me posing for a picture

Mom holding Maureen on the Grand Concourse

Uncle Pat and Aunt Catherine on the occasion of the baptism of Maureen at St. Angela Merici Church

Mom with her dear friends. *From right to left*: Delia Doyle, Ann Vaughan, Paddy Vaughan, Mom, and Mrs. Hoffman

1953–54: Working at a typewriter with classmates on Bishop Dubois yearbook

1954 yearbook: My graduating class, with me in the far rear

Mom and Pop at my eighth-grade graduation with Donald and Kevin

Patrick Boyle and Maria Boyle (née Moran),
Mom's parents

Uncles Pat and James with their mother, c. 1948

Pop's mother, Ellen McDermott
Feerick, and her son Martin

A joyous occasion in Ireland for Uncle Pat with nieces and nephews and other family members

Pop with Uncle John Boyle outside the basilica at Knock Shrine, County Mayo

Aunt Catherine (*center*) welcomes to her home Pop's sister Margaret and daughter Mary Allen

Donald and Kevin meeting in Birmingham, England, with Pop's brother Michael (*far right*) and his family members, with Kevin Boyle at the left

May 2019: Kevin, Anne, me, and Maureen at the home we built for Mom and Pop in Lake Carmel, New York

From left: Governor Malcolm Wilson and Attorney General Louis J. Lefkowitz

Left: Irene and Denis McInerney '51, a grand couple
Right: Katherine and Archibald Murray '60, a grand couple

2010: Dennis Kenny and me with Bishop Matthew in Ghana to discuss establishing a conflict-resolution center

Alumni trip abroad. *From left:* Diane Keenan, John Keenan, Connie and Jack Vaughan, and Emalie and I

Celebrating Skadden's Barry Garfinkel (*second from left*) on his ninetieth birthday with his family members and Skadden's Tony Arbisi (*far right*)

April 1982 at Skadden, with Flom and Mullen in the first row on the right and Mulligan, Arps, and Garfinkel right behind them

My brother Donald

he encouraged, and pay attention to the hardworking applicants who fall short on LSAT scores); Dean Hanlon, a master of registration and enrollment, who possessed an extraordinary flair for writing (e.g., the 75th anniversary booklet on the history of the Law School and an elegant honorary degree citation for Justice Sandra Day O'Connor); Professor Hollister, a superstar who set the standard for her successors as dean of students[13] and later defined the position of administrative associate dean; James McGough, who always found a way to help students in financial need and received the Eugene J. Keefe Award in 1995; Assistant Dean Robert Reilly, a larger-than-life spokesperson for the school with its alumni, students, the university and other constituencies; Assistant Dean Andrew Rivera, a somewhat recent and older student himself, who served students with compassion and sensitivity to their needs; Estelle Fabian, whose remarkable work and caring for LL.M. students left a huge legacy for the school; and Susan Santangelo, director of faculty administration, who served magnificently until retiring in 2015.[14] Other administrators who made outstanding contributions were Helen Herman, director of academic programming; Jennifer Atherly, director of network services in the Office of Information Systems and Technology; Kit Kreilick in the library; Kevin Downey as director of admissions; Mary McKee, an incredible resource for all of us in the library; and Kenneth Prokowski as the registrar, as well as the members of their departments.

Then there were the remarkable individuals who served in areas of career services — Maureen Provost, Carol Vecchio, Kathy Brady and Michael Schiumo, and those who served with them, including Thomas Schoenherr, whose center became a defining part of the school. Maureen and Kathy gave national expression to the school as presidents of the National Association of Law Placement, as did Tom Schoenherr later in his own way among his public service colleagues.

Development officers of great talent helped take fundraising at the school from a few hundred thousand dollars to many millions by the end of the 2001–2002 school year. This terrific group included Arthur Peterson, Midge Stulberg, Tina Guererro, Lorraine Zamora, James Campbell, Timothy Barr, and Fran Sheeley, all with important backup support from others.

Behind the Scenes

The school's success was also dependent on the people who served behind the scenes as faculty secretaries and in the principal offices of the school. I came to know quite well those within the immediate vicinity of my office, and I am forever in their debt. Prominent in this group, to whom I owe the deepest of gratitude, were Marilyn Force, Barbara McFadden, Marta Hrycyn, Sarina McGough, and Mary Kiernan. Kathy Keenan, an extraordinary chief of staff for Dean McLaughlin, became for me the principal overseer of financial aid for students by way of loans and rendered truly extraordinary, outstanding service. Marilyn Alexander was an exceptional leader of the secretarial staff, which included such stalwarts as Mary Whelan, Pat Erts, Ann Smith, Kathleen Smit-Ruggiero, and Lourdes Ramirez (who has continued to work at the school since joining the staff in 1983). Loretta Richardson and Valerie Richards served as faithful stewards in the Registrar's office, as did Mary Conlon in the admissions office, and Michael Slauenwhite in financial management.

The Library and IT

And I can't ignore the sweeping changes in the library. When I was a third-year law student, as earlier noted, I helped out part-time in the Fordham Law library. I came to know where almost every book was located as the collection was quite small. Eugene Wypyski was the director in charge, assisted by a few other librarians and a part-time student.[15] This was a time when students researched cases by using the volumes of Shepard's case digest, the standard source of legal case history.

When I left the school as dean, the library bore the name of Leo Kissam, who, as of 1980, had made the largest gift in the school's history. The staff had grown considerably, with Victor Essien (who emigrated from Ghana) charged with overseeing our foreign law collection, another member helping expand information technology, and others, such as Nilda Elias, working in the library assisting students and faculty with their research. The school had also developed relationships and interchanges with libraries of neighboring schools and Jesuit law schools, all of which expanded the resources available to students, faculty, and alumni.

The size of the student body had doubled since the school was located at 302 Broadway. The school's physical plant, as expanded, provided room for more than five hundred thousand books, tenfold the number of 1961. There were two spacious library levels, each with seats and carrels that were wired for laptops as part of the library expansion that began in 1984. Because of the gifted leadership of Professors Teclaff and Janet Tracy and their dedicated staff, the library kept pace with the world at large despite the limitations of space. The mode of research via bound Shepard's had given way to the Internet, because of the pioneering work of companies like Lexis and Westlaw.

Tracy brought that know-how to Fordham from her previous work at Lexis. But when she took charge in 1986, she had to confront such issues as excessive heating in the library and, for security reasons, cuts to operating hours. (Up to that point the library had been open 24 hours a day.) She was successful in meeting these challenges, recalling that on her first workday I said to her: "I know nothing about law libraries. Your job is to give us a library for the future and let me know how I can support you." She said: "That made you the perfect dean for a library director, giving me total discretion." Tracy also made possible the establishment of the Information Systems and Planning Department and oversaw the construction of the school's networking infrastructure.

Off the Radar

Operating below the radar screen was Addison Metcalf, the faculty law clerk. He worked alone in the library and would deliver mail to the faculty and keep deans up to date. He would later give the school gifts that led to the establishment of scholarships at the school. Another individual was Robert Cooper, who was tireless in assisting me with the drafting of remarks and speeches, serving as an assistant in the library. He also served as a legal writing instructor, as well as a counselor to LL.M. students and undergraduates interested in attending law school. Others who gave quiet service included a security guard, Luke Carolan, who spoke in quotable verses. If one had time, he would provide a rendition of a poem he had composed. Small in size, he could not help but be noticed because of his oversized uniform, distinguished by a cap larger than his head, his freckled face, charming personality, and efforts to befriend everyone entering the building.

Murray Sewdass was an equally unforgettable presence. Born in Trinidad and Tobago, he set a very high benchmark in the mail room. When he retired after my tenure as dean, I celebrated his service along with faculty and staff at his farewell ceremony, where we let him know how much he meant to us.

Father George J. McMahon, S.J.

Father George J. McMahon, S.J., vice president of administration at Lincoln Center, whom I called the "Good Shepherd of Lincoln Center," played a major role in my life when I served as dean. I sought his help with students facing personal challenges, with physical plant issues, and on matters involving the university. Robert Grimes, S.J., on Father McMahon's induction into Xavier High School's Hall of Fame, said of him, "In his heart of hearts, he was a Jesuit and a priest, working joyfully from morning until night for the good of all of those around him."

I invited him to give the invocation at each law school graduation I presided over and at each annual luncheon of the alumni association. I stood next to him when the McMahon residence hall was dedicated in his honor at Lincoln Center and witnessed how moved he was. At my last graduation as dean, his health had declined so much that he was unable to give the invocation, but I couldn't say goodbye without his presence on stage. I thus took it upon myself to ask him to offer the benediction at the end of the ceremony, which he did; it was his last appearance at a law school graduation. He died a few years later, and after his funeral at the Rose Hill campus, I broke down and cried on the shoulder of Father McShane. I experienced the same level of grief years before on the day of Joe Crowley's funeral when I saw in his home the cap he often wore. The two were special heroes of my deanship years.

Postscript—An Unsung Hero

In all of my roles, I received invaluable support from Dean Robert Reilly, who embodies the Jesuit ideal of *cura personalis*. He served as assistant dean of alumni relations, assistant dean of students, assistant dean of external relations and communications, and in many other roles without official titles. He also responded to the many hundreds of calls each year from graduates with questions or requests, and assisted students in countless ways, especially in their times of great need. He never said no when it came to helping me discharge my responsibilities as dean. I recall the important role he played in helping the school develop and implement conflict resolution and alumni programs in Ireland.

When I left as dean, Dean Reilly continued to work alongside me for an additional sixteen years at the Center for Social Justice. Retiring from Fordham in June 2018, his role was critical in the establishment of the center. He developed a board of visitors when the school had none, made important to me personally because I then chaired the ABA's board of visitors committee. He accompanied me on visits to prominent graduates from whom we sought support. He implemented the Supreme Court Bar Admission Ceremony (with the enormous help of Katsoris) and assisted in the development of the Annual William Hughes Mulligan Scholarship Golf Outing (under the towering leadership of George Ross). He made an indelible contribution to Fordham. No award can express his incredible legacy.

18

Commitments, Challenges, and Special Moments

Run at full speed toward perfection — no commonplace achievement will satisfy the great obligation we have to excel.

— IGNATIUS LOYOLA

As dean, I made central to my tenure a commitment to the Jesuit ideals of intellectual rigor, service, social justice, and ethics. In the 1970s, the university had transferred its legal control from a religious order to a lay board of trustees in order to qualify for certain government aid programs. These changes occurred with consequences, such as the removal of religious symbols from the walls and classrooms of the various schools.

But respect for religion remained ever present. In 1982, two members of the Society of Jesus served on the full-time faculty, as well as a former Jesuit. They were Fathers Charles Whelan, S.J., and Donald Magnetti, S.J., and Professor Thomas Quinn. They were terrific teachers and scholars and contributed greatly to the spirit of the school in countless ways. I wanted to build on that history. As time went on, the school increased its sensitivity to the multiplicity of faiths represented, and groups for Catholic, Jewish, and Christian students emerged.

A major turning point occurred at the turn of the century with the establishment of the Institute on Religion, Law and Lawyer's Work, which was made possible by the extraordinary work of Professor Russell Pearce. By 2000, Professor Pearce had already organized nationwide programs on law and religion in American legal education.[1] I suggested that we establish something permanent, and so the institute was born.

The institute was inaugurated in the fall of 2001 with a program featuring a lecture on "Catholic Social Teaching and American Legal Practice" by Avery Cardinal Dulles, S.J., the first American theologian to become a Cardinal. He said that Biblical and Christian social teaching "is an excellent resource that no publicly minded lawyer can afford to ignore," and urged that law students and lawyers acquire a greater interdisciplinary understanding of such teaching, particularly in law schools operating in universities with a religious heritage.

I offered a response to Cardinal Dulles' lecture, along with Jennifer Mone, a graduate of Fordham Law, class of 1993. In my remarks I tried to show how the school reflected Jesuit values, while Jennifer spoke about her own values, saying, "Discretion by a Catholic lawyer will be guided by faith, because that faith is so much a part of who you are."[2] The Institute has since been replicated at other law schools, filling a need in legal education to include courses and programs linked to the spiritual dimension of student life and development.[3]

A few years earlier, a small group led by Dean Reilly sought an appropriate motto by which Fordham Law School might express itself. He solicited alumni, faculty, students, and others for their views as part of the school's celebration of its 90th anniversary. From this undertaking, the motto "A School in the Service of Others" emerged. It was Jesuitical in its history, but reflected more than anything else where the school stood at this point in time, with the emergence of a legal ethics curriculum and a public interest resource consortium.

Father Whelan, S.J., remarked to his Jesuit community that he had never seen the Law School more anchored in the university's Jesuit heritage. He was peerless in the field of church/state law and gave important service in the writing of amicus briefs in such cases. As I noted at his funeral, referencing a remark made by Sister Bernadette Kenny, "Father Whelan is truly Fordham's own version of Chaucer's Oxford Scholar: 'Not one word spoke he more than was his need;/And that was said in fullest reverence/And short and quick and full of high good sense./Pregnant of moral virtue was his speech;/And gladly would he learn and gladly teach.'"[4]

The Introduction of Gay Rights

In the 1980s, a group of Fordham law students approached me with a petition to establish the school's first student gay rights group. They had a draft charter to accomplish this purpose, and I arranged for their leader to meet with Father O'Hare, who, after the meeting, called me to say that the Law School could decide on the establishment of such a group. He said that the university had no objection, because of changes the students were willing to make in the proposed charter as to their social activities. At the time, the issue of gay rights was an explosive one at other religious institutions, but the group's assimilation at Fordham Law occurred without fanfare.

Military Recruitment

In the late 1980s and early 1990s, the subject of military recruitment became an issue on school campuses around the country because of the military's policy of discriminating when it came to the enlistment of citizens who were gay. Before I knew it, I'd received petitions from faculty and students requesting that the school ban the Judge Advocate General's Corps (JAG Corps) from recruiting on Fordham's campus.

Those who strongly opposed any ban believed that the Law School had a duty to the country and to those who had served to allow the military on campus. Some opponents also believed the school shouldn't become involved in charged political issues. Yet, understandably, for gay students, faculty, and administrators it was a matter of respect. I knew that any resolution of the issue would have repercussions in the broader community. I felt we needed to take a stand on the subject.

I sought the counsel of alumni leaders and university administrators. The division among graduates became clear, while support for the ban sought by students and faculty grew. Archibald Murray '60, asked if segregation based on race was morally wrong before the Supreme Court's decision in *Brown v. Board of Education*. If so, he suggested, it was morally wrong to discriminate against others based on their being gay. It was clear that he supported the ban.

I reached out to Denis McInerney, a distinguished Fordham College and Fordham Law School graduate and a veteran of the Normandy invasion. His view was also clear and, as always, quietly and eloquently stated. The school had to provide continued access to the military, he said, but he suggested that it could be done in various ways, including through forums, programs, and the like. Without continued access, Denis indicated, the Law School community would be ripped apart.

I implemented the ban on interviewing on campus but allowed the JAG Corps continued access to the school for programming. Many on both sides of the issue were unhappy with this solution, but the approach held. Forums on military education were held, and JAG Corps officers continued to interview Fordham students, but off-campus. Later, I received a visit from several graduates of senior ranks in the military, including the Army's then Judge Advocate General, Michael Nardotti '76, and Henry White '76, an admiral in the Navy Reserve. They indicated that the military wouldn't make an issue of the matter.

For a while, students and faculty members continued to protest peacefully whenever JAG Corps officers arrived on campus for a program. Once someone came into my office and yelled that faculty members and students were picketing outside the building. Exasperated by the interruption, I replied, "They had a right to picket if they chose to do so."

But it wasn't long after this resolution that a new law was passed requiring schools that received funding from the federal government, through financial aid and other programs, to allow interviewing.[5] The JAG interviewing therefore resumed at Fordham, with students and faculty in favor of the ban accepting the realities of the situation. Several members of the Fordham community played an important role throughout this turbulent period, assuring that the school community was not damaged. The school was also helped by leaders of the students' gay rights group and by members of the faculty and administration.

The school's openness to the creation of a gay students group and the prominence of its bulletin board played a helpful role in navigating this challenge, as did individual student leaders who were constructive in all of their dealings with the school administration.

Disciplinary Complaints

In every academic setting, administrators are confronted with issues of a disciplinary nature. Fordham is no exception. It has a code to assure fairness for students who find themselves on the receiving end of a complaint. Sometimes the allegation involved plagiarism or a violation of another standard. During my tenure, more than ten thousand students attended the Law School, and I estimate that fewer than two hundred disciplinary complaints were filed in my office.

Upon a finding of probable cause, a student would have the opportunity to receive a proposed disposition by the dean (or a designee) which, if accepted, would end the matter or, if not, would lead to a hearing in which the dean was not involved. I personally considered each matter that came into my office. I met with each student, and assured myself that the school had conducted its investigation appropriately. Only once did a student not accept my recommendation. Although handling complaints against students was difficult, I left each case feeling that I'd done my best to be fair, understanding, and merciful. From the beginning to the end, the school's outstanding dean of students, Nitza Escalera, provided enormous assistance to me.

Graduation and Other Speakers

In the 1980s, the Catholic Church in the United States began to object to schools within their tradition hosting speakers who held points of view that the church didn't support. When I received suggestions from students and faculty for speakers who held controversial positions, I respected their requests, given the academic nature of the school, but I strongly encouraged them to have the different points of view reflected in their programs.

All of this came to a head in 1992 when the students in the graduating class recommended that Geraldine Ferraro '60 be their graduation speaker. Ferraro was a Democrat in the House of Representatives and the first woman to serve as a vice-presidential candidate for a major political party, running with former vice president Walter Mondale in 1984. She was also an extraordinarily devoted graduate of Fordham in her support for the school, and time and time again she would accept invitations to speak and participate in school events and programs.

When I first met with the student graduation committee about possible speakers, I was presented with a list of male luminaries, including the president and the chief justice of the United States. I pointed out the practical difficulty of securing either one. I also suggested that women should be included on the list before we made a final decision, as the school, as far as I knew, had never had a woman as its graduation speaker. The committee, consisting of women, returned a few days later with another list in hand, this one consisting only of women speakers with Ferraro as the top pick. She was the right choice for me.

However, for the next several months, I was pilloried by clergy and lay Catholics for choosing Ferraro, a Roman Catholic who, although personally opposed to abortion, supported a woman's right to have an abortion as a matter of public policy. The critics were relentless in attacks on me and on the president of the university. I was dumbfounded by the continued criticisms, some coming from church pulpits in the Archdiocese of New York. I received, by my estimate, more than a thousand letters of criticism, each of which I responded to.[6]

At the graduation, protesters could be seen picketing outside Avery Fisher Hall on Columbus Avenue. As I began to introduce Ferraro, screams and the word "excommunication" could be heard inside. The protesters were quietly removed by two members of the Fordham community, Thomas Liddy '92, and Raymond Liddy '93, the sons of Gordon Liddy '57, who was sitting on stage to present his son Tom with his diploma.

When Ferraro took the podium, the graduating class stood *en masse* and gave her an enthusiastic greeting, after which she went on to speak about the nobility of public service. In 2002 she would be honored by the Law School with its Dean's medal of recognition, and in 2005 she would receive the alumni medal of achievement. After her death in 2011, her name was inducted into Fordham University's Hall of Honor, and the Law School's clinical education center now bears her name as well. The National Women's History Project also honored her during Women's History Month in 2018. These recognitions vindicated the class of 1992's choice, although given her career and her devotion to the Law School, validations were hardly needed.

Uplifting Moments

My moments of challenge paled in significance in the face of the many wonderful moments I experienced as dean. These included the 75th anniversary celebration in 1993 of the admission of women to Fordham Law School in 1918; the inauguration of the William Hughes Mulligan Chair in International Studies in 1995; the announcement of the Archibald R. Murray Chair in Law in 2000, with Professor Gail Hollister as the first occupant, and also that year the establishment of the Joseph M. McLaughlin Chair, with Professor Maria Marcus as the first occupant; the Millennium Tribute in 1999 to the Fordham Law faculty past and present;[7] and many wonderful volumes of our six student journals and the successes of our moot court teams.

By the turn of the twenty-first century, the *Hispanic Business Times* of 2000 placed the school among the top 10 in the United States in its receptivity to students of Hispanic backgrounds, the only law school in New York State to be included in that listing. About two years before, on May 15, 1997, I accepted on behalf of the school a similar recognition from the New York Hispanic Judges Association, presented by Justice Sonia Sotomayor, then a member of the Second Circuit.

In *Fordham University School of Law: A History*, Professor Kaczorowski stated that, in 1994, ABA inspectors concluded that the Law School "'can be proud of its progress' in recruiting 'an ethnically diverse student body.' Recruitment procedures produced 'dramatic results, especially in enrollment of African Americans, which more than doubled from 25 in 1992 to 55 in 1993.'"[8] During the 1995–1996 school year, Professor Kaczorowski noted, "Among ABA approved law schools, Fordham ranked eighth for African Americans, nineteenth for Hispanic Americans, and twenty-fifth for Asian Americans."[9] As the twenty-first century began, the Law School ranked among the top 5 percent of law schools with the most diverse student bodies, in both racial and gender diversity.[10]

In 1991, I led a project at the school to install throughout its building portraits of faculty and distinguished graduates in celebration of Fordham University's Sesquicentennial. Justice Sandra Day O'Connor once remarked that the portraits were "absolutely stunning," rivaling, she said, what could be found in the U.S. Supreme Court. Without my realizing it, in secret, a portrait was made of me, commissioned and paid for by Louis Stein. More than twenty years later, on April 2, 2014, it was unveiled as the school was preparing to move to its new building.[11] On that occasion, I shared these remarks:

> I am the firstborn of two Irish Immigrants, Mary Jane Boyle and John Feerick. They would have been absolutely astonished that you would want to hang a portrait like this of one of their children. . . . I never sat for this portrait. . . . The principal artist of those portraits, Frank Peterson, was in and out of my office throughout this period and, unknown to me, studied me and painted the portrait that has been unveiled tonight. I was shocked when I saw this ever so briefly in 1991 and requested that it be put away in a closet and to never see the light of day while I was still around. I frankly had contemplated that it would probably go up after I died. It remained hidden in a closet until Dean Treanor became Dean . . . I think he needed the closet space!

At orientation each new school year, I described in my remarks the keys to success grouped under four H's — helping others, hard work, harmony (i.e., staying balanced), and honesty. The four H's became my trademark. When students graduated, I added a fifth "H": May you achieve your "highest aspirations."

A constant theme of mine in conversation with students was, "Someday you'll have your own story to tell." Overall, the most important moments of my tenure occurred in meetings I held with students and graduates and at the events and functions of the student groups. It was always an honor to offer students mentorship and support, as I knew, to quote Father McShane, Fordham students are "men and women who make a difference in the world."

19

The Many Hats a Dean Wears

A Fordham Law School Dean is not doing his job unless he is on the edge of being fired.

— JOSEPH A. O'HARE, S.J.

Father O'Hare served as president of Fordham University from 1984 to 2003, longer than any other president in the university's history. He was an inspiring leader who enabled the Law School to grow and prosper nationally. He also was a magnificent speaker with a wonderful sense of humor and was an exemplar in his public service commitments. He served in many important public positions, including as the founding chair of the New York City Campaign Finance Board, whose mission was to administer the largest public financing program of its kind in America. Luckily for me, I served as dean for eighteen of his nineteen years as president.

Relating to Students

In my first year as dean, nothing had prepared me for the "demanded" actions made by the student newspaper, from the quality of the cafeteria food to the inadequacy of student lockers to the limitations of the physical plant itself. Students also wanted new journals, new student groups, enhanced career services, and more diversity. I immediately assembled my administrative team to help me respond to the students' requests.

The students accepted the limitations of space and appreciated being taken seriously when they made suggestions. I, in turn, made it a point to explain matters to them and to attend, to the extent I could, all their major functions.

I also sought out their help when we were unduly challenged, such as when dealing with a decline in the school's *U.S. News* ranking or when a derogatory symbol appeared on a wall or bulletin board at the school.

I'll forever appreciate the students' help in encouraging and broadening diversity on campus and for expressing the values of public service. In sadder moments, as students experienced personal tragedies and hardships, I was inspired by how the school came together. As Rabbi Chanina reflected in the Talmud, "I have learned much from my teachers, and from my colleagues more than from my teachers, but from my students more than from them all."

Law School Faculty

When I began as dean, it became painfully obvious that faculty had strong feelings about salary levels, given the higher levels at other law schools, and about insufficient support for faculty scholarship, an area that drives schools' reputations. Over the years of my tenure, salary comparisons with other schools became more favorable, as did support of scholarship through summer writing grants and the establishment of chairs and professorships in law.

A faculty collective bargaining committee contributed to the stability of the school, meeting annually with me in hopes to secure more financial support from the administration. Professors Frank Chiang, Donald Sharpe, and Earl Phillips ably represented the faculty in presenting faculty requests. Several senior faculty accepted a salary cap I proposed as a way of transferring what otherwise might be their due via a merit increase to younger faculty members. I considered their agreeing to the cap as among the most selfless acts I ever encountered. I also placed a premium on annual merit increases tied to scholarship productivity.

The faculty also sought more involvement in the school, and as a result more faculty committees were formed, leading to innovations in faculty hiring, clinical education, relationships with schools abroad, centers and institutes relating to the faculty's work, and dual degree programs with other parts of Fordham University. Especially helpful to the school were visits by prominent faculty from other schools.

Dealing with University Administrations

Father O'Hare's larger message was that of the Jesuits' concern for the welfare of every member of the community. His comments about law school deans "on the edge of being fired" drew laughter, but I suspect that at times he felt that temptation in dealing with me and my team over financial matters. There was no year in which we didn't press hard for a greater share of tuition revenue or a reduction in overhead and indirect charges. These annual discussions were often wearing, as the Law School was bursting at the seams in becoming more national and international in scope with a limited endowment.

The university responded positively to our requests, loosening the rigidity that existed in line budgeting, providing the school with a greater share of tuition revenue, and giving us more freedom to fix tuition rates and allocate tuition among the school's constituent parts. In the latter years of my tenure, however, the annual budget discussions became more difficult as university cost allocations grew and university surpluses declined.

Dealing with Accreditors

Law schools all over America interact with the ABA in its accrediting of law schools. The consultant to the ABA Section on Legal Education and Admissions to the Bar was the single most important person in the process for me. From 1973 to 2001, that person was James White.[1] As the late Mary Daly wrote, the Council to the section "is a flashpoint for critics of legal education and is in the unenviable position of never being able to satisfy these critics. At the center of the debate surrounding legal education, the Council is condemned by some for alleged excesses of regulation while simultaneously accused by others of regulatory cowardice."[2]

In 1982, I inherited some issues arising from an inspection visit by the ABA with respect to the financial relationship between the university and the Law School.[3] The basic question was whether the university was doing enough financially for the school to help it grow. The university's relationship with the ABA had reached a boiling point, so much so that Fordham was considering joining other major universities in a lawsuit against the ABA on the ground that it was exceeding its proper role in the accreditation process.[4]

I asked Father Finlay not to pursue such a suit, and he agreed to follow my request. I thought that we could work through the issues with the ABA amicably, which we did, but not without the university agreeing to take some necessary steps, such as undertaking a major building expansion. By 1986, we had moved through this period and were on our way to bigger and better things.

I became deeply involved in the work of the ABA Section on Legal Education and Admission to the Bar, believing that it was important that a Fordham dean have a presence in this area. At the start I felt uneasy in such academic involvements because of my background as a practicing lawyer, but I persevered. By 2001, I'd served on many programs of the section, regularly attended its annual and semiannual meetings of deans, and served on accreditation reviews of other law schools. Because of my longevity and involvement, I was chosen to chair its Academic Standards Review Committee, its Professionalism Committee, its Committee on Boards of Visitors, and one of two subcommittees of the Wahl Commission.

The Wahl Commission

The ABA came under federal investigation in 1994 when the Department of Justice launched an inquiry to determine whether the standards it used for accrediting law schools were unfair and anti-competitive. The matter was ultimately resolved with a consent decree.[5] But before even reaching the settlement, the ABA's Board of Governors established the Commission to Review the Substance and Process of ABA's Accreditation of American Law School, also known as the Wahl Commission, to review the matter and make recommendations. I was chosen to serve as a member of this commission.

The commission took its name from its chair, Rosalie Wahl, the first woman named to the highest court of the state of Minnesota. Wahl was an outstanding chair who made sure that each of us became immersed in the work of the commission. She asked me to chair the subcommittee on academic standards. The subcommittee examined each of the accreditation standards and determined whether they continued to be appropriate.

The subcommittee made many recommendations that were adopted by the full commission, but the one I was most proud of was a new preamble to the existing standards to focus on the goals of legal education. It stated that the minimal goal is to ensure that every law school graduate "understands that law is a public profession requiring the performance of *pro bono public* legal services."[6] The commission's recommendations were adopted by the ABA.

Of Rankings

Each year, law schools, colleges, and other educational institutions are subject to evaluations by publications such as *U.S. News and World Report*. These rankings can make school administrators crazy, and can make students, faculty, and alumni happy if the school does well or alarmed if the school's ranking declines.

Rankings hardly capture the spirit of a school or the quality of its students, faculty, teaching, and scholarship, not to mention the benefits that flow from successful sports programs and other prestigious schools within a university. Rankings are, however, a fact of life in contemporary higher education, and presidents and deans must deal with them as best as they can.

In my first six years as dean, rankings appeared in publications that lacked the splash of *U.S. News and World Report*, such as the *Gourman Report* and the *Princeton Review*. We fared well in such evaluations. When *U.S. News* began reporting on law schools in 1987, however, the rankings were limited to the top 25 law schools as determined by the magazine's criteria, and Fordham Law School was not included, although it was among the top 25 law schools in the *Gourman Report*. In March of 1994, *U.S. News* added another 25 law schools, with Fordham ranked at No. 34. In 1994, additional listings called "The Rest of the Rankings" were included, grouping them as "Third Tier," "Fourth Tier," and "Fifth Tier." Altogether, 176 schools were ranked in 1994, but it is doubtful that anyone was entirely happy unless listed as No. 1, an honor that went to Yale Law School, with an overall score of 100.

Fordham moved up to No. 33 in 1995 and to No. 28 in 1996. In 1997, Fordham was 25th, tied with the University of Washington. This was a heady moment for Fordham consumers of *U.S. News*, but it didn't last long. A year later, the school dropped to No. 40 because of changes in the ranking criteria. And yet, I knew the school was better at No. 40 than when it was at No. 25; however, I had to deal with the agony of explaining the dip to students, faculty, alumni, and university administrators. Fortunately, the dip had no effect on admissions, student employment, or alumni generosity. Fordham climbed back up to No. 32 in my last year as dean and to No. 31 the following year, as a result of the efforts we made during my final year as dean.

Appealing to Alumni

I cannot do justice to all the graduates who made a difference in the life of the Law School. Some senior to me in age and experience became my mentors. Among these graduates were Paul Curran, who had a distinguished career in law and politics and was then president of the alumni association; William "BJ" Harrington, an extraordinary citizen-lawyer in Westchester County with a reputation for helping religious institutions; Frances Blake, a beloved secretary of the alumni association; Denis McInerney, who had established the school's annual fund of unrestricted giving and chaired for me campaign after campaign;[7] and George D'Amato, who excelled in the field of insurance law, and whose extraordinary generosity to the school and willingness to provide employment opportunities to students set a special benchmark.

And to add to this list, let me include: the late James "Jim" Gill, a superb lawyer and public servant extraordinaire;[8] Michael Stanton Sr., a highly successful lawyer and graduate of three schools of Fordham, who had few equals in his devotion to the Law School; and Jack Vaughan, an outstanding lawyer with a wonderful sense of humor, who left behind a legacy of good works in the law and at Fordham. Several senior graduates in my early years as dean helped build the school's financial aid and scholarship endowment. These included all of the above and E. Ernest Stempel, M. James Spitzer, and Simon Gluckman.

For twenty years I called on graduates for assistance. Some said that I was the most expensive friend they had. Nonetheless, they gave generously and were incredible in their service to the school. Paul Curran helped secure public speakers for school and alumni events. BJ opened doors for students without jobs and graduates in transitional situations. He was also extraordinary in his commitment to and support of the school's building and program expansions.[9] His final cause at the school was the Institute on Religion, Law and Lawyer's Work, which, for him, expressed the school's core values. Others later followed their lead during my tenure, among them Thomas Kavaler, Denis Cronin, George Ross, and William Frank. As presidents of the alumni association, they gave generously with their time and support of the school's fundraising campaigns.

Many other graduates made remarkable contributions to the school during my tenure, such as establishing (or helping to establish) scholarship and fellowship programs, chairs and professorships in law, centers, institutes, and a million-dollar annual fund. Others, through extremely large gifts, established a special scholarship for women students (Margaret Hill and Patricia Hynes); an extraordinary student trial advocacy program (Thomas Moore); a public service endowment fund to support students in such activities (fourteen graduates were the founders);[10] a unique human rights program in memory of Professor Crowley (James Leitner being principal among such graduates); a national scholars program (Frances Mulderig); and a major endowed scholarship program.

Louis Stein

Louis Stein, a 1926 graduate of Fordham Law, set an early benchmark of generosity to the Law School. After achieving success in business, he gave back with enormous generosity to Jewish causes, the educational institutions he attended, and a vast array of other causes. His initial gifts to Fordham Law School established a scholarship, a loan fund to assist students, and the *Urban Law Journal*.

As the Watergate crisis permeated and damaged the American legal profession in the mid-1970s, Stein saw a need to call attention to the best of the profession and suggested that Dean McLaughlin create a Fordham Stein Prize, providing money to support such an honor. The prize has honored justices of the U.S. Supreme Court, circuit and district court judges, the chief judge of New York, and lawyers who have served as Secretary of State or in Congress or other public positions. Three of the judges so honored graduated from Fordham Law School: Deans Mulligan and McLaughlin, and Judge John Keenan of the U.S. District Court for the Southern District of New York. All were exceptional jurists who expressed deep loyalty to the school in attending functions, judging moot court competitions, and hiring students as their law clerks, as well as through the distinctiveness of their public service.

In March of 1982, as I was preparing to become dean, Stein, still alarmed by Watergate's effects on the legal profession, told me that he wanted to make a gift to help the school become a leader among law schools in the field of legal ethics. He had a dream, and several faculty members came together to help achieve this dream, including Joe Perillo, Mary Daly, Bruce Green, Russell Pearce, and Matthew Diller. Others joined in the efforts later in my deanship. Stein asked for regular accountings of what we were doing, made suggestions, and responded with even more financial support, which his wonderful daughters and grandchildren have continued since his death.

Thanks to Stein's generosity, Fordham Law School today enjoys an unparalleled reputation in the field of legal ethics. The Stein Scholars Program, an idea of Professor Bruce Green, has made the school highly attractive to prospective law students. In 1995 in an unusual action, the Law School surprised Stein by placing his name with the purpose of his center on its building to acknowledge his generosity and vision. I stood next to him as he sat in a wheelchair looking up to the roof of the building as a covering was removed, leaving for all to see the words: "The Louis Stein Center on Law and Ethics." To say he was humbled understates this tearful moment. The new law school building carries forward his name on its exterior.

Annual Luncheon

The Fordham Law Alumni Luncheon has taken place for six decades, with a turnout ranging from 600 to 1,200 people. Prominent speakers have addressed the assemblage. At the luncheon, the alumni medal of achievement, the school's highest honor, is presented to a graduate (and on occasion to two graduates). I particularly remember a few of these events.

Graduate Donald Dunn, the guiding partner of what was then the Alexander & Green law firm, accepted the medal, said thank you, and immediately sat down to the largest applause I can recall. More somber was Frances Berko's response. Berko was afflicted with cerebral palsy. In her acceptance speech, she spoke haltingly about her career and how hard it was to keep going. Despite her disability, through hard work and determination, she became a leader in her field and used all of her resources to open doors for other people with disabilities.

In her speech, Berko mentioned how her father had encouraged her to believe that she could do anything she set her heart on. He, too, had attended Fordham Law School and urged her to try for a career in the law, which was why she applied to Fordham. In accepting the award, she strenuously lifted herself out of her wheelchair and said, "Daddy, this is for you." He was long gone, but I'm sure he heard her. Judge Lawrence Pierce described Berko as "a living symbol of achievement despite adversity," which her acceptance speech illustrated to all of us. There wasn't a dry eye in the house.

The year before, Federal Judge John Cannella, a legendary Fordham and Giants football player, was honored. He expressed gratitude and spoke about how much Fordham meant to him. He finished by speaking about his true love, his wife of many years, who had recently died, and slowly recited from memory a love poem he had written to her when they were both young. Once again, there wasn't a dry eye in the room.

It was a particular honor for me to have a role at twenty-five of these luncheons, including as the recipient of the medal of achievement. On the latter occasion, in 1980, as Father Finlay spoke, my young children, sitting at a family table up front, got up in the middle of his remarks and walked out, appearing to find what he said about me rather boring, to which Father Finlay immediately remarked, "They have very good judgment."

And I will always remember an occasion honoring Thornton Meacham Jr., '42. Meacham, a close friend of Rev. Martin Luther King Jr., broke down many racial barriers to become one of New York's most celebrated legal advocates. He used his acceptance speech to advocate for racial diversity and inclusion in the legal profession.[11]

Another graduate honored at one of these luncheons was Peter Campbell Brown, who served in President Truman's Justice Department and as corporation counsel of New York City. He was equally passionate in his dedication to the school, in his later years coming to each luncheon in a wheelchair, pushed by his sons, Peter and Robert, who both graduated from Fordham Law. Getting to know such graduates is one of the great joys of being a law school dean, former dean, professor, and graduate.

20

Fordham Law Goes to Ireland

I believe the people of Northern Ireland will make their choice and leave behind those mired in violence and hate.

— DAVID TRIMBLE

History has placed a challenge at all our doors. We must succeed, for all our people and for the generations yet to be born.

— JOHN HUME

When I became dean in 1982, Ireland was not on the school's agenda. However, Ireland was part of the fabric of Fordham University, with many of its presidents, deans, and graduates having deep roots in the country thanks to their Irish ancestry. My predecessors as dean, Mulligan and McLaughlin, were renowned for their Irish wit and humor and their stories of Ireland. Irish American professors populated the Law School faculty and the leadership of its alumni, and the school's Corporate Law Institute and Sonnett Lecture Series sometimes expressed a connection to Ireland in their choice of speakers.[1]

A few months after President Clinton's inauguration on January 20, 1993, I received a request from the Secret Service to help them find an office at Lincoln Center where the president could meet with benefactors and supporters. Since Lincoln Center was across the street from the law school, I offered my office to the president. Unknown to me at the time was President Clinton's interest in the country of my parents.

After an inspection by the Secret Service, the school was selected. When the president arrived in June of 1993, I mentioned to him that law students were in the lobby hoping to shake his hand. He obliged us, making it a joyous moment for all present.

In the following year, I received a request from the Irish consul general in New York to host a talk by Dick Spring, the leader of the Labour Party in the Republic of Ireland, who was playing an important role in the process intended to achieve a peaceful solution to the conflict between Northern Ireland and the Republic of Ireland. The event went well, and a day or two later, to my surprise, Spring sent me two tickets to see Ireland play Norway in a World Cup. Dean Reilly and I went to that game, a first for me and a thriller, ending with a 0–0 tie.

In the late fall of 1994, I received a request to host a luncheon for an Irish dignitary, John Hume, a founding member of the Social Democratic and Labour Party. The request came in the form of a call from John Connorton, a distinguished Fordham graduate who had chaired Al Gore's New York primary campaign for president. Connorton said that Hume was playing an important role in the peace process in Northern Ireland.

I was familiar, of course, with Hume's nonviolent approach to peace in the North, but at the time that seemed like an elusive dream. However, I arranged a lunch and invited several of the school's Irish-American graduates to attend.

The event was pleasant enough. What I didn't expect, however, was Hume's parting request: "I appreciate the lunch, but I want more from you." He paused, then added, "Please come and visit Northern Ireland." The sincerity of his words touched both me and our luncheon group, and as I often did, I reached out to Dean Robert Reilly, asking him to give some thought to organizing an alumni travel program to Ireland, North and South. Then, upon seeing a U.S. Information Agency communication seeking conflict resolution proposals for several countries, including Northern Ireland, I reached out to Professor Jacqueline Nolan-Haley to ask for her help in developing a program that would provide conflict resolution training for local citizen groups in Northern Ireland. This seemed like a long shot to me, but the former idea, with Reilly behind it, seemed quite doable, given our alumni history.

The work in putting together the grant proposal, led by Professor Nolan-Haley, was arduous, as we envisioned a program that would bring Protestant and Catholic citizens of Ireland together in New York. Of enormous help in this endeavor were Professor Maria Volpe of John Jay College and also Connorton, who suggested that we try to get Ulster University to partner with Fordham on the program. We acted on his idea and reached out to Seamus Dunne, head of the Centre for the Study of Conflict at University of Ulster, Coleraine, who said he'd be pleased to participate. Dunne made suggestions regarding Northern Ireland that should be reflected in any proposal and said that if we received the grant, he would help us select a group for the program and advertise it in Ireland.

The proposal called for social workers, personnel managers, teachers, police officers, union members, members of the bar and judiciary, and housing officials from Ireland to come to New York for conflict resolution training, which would involve visiting community resolution centers and attending workshops on mediation and methods of conflict resolution. At Fordham, we planned exercises in active listening, nonjudgmental questioning, perception analysis, trust-building and cross-cultural understanding. We also planned extensive role-playing on culturally specific situations. We were thrilled when we learned from the White House that we had been selected for a U.S. Information Agency grant of $123,420, the only grant awarded for Northern Ireland. The announcement was made on May 25, 1995 at a White House conference that focused on organizing economic and humanitarian efforts to mitigate the crisis in Northern Ireland. Undoubtedly, we wouldn't have received the grant without our having a local partner in Ireland.

Professor Nolan-Haley and I traveled to Northern Ireland over Halloween of 1995 to begin discussions and planning with Dunne. Dean Reilly lent his support to the conflict resolution program as well, and we also made a trip to Northern Ireland to further develop the program. We met briefly with Gerry Adams and Martin McGuiness and were referred to Mark Durkin, a leader of the Social Democratic and Labour Party, for a more extended discussion on peace in Ireland. The following June, a distinguished group of citizens from the North, equally divided between Protestants and Catholics, came to Fordham. It was fascinating to witness the conversations and discussions among them during program sessions. Among the subjects discussed were the use of symbols and colors in Northern Ireland and their provocative nature.

"I was struck by the fact that after several days of quiet, almost non-conversation with each other, they opened up with frank discussions about what was occurring back in Northern Ireland," Professor Nolan-Haley said. "Some of them told me that they had public conversations here at Fordham that would not have been possible in Northern Ireland."[2] Participants in our program later went on to form a Fordham/Belfast Conflict Resolution group for the purpose of exchanging information and aiding each other in their work.

The program received favorable attention in a number of publications, including the *New York Times*, the *Irish Echo*, and *Catholic New York*. Clyde Haberman's *Times* article of July 2, 1996, focused on one of the participants, a prominent human rights lawyer in Northern Ireland named Paul Mageean, who was quoted as saying: "I must say that I approached this program with a great deal of skepticism. . . . The idea of mediation is to find a middle ground, and that was difficult for me to get my head around."[3]

"I still don't think that you can mediate the terms of the investigation of a police shooting," Mageean continued. "But I think you can bring people together to see if you can keep things from getting out of hand."[4] He added that "contacts were made that would have been close to impossible back home," and mentioned some bar-hopping that he, a Catholic lawyer, had done with Richard Russell, a Protestant chief inspector with the Ulster police.[5]

The issue of *Catholic New York* for July 4, 1996, quoted Professor Nolan-Haley. "We thought it would be great to piggy-back on the peace process because there were so many hopes and aspirations there," she said. "We tried to break the culture of silence." And the article went on to say: "[Nolan-Haley] said that many participants would not have been able to have in Northern Ireland the conversations they had here, either because they were from institutions in direct conflict with each other or because of a lack of trust, opportunities or permission." Professor Nolan-Haley also said: "We told them, it's for you to decide what will work in your own contexts."[6]

The article also mentioned Dunne: "Dunne hopes participants will try to persuade the people they work for that conflict resolution is valuable and that the 'bug' of mediation will spread in Northern Ireland . . . 'People lack listening skills,' he said. 'It's remarkable, when people listen and have a clear structure for dialogue, how they discover how close they really are in their positions.'"[7]

Ireland continued to grow in importance to Fordham Law. After we received the grant, I was thrilled to receive an invitation from President Clinton to join him on his maiden voyage to Northern Ireland in late November of 1995. Under Reilly's leadership, the Law School also began an annual alumni travel program, with Northern Ireland as the first venue.

Other opportunities came our way. We received a request, sometime before the Good Friday Agreement was reached in 1998, from the British consulate to host a meeting for David Trimble of the Ulster Unionist Party, and we were asked after the peace deal was reached to participate in programs related to the peace process held at John Jay College and at the British consulate.

The Trimble meeting took place in my office. Professor Martin Flaherty attended and challenged Trimble on human right standards. Based on what Trimble said in response, I had a sense that, notwithstanding the current lull in the peace process caused by a bombing incident in the North, an agreement would eventually be reached. In response to a question I posed, Trimble said something like, "We can't go backwards."

In late 1999, against this background, I discussed with Flaherty and other faculty members the idea of developing a Fordham summer law program in Belfast and Dublin. They were encouraging, and I received an enthusiastic response from the faculty. The program was made possible by the willingness of Dean John Jackson of Queens University Law School in Belfast and Dean Paul O'Connor of University College Dublin to join together with us in a formal relationship, a first of its kind between the major law schools in Belfast and Dublin.

With faculty approval, I traveled to Ireland to visit with Dean O'Connor, who liked the idea of such a partnership. I then traveled by train to Belfast to meet with Dean Jackson, who also readily embraced the idea. On that ride, I thought of how Mom and Pop could never have gone to the North in their youth, as they, like countless numbers of their countrymen and countrywomen, would have encountered border-crossing checkpoints, and maybe worse, along the way.

Fordham's summer law program began in 2001, with a supporting visit from Senator George Mitchell, then the chancellor of Queens, and the next year by Justice Sandra Day O'Connor, who joined the program for several days as a visiting faculty member. We were off to a great start, attracting many law students from Fordham and a few from other American law schools. From its beginning to 2019, more than six hundred students have attended the program, including in recent years students from Queens and University College Dublin.[8] I joined the teaching faculty in this program after I left as dean and have continued to serve in this capacity, with the help at times of Professors Nolan-Haley and Kathleen Scanlon and Michael W. Martin.

President Clinton's Visit to Northern Ireland and Ireland, November 29 – December 2, 1995

President Clinton's trip to Northern Ireland on November 29, 1995, was the first by an American president. The delegation was chaired by Ronald Brown, U.S. Secretary of Commerce, and Richard Riley, Secretary of Education. I was one of three members of the group identified with an educational institution. The others were Mary Boergers, senior fellow of the Ireland U.S. Political Leadership Program at the University of Maryland, and William Kennedy, the novelist and director of the New York State Writers Institute at the University at Albany. I felt privileged that Fordham University, founded in 1841 by John Hughes, a native of Northern Ireland, was represented on this trip.

After a briefing in the White House on November 29, 1995, we left for Andrews Air Force Base and boarded a plane used by the U.S. Air Force for VIP transportation to Belfast. The briefing book we received noted: "Ireland is well known throughout the world as a country that extends a warm and friendly 'cead mile failte,' a hundred thousand welcomes to all its guests."

It continued, "The protocol tends to be informal and sometimes in an exuberant enthusiasm to be friendly, it can get a little 'over the top,' with back slapping. This is done with the greatest sincerity and is never intended to be disrespectful." And it added: "Irish people love to talk and most of the time they are very articulate. There is a distinctive difference of accents. North, south, south-west, west and east all have different accents, but all speak in English." The background section concluded, "Formal gifts presented to guests are usually given at the beginning or end of a function and are on display, not gift wrapped."[9]

The next day began with a breakfast at the Ford Motor Company's Belfast plant. We were then taken to the Mackie plant to be part of the president's first major event in Northern Ireland. According to the briefing book, Mackie was the last large-scale engineering plant left in West Belfast, located on a site next to the Protestant and Roman Catholic communities. "It is widely respected for its efforts to ensure fair practices," the book said of the plant, "and to maintain a neutral environment where members of both communities can work together."

The president was introduced, movingly, by a young boy and a young girl, one Protestant and one Catholic. His speech of hope and promise for Northern Ireland challenged both communities to embrace peace and open the door for greater economic development in the North and the employment that would follow. Upon leaving the plant, I noticed security everywhere, including armed personnel on the surrounding buildings, much as it was throughout and surrounding Fordham Law School when the president visited Lincoln Center in June of 1993.

President Clinton's message at the Mackie plant was repeated in many ways by Cabinet Secretaries Brown and Riley, the leaders of our delegation, during our community outreach events. These events included a visit and lunch that day at Springvale Learning, a community-based job-training center serving predominantly Catholic West Belfast; a tour and briefing at the Argyle Business Centre; and a tour and briefing at Shorts, a company with a historic record of aircraft production, including the world's first aircraft production contract involving the building of Wright flyers. We then joined the presidential motorcade en route to Belfast City Hall.

The Christmas tree lighting ceremony held at Belfast City Hall that day was inspiring, as thousands of people of all ages and from many different communities greeted President Clinton and the First Lady with an enthusiasm I'd never before experienced. Young children were hoisted onto the shoulders of parents, and cheering and screams of joy filled the air. Seeing thousands of small American flags waving everywhere gave me chills. There were also flags of Britain and the Republic of Ireland. And President Clinton and the First Lady did not disappoint in their remarks that evening.

After the ceremony, a reception for them took place at Queens University, made special by the presence of leaders from different communities and political parties (with the exception of Ian Paisley, the founder and leader of the Democratic Unionist Party).[10] The late David Ervine, the leader of the Progressive Unionist Party, remarked to me that he had never seen in Belfast a reception like this one, attended as it was by people from every part of the larger community.

I met First Lady Hillary Clinton that evening for the first time and passed on to her a statement made by Uncle Pat concerning her tenure in the White House. He asked me, if I met her, to let her know that he had been in America for nearly seventy years and considered her the finest occupant of her position he'd ever seen. She asked me for his name and address, and a week or two later I was astonished to receive a call from Uncle Pat, excitedly telling me that he'd received from the White House an autographed photograph of the First Lady bearing the words: "Patrick Boyle, With Best Wishes, Hillary Rodham Clinton." That picture remained on his dining room table until the day he died and is now one of my family's treasured possessions.

On December 1, our delegation left Belfast for Dublin. As soon as we arrived we were rushed to the Bank of Ireland building, adjoining Trinity College, where President Clinton delivered a speech to the people of Ireland. Clinton followed the speech with an address to Parliament and a stop at Cassidy's Pub.

At the speech at Trinity, I stood with two other members of the delegation, John Sweeney, then president of the AFL-CIO, and his predecessor, Tom Donahue. One of them offered words to the effect of, "Not bad for three boys from the Bronx."

I'll never forget President Clinton's interaction with the former prime minister Albert Reynolds during his speech to the Parliament. Reynolds had recently left his position under difficult circumstances. The president spotted Reynolds, waved to him, and praised him in his remarks. Upon completing his speech, the president looked again at Reynolds who, in return, made a victory sign. I was moved by the rapport between them. Later, at Cassidy's, I was deeply impressed by the human qualities expressed by President Clinton as he relaxed, shook hands, ordered a drink, and chatted, seeming both youthful and exuberant.

As with the visit to Belfast, the visit to Dublin ended with a crowning event—a formal dinner given by the Irish Government for the president in Dublin Castle. Prime Minister John Bruton and President Mary Robinson were among the Irish leaders present. I was honored to be placed between chief justice of Ireland Liam Hamilton and Patrick Hillery, the former president of Ireland. This placement allowed me to invite the chief justice to Fordham to deliver the John F. Sonnett Memorial Lecture, which he did on March 28, 1996,[11] and gave me the opportunity to introduce him to President Clinton as the president made his way out of the castle later that evening. The chief justice seemed somewhat hesitant, but I urged him forward and called the president over, saying, "Mr. President, this is the chief justice of Ireland." They graciously exchanged greetings with each other. The evening was filled with much joy, beautiful music, and a wonderful speech by the president, who appeared to speak off the cuff but with great effectiveness.

Saturday, December 2, was our last day in Ireland. I attended a breakfast at the Berkeley Court Hotel, where we were staying, to listen to Secretary Brown speak to a hundred or so members of the Irish Chamber of Commerce. He spoke without notes and was brilliant, I thought, in discussing peace, trade, and investment. The night before, when I ran into Secretary Brown in the hotel, I asked how the trip was going from the president's perspective. I remember him saying how singular an experience it was for the president, comparing it, in terms of excitement and enthusiasm, with the 1994 inauguration of President Nelson Mandela in South Africa. He also used the word "inspiring" in describing the trip to Ireland. After breakfast the delegation toured Ambassador Jean Kennedy Smith's residence, the famous former prison Kilmainham Gaol, and the Guinness factory.

It was hard to say goodbye that afternoon as we headed back to the United States, each of us realizing that being part of this historic trip represented the opportunity of a lifetime. In an address at the White House Irish-American state dinner on June 13, 1996, President Clinton said of the visit: "It was, I think it's fair to say, two of the most extraordinary days in the lives of all of us who went."[12] President Mary Robinson of Ireland was honored at that dinner,[13] which I attended, joined by my daughter Jean.

At the White House, I told Jean that she'd be meeting President Clinton and the First Lady on the receiving line. I added that the greeting would be very brief as the line would be long and moving quickly, and that if she wanted to get the president's attention she had to say something catchy. I shook the president's hand, briefly introduced myself, and moved on. Jean, on the other hand, introduced herself and exclaimed, "We share two universities in common!"

"He lit up," Jean recalled, "and asked me which schools. I said George-
town and Oxford. He asked which college at Oxford and I said Brasenose.
As I walked away, he called down the line, mentioning my name, asking if
I had seen the special Lincoln manuscript at Brasenose. I said no, but that I
was aware, being a scholar of Renaissance literature, that there was a famous
Robert Burton Renaissance manuscript there."

Animated by this conversation, Jean found the rest of the evening an
"amazing experience," seeing celebrities everywhere, including her particular favorites, Paul Newman and Meg Ryan. Jean also loved the singers who
performed, among them Mary Black and Mary Chapin Carpenter. President
Robinson spoke on this occasion and "was incredibly eloquent," Jean said.
The night ended with President Clinton surprising his guests with good news:
"President Robinson," he said, "brought America a little of the luck of the
Irish. I'm pleased to say that while we were eating here, the standoff . . . with
the (Montana) Freemen ended peacefully."[14]

At the invitation of the president, I paid another visit to the White House
on St. Patrick's Day of 1997, this time joined by my daughter Rosemary. While
I visited with colleagues, Rosemary had the opportunity to meet many well-
known Irish Americans, sample the fine food, and admire the White House
artwork. Once again, we went through the receiving line and met the Clin-
tons. Rosemary, who had recently traveled to Haiti, took that opportunity to
ask the president to work for real justice for the people there, and he replied
that he would. I only regret that Mom and Pop were not alive to share the joy
of such moments. They would have been thrilled.

21

Leaving the Deanship

In memory of those whose spirit shines in the darkness. May we never forget.

— MOURNING CARD, SEPTEMBER 11, 2001

When I began as dean, Albert Sacks, the dean of Harvard Law School, told me that it usually takes ten years to have an impact. I couldn't tell what my impact was at the ten-year point, when I was then 55, but I certainly felt empowered by the faculty and students and by the alumni's growing financial support of the school. There was exciting innovation taking place at the school. Fordham University and its various schools were enjoying growth as well, with the university having completed a wonderful celebration of its 150th anniversary.

In 1997, my fifteenth year as dean, I discussed with Father O'Hare the question of my longevity as dean. I wanted to be sure I had time left for another career. "Unless you have something else you want to do, keep doing what you are doing" had been his annual response, and it never changed.

During this time, the space needs and limitations of the school became pressing. I finally felt pressure to raise the subject with the university's academic vice president, Father Vincent Potter, at our year-end meeting of 1996 or 1997.[1] I told him that the present building would be inadequate for the space needs of the students by the twenty-first century and that an additional building would be needed. Not long after our meeting, Father O'Hare asked if I was open to the Law School leaving its present building and, not having thought of that as a possibility, I said yes, although I thought that an additional, adjacent building would do the job and that we could raise the funds to cover its costs toward that end.

Confident that there would be a new building, I set up a committee, chaired by Associate Dean Michael Martin, to study physical plant developments at other law schools and generate ideas for the new building. I suggested as well to Dean Martin, in his capacity as chair of the Law School self-study committee, to focus on this critical need and give it priority in the self-study[2] for the 2001–2002 ABA accreditation inspection.

To further the building expansion program, I turned my attention in my last two years to fundraising for such an eventuality, believing that if we could raise $12 million to $14 million right away, the university would give the need its highest priority. Graduates and others I reached out to responded with extraordinary gifts, pledges, and statements of support.[3] As I was engaged in this effort, Father O'Hare reiterated that the university was committed to a new building for the school but that it couldn't be built for at least five years.

As all of this was occurring, I was approaching the age of 65. It seemed like a good time for the school to consider a successor. The new dean would be able to focus on exciting steps in the future of the school, such as the centennial celebration and the new building program. With that in mind, I entered my meeting with Father O'Hare to inform him of this decision. He suggested at the meeting that I stay in place until I decided on an alternative career. When I asked him how long he'd be staying as president, he said he'd be leaving on June 30, 2003. Upon hearing this, I said that July 1, 2002, one year before he retired as president, was the right time for a new dean, and that he'd be able to choose my successor. He then accepted my decision, but from time to time thereafter would ask if I wanted to change my mind. I decided to make the announcement of my decision on September 17, 2001, Constitution Day, but the tragedy that occurred on September 11, 2001, delayed the announcement.

On September 11th, faculty, staff, and students, assembled as a community in the James McNally Amphitheatre. We watched on a screen the collapse of the World Trade Center and prayed for those who had lost their lives. A prayer service was led by Father Damian O'Connell, S.J., and Psalm 121 was read by Eliezer Drew, the leader of Fordham's Jewish law students association. He read, in part:

> I will lift up mine eyes unto the hills, from whence cometh my help.
> My help cometh from the LORD, which made Heaven and earth.

By late afternoon on September 11th, most students, faculty, and staff had left to join their families. I hesitated to leave that evening, as I wasn't sure if there was anyone else to whom I should reach out. A week later, I sent the Fordham Law School community a letter that stated, in part:

I really don't know where to begin in sharing some information about our School and how it has been impacted by the tragic and disastrous events at the World Trade Center. I would say at the very outset how deeply affected we all have been by the loss of life and the pain suffered by many families. They all have been in our prayers and thoughts individually and at a number of services held within the Fordham University Community. . . . Several students have lost loved ones and others are suffering the loss of friends who worked at the World Trade Center. While we had over 150 alumni who worked at the World Trade Center, we are thankful that almost all have been reported as safe. Our sadness is running deep concerning members of our alumni and their families who are not accounted for . . . and they are very much in our thoughts and prayers.

The school had taken steps to minister to students and others affected by the tragedy and had made available its facilities to colleagues and organizations displaced by the attack. In my statement, I also noted that "every office and every member of our staff and faculty is involved in trying to be helpful" and asked the larger community for their suggestions. "We hope that you will let us know of members of the Fordham family who are injured or missing in the attacks," I concluded, "so that we can reach out to them and their families."

I decided to announce my decision to leave as dean on November 2, 2001, All Souls' Day, or the Commemoration of All the Faithful Departed, in the Catholic faith. I assembled everyone who was around that day and read a written statement in the James McNally Amphitheatre. It said in part:

Twenty years, in a position I intended to take for only five years, is a long time. . . . The decision I have made is not easy. . . . It is one I long knew I would make someday and I have not been anxious to rush the years of my life to get there. But a great many years have passed since I came here with the energy of a 45-year-old. . . . The years since have been wonderful ones because of the opportunities to come to know each of you and work with you in building the great law school of which we are all a part. I will miss this honorable position very much, but it has always seemed to me that I should pass the baton when the School was strong and the challenges ahead were exciting. . . .

What makes this decision most difficult is the fact that the school is in the beginning stages of a campaign to support the development of a new state-of-the art building. We already have been the recipient of extraordinary gifts to that campaign by a dozen graduates, and the alumni leadership of the campaign is now in place. The challenge to lead that campaign is a tempting one, but it would require a commitment of many years and that would make it difficult for me to address, in any meaningful way, professional and personal interests that I have been wanting to dust off and express in some measure. . . . On a personal side, they include a little more time with my eight grandsons and, of course, my wife, Emalie, and our six children.

I expect to remain very active in the life of the School, helping it and my successor in whatever quiet ways I can. I hope always to be a resource for the School and our students. The School gave me my start as a lawyer and in so many ways has defined a most important period of my life. Nothing I have done or can do will ever repay the debt I owe the School and my teachers. I have had two periods of twenty years each of involvement in the life of the School and I look forward to at least another twenty in different capacities.

I then left the room and cried. My plan to retire as dean on June 30, 2002, went forward with many difficult farewells.

In June of 2002, as in the past, I sent Father O'Hare a memorandum about events during the year, which I dedicated to the four Fordham Law graduates who had died in the attacks on the World Trade Center on September 11th. They included Dwight Darcy '81, a labor relations lawyer for the Port Authority of New York and New Jersey, who left behind a wife and two children; Kevin Cleary '91, a stockbroker for Euro Brokers, who had recently started a second career as a part-time theater actor; Linda Lee '94, a senior associate at Jennison Associates, a financial services firm; and John M. Moran '94, a fire department battalion chief who left behind a wife and two children.[4] I knew Kevin (whom I had recommended to the school), Dwight, and John personally and deeply lamented the loss of all four graduates.

All told, thirty-nine men and women of the Fordham community lost their lives that day and more than thirty additional Fordham families were touched by this tragedy. There were many tributes to those who lost their lives, and I, like many others at Fordham, made it a priority to attend these tributes, including a dedication ceremony for a monument in memory of those individuals at the Rose Hill campus.

The 2001–2002 school year ended with an alumni trip to Germany to celebrate the 13th anniversary of the school's LL.M. program and to establish an alumni chapter. At the end of June, I traveled to Ireland to participate in the school's summer law program in Belfast and Dublin, where Justice O'Connor was a special visiting faculty member for a few days. She was fully engaged in the undertaking, going on a Sunday bus tour with the students, speaking to them in the most personal of terms, and inscribing for each a copy of her book, *Lazy B: Growing Up on a Cattle Ranch in the American Southwest.* My copy will forever be a cherished reminder of the occasion.

Justice O'Connor told students she had two callings in life: to be a mother and to have a profession. She was able to pursue both callings, becoming the mother of three children and establishing a career in law which she said proved rewarding in ways she never could have expected. She encouraged the students to see the law as a noble way to serve others.[5]

During my last year as dean, Skadden asked me if I had an interest in returning to handle alternative dispute resolution matters or to engage in pro bono service, or anything else I'd like to do. The opportunity to return to the place where my career began and that I had considered home for many years had emotional appeal. Another firm also asked if I'd join it as counsel, working at an office they'd set up not far from my home in Larchmont.

Chief Judge Judith Kaye at the same time asked if I'd consider becoming dean of the new Judicial Center that New York State was opening at the Pace University campus in White Plains. After reflection, I concluded that it would be hard to undertake another deanship. Then two prominent members of the New York Bar, whom I esteemed greatly, asked if they could advance my name for consideration for a vacancy on the U.S. Court of Appeals for the Second Circuit. I told them that I didn't wish to put myself through the politics of the confirmation process at my age. Since I had a year-long sabbatical, I decided instead to mark time until I had to make a decision about my future, giving weight to a career that would allow me and Emalie to have more time together.

And so I began my transition.

22

Becoming a Classroom Teacher

Genius is one percent inspiration and ninety-nine percent perspiration.

— THOMAS EDISON

During my sabbatical, I began a Fordham teaching career, starting with a course in the fall of 2002 for foreign LL.M. students providing an introduction to the U.S. legal system. It was hard for some in this period to accept that I was no longer serving as dean. I received requests about applicants, and some within the school tried to involve me in personnel issues. I even got a call from a former American president about an applicant, but I directed him as well to speak to our new dean.

I asked for an office in a building across the street from the Lincoln Center campus and removed myself from faculty meetings and other gatherings. It was my sense that successions worked best when those who have served leave the stage in a timely fashion and allow their successors to enjoy the limelight. As Chief Judge Kaye said to me, there's very little training for predecessors. You have to figure it out, and I did. Some people were surprised that I remained at Fordham as a full-time teacher. Others thought that I had retired, despite the fact that I was probably as busy as I'd ever been as dean.

The following semester, I taught a course on the history of law in the Political Science Department of Fordham College. I enjoyed returning to the college and getting to know the students. To broaden their perspectives, I arranged for a trip to the U.S. Supreme Court so the class could listen to a few oral arguments. Immediately after the court adjourned, Justice Ruth Bader

Ginsburg accepted an invitation to address the class in an anteroom. This was a thrill for all of us, and she gave a wonderful speech about the Supreme Court and its history. The trip with the students on the small bus to and from Washington that day was also a highlight for me on this teaching excursion, and perhaps for the students as well.

This class was reminiscent of an undergraduate course I'd taught at Georgetown College in Washington in 2000 as the first occupant of its Peter P. Mullen Visiting Professorship. When invited to teach there by Professor Robert Katzmann, now chief judge of the Second Circuit Court of Appeals, I couldn't refuse because of my esteem for Peter and because three of my children had graduated from Georgetown. The course was challenging to teach as I left New York early each Monday by train for Washington, prepared for the class on the trip, and returned to New York very late at night. I was often too exhausted to make the journey back home to Mount Kisco and would sometimes stay in an apartment next to Fordham to make it in early for work the next day. Despite these challenges, teaching this class was a wonderful experience.

From 2004 to 2007, I co-taught a range of courses at the Law School, including institutional reform by court litigation, ethics in alternative dispute resolution, and the language of the Constitution. The latter course was my most enjoyable teaching experience, and through it I learned more about the Constitution than I could ever have imagined. I appreciated the interest shown by the class in learning more about the debates at the Constitutional Convention of 1787. I stressed to the students, as future lawyers, the importance of being familiar with the text of the Constitution and encouraged them to share their education with other students, whether in elementary or secondary schools.

I again taught the Language of the Constitution early Monday mornings in the spring of 2010. Twelve students signed up, and they never missed a class, even after snowy weekends. They were a delightful and engaged group, and I worked hard to be a good teacher, plowing through my accumulated materials on the Constitution every weekend before class. I had a hard time giving less than an A grade to every one of them.

In the 2010–2011 school year I helped the *Fordham Law Review* sponsor a major symposium on presidential succession, the papers from which were published in a volume entitled "The Adequacy of the Presidential Succession System in the Twenty-First Century: Filling the Gaps and Clarifying the Ambiguities in Constitutional and Extraconstitutional Arrangements."[1] A wonderful array of public servants and scholars participated, among them former

Senator Birch Bayh; Fred Fielding, counsel to three presidents; and Benton Becker, counsel to President Ford. I presented a paper titled "Presidential Succession and Inability: Before and After the Twenty-Fifth Amendment."[2]

That paper had been preceded by a talk I gave that was published in the *Houston Law Review*.[3] I had given the talk at the invitation of Yale Law School Professor Akhil Reed Amar. I commented on a lecture of his on the defects in our succession and electoral systems.[4] I happily agreed to do so as I was eager to have him join us at the Fordham symposium, which he ultimately did.

After the symposium, Dean Treanor suggested that I create a clinic on the presidential succession system, and I did so in the fall and spring semesters of 2010–2011. I co-taught what became known as the "Treanor clinic" with Dora Galacatos and Nicole Gordon. We chose nine students from an applicant pool of twenty and together we helped the students develop their agenda of reforms. The clinic studied three distinct areas: presidential and vice-presidential inabilities not provided for by the Twenty-Fifth Amendment; the desirability of the present line of succession; and succession in the pre-inaugural period. The students seemed to have enjoyed the learning experience, and the document they wrote represents an achievement worthy of consideration by our nation's lawmakers.[5]

In the academic years between 2012 and 2019, I continued teaching courses on the Constitution, ethics, and conflict resolution. In 2016, I added a new seminar on the skill of facilitation, which I co-taught with Professor Linda Gerstel, and another clinic on presidential succession, as suggested by Professor John Rogan who co-taught the course. Professor Rogan and I also co-taught a seminar on the electoral college system in 2017 and a clinic on democracy and the Constitution in 2018 and 2019. In fall of 2017, 2018, and 2019, I also co-taught a class with Professor Kathleen Scanlon on professional responsibility and ethical issues in alternative dispute resolution.[6] During this period I continued to write and speak on subjects of my background. These years were also filled with public service undertakings (more on them later). In addition, beginning in September of 2006 and continuing to the present, I've devoted considerable time to social justice activism. And since 2002 I've been researching and writing this book.

Center for Social Justice

In the Law School's centennial school year of 2005–2006, Dean Treanor announced as his principal academic initiative the establishment of a Center for Social Justice and Dispute Resolution, with me as its founder. I agreed to allow my name to be placed on the center, and I've been proud and privileged to be associated with the dedicated group that runs the center's day-to-day operations — namely, Dora Galacatos as executive director, Professor Elizabeth Cooper as faculty director, Robert Reilly as assistant dean (until his retirement in July 2018), and Wilma Tamayo as administrative assistant. The center is ably guided by a distinguished advisory committee, chaired by Fern Schair, the first woman to receive the New York City Bar Association's President's Medal. Derek Hackett, my administrative assistant, offered invaluable help until he retired in 2018. Clementine Schillings has now stepped in to support me and the center.

Students, AmeriCorps VISTA members, recent graduates of Fordham Law School known as dean's fellows, volunteer lawyers, and others contribute substantially to the center's work. They seek to address the problems of poverty through education and partnerships, and by working on specific issues that might be resolved without litigation.

The center began its work by helping to expand a program in New York City called Homeless Experience Legal Protection (HELP), designed to serve people who are at risk of homelessness by providing them with limited legal advice on a range of issues. Participating HELP law firms and attorney volunteers served at various centers in Manhattan. The center's assistance, thanks to Thomas Bisdale, consisted of coordinating schedules of volunteer lawyers and organizing training programs on issues involving public benefits, disability law, landlord-tenant matters, creditor-debtor law, and child support issues.

Another early program sponsored by the center helped develop a conflict resolution center in Ghana, with the help of law professors and volunteer lawyers. The center also facilitated, with the help of six law students, a national dialogue about a new way to handle union organizing campaigns in the Catholic Healthcare System.[7]

Throughout its history, the center has organized and hosted conferences, meetings, forums, lectures, fact-finding sessions, mediations, and facilitations on many social justice issues faced by low-income New Yorkers. The center has several areas of major focus, including the Civil Legal Advice and Resource Office (CLARO) program, the Attorney Emeritus Program (AEP), and the Dilley Pro Bono Project.

Through a weekly clinic, the CLARO program helps New Yorkers involved in debt collection cases in New York City Civil Court. The program relies on volunteer lawyers to counsel litigants, volunteer consumer law experts who provide on-site assistance and guidance on challenging consumer debt issues, and volunteer law students who provide administrative and programmatic support. Thousands of low-income, otherwise unrepresented people have been helped by these volunteers. In conjunction with other organizations, the center supports the operation of the CLARO program in the Bronx, Manhattan, and Staten Island and encouraged the creation of such programs in upstate New York, Long Island, and Westchester County.

The AEP was developed by our center under the leadership of Fern Schair, working closely with Dora and students from Siena College, a Catholic institution near Albany. The concept for the program was presented to New York Chief Judge Jonathan Lippman, and the effort became part of his far-reaching efforts to help address the civil legal services "justice gap," which affects unrepresented people faced with litigation in the civil courts of New York. In its simplest terms, the AEP facilitates pro bono services by senior attorneys (at least 55 years of age who have practiced law for a minimum of ten years) willing to provide limited-scope legal assistance to low-income New Yorkers, working in tandem with courts and legal service providers. More than one thousand of these senior lawyers have been enrolled in the program.

The center's initiatives also include the Unaccompanied Immigrant Children and Immigrant Families Project in Dilley, Texas. The project supports coordinated efforts to improve state and local policy on immigration through partnerships with stakeholders in fact finding, policy advocacy, resource development, and capacity building efforts. Additionally, the center organizes service trips to Dilley, Texas, where Fordham Law students, alumni, staff, and other volunteers assist asylum-seeking women and their children through the Dilley Pro Bono Project. The project reflects the initial great work of Olga Byrne and then Bree Bernwanger, both of whom now have important positions in the field of human rights.

In 2006, the center launched the Domestic Violence and Consumer Law Project. In partnership with other legal services providers, the project examines the unique financial issues faced by domestic violence survivors, including economic abuse, inadequate financial literacy, accumulation of consumer debt, and identity theft, with a view toward helping expand service providers' capacity to address these concerns.

Since 2012, the center has received grant funding from the Corporation for National and Community Service (CNCS) to support the development of several programs, including Volunteer Lawyers for Veterans (VLV), and the Legal, Economic and Educational Advancement Project (LEEAP). The mission of VLV, launched in 2017, is to recruit volunteer lawyers to assist low-income veterans who have civil legal needs in the areas of consumer laws and VA benefits. LEEAP uses experienced lawyers and professionals to assist underserved students and their families' access to high-quality secondary and higher education.

Past programs include the Fordham University Consortium on Social Justice, which linked all the schools of the University in coordinated and collaborative activities related to social justice.

I've been astonished by the growth of the center under the inspiring leadership of Dora Galacatos, Elizabeth Cooper, and Dean Reilly, staff members, students, the school's alumni, volunteers, partners, and the advisory board, especially its chair.

Beginning in 2011 and continuing each year thereafter, the center has sponsored an annual awards and benefit function to recognize individuals of accomplishment in various areas of social justice and at the same time generate substantial revenue to cover the costs of operations. These recognitions include a Spirit of Service Award, a Life of Commitment Award, a Champion of Justice Award, James F. Gill Spirit of Hope Award, and the George J. Mitchell Lifetime Public Service Award. Senator Mitchell was the first recipient of the award that bears his name and has returned to present that award.[8]

The 2014–2015 School Year

Every school year has its unique challenges for faculty and school administrators. This was especially true of the 2014–2015 school year for me. My focus on two major endeavors, chairing the Law School's search for a new dean and coordinating a pastoral transition effort related to collaborations among Catholic parishes in the Archdiocese of New York, became humbling experiences. But as one of my students reminded me, quoting her grandmother's wisdom when I spoke of these challenges, "All will be well." And how right she was.

Dean's Search

The search for a new dean began in May of 2014 when Father McShane met with a search committee of three trustees of the university, six law school professors, two law school deans, the president of the law alumni association, the president of the student bar association, a former interim dean and professor at another law school, a former dean of Fordham's School of Social Service, and me. He asked us to recommend at least three people for the position.

With the help of a search firm (Witt/Kieffer), the search committee put advertisements in various publications and communicated with deans and associate deans of American law schools, alumni of Fordham Law School, prominent members of the Bar, the ABA section of legal education and admissions to the bar, and other groups. We put together an 18-page packet describing the law school, complete with pictures. While teaching in Ireland in June of 2014, I recall spending almost every evening at a computer communicating with the law school and the search firm regarding this undertaking.

The school's alumni were provided with an unprecedented role in the process. The president of the alumni association appointed a committee of six distinguished graduates, men and women, which drew input from graduates around the world. The committee produced a 13-page memorandum and was invited to meet with the entire search committee before it began its deliberations. This singular involvement of alumni, under the leadership of alumni president Michael Stanton Jr., attested to the importance of the alumni to the future of the school.

To help the search firm with their outreach, we held separate meetings with faculty, administrative staff, librarians, and students, asking, among other things, for their input on a range of issues: What were the major challenges of and opportunities for the Law School over the next several years? What will a new dean be expected to accomplish, and how will that person's success be measured? What should be the professional credentials, executive competencies, and personal characteristics of the next dean? What specific suggestions can be offered to the next dean? How might the next dean enhance the school's reputation? The student member of the committee did the same through an e-mail to the entire student body, making sure that students had a chance to participate in the process.

Throughout the process I was sensitive to the need for faculty input. I asked faculty members of the search committee to keep their colleagues informed as to how things were progressing. By September the search firm had communicated with more than seven hundred people. From about sixty serious candidates, the committee chose to interview thirteen of them.

The interviews took place over three long days. They were held in locations where the candidates' identities would be protected, even from one another. After the interviews, we chose to bring several of the thirteen to the school. It was painful for me to inform those not chosen, some of whom I knew personally. Those who came to the school had to pass through a gauntlet of sorts over two days — meeting with faculty, administrators, librarians, students, alumni, the provost, the dean, and other administrators. They were also asked to give a presentation to the faculty and administration as to how they viewed the challenges ahead for the Law School and legal education in general, and how they would address them.

After all the candidates had come to the school, I met with the faculty and the administrative and library staff for a general discussion concerning the candidates. After that meeting, the committee narrowed down the group of thirteen to a selected few to be presented to the president. I then presented the names to Father McShane and Provost Stephen Freedman and gave Father McShane a binder containing detailed information about the candidates. The committee didn't rank the candidates so as to give the president full scope to make his choice.

After Father McShane received our recommendations, he met with each candidate for a few hours and arrived at his choice on December 26, 2014. The person he chose, Matthew Diller, then dean of Cardozo Law School, had spent his first sixteen years in academia as a faculty member at Fordham Law, including several years as the school's associate dean. He and the president and provost had subsequent meetings and discussions, and his appointment was announced on January 5, 2015.

When the school year ended, Dean Martin, at his final faculty meeting as dean, thanked me for pulling together all parts of the Law School community in the dean's search, for never imposing myself during his deanship, and for always being available to help. I couldn't have been more grateful for his remarks given how exhausted I was by the process. As for when I became dean at an earlier, perhaps ancient time in history, I invite the reader to examine the section describing the dean's search of 1982 in Professor Robert J. Kaczorowski's comprehensive history of Fordham University Law School,[9] described by Professor William Nelson as "one of the best books written." All I will add is that there's nothing like the search for a law school dean.

PART V

The Vocation of Service

I don't know what your destiny will be, but one thing I know: The only ones among you who will be really happy are those who will have sought and found how to serve.

— ALBERT SCHWEITZER

The call to serve involves something special, to which we must be attentive. Serving others chiefly means caring for their vulnerability. Caring for the vulnerable of our families, our society, and our People. . . . Service is never ideological, for we do not serve ideas, we serve people.

— POPE FRANCIS

PART V

The Vocational Service

23

Serving Others

What is merely average will not satisfy the great obligation you have to
do good.

— ST. IGNATIUS LOYOLA

Ye cannot live only for yourselves; a thousand fibres connect you with
your fellow-man, and along those fibres, as along sympathetic threads,
run your actions as cause, and return to you as effects.

— HENRY MELVILLE

The idea of serving others was instilled in me by Mom and Pop. As their oldest
child, I was expected to show leadership in the family, which meant keeping
an eye on my younger siblings. I played the same role in my neighborhood,
where I often played with children who were younger than me. At times they
looked to me for guidance and protection against neighborhood bullies. Back
then I had a pretty fierce headlock move and sometimes had to use it, but the
threat of doing so was often enough to smooth over the situation.

When I went to college, I understood the necessity of working part-time
to help Mom and Pop deal with the family's finances, and opportunities to
display responsibility in other contexts emerged.

My teachers influenced me in the way they cared for students, both in and
out of the classroom. When I graduated from law school, I saw a life in the
law as embracing a larger service, although what that meant wasn't clear to me
at the time. Fordham's values didn't emphasize making money as a life goal,
nor did Mom and Pop, who lived simply and frugally, and I had no burning
passion to accumulate wealth. I still recall my college classmate Bob Bradley

saying that I had the potential to someday earn $40,000 a year, but I really didn't know what that meant. I often thought in those years that if I could only make it to age 35, the age of Lawrence Reilly, my role model, and have a chance to repay Mom and Pop, my life would be complete. And so off I went, wet behind the ears and naïve about so many aspects of the world.

Will Durant's *The Story of Philosophy*, which I read in my third year of college, was a benchmark of sorts for me, helping me reflect on the meaning and purpose of my life through the views of many great thinkers. But as things turned out, I had an innate incapacity to choose and focus, thereby accepting all kinds of requests. As a lawyer for more than fifty-eight years, I must have spent nearly half of my time involved with some form of volunteer service (including my writings). My service activities have ranged from committees of bar associations, to government bodies, to not-for-profit and community organizations, to educational and religious institutions, to boards of public companies, to participation in politics, to service in other countries (Ireland and Ghana), and to helping individuals cope with personal challenges. It's hard to find a common denominator, other than the model of a vocation of service presented to me by Mom and Pop, and the priests, Ursuline Sisters, and Marist Brothers who taught me.

I came to particularly enjoy service in the form of writing, in which I was able to advocate, educate, offer points of view, and honor others. In time, I'd write law review articles, books, book reviews, op-ed pieces, articles for encyclopedias and bar journals, bar association reports, testimony for legislative hearings, opinion letters, briefs, memoranda, and speeches, including eulogies, remarks for programs, and many hundreds of tributes to others on special occasions. The opportunity to speak positively about another person gave me particular joy. I sought to find in each person's story their uniqueness, and I often found myself inspired by their example.

Politics, I would have thought, might have engaged me more fully, as in college I enjoyed the opportunity to serve students through student government positions. I believed that I might have some kind of political career, but the opportunities to be involved in constitutional reforms of our presidential system took me in another direction. I'm not sure I would have lasted long in elective politics anyway, given the attacks often associated with such participation, along with the need to raise enormous sums of money and the pressures and expectations associated with such fundraising — all of which has increased exponentially over the years.

I would also have had trouble dealing with the nastiness of modern-day politics. Yet, despite everything, political life can be a noble and critically important calling, one that sits at the heart of our democracy. At times I've wondered whether I should have given it a chance. My service was on the fringes of the system in areas of government reform, although at times my participation was more direct.

One of my most enjoyable political excursions came from volunteering on the 1965 mayoral campaign of John Lindsay, a Congressman from New York City's "Silk Stocking District." Some people saw him as a future president. My principal job involved drafting position papers on issues of importance to the community of Riverdale, in the Bronx. This involved speaking to local residents to identify issues, writing a short paper on each issue advocating reform, and then clearing the papers with the upper echelon of the campaign leadership.

In this capacity I studied and made recommendations on parking congestion, traffic control, and park space development. I also wrote Lindsay a letter suggesting "a program under which a New York City Heroism Medal be given to those who perform a heroic act deserving of recognition." Later in the summer our volunteer group acquired an old bus, decked out in red, white and blue, to drive volunteers to campaign stops and to street corners to hand out flyers. Lindsay himself came along when he visited Riverdale. On Election Day I served as a poll watcher. I was thrilled to learn at the end of the day that Lindsay had won the election, becoming the 103th mayor of New York City. He went on to serve two terms in that office.

My next excursion into politics was less successful.[1] In 1976, Indiana Senator Birch Bayh ran for the Democratic nomination for president of the United States. In this time period, I set up a nonprofit entity in New York called Bayh-Partisans Inc. with Lionel Hest, a talented young lawyer from the firm of Debevoise & Plimpton. But it ceased to exist when he withdrew from the race. We engaged in some activities to promote the senator's primary campaign in New York, but after his showing in an earlier primary in Massachusetts he withdrew his candidacy. It was empowering, however, to have engaged in such activity, believing as I did that Senator Bayh would have made an excellent president. I recall him saying on a visit I made to his office, "I don't feel worthy of such a position, but when I consider the other candidates, I think I can do at least as good a job, if not better." I am sorry he didn't have the opportunity to add to his contributions to America.[2]

But let me back up with an overview:

My time at Fordham Law helped me understand the larger dimensions of a life as a lawyer. Dean William Hughes Mulligan and the small faculty he'd assembled challenged us to be good lawyers, and we understood that to include some form of public service. Service to our country was also inspired by the graduates who fought for the country in World War II and the Korean War, and by the requirement that we serve in the Armed Forces.

We also learned about the successes of graduates in the private practice of the law and in public life. I left Fordham with a desire to make the school, and Mom and Pop, proud and with the knowledge that the greatest success may be in the multiple ways we give back to the world in which we find ourselves.

Upon graduation, I joined Skadden, which, despite its small size and uncertain future back then, stressed the importance of service to the profession. I was on the job only a short while when Barry Garfinkel, a partner at Skadden, urged me to join the New York City Bar Association and become active in the association. I also became a member of the New York State Bar Association and the American Bar Association. Later, Skadden's Joe Flom would encourage me and other lawyers at the firm to give back to the community through, for example, service on not-for-profit and community boards.[3]

In these activities, I learned about the importance of serving our communities, cities, states, and country. I also became exposed to issues involving discrimination, oppression, and unfair treatment within the legal system. It was clear I had to do my part, and that doing so involved more than serving on a committee. Over the years I took on the representation of individuals in non-compensated settings and used various platforms to promote public service.

Without performing some type of public service, lawyers miss out on the full potential of their professional lives. There are so many opportunities available to represent people, to work in nonprofit and government offices, to advance the state of the law, and to teach and educate the next generation. Archibald Murray did so as the attorney in chief and executive director of the New York Legal Aid Society. Fordham law graduates Malcolm Wilson, the fiftieth governor of New York, and Louis Lefkowitz, who served as attorney general of New York, did so through decades of service to the state. Former New York Court of Appeals Chief Judge Judith Kaye's public service changed the justice landscape by effectuating jury reforms, establishing problem-solving community courts, enhancing access to justice for those unable to afford counsel, and increasing diversity in the courts.[4] James Gill did so through his commitment to pro bono service for individuals in need of help, nonprofits requiring volunteers, government officials seeking active citizen engagement, and the causes of the Catholic Church and the schools that educated him. Law firms and corporate legal departments have also made impressive commitments to serving the underserved.[5]

I have found the lawyers I know to be generous with their time in helping others through their knowledge of the law and their legal skills. Their services are often misunderstood or largely go unnoticed by the larger public. I became exposed to that tradition of service often at Skadden and because of my father-in-law, William Platt, who gave freely of his time to neighbors and strangers in Southampton. I tried to do my part, something that has brought me much happiness, particularly when I was able to provide representation for an individual or give help in other ways. Of my experiences helping individuals, two examples, thirty years apart, jump to the surface.

Miguel Valentin

Miguel was a first sergeant in the Army's 77th Infantry Division. We met in the 1960s when I attended weekly Army Reserve meetings. Miguel had joined the U.S. Army, spent two years in Berlin, then continued his service as a member of the 77th Division. One day he approached me to ask if I could help him gain admission to the New York City Police Department.

Miguel explained that when he was a teenager living in Puerto Rico, he and a few of his classmates, out of curiosity, had taken a day off from school to attend a meeting of the Nationalist Party, whose goal was to fight for Puerto Rican independence. The students were subsequently investigated, although nothing came of the investigation. In his application to the police department, Miguel answered a question that asked if he'd ever been investigated by mentioning his attendance at the meeting and the subsequent investigation. This resulted in his being rejected by the department for what was termed "subversive activities," even though he had passed all of the necessary tests.

I knew Miguel to be an outstanding member of my reserve unit. I said I'd help, and together we went to see his New York City Council member, who told us that there was nothing he could do because the police commissioner had complete discretion when it came to omitting a certain number of applicants from consideration. We decided to sue to overturn the law. We included in our court letters of support for Miguel, including one from Puerto Rico's then-attorney general, who, in a conversation with me, rejected any suggestion that Miguel had been involved in subversive activity.

I subsequently received a call from a lawyer in the office of the New York City Corporation Counsel to let me know that the papers we'd filed were essentially frivolous (or words to that effect). I pressed my point of view and was gratified when the lawyer promised to look into the matter and get back to me. Sometime later he called to advise me that the "block" placed on Miguel's application to the Police Department would be removed. I was ecstatic. The lawyer had obviously been affected, as was I, by the injustice that had been wrought.

Thanks to the lawyer, Miguel became a police officer. Years later I was happy to read an article in the *Daily News* describing his heroism in trying to rescue a person from the subway tracks. Another article, a few years later, identified him as having broken up a drug ring in Manhattan. Miguel eventually reached the rank of detective and retired after twenty years of service. Two of his children have followed him into the police force.

Neal Wiesner

Another opportunity to help an individual occurred unexpectedly in the 1990s when I was serving as president of the City Bar. I received a letter from CUNY Law School student Neal Wiesner regarding a question on the association's admission application as to whether the applicant had ever been convicted of a crime. Wiesner said the question discouraged law school graduates from applying to the City Bar, even though they had become lawyers in good standing.

Wiesner said that some law school students, like himself, had done wrong growing up and had served time in criminal justice institutions. He added that such lawyers would be discouraged from applying to the City Bar in the belief that by doing so, a further review of their past history would take place, despite their good-standing status.

I discovered the association did not have a practice of further reviewing applicants based on affirmative answers to the former-crimes question, and I arranged for Wiesner to meet with the association's Civil Rights Committee. The committee recommended that the challenged question be eliminated from the form. What was required for admission was simply being a member of the bar in good standing. I agreed and in my last annual meeting as president, the question of previous conduct was removed from the application. Through his actions, Neal Wiesner had made an important difference for others.

To become a member of the City Bar, however, Wiesner had to first be admitted to the New York State Bar. Not long afterward, I was asked by Haywood Burns, dean of CUNY Law School, to testify on behalf of Wiesner at a hearing of the Character and Fitness Committee of the First Judicial Department. He was representing Wiesner at that hearing as to his fitness to be admitted to the bar.

I gave supporting testimony based on my experiences with Wiesner, noting in response to a question by a committee member my belief in second chances: "I am a believer in redemption," I testified, "and I am a believer in the greatness of the American democracy, which is willingness, once you have paid your price and dealt with that issue, to be judged based on what you subsequently do and take an account of the totality of your life." My testimony and that of others was not sufficient to gain Wiesner's admission to the bar, although the chair of the Character and Fitness Subcommittee before which I testified, a distinguished law partner of the late Senator Jacob Javits, supported his admission, dissenting from the report that favored his denial, 2 to 1.

Wiesner later brought a case in the New York courts to overturn that ruling. He was represented by Haywood Burns and two other distinguished African-American lawyers, one a former member of the New York Court of Appeals and the other a former ambassador from the United States to Ghana. When Burns died tragically in Africa while Wiesner's appeal was pending, I was asked by his co-counsel to take Burns's place, which I did. Wiesner, however, lost his case and was denied admission to the bar. The denial was based on the seriousness of past crimes, the short period of time that had passed since the crimes had occurred, and uncertainties about his explanations of his state of mind in using his firearm.[6]

To my surprise, in 2006, Wiesner called and asked me if I were willing to go to New Jersey and offer testimony supporting his admission to the New Jersey Bar. Although he didn't press the point, there was something within me that said, "You can't walk away from him now." I decided to go in order to explain to that bar's representative my role and views in the matter. Wiesner called me a few months later to say that he'd been admitted. He certainly earned it based on his grit and determination.

In March of 2012, I learned the Appellate Division First Department granted his tenth application to become a New York lawyer. I was in disbelief, given how many times Wiesner had tried unsuccessfully to become a member of the New York Bar since 1995. The court concluded that "there is no sound basis to further impede petitioner's quest to be admitted to the bar in the jurisdiction where, in an earlier life, he violated the law."[7] And the court added: "Although our approval in the past was impeded by the brevity of time, a sufficient time period has now passed without incident in petitioner's life — during which he has been a practicing attorney in good standing and has contributed to society — that we are now persuaded that a change in circumstances warrants a different result."[8]

The court, in an opinion by its presiding justice, Peter Tom, started its review of the record by referring to my earlier testimony and my emphasis on the importance of redemption. New York thereby joined New Jersey in admitting him to their bar.

For me, mercy has a place in justice. I found this belief present in the Valentin and Wiesner matters.

24

The Voluntary Bar

Life's unfairness is not irrevocable; we can help balance the scales for others, if not always for ourselves.

— HUBERT H. HUMPHREY

Service in the organized bar, starting with the City Bar Association's Committee on State Legislation, was a highlight of my life as a lawyer. The committee met frequently, offering comments on the pros and cons of proposed New York State legislation. I still think fondly of the late hours spent on Monday nights with other committee members debating the merits of various legislative proposals. I was young and committed to improving the rule of law.

Some of these members, like Arthur Liman and Floyd Abrams, would develop reputations as being among the greatest of America's lawyers, and with good reason.[1] I was especially impressed by the committee chair, Raymond Falls of the Cahill Gordon law firm. He worked throughout the night and into the morning to make sure the reports reached the legislative leaders in Albany in time to be considered. He set the pace for the rest of us. I felt I was making a difference through this service, even though many of the committee's recommendations were not acted upon in Albany.

I continued this bar activity throughout my career at Skadden, going from service on one rewarding committee opportunity to another, among them the Young Lawyers Committee, where I helped develop the hypothetical case for a national moot court competition; the Special Committee on the Constitutional Convention of 1967, where I chaired its Suffrage and Elections Subcommittee and was exposed to many giants of the legal profession; the Federal Legislation Committee, of which I was a member for three years[2] and then its chair for three more years, which enabled me to help draft major reports, testify before or submit committee statements to congressional committees, and participate with brilliant lawyers on issues of civil rights and law reform.

Others included the Judiciary Committee, which thrust me into evaluating the qualifications of candidates for the judiciary; an ad hoc Lawyers in Transition Committee, chaired by Madeline Stoller, which supported the creation of New York's first wide-ranging program of the organized bar to help lawyers in transition facing difficult life circumstances;[3] the Executive Committee, which opened my eyes to the challenges of governance; and in 2001, a twenty-four-member Commission on Campaign Finance Reform, where I served as co-chair with two of the great lawyers of my generation, Cyrus Vance Sr. and Robert Kaufman, both former presidents of the bar association.

The report of the last committee, appearing in book form thanks to Fordham University Press, was dedicated to the memory of Vance, "whose . . . life in public service has been a model of the legal profession at its very best."[4] The committee made recommendations for public funding for congressional elections, adjustments to existing contribution limits, controls on soft money and political parties, redefining electioneering speech to prevent so-called issue advocacy advertising, and reforming the Federal Election Commission.

I also served in the New York State Bar Association as a member of its House of Delegates and Nominating and Executive Committees. It was meaningful to participate in the work of the Nominating Committee, serving as one of its two members from the First Judicial District. This position allowed me to cast affirmative votes for Maryann Saccomando Freedman, who became the first woman to serve as president of the New York State Bar Association, and, later, for Archibald Murray to be a member of the Executive Committee.

Also memorable was serving as chair of the association's Federal Constitution Committee as Congress considered legislation to broaden the grounds for removal of federal judges. The committee found the legislation to be unconstitutional, and I communicated the bar association's position to the judiciary committees of Congress. I believe that its view contributed to the rejection of such legislation.[5]

But there were also challenging moments. On one occasion I supported the adoption of the ABA Model Rules of Professional Conduct, only to see the idea overwhelmingly defeated in the state bar's House of Delegates. On an occasion involving the opening of disciplinary proceedings against lawyers after a finding of probable cause, I presented a supporting statement from the City Bar as its president, but I could find no support for the position in the House of Delegates. In fact, I could hardly find someone to second a motion to consider such a proposition. Thanks to the gracious chair of the house,

Archibald Murray, the motion carried, but he urged me to move along the discussion, which I did, resulting in very few votes for the City Bar's position. Fifteen years later, however, the state bar adopted the Model Rules with a few changes.

Among my bar days, the most fulfilling were spent working with Dean Robert McKay when he was president of the City Bar. He made his mark on just about every area of law, including legal education, admission to the bar, ethics, lawyers' disciplinary standards, and law reform. He spoke of the law as a profession with moral imperatives and of lawyers as setting the moral tone for justice and fairness. "No calling is higher, no obligation is more demanding," he said, "than for each of us to serve that rigorous master whom we call justice." He added, "The path is not easy, nor is the path altogether clear. But we must all join hands in that glorious search."[6]

Bob McKay, like Whitney North Seymour Sr., by words and actions, expressed a vision of the profession worth reflecting upon in times of challenge. McKay's vision was not complicated: it was to represent clients honorably, to show respect for the legal system and each other, and to engage in activities that served the public interest.[7]

The New York County Lawyer's Association was also important to me. As a law student I used its library, and as a young lawyer I attended its continuing legal education programs, but not until I was leaving as dean did I have an opportunity to serve this association, which was a pioneer in providing access to minorities and women.

I was asked by Craig Landy, its then president, to help develop and implement a justice center focused on issues of the urban poor. The center was a vision of Barry Levy's, a law school classmate and an unheralded but truly great bar leader. A small group of us studied the problem and then created such a center, for which I served as its first chair.

Among my bar opportunities, apart from my service with the ABA's presidential succession group, the one that had the most impact on me professionally was serving as president of the City Bar Association from 1992 to 1994. I became its fifty-sixth president, the consecutive-game-hitting number of my favorite baseball player, Joe DiMaggio.[8] A front-page article in the *New York Observer* for June 8, 1992, headlined "Incoming Head of City Bar Is a Bronx-Bred Quixote," said of the occasion:

> With only stereotypical preconceptions to go by, you might predict
> that John Feerick will be a very different head of the City Bar Asso-
> ciation than he is probably going to be. You might expect a white
> president to be less sensitive to the inequities experienced by minority

lawyers than was the black president he succeeded, Conrad Harper.
You might expect an Irish Catholic to be conservative on issues such as
improving conditions for female lawyers and making gay and lesbian
attorneys feel more welcome in the profession. You might expect an
academic who has been the dean of Fordham University Law School
for a decade to be out of touch with the day-to-day issues affecting
practicing attorneys.

As these articles predicted, these stereotypes were not accurate in my case.
And it concluded by noting that after my bar tenure I was "looking forward to
slowing things down — perhaps having more time to attend Jets football games
in below-freezing temperatures, which is one of his rare indulgences." That
was my dream, although it never came true to the extent I'd hoped.

As president of the City Bar, I placed my emphasis on such issues as serving
the public, enhancing the conflict resolution work of the bar, and involving
law schools and law students in the work of the voluntary bar. The headlines
of my monthly president's columns in the association's journal, *44th Street
Notes*, gives a glimpse of what was important to me: "Serving the Public"; "A
Commitment to Professionalism"; "New York's Continued Failure to Commit
to Ethics Reform"; "A Public Profession if We Can Keep It"; and "The Bar
and Legal Education: Joining Hands."[9]

I found especially memorable the opportunity to present the association's
views on the nomination of Ruth Bader Ginsburg to be Associate Justice of
the Supreme Court in 1993. It was a privilege to testify in support of her confirmation before the Senate Judiciary Committee, then chaired by Senator
Joseph Biden.

At the hearing, Biden stated, "I have often wondered whether or not the
origins of the practice of the bar of New York City of looking into judicial
nominations was a response to the patronage system and concern about it that
existed in the days of the late 19th century."[10] He was correct in pointing to
corruption in New York as being a precipitating cause of the founding of the
association. I followed up with him, discussing the long history of the city bar
with respect to judicial nominations, and why the city and not the state bar is
represented at the hearing: judicial nominations had been part of the history
of the city bar before the state bar was created.

As I concluded my tenure, the City Bar Association began a celebration
of its 150th anniversary, made splendid by my successor, Barbara Robinson,
the first woman to serve as president of the association, and by the chair of
the Celebration Committee, my esteemed former partner Barry Garfinkel.

Before the end of my term, I reached out to then Chief Justice of the

United States William Rehnquist to see if I could persuade him to preside at a mock trial of Thomas Jefferson on charges that his reputation was unduly inflated. Professor Charles Ogletree of Harvard Law School would represent the prosecution and Solicitor General Drew Days III the defense. The chief justice was believed to have a strong Jeffersonian interest. Intrigued by my request, his chamber granted me five minutes over the telephone to persuade him to accept the invitation, and I proceeded to build an argument around his scholarship on Jefferson, with which I had familiarized myself because of its relevance to the proposed trial. To my astonishment, the chief justice accepted our invitation.[11]

Whether I would have done as well in an actual argument before the Supreme Court, I will never know, but this one argument succeeded gloriously. Later, I presented Chief Justice Rehnquist with Fordham Law School's Stein Prize and chatted with him briefly, finding him exceedingly thoughtful and gracious.

When my service to the City Bar Association ended in May of 1994, I reflected on how lucky I was, among all of the outstanding lawyers who serve the bar, to have been a Fordham graduate chosen to serve as the group's president. As I started my tenure, a book had just been published that was critical of the association for its claimed elitism and continued dominance by the corporate legal elite, noting a lower rate of participation by graduates of "local schools" such as Fordham.[12] Then as now, Fordham would dispute the use of the term "local" and its second-class implications.

Archibald Murray, also a Fordham graduate, would later become the first African American president of the New York State Bar Association; another graduate, Patricia Hynes, the third woman to serve as president of the City Bar Association; and yet another graduate, Barbara Opotowsky, would be appointed chief administrative officer of the City Bar, followed in that position by another Fordham graduate, Bret Parker. William Carroll, a Fordham College and Bishop Dubois graduate, served with great effectiveness as the longtime executive director of the New York State Bar Association. As America has grown in its inclusiveness, so too has the bar.[13]

25

Public Service: From Carey to Koch to Cuomo to Bloomberg to Kaye

It is not the critic who counts; not the man who points out how
the strong man stumbles; or where the doer of deeds could have
done them better. The credit belongs to the man who is actually in
the arena.

— THEODORE ROOSEVELT

My services to New York State government organizations were all as a volunteer and "part-time." The earliest of these opportunities was serving, at the request of Mayor Edward Koch, as one of two New York City representatives to the New York City Board of Collective Bargaining, now known as the Office of Collective Bargaining. The other representative on the board was Edward Silver of the law firm Proskauer Rose. The agency enjoyed a long history of providing stability to labor relations between New York City and the unions with which the City had collective bargaining relationships.

When I was appointed to the board on May 30, 1980, it was chaired by Arvid Anderson, an inspiring presence who excelled at building consensus. I caused some consternation at the beginning of my service when I felt I should dissent from a decision to be issued by the board. A dissent was not in Anderson's vocabulary, but on further consideration, I found I could concur in the result and didn't have to dissent. I was sorry to resign from the position in 1987 to undertake the chairmanship of the New York State Commission on Government Integrity, believing that there could be a conflict of interest if I served on a board to which I'd been appointed by the mayor. As it turned out, conflict did develop as the commission investigated a city agency located in City Hall.

I was also appointed by Governor Hugh Carey to serve as a member of the New York State Law Revision Commission, which enjoyed a noble history of law reform in New York State.[1] I very much enjoyed this service, which included an opportunity to study gubernatorial succession in New York State and to determine ways to deal, prospectively, with a vacancy in the office of lieutenant governor and the disability of a governor.

The commission's unanimous recommendations were expressed in the form of a proposed constitutional amendment, supported by a detailed report. The proposal provided for filling a vacancy in the office of Lieutenant-Governor. The amendment didn't move through the legislature. I was later informed that the senate majority leader, next in line of succession when there was no lieutenant governor, did not favor it, perhaps because it would diminish the likelihood of future senate majority leaders serving as acting governors.

Following these services, I was asked by Chief Judge Judith Kaye to chair the Judiciary's Cameras in the Court Committee, ably assisted by Alexandra Lowe as counsel. I also served as a member of the New York State Judicial Salary Commission, the New York State Committee to Promote Public Trust and Confidence in the Legal System, and as a charter member of the New York State Continuing Legal Education Board, which put a system in place requiring the continuing legal education of lawyers in New York.

My work on the Cameras in the Courts Committee had a disappointing conclusion. The committee, by a vote of 11 to 1, recommended to make permanent a temporary program allowing cameras in the courts, but the legislature rejected the recommendation. The effects of the O.J. Simpson trial, then taking place in California, and opposition from trial lawyers in New York combined to dismantle this program, despite the fact that it had appeared to be a success over a ten-year period.

Our report was issued in April 1997 after an in-depth examination of the experiment allowing media coverage of court proceedings in New York State. The core of our reasoning was contained in this passage from the report: "We find instructive judicial decisions on the nature of a trial and the values served by the principle of openness of the judicial process, assuring that proceedings are conducted fairly, providing the public with information about the workings of the judiciary, and satisfying the appearance of justice."[2] As to the O.J. Simpson trial, the report noted:

> Camera proponents assert that televised coverage of that proceeding
> made an important contribution to the public's understanding of
> the judicial process and fundamental legal principles, such as the

presumption of innocence, proof beyond a reasonable doubt, and the suppression of illegally seized evidence. Camera opponents have argued that the Simpson case personifies the evils of cameras in the courts: television programming that sensationalized the judicial process and turned a murder trial into a mass-marketed commercial product which, in the eyes of some observers, brought the American legal system into disrepute.[3]

Post-Deanship Opportunities

Family Homelessness

In October of 2002, Steven Banks of the New York City Legal Aid Society reached out to ask if he could propose me as a mediator of controversies then raging between the City and the Legal Aid Society concerning the shelter system, particularly in a lawsuit involving homeless families. The Legal Aid Society had sued the City in 1983, with Yvonne McCain as the lead plaintiff. McCain and her children, having fled their home because of domestic violence, were left homeless and were offered temporary housing through the City at a hotel in deplorable condition. The goal of the lawsuit was to ensure that homeless families like hers had access to decent shelter.

There appeared to be little communication between the City and the Legal Aid Society other than through litigation. The litigation, one of the longest-pending lawsuits in the state courts at the time, had resulted in many orders protecting homeless families, and in the recent past, there had been a contempt motion against both Mayor Michael Bloomberg and the commissioner of homeless services. Banks, who was open to a mediation resolution, believed that I would be an acceptable mediator to the New York City corporation counsel, Michael Cardozo. I agreed to serve as mediator for the City and the Legal Aid Society on a pro bono basis.

I had no background in the shelter system but served alongside two preeminent social workers, Gail Nayowith, then executive director of Citizens' Committee for Children, and Daniel Kronenfeld, a founder and former director of the Henry Street Settlement. Both were incredibly dedicated individuals, and it was through them and the people they introduced me to that I came to learn about poverty and the shelter system.

Over several months we brought representatives of New York City and the Legal Aid Society together, day and night, and sought to find a basis for temporarily halting the litigation while searching for an overall approach to family homelessness in the City. The discussions were difficult, but in the end the parties agreed to the creation of a Special Master Panel on Family Homelessness with wide-ranging authority to adjudicate disputes.

Then, in December of 2002, I learned that Emalie had breast cancer. The decision to continue with this service was excruciating for me, but with her encouragement, I remained active in the mediation. On January 17, 2003, a mediation agreement was approved by the New York State Supreme Court, which appointed Danny, Gail, and me to serve as special masters on the panel. We were given two years to examine the system and make recommendations for reform.

The appointment also entailed resolving issues that might arise, as they did, between the City and the Legal Aid Society and denied direct resort to the courts unless our panel acted in an arbitrary or capricious manner. We met separately with the parties on a regular basis, and sometimes convened a joint meeting of senior principals of the parties to obtain their help in resolving sensitive issues and to explore their views as to reform of the system. All of us devoted an enormous amount of time to this undertaking over the two-plus years.

It remained a difficult period. Emalie underwent two surgeries, chemotherapy, and, for several months, radiation several times a week, all while I was also teaching full-time at Fordham Law School. I regretted how time-consuming my commitments were. Happily and mercifully, Emalie was given a clean bill of health and fully recovered from this challenge.

It's hard for me to describe how deeply I was affected by this public service. I visited many homeless shelters and was particularly troubled by the terrible conditions at a facility called the Emergency Assistance Unit (EAU). The EAU served as the family intake center for the City's homeless shelter system. Located at 150th Street and River Avenue in the South Bronx, the facility was just a few blocks south of where I grew up.

I witnessed people, many of them children, being processed at the EAU and then made to wait among hundreds of other families for a bus to take them to a shelter somewhere in the city. Many returned the next day, hoping to be found eligible and assigned to an appropriate temporary shelter on the path to securing affordable housing. The situation was deplorable, and I knew, as did my panel colleagues, that the City had to address the matter in a major way, and thankfully under Mayor Bloomberg's leadership it did.

Throughout this service, I had many conversations with homeless families. Some had lost their jobs, including government jobs; some had been evicted from their homes; some were veterans; and others were victims of domestic violence. Many appeared beaten down, forgotten, or ignored. I could feel their frustration and anger and see the anguish on their faces, and I sensed an unusual degree of appreciation when the panel took the time to listen to their stories.

I saw many hundreds of children in these shelters. These homeless children were no different from my own grandchildren, but I knew many of them would not have the opportunities my children and grandchildren enjoyed. Of my many meetings with homeless families, a few stand out. On a visit to a temporary shelter in Upper Manhattan, I met a young boy named Pedro. He was about 10 or 11, in a family of five children. They lived on the top floor of their building. After his mother showed me their living accommodations, I thanked her, and I gave Pedro and his siblings a dollar each to buy an ice cream.

As I was leaving, Pedro asked if he could show me the way out. As we walked down the stairs together, he took my hand and held it. I asked him what he wanted to be when he grew up, mentioning a number of occupations. He looked up at me and said, "I want to be like you." On another occasion a little girl, also homeless, gave me a drawing with the words "Don't forget me." It was another piercing moment for me.

My service on the Special Master Panel was among the most fulfilling experiences of my life. In a series of reports, the panel recommended closing the EAU, a greater commitment by the City on preventing homelessness, and redesigning the eligibility process for the city's homeless families seeking temporary shelter.[4] Mayor Bloomberg responded positively to our recommendations. In 2011, after our service as special masters ended, he invited me and the other panel members to the opening of an entirely new processing facility for families, the EAU having been abolished and replaced by a modern, eco-friendly building that was accessible and had the capacity to assist families in need.

The members of the panel, along with the mayor and others, cut the ribbon for the new building, creating for those present a proud moment in the City's history. On that occasion I said to the mayor that in the Catholic faith, what a person does for the least among us, that person does for God. I told him he had done something transcendental, principled, and wonderful, even if he received little public recognition for it.

In 2005, as a final item of business, the Special Master Panel tried to resolve the litigation controversies between the City and the Legal Aid Society through mediation. Despite extensive efforts, we weren't successful in this effort. In 2008, however, the City and the Legal Aid Society did reach a resolution, and I learned that the panel's earlier discussions were helpful in achieving it. When McCain, the lead plaintiff, learned of the settlement, she said: "When [Banks] told me that, under the settlement, there would be a permanent right to safe, adequate shelter for families like mine, I was so happy and relieved. This is what we went to court for so many years ago, and I am so glad that I lived to see it happen."[5]

Despite settlements and improvements, the problem of homelessness remains. As the panel noted, it is a problem of enormous proportions. But as we said in our final report, this much was clear:

> Solving the problem of family homelessness requires the broad engagement of not only all sectors but also of every citizen. . . . How we deal with this moral issue both reflects upon us and defines us as a society. . . . New York City has a rich history and experience, anchored in the New York State Constitution, of providing shelter to homeless persons. We must never walk away from this tradition . . . we should reaffirm that commitment and provide shelter decently, humanely, and thoughtfully.[6]

Judicial Elections

In late 2002, I was asked by Chief Judge Judith Kaye to help her create and then chair the New York State Commission to Promote Public Confidence in Judicial Elections. Concerned about the impact of campaign contributions and low voter turnout on such elections, Chief Judge Kaye wanted to do all she could to build greater confidence in the system.

The Chief Judge noted that the 1987 Commission of Government Integrity I chaired had recommended an overhaul of judicial elections in favor of an appointive system, but that it had received little political support. She wanted this new commission to focus on what could be done to promote public confidence in judicial elections and promised to put the full weight of her office behind whatever the commission recommended. I agreed to serve on what would eventually become a twenty-nine-member commission, which included at least one member from every judicial district in the state.

The commission began its work in 2003 and presented its final report to the Chief Judge in February of 2006. The commission made an intensive inquiry into all aspects of the judicial election system. Statewide, it held public hearings; conducted focus-group meetings; sponsored a public opinion poll by the Marist Institute for Public Opinion; conducted a survey of sitting judges; met with political leaders; addressed bar, judicial, and civic groups; testified before the New York State Legislature; and heard from many citizens in private meetings. The commission also conducted extensive research on the history of judicial elections in New York State and elsewhere. Based on its work, the commission issued three major reports containing many integrated recommendations.[7]

The commission's 2003 Interim Report recommended establishing independent commissions to evaluate the qualifications of judicial candidates throughout the state; amendments to the Rules of Chief Administrator of the Courts governing judicial conduct with respect to campaign speech restrictions, disqualification, and campaign expenditures; the creation of a campaign ethics and conduct center; the expansion of judicial campaign finance disclosure rules; and the publication of a state-sponsored voters' guide to judicial elections.

The commission's 2004 report expanded on these recommendations and addressed issues of public financing, voter education, retention elections (allowing voters to determine whether a judge was fit to remain in office), and the enforcement of the rules of judicial conduct. The commission's final report recommended the public financing of judicial elections, and if there was no public financing, to replace the existing primary system with a modified judicial nominating system. We believed this would make judicial elections more transparent and effective and decrease the problems associated with private contributions to judges.

Although the commission's recommendations drew varied reactions, the leadership of Chief Judge Kaye led to the judiciary's adoption of many of the recommendations, including the creation of a statewide system of independent judicial election qualification commissions and the creation of the Judicial Campaign Ethics Center.

In areas requiring legislative approval, the Chief Judge pressed for the adoption of the recommended changes, including one related to timely, electronic disclosures of campaign finances. In her State of the Judiciary address of February 6, 2006, Chief Judge Kaye praised the work of the commission, stating that its reports "represent a body of work unprecedented in depth and quality," and adding that "[w]e are all indebted to . . . the Commission for this comprehensive picture of our Judiciary system and how to improve it."[8]

Of my many memories from this service, one experience that stands out to me involved meetings with the commission's dedicated counsel, Michael Sweeney, along with judges and bar leaders, concerning the recommendations on limiting campaign contributions to judicial candidates and requiring that judges who had received significant donations from parties appearing before them recuse themselves from hearing such cases. We took a lot of heat for those recommendations. It was interesting, however, to learn in 2009 of the U.S. Supreme Court's decision in *Caperton v. Massey*[9] and of renewed interest in the subject of recusal as a way to protect and promote confidence in the judiciary.[10]

Committee for Fiscal Equity

In the summer of 2004, while the work on judicial election efforts was in progress, I was appointed by New York State Supreme Court Justice Leland DeGrasse to serve as one of three judicial referees in the lawsuit titled Campaign for Fiscal Equity against New York State. Our committee was asked to deal with the level of public funding for New York City's public schools. Also appointed were two distinguished former New York State Supreme Court justices, E. Leo Milonas and William Thompson.

The appointments were made in response to recent decisions by the New York Court of Appeals. The first decision, in 1995, determined that the state constitution guarantees all children a sound basic education.[11] The second, in 2003, found that the funding for public education in New York City was inadequate to provide children a sound basic education and gave the state a period of time to comply with the law.[12]

Governor George Pataki responded by appointing a commission, which recommended a five-year phase-in of between $2.5 billion (including $1.93 billion for New York City) and $5.6 billion from state, local, and federal sources. The legislature, however, passed a law providing only $300 million in aid for New York City and otherwise had no plan to bring the state into compliance. In appointing the three referees, the court directed us to "hear and report with recommendations on what measures defendants have taken to follow the directives [of the 2003 decision] and bring this State's school funding mechanism into constitutional compliance insofar as it affects the New York City School System. The referees shall also identify the areas, if any, in which such compliance is lacking."[13]

We proceeded to conduct a public hearing at Fordham Law School regarding the amount due from the State to ensure constitutional compliance for public education in New York City. Mayor Bloomberg was among those who testified and was impressive in making the case for the City in terms of its needs for operating and capital funds. The State, reflecting the position of Governor Pataki's Administration, urged that $1.93 billion in funding over four years would bring the State into compliance, but we rejected the State's position and found in favor of the City, awarding $5.63 billion in operating funds over four years and $9.179 billion for capital projects.

Our report was adopted by the lower court as its judgment, but the lower court's decision was vacated by the appellate court, which found the capital improvement plan of $9.197 billion unnecessary and directed that the State appropriate to the City at least $4.7 billion in additional operating funds over four years.

A further appeal was taken to New York's highest court regarding the operating funds. The court, with Chief Judge Kaye[14] and Judge Carmen Ciparick dissenting, agreed with the Pataki Administration's position, and said that the constitutionally required funding for New York City included $1.93 billion in additional operating funds. As the litigation was proceeding, the capital fund issue became academic from the standpoint of both parties, because the state acted to remedy deficiencies in the city's facilities. In time the city would receive the additional funding it had sought for in operating needs.

In the report of the Judicial Referees, we thought it important to remind everyone of the U.S. Supreme Court's decision in *Brown v. Board of Education*:

> [E]ducation is perhaps the most important function of state and local
> governments. . . . Today it is a principal instrument in awakening
> the child to cultural values, in preparing him for later professional
> training, and in helping him to adjust normally to his environment. In
> these days, it is doubtful that any child may reasonably be expected to
> succeed in life if he is denied the opportunity of an education.[15]

This statement remains an overarching benchmark for a society still mired in pervasive poverty and racial discrimination.[16]

Judge Judith Kaye, Chief Judge of New York State (1993–2008). See *Judith S. Kaye In Her Own Words*, published by State University of New York Press, Albany (2019).

26

Boards of Not-for-Profit, Charitable, and Public Institutions

For we are a nation of communities . . . a brilliant diversity spread like stars, like a thousand points of light in a broad and peaceful sky.

— GEORGE H. W. BUSH

In my professional life, my associations have been wide-ranging, extending from legal services and civic groups, to educational and religiously based organizations, to boards of public companies.

As I grew older, my associations grew far beyond the organized bar to include Fordham University; the Archdiocese of New York; the Jesuit School of Theology in Berkeley, California, now part of Santa Clara University; the School of Holy Child in Rye, New York; Brooklyn Legal Services; New York Medical College; the American Arbitration Association; the Fund for Modern Courts; Citizens Union Foundation; the Center for Information on America; Angela House; the Elizabeth Seton Pediatric Center; the American Irish Historical Society; the Irish Hunger Memorial Foundation at Battery Park City; MedShare Inc.; EmblemHealth; and a few public companies.

Many organizations need financial help to subsist, and sometimes my board service for charitable and not-for-profit organizations involved fundraising. Annual fundraising events allow organizations to discuss and celebrate their work, and on these occasions, individuals are oftentimes recognized and honored for their services.

It is an honor to be recognized by an organization as deserving of an award, but in the beginning, I hesitated to accept awards, believing that by doing so I was calling attention to myself. I recall delaying for almost twelve years the acceptance of an award from a legal services organization I was involved in, and, in another case, feeling it inappropriate to accept the first annual award from an organization I wasn't involved in. I relented in the latter case when Fordham graduate Jack Vaughan called and persuaded me that I should accept the award because of the organization's role in providing pro bono legal services to low-income Americans.

In time, I recognized that award ceremonies are beneficial for fundraising purposes. The individual being honored calls attention to the fiscal supports needed to sustain the organization's mission, which brings in contributions from friends and family and from those who believe in its work.

On another occasion, upon accepting a request to chair the board of the Fund for Modern Courts, I learned that the organization's revenues were not sufficient to sustain its payroll on a long-term basis. The solution seemed obvious — introduce a fundraising program in connection with its annual award. I met with the forthcoming recipient of that award, Robert Kaufman,[1] who had asked me to serve as chair, along with Fern Schair, and sought his approval to expand the award presentation to include fundraising. He agreed, and the event that followed was a great success.

Among the most meaningful of my services involved two organizations no longer in existence: the Center for Information on America and Angela House. Each was led by remarkable individuals who worked, in the first instance, to further American democracy, and in the second, to help the poor.

The center generated publications, known as *Vital Issues* and *Grass Roots Guides*, on issues involving democratic government. I was introduced to the group in 1967 by Orison Marden, who asked me to write an article for *Vital Issues* on the electoral college system, which I happily did. I then was asked by the center's founder, Townsend Scudder, to serve as a member of its board and later as its chair.

Year after year, Scudder single-handedly obtained foundation grants to cover the costs of the center's publications. He invited people knowledgeable in various subject areas to write articles. He received very little compensation for his commitment to this organization, and it was painful for me to see a lessening in the center's support as he aged. My successor as board chair, Letitia Baldrige, who served as the White House social secretary to Jacqueline Kennedy, was remarkable in her handling of the issue, showing great sensitivity to Scudder, someone we both loved, when the center finally did have to close its doors. His spirit of concern for his fellow citizens lives on within me.

Angela House was the inspiration of Sister Winifred of the Ursuline Sisters, the order that educated me at St. Angela. She and the late Sister Dorothy

Ann Kelly of New Rochelle College asked me to host a reception at Fordham Law School in 1991. They hoped to use the reception to speak about an idea Sister Winifred had about opening a residential transitional program for homeless women and their children in the Bronx.

I thought it inappropriate to use the forum of the Law School to support a non-school-related cause, but the Sisters insisted on meeting with me. In the meeting they explained that they were offered space in a building of Montefiore Hospital for five years, free of charge, to accommodate such a facility, but to obtain the gift, they had to show that they could sustain an annual operating budget of about $150,000.

Despite my reluctance to introduce a new cause to alumni, already beleaguered by my fundraising requests, I nevertheless decided to do so in this case. To my pleasant surprise, the resulting breakfast reception was well attended, and a sum of $30,000 was raised. This, however, was clearly not enough. One of the most generous people I've ever met, Margaret "Peggy" Hill of Fordham Law School, class of 1964, came forward and added another $100,000. Her dramatic gift led to the opening of the home, and when the original lease ran out, Peggy helped to secure another location for the home. Ten remarkable years followed, during which many homeless women were able to transition to affordable housing.

Sister Winifred's dedication to serving those less fortunate and her inspiring leadership remain with me. The families and children she touched will never forget the lift she gave to their lives. I'll never forget Peggy's extraordinary intervention, nor Sister Winifred and graduates like Michael Stanton Sr. who helped through service on the program's advisory board.

As with the organizations led by Townsend Scudder and Sister Winifred, I witnessed the difference one individual can make in other settings. The School of the Holy Child in Rye, New York, from which my daughters Rosemary and Margaret graduated, reached a low point in its enrollment during the 1980s, raising the question: If its enrollment continued to decline, could the school continue to cover the costs of operation?

I served on the school's board at the time and reluctantly, because of my fundraising at Fordham Law School, accepted the challenge of chairing its capital campaign, whose purpose was to retire a seven-figure debt. Under the leadership of Sister Jean O'Meara, the school's principal, it was able to do so. She was indefatigable in her fundraising efforts, and board members and others responded with great generosity. Whenever the campaign sagged, I asked the board to make additional gifts in support of her efforts, and they did so on each occasion. On her recommendation, the school opened a middle school which reversed the financial decline and led the school to many years of popularity and success. Serving under her leadership as a board member for more than ten years was a privilege.

I also watched William Slate lead the American Arbitration Association (AAA) through the many challenges it was facing in the mid-1990s. The AAA is among the oldest leaders in the field of dispute resolution, but the emergence of new competitors was the source of some of its challenges. Slate became president of the AAA in 1996 after a search committee I served on passed his name along for consideration.

With the help of an able staff and board, Slate embarked on many initiatives. He streamlined the group's office structure in the United States, diversified the leadership of its board, and expanded the association's reach globally. I was privileged to serve under his leadership when the association opened its first overseas office in Dublin. In September 2011, Slate passed the reins to a very able successor, India Johnson, who had made a distinguished career for herself within the association over the thirty-eight years prior.

Brooklyn Legal Services, another not-for-profit organization I've been involved with, plays a major role in helping communities in Brooklyn. Each year the organization raises money from private sources to sustain its mission. The organization was ably led for more than thirty years by Martin Needleman. Although recently retired from his leadership position, he continues to plow ahead in his fundraising efforts for the organization. He's an example of a lawyer who excels in his commitment to the underserved.

All my children, I'm proud to say, have made service to others a core value in their life. My daughter Rosemary, for example, is the leader of a not-for-profit ministry called Wisdom and Money (previously, Harvest Time), designed to help those in need. My son Bill has developed a summer educational and recreational enrichment program for young children living in poverty in Brooklyn.

I should add a word about my experiences serving on public boards such as Wyeth Pharmaceuticals (formerly American Home Products) and the Sentinel Mutual Funds in Vermont, the learning of which assisted me in my managerial work as dean. It was humbling for me to serve on the Wyeth board with Clifford Alexander Jr. (the first African American Secretary of the Army), Robert Sarnoff (a pioneer of radio and television broadcasting), William Wrigley (the principal owner of the Chicago Cubs), Frank Bennack Jr. (the chairman of Hearst Communications), Ivan Seidenberg (the CEO of Verizon Communications Inc.), and Jack Stafford (the CEO of Wyeth).

I equally enjoyed my service as a director of the Sentinel Mutual Funds of Vermont[2] and as a member, and now chair, of the board of EmblemHealth, with CEO Karen Ignagni, during a transformative period in the company's existence. The members of all these boards set a powerful example for me as I watched them consider management reports, examine financial data, ask challenging questions, seek additional information to better inform themselves, and make sure that problems were addressed with the help of lawyers, accountants, and other experts.

Margaret M. "Peggy" Hill '64, an extraordinary graduate.

27

The Catholic Church

[The laity] live in the world, that is, in each and in all of the secular professions and occupations. They live in the ordinary circumstances of family and social life, from which the very web of their existence is woven. They are called there by God that by exercising their proper function and led by the spirit of the Gospel, they may work for the sanctification of the world from within as a leaven.

— DOGMATIC CONSTITUTION ON THE CHURCH

Growing up, I saw things in limited terms. I saw marriage as a life-long commitment between two members of the opposite sex. I believed in the nuclear family. I planned to one day be a father, unless I decided to become a priest, and a grandfather if I lived that long. And I embraced the view that I needed to be a Roman Catholic in order to reach Heaven, preceded by a stay in Purgatory.

As a world outside of my neighborhood in the Bronx opened up to me, this worldview changed. I became exposed to different cultures, different ways of living, and different worldviews and belief systems, and I learned that other faiths offer other routes to revelation and salvation, as reflected in the 1962–1965 work of the Second Vatican Council. I came to know single mothers with children. I saw friends leave their marriages, divorce, and remarry. I became friends with individuals in relationships with others of their own sex, some of whom entered civil unions and marriages and some of whom raised children. I learned of people changing their sexual identity. I became aware of members of my own faith supporting the use of contraceptives and choice in the matter of abortion, both practices prohibited by the Catholic Church. I realized that some among my Catholic friends did not regularly attend Mass on Sunday and possessed, often strongly, points of view very different from my own.

The variations in our culture raised questions for me as to what was right and what was wrong and whether it was right for me to judge others according to my beliefs. And so I adopted a quiet posture in these matters, respecting other people's individuality.

In the fall of 2014, a report was made public following a synod of Bishops convened by Pope Francis in Rome. Its words seemed to reflect my own thoughts on these diverse realities of the world.

According to a November 11, 2014, article by Jacob Lupfer, "This month's Synod of Bishops reveals that Catholic leaders are considering more conciliatory language toward gays and lesbians, divorced and remarried Catholics, and couples who live together before getting married." It continued, "[T]he conflict between conscience and authority is the pre-eminent battle underlying the synod's debates." It noted that one Cardinal at the synod worried that couples "do not believe that the use of contraceptive methods is a sin and therefore they tend not to speak of them in confession and so they receive Communion untroubled."[1]

While the Synod's final report downplayed the language of an earlier draft, the subject was discussed and debated again in a three-week Synod in October of 2015. The resulting report, summarized by *Catholic New York*, the official newspaper of the Archdiocese of New York, "highlighted the role of pastors in helping couples understand Church teaching, grow in faith and take responsibility for sharing the Gospel." The report also "emphasized how 'pastoral accompaniment' involves discerning, on a case-by-case basis, the moral culpability of people not fully living up to the Catholic ideal."[2]

The paragraph dealing specifically with leading divorced and remarried Catholics on a path of discernment passed with only one vote beyond the necessary two-thirds. The final report also noted the changing role and importance of women in the Church's future. I remain hopeful that such a role can be spelled out beyond the ninety-four paragraphs in the report.

Pope Francis spoke to me from afar when he said that it wasn't for the Catholic Church to "hand down condemnations or anathemas, but to proclaim the Mercy of God." Clearly, the Pope has broadened horizons, encouraging Catholics to listen to and learn from each other. What occurred at the Synods of 2014 and 2015 reflects a change of emphasis that is more understanding of people's various life circumstances.

I had arrived at this approach for myself because I saw all the good things being done by friends and others who fell into classifications that had brought condemnations from some church leaders. They worked hard, cared for those less fortunate, and treated other people with respect. The words of Pope Francis, "Who am I to judge?," seemed right to me.

My faith has helped me enormously in times of pain and suffering. I often carry with me a set of rosary beads, or another religious object, to which I turn both in joyful moments and in times of distress and sadness involving myself, loved ones, or strangers. My faith has provided me refuge most especially in moments of stress and challenge.

During my adult life I've felt a responsibility to live my faith, in particular, by being faithful to my local Catholic church and, more expansively, by participating in activities involving the church. God implores me to be caring of others, especially to those being discriminated against. God calls me to respect the dignity of every person and to be charitable in sharing and giving and to do what I can to make this a more peaceful and just world.

The Archdiocese of New York

In the early years of our married life, Emalie and I were members of St. Gabriel's Parish in Riverdale, where three of our children were baptized. I gave financial support through the Sunday collection and attended Church Masses and sometimes parish events, but for the most part, that was the extent of my participation.

In 1969, when we moved to Mount Kisco and joined the parish at St. Francis Assisi Catholic Church, I took on a slightly more active role. I recall the chair of the new parish council asking if anyone had experience drafting a constitution. I did. I volunteered to write the first draft of that parish charter. Emalie assumed a much more active role, becoming a religious teacher at the church, volunteering as a driver for those in need, and collecting and bringing food to the church to distribute to the poor. Her service set an example for me in the decades to come.

In the 1980s, I served on a small committee convened by Terence Cardinal Cooke to advise him on criminal justice matters and responded to requests from John Cardinal O'Connor and Edward Cardinal Egan to help the Archdiocese put in place an alternative dispute resolution program. The program would familiarize priests and employees of the church with methods of resolving disputes, such as mediation and arbitration. The American Arbitration Association, whose board I had chaired, helped by asking some of its experienced trainers to conduct training sessions for prospective neutrals who worked in church settings.

Clerical Sex Abuse

In the fall of 2002, Edward Cardinal Egan asked me to serve as a member of
a small committee reviewing allegations of child abuse lodged against priests.
He asked us to make recommendations as to whether these priests should remain in active ministry. The allegations in some cases went decades back and
proved shocking and deeply troubling. The committee did its work carefully.
It was aided by the legal staff of the Archdiocese, which provided background
information, reviewed documents, and gave complainants and priests an opportunity to meet separately with the committee to present their points of view
and answer questions.

Our recommendations went to Cardinal Egan. Working with him, we
developed protocols for handling future allegations. He respected the committee's work and enabled us to do our work independently. Nevertheless, I
found participating on this committee to be painful and difficult. To hear and
weigh allegations of sexual misconduct by priests against young children was
appalling. Like the vast majority of Catholics, I placed priests on a pedestal,
regarding them as God's servants in the world and as models of the Church.

Nor were these issues of abuses isolated. Countless cases of abuse can be
found throughout America and the world involving both dioceses and religious organizations. Costly settlements were entered into, and in some matters courts reached decisions that collectively shook the foundations of the
Catholic Church of America and undermined its support among the laity
and beyond. Serious mistakes were made in the handling of these issues, and
efforts are continuing to deal with these abuses and prevent their recurrence.

Inner-City Youth

I was pleased to serve for a decade as co-chair of the Inner-City Scholarship
Fund Lawyers Division, which helps generate monetary and other support for
Catholic schools in the Archdiocese of New York. The schools educate more
than sixty-seven thousand students,[3] many of whom are not Catholic, in rural
villages, suburban enclaves, and inner-city communities. Seventy percent of
the students live near or below the poverty line, yet an astounding number
go on to college thanks to the rigor of these institutions and the values they
express.[4]

In 2014, Edward Cardinal Egan, the "old man on the block," as he would
call himself, spoke of the founding roles played by Jim Gill, Paul Curran, and
me in this area, describing us as the "Tres Amigos." He later sent me a letter
that said: "Your [family's] support of Saint Angela Merici School is deeply

appreciated. It is one of my favorite places in the world. If someone wants to see genuine compassion for the neediest in our midst that is the place to go." Tears welled up in my eyes when I read his letter, and again when he died a short time later.

Church Realignment

Another important opportunity to serve the church came in 2007, when I was invited to join a Committee on Realignment, chaired by Auxiliary Bishop Dennis Sullivan. After a lengthy review, the committee issued a report recommending expansions, closures, and consolidations of churches. For me, the litmus test was how the South Bronx would fare. Because so many people lived in poverty in the South Bronx, expecting the majority of the economic support for the Church to come from the community and congregation was not practical. When asked by Bishop Sullivan for my view on the draft report, I said, "It is in the South Bronx that Jesus Christ is to be found." I was pleased to join with other members of the committee in underscoring the importance of maintaining church institutions in that part of the city. One of those institutions is the parish of my youth, which remains a vital institution in the South Bronx.

Catholic Church Nationally—Social Justice Activities

The Law School's Center for Social Justice has provided me with a unique opportunity to serve my church. Perhaps the center's most significant undertaking in its first five years was aiding in the development of a historic document for the American Catholic Health Care System called "Respecting the Just Rights of Workers: Guidance and Options for Unions and Management in Union Organizing Elections." The center was asked to moderate and mediate a dialogue among these groups on the subject of workers' rights in union organizing campaigns to see if a model or option could be developed for nationwide consideration.

With the help of six law students and the active engagement of Professor Elizabeth Cooper and Dean Reilly, we studied the background of the issues involved, met with representatives of the parties to get their views, conducted meetings of the parties to facilitate exchanges among them, and discussed proposals with them.

I found the discussions about Catholic health compelling because they revolved around Catholic social teaching and its emphasis on the rights of workers in the modern-day workplace. The final document is filled with principles and understandings that resonate with Catholic social teaching. Indeed, the document's final title, "Respecting the Just Rights of Workers," can be found in writings issued by the Vatican. Among its many provisions is a preamble of principles, one of which recognizes the right of a worker to join or not join a labor organization.

Ghana

My work in Ghana began at the request of Dennis Lynch, a graduate of Syracuse Law School.

He asked me to support his newly created Giving to Ghana Foundation, which I agreed to do, and I asked my dear friend and law school classmate Dennis Kenny to join me in these efforts. This undertaking led to several annual trips to Ghana between 2011 and 2013, with colleagues from Fordham and St. John's Law School, to help establish the Marian Conflict Resolution Centre. We conducted annual, forty-hour alternative dispute resolution (ADR) training programs over several years at the Centre. The program provided education and training in mediation and arbitration to priests, seminarians, tribal chiefs, lawyers, and judges, among others. Then Chief Justice of Ghana Georgina Theodora Wood welcomed the participants, and two leading ADR lawyers in Ghana — Nene Amegatcher, then president of the Ghana Bar Association, and Michael Owusu — assisted in facilitating the program.

Everywhere I went I saw people working land that would yield their food and selling their harvest and other items to generate a few dollars of income. Dennis Kenny, obviously affected by the experience, helped build a well sorely needed by local residents, put a roof on a Catholic church that had needed one for more than a decade, and arranged for computers to be sent to a new girls' high school. I joined him in some of those efforts.

Making All Things New

Fordham Law's Center for Social Justice's services to the Archdiocese of New York didn't lessen, despite this overseas undertaking in Ghana. In 2012 I was asked by Cardinal Dolan to serve on a pastoral planning initiative called "Making All Things New." The forty-member pastoral advisory committee was tasked with reviewing the then 368 parishes in New York City and the parishes in counties to the north. Eighty-eight of these parishes were in Manhattan, where the Catholic population represented less than 12 percent of the 2.8 million Catholics living in the Archdiocese, which covers Manhattan, the

Bronx, and Staten Island, along with seven upstate counties. Cardinal Dolan encouraged the entire Archdiocese to become involved.[5]

This process led to decisions by the Cardinal in November of 2014 to close some parishes, consolidate others, create new parishes, and encourage greater collaboration among parishes. As the committee was finishing its work, I was asked if the Center for Social Justice could assist with the implementation of the Cardinal's decisions involving parish mergers, and with the help of eighteen volunteers, we did so. These volunteers reduced the pain and anger felt by some parishioners and helped parish implementation teams come together to form new parish communities.

Merger Facilitators

One of these mergers I observed up close. On September 20, 2015, along with two Fordham Law colleagues, Lucy Brusco and Frank Manchisi, I attended the opening Mass of two recently merged parishes in Mamaroneck, New York — the parishes of St. Vito and Most Holy Trinity. The Mass and attendant music by parishioners of the two merged parishes, with scripture readings in English, Italian, and Spanish (reflecting the varied nature of the two communities), made this moment incredibly special.

Six months earlier I had met with the pastors of these communities and learned of the hurt being experienced by them and their parishioners because of the merger decision. The pastors understood Cardinal Dolan's decision that by August 1, 2015, a new parish community embracing the two former parishes would have to come into existence, with St. Vito Church continuing as an active place of worship for the new community. Lucy, Frank, and I met with these pastors and their implementation teams to help them achieve a merger that would result in a robust new parish community. The chosen pastor for the new community was Monsignor James White, previously the pastor of St. Vito.

The cover of the program for the first Mass celebrated by the new religious community bore the words: "Saint Vito — Most Holy Trinity — Unity Mass." The inside of the program declared, "As the Archdiocesan merger of parishes is now a reality, the parishioners of Saint Vito and Most Holy Trinity come together this weekend as one faith-filled parish and community. After months of preparing for this orderly transition, representative members of both parishes have prayed together, deliberated together and, in many instances, shed tears of sorrow as well as of joy together. We now unite our minds and hearts in prayer as one family. The new wine is now poured into new red wine skins."[6]

Lucy, Frank, and I were invited to attend this Mass by parishioners of the former parishes whom we had come to know and like. They wanted us to sit in the first row with Mamaroneck's mayor and deputy mayor to thank us for our service as, in their words, "merger facilitators." All three of us experienced a beautiful moment. The new parish community was a tribute to Monsignor White and Father Henry, the two pastors involved, and the implementation teams they had assembled. I left the reception after the Mass with our reserved seat card, which read "Merger Facilitator." I asked Lucy, Frank, and Monsignor White to sign it. "It doesn't get better than this," I said to them.

PART VI

Peacemaking and Problem-Solving

I believe there's no such thing as a conflict that can't be ended.
They're created and sustained by human beings.
They can be ended by human beings.
No matter how ancient the conflict, no matter how hateful,
no matter how hurtful, peace can prevail.

— GEORGE J. MITCHELL

PART VI

Peacemaking and Problem Solving

28

Learning the Art of Conflict Resolution

The probability that we may fail in the struggle ought not to deter us
from the support of a cause we believe to be just.

— ABRAHAM LINCOLN

As a practicing lawyer I was introduced to the principal methods of resolving
disputes: negotiation, fact-finding, mediation, neutral evaluation, arbitration,
and litigation in state and federal courts and before administrative agencies. I
also gained experience as a volunteer arbitrator for the American Arbitration
Association, handling commercial matters as a sole arbitrator or as part of a
multimember panel, as early as 1963.

A particularly significant experience came in the late 1970s, when I was
appointed by Judge Kevin Duffy[1] to serve as an arbitrator of labor disputes between the Greater New York Health Care Facilities Association Inc., and Local 144, Hotel, Hospital, Nursing Home & Allied Service Employees Union,
SEIU, and AFL-CIO. Although I was reluctant to take on this assignment, the
good judge opined that I would dispose of the matter in a few days.

I accepted the request and then spent much of the rest of the year holding
hearings and issuing awards in an acrimonious context involving the parties
and their counsels. To accommodate the lawyers' multiple demands from
other clients, which made it hard to find dates for hearings, I had to schedule
hearings on Friday nights, weekday nights, and weekends, a schedule that
eventually brought the matter to an end.

December 17, 1980, marked the conclusion of this effort with the issuing of
my final award, to which I attached three entirely new collective bargaining
agreements reflecting the awards in contract language. The awards added up

to 291 pages.[2] As it turned out, one party declined to pay my fee (which I would have turned over to the firm). I expected a motion to vacate the awards. Instead I received an unusual call from Howard Squadron, the association's then lawyer, who said he had been asked to make such a motion but concluded that it wouldn't be successful and therefore wasn't going to do so.[3]

In accepting requests to help resolve disputes, I made sure that they didn't interfere with my school responsibilities. I often used weekends, holidays, and vacations for such purposes. Not infrequently, I donated my compensation to the school. The matters in which I was involved covered a wide spectrum, including issues of discrimination based on age, color, and gender; commercial and business issues such as the scope of insurance coverage; and the entitlements of partners or former partners in legal, accounting, and business contexts.

Some matters were of public importance, such as serving as a pro bono mediator of the 1995 transit negotiations and dealing with the threatened closure of New York City's subways and buses; as a pro bono mediator, at the request of New York's then Chief Administrative Judge, Jonathan Lippman, and Westchester County Executive Andrew Spano, of a dispute involving the county, the Office of Court Administration, and the Dormitory Authority concerning the building of a courthouse in Westchester, a project that had been shut down because of cost overruns; as mediator of a dispute between the National Collegiate Athletic Association (NCAA) and the National Invitation Tournament (NIT)[4] over post-season tournaments; and as mediator of a much-publicized lawsuit brought by former Yankees catcher and coach Yogi Berra.

These disputes were interesting, and, I'm glad to say, were resolved amicably. I was happy to slip into the background each time the parties announced final settlements. It was enough to be a contributor and a problem solver.

I also had opportunities to serve under innovative and carefully designed procedures. The first of these was at the Jacob K. Javits Convention Center in New York City. The unions working at the Convention Center developed a process to resolve labor disputes. I was to oversee that process as the arbitrator of labor disputes.

On December 19, 1985, the management of the $487 million center approved an operating agreement with more than a dozen unions that was designed to make the new center for shows and exhibitions economically competitive. The agreement contained a "no-strike" clause prohibiting "work stoppages of any kind," a provision that no show or exhibit would require more employees "than actually needed to do the work to be done," an expressed "principle of a day's pay for a day's work," and a dispute resolution procedure involving the "Office of Czar" with authority to deal with jurisdictional disputes and work practices, especially those involving featherbedding, guaranteed overtime, and gratuities. I disliked the title of Czar and insisted that everyone call me arbitrator or chair. I also asked that all fees for my services go to the Law School.

Over the next several years, I decided many cases involving the Javits Center, striking down practices from the old Convention Center and giving voice to the promise of this acclaimed, historic agreement. In one decision, I ruled that the center didn't have to schedule a standby crew for freight handling on days when there would be no freight deliveries. In another decision, made difficult because of a long history of compensation for meal periods, I ruled that the center didn't have to pay for a meal period occurring during an eight-hour workday under the unique provisions of the agreement.

In yet another case, I ruled that the center didn't have to recognize a particular union's claim of jurisdiction over cleaning functions. Finally, when a show manager argued that his security personnel were sufficient to handle the work of checking the badges of visitors to a show, I sustained a union's grievance that its members were entitled to this work based on the union's traditional jurisdiction, finding no duplication of work in the facts presented. Scandals occurring at the Convention Center, however, led to the agreement's demise in the 1990s, during the administration of Governor George Pataki.

Because of the innovative use of dispute resolution procedures under the Convention Center agreement, I was asked to serve as impartial chair of disputes at the Democratic Convention of 1992 and the Republican Convention of 2004, both held in New York City. I agreed to do so on a pro bono basis. The resulting agreements were entered into by the respective national political parties, the City of New York, and the various operating unions at the conventions.

The aim of the agreements was to avoid work-related disputes at the conventions. The agreements provided for expedited hearings, by telephone if necessary, and rulings delivered orally and in abbreviated form. Jurisdictional disputes were also subject to rulings, but recognizing the incendiary nature of such disputes, the parties limited the effect of such rulings to the period of the convention. Thereafter, the parties were free to re-arbitrate these disputes without being stuck with a precedent.

Not surprisingly, there was no business for me at the 2004 Republican Convention, and only one or two cases involving lighting at the 1992 Democratic Convention were presented to my deputy, Carolyn Gentile. It was clear both times that the existence of the process itself served as a deterrent to conflict. The parties were encouraged to reach their own settlements rather than chance a resolution by a third party and the resulting precedent.

The most publicized of my ADR undertakings came in the area of sports, first as the initial salary cap arbitrator of the NFL, then as the grievance arbitrator for the NBA, and then as a member of an arbitration panel of the NFL after another member was replaced because of a particular decision. In these roles, I handled a number of much-publicized matters and had to accept the heat that goes with decisions that are not well received by one of the parties or the public. I served for one term in each of these positions, since either party could strike you from the panel at the end of the contract term, as was likely to happen after an unpopular decision.

The salary cap role involved issues arising under a federal consent decree (in *White v. National Football League*) and its embodiment in a collective bargaining agreement. My very first case involved the modification of the contract of Dallas quarterback Troy Aikman the day before the cap went into effect, raising the issue as to whether the modification could stand. I decided it could, and that became the precedent for other pre-cap modifications.

Another decision, which had to be decided on the very day that the matter came to me, hinged on whether the Oakland Raiders could change a "Transition Player Designation" of cornerback Tim Brown to a "Franchise Player Designation," with consequences for both parties at the end of the player's contract. I ruled that the designation couldn't be changed by the club, but as it turned out, Oakland and the player concluded another agreement, and Brown went on to enjoy a super career with Oakland.

My NBA decisions involving the player Latrell Sprewell and the NBA lockout, which I discuss later, were the stuff of high drama. The response to the Sprewell decision was thunderous, while the lockout decision, which had profound importance for the sport, was accepted by both parties. Counsel for the players' association, as quoted in the press, said, "The arbitration was a little bit like a tie game and we took a 40-foot shot at the buzzer."[5] Others criticizing my lockout decision said words along the lines of, "What else can you expect from a labor arbitrator?"[6] Although both parties to the collective bargaining agreement accepted the Sprewell decision, the player did not, bringing a lawsuit in the Federal Court in San Francisco against the NBA, a suit that was eventually dismissed.[7]

The last of my arbitration services for the NFL involved several challenging matters, but none more so than a case involving the late Steve McNair. Briefly stated, the case involved a refusal by the Titans to allow McNair to participate in its off-season program at its stadium.

But the context was larger. The player and the club were at odds over a renegotiation of McNair's contract; a new quarterback had been recruited by the club, and another team, the Ravens, was interested in McNair. After sorting out the facts as presented at a hearing, I ruled that the Titans had to allow the player to participate in its off-season program, concluding: "The Undersigned finds, in the unique and special circumstances of this proceeding, a violation of the obligation implied in this Player's contract not to impede or hinder his right to receive its fruits and benefits."[8]

After the decision was issued, McNair was traded to the Ravens and enjoyed a few seasons with that team. I was sorry to have to move on from this NFL service in 2007, but my acceptance of the chairmanship of the New York State Public Integrity Commission made the move inevitable. It saddened me to later learn of McNair's tragic death in 2009, at only 36 years old.

In 2014, I was asked to serve as the mediator of New York City's contract with the Uniformed Superior Officers Coalition, which consisted of a number of associations, including the NYPD Captains Endowment Association. The mediation came at a time of increasing hostility between the city administration and the police springing from civil unrest in response to the killings of two unarmed Black citizens, Eric Garner in New York and Michael Brown in St. Louis.

I was asked to serve as mediator by two key negotiators, Robert Lynn, the City's commissioner of the Office of Labor Relations, who had worked with me at Skadden after he graduated from law school, and the president of the Captains Endowment Association, Roy Richter, who was a student of mine in the evening division at Fordham, class of 1998. Both were comfortable with me serving as a mediator, and the trust that flowed from that enabled me to help facilitate communications between the parties during the mediation and, when necessary, offer my own thoughts on their deadlock issues. They hammered out a compromise sufficient to conclude a mediated agreement, which was later ratified by the coalition members.

I was thanked for my services by Mayor de Blasio and the coalition presidents in a private ceremony in a box at Citi Field. The letter the mayor gave me is one of my most precious possessions. In it he described the agreement as the first in his administration with the uniformed forces and therefore "historic." He spoke of the "magic touch" provided that helped to advance a dialogue based on mutual respect between labor and management and achieve meaningful gains for both parties. I was glad to have been part of the process.

In May of 2016, I was asked to mediate a labor contract dispute at Sarah Lawrence College in Yonkers, New York, after a three-day student occupation of college offices in support of increased wages and benefits and other provisions. The goal was to negotiate a first-time collective bargaining agreement for the college's recently unionized facilities employees. When the college agreed to mediate, the students withdrew.

My daughter Maureen played an essential role in the matter as a co-mediator. I asked Maureen to co-mediate because I thought she could provide an analysis of the numbers associated with wage classifications and vested benefits. An analytical mind would be needed if called upon to offer mediator suggestions for the parties to consider. Maureen's expertise in financial matters were wide-ranging, having served as a former assistant vice president of the Federal Reserve Bank in New York and as a member of the library board in Larchmont, where she dealt with budgetary and labor issues. She provided essential help in a fast-moving situation, which involved separate, back-and-forth discussions with the parties. Our efforts, for which we declined compensation, succeeded after thirty-nine hours of work spread over several days and evenings.

In a letter of thanks, the president of the college wrote: "Additionally, I wanted to thank your daughter for assistance in this process and her commitment to attend several mediation sessions here at campus, with some lasting late into the evening." On Thanksgiving Day 2016, Maureen and I received a card signed by the workers and students thanking us as well.[9]

In 2017, I undertook, with Linda Gerstel as a co-mediator, on a pro bono basis a sensitive matter involving a long-standing lawsuit by New York City against New York State, with a class action subsequently added to the case on behalf of developmentally disabled children in the foster care system.

29

Conflicts in the Public Eye

There comes a time when one must take a position that is neither safe, nor politic, nor popular — but he must take it because conscience tells him it is right.

— REV. MARTIN LUTHER KING JR.

Of my problem-solving experiences, a few stand out above the rest.

The Armonk Byram Hills Teachers

I wasn't ready for my first experience with labor relations in the public sector. One evening in early 1970s as my children slept, I received an unexpected telephone call from a friend about the teachers of Armonk, New York, a community not far from my home in Mount Kisco. He asked if he and a few teachers could get my advice regarding a problem they were facing.

The teachers had begun, without a lawyer, a labor negotiation for a new collective bargaining agreement with the Armonk School Board, which was represented by very able counsel. They explained that they'd made a contract offer that they now regretted. Since the offer was taken under consideration by the school board for 48 hours and was not accepted, the teachers could still withdraw it.

On my advice they did so by telegram that night, and I agreed to represent them in the ensuing negotiations for a fee of $2,000, which was all they could afford. As it turned out, I devoted a few hundred hours to this matter, with another Skadden colleague also helping me, making the agreed-upon fee a "disaster" from a firm billing standpoint. (My hourly billing rate was about $70 at the time.) Still, the firm stood by my decision to undertake the representation.

The matter became a whirlwind of point, counterpoint moves. The school board refused to negotiate unless the offer was put back on the table, an offer that the board would have accepted. A state-appointed mediator entered the negotiations and told me that the offer had to go back on the table. We declined to cooperate, and the mediation collapsed.

The state then appointed a fact finder who conducted hearings at which we earnestly made the case that the teachers were entitled to a pay increase and other benefits. We were pleasantly surprised with his decision, a principled and courageous one I thought, in which he did in fact recommend a salary increase. The school board, however, immediately issued a message of disapproval and a notice of a public hearing. Support for the teachers grew, a development we did not discourage, and happily for us, on the eve of the hearing the fact finder's report was accepted and became the basis for the new contract.

This, however, wasn't the end of the matter. As we were drafting the contract language with counsel for the school board, President Nixon imposed in August 1971 a national wage freeze, prohibiting any wage increases except for executed contracts but providing for a process of exceptions administered by the Internal Revenue Service. We decided to negotiate language in the draft contract specifying that if the teachers could secure such approval, the salary increases would be retroactive, with interest.

A hearing before the Internal Revenue Service took place, with scores of teachers in attendance. Some weeks later a decision was issued approving the increases retroactively, with interest. To say there was joy among the teachers and relief on the part of their lawyers would be an understatement. (I wasn't privy to the reactions of the school board and its counsel.)

What I didn't expect was the knock on my kitchen door one morning in November of 1971. I opened the door to find Walter Ruthizer, chief of the teachers negotiating committee (and later teacher of the year at Byram Hills High School). Ruthizer gave me a letter of gratitude signed by the teachers to their lawyers at Skadden and told me that they had decided to increase our fee from $2,000 to $4,000. I never felt more appreciated, even though the number of hours spent on the case resulted in an hourly compensation rate of probably less than four dollars.

The New York City 88-Day Newspaper Strike of 1978

In 1978, I served as senior outside counsel to the New York Newspaper Printing Pressmen's Union and was confronted with the most challenging of labor situations, a strike, which closed the major newspapers of New York City (the *Times*, the *Daily News*, and the *Post*) for 88 days. Representing the union in this matter was among the most complex, consuming, and exhausting of all my experiences representing clients in labor matters.

As economic costs soared and the problems of running a modern newspaper mounted, publishers began to push their labor unions to give back some of what they had achieved in collective bargaining and shop practices over the years. There ensued in some areas of the country a series of confrontations between management and labor in the newspaper field. Some of these confrontations involved strikes and lockouts, and one dispute saw a pressmen's union lose its representation at the *Washington Post*.

When the New York City newspaper negotiations ended in 1975, word went around that the pressmen's union would be the object of special attention in the 1978 negotiations. In 1976, I was asked by William Kennedy, president of the pressmen's union, to represent his organization. After I conferred with Skadden colleagues, the firm agreed to provide representation.

Soon I was to discover that Kennedy had a keen focus on the 1978 negotiations and the eventuality of a strike or lockout. He spent practically every working hour, some in my office, thinking about the forthcoming collective bargaining negotiations. He hoped to negotiate a contract and informally explored ways to achieve that objective. He and the large bargaining committee he had put together were prepared to recommend reasonable concessions but were also determined not to compromise practices essential to the welfare of the union and its members. One of these practices involved the concept of "unit manning," or the number of employees required for each printing press of the newspaper.

It is difficult to describe the tension, crosscurrents, pressures, and confusion of a strike in which thousands, even millions, of people had an interest. When the 1978 newspaper confrontation unfolded, Kennedy was suddenly catapulted into a role that would test both his mettle and mine as his counsel.

When the strike began on August 10, 1978, Kennedy took the buffeting of adverse public opinion and bore all the abuse heaped upon him for his refusal to deviate from what he believed to be in the best interests of his union. Throughout the strike he displayed both initiative and restraint. He was tough, extremely tough, in adhering to those issues that couldn't be compromised on because they involved either the welfare of his fellow pressmen or the continued viability of his union. He patiently waited for others to realize that he wasn't going to waver. He was always the leader, strong, intelligent, courageous, and dedicated to his members. He never lost sight of the trust his union had placed in him.

Through all the tumult, Kennedy, his bargaining committee, and his membership functioned as an extraordinarily cohesive, loyal, and effective force aimed toward the objective of achieving a decent contract. Kennedy was the key strategist, and at the bargaining table, there was no one more knowledge- able about the operations of the pressroom or more articulate when it came to explaining the union's bargaining positions. He was always solicitous of the advice of counsel and was respectful of my bent to minimize the damage of a strike and to find a solution as quickly as we could.

I made suggestions, which he and his executive committee considered. He also accepted my suggestion to meet off the record with the labor representa- tives of key publishers, even though he didn't believe that the meetings would be successful. Shortly after the strike began I reached out to John Mortimer, the *Times*'s senior vice president for personnel and industrial relations, to see if we could make some progress. Often, in disputes involving automation and other issues, he had made such calls to me.

Mortimer, however, said that his hands were tied, apparently because oth- ers were directing the publishers' strategy in that confrontation and didn't want to meet. I recall saying to Mortimer that if we didn't meet, the situation would grow in intensity and the strike would be a long one. Kennedy was right that the timing was not ripe, and I was right that the strike would last a long time.

Rugged, indeed, was the path for all of us in 1978. The first major break came from Rupert Murdoch, owner of the *New York Post*. Howard Squadron, Murdoch's counsel, called me to say that his client wanted to meet with Ken- nedy and me. We met at Peter Luger, a famous New York City steakhouse, and agreed to resume negotiations, subsequently achieving an agreement after a long night of negotiations in Squadron's office.

This agreement constituted a breakthrough since the reappearance of the *Post* put pressure on the other publishers to come to the bargaining table. They did so, and with the help of Ken Moffett, a federal mediator, and the incomparable labor mediator Ted Kheel, an agreement was reached. By early November the other papers were publishing again. The last week of the strike was filled with round-the-clock negotiations for what felt like days on end, driving us all to the point of exhaustion. I had anticipated this possibility and kept in reserve a colleague named Edward Imperatore, whose work would become key.

When in the final days of the strike both parties needed help in drafting a document containing the agreed-upon terms, Imperatore was the unanimous choice. He knew the old contract and the operations of a pressroom as well as anyone, and he quickly developed a draft. To this day, I believe, the contract with the pressmen bears his fingerprints. Interestingly, the agreement reached in 1978 was not too different from the one the union had placed on the bargaining table for the industry to consider the night the strike began.

The Sprewell Decision

In 1998, I served as the NBA Grievance Arbitrator in a case involving the NBA, the Golden State Warriors, the National Basketball Players Association, and the player Latrell Sprewell. The media coverage of and public response to my decision was extensive, and some of it viewed the case through a racial lens.[1] I was severely criticized by some on the grounds that I had been too lenient on Sprewell. For a time, it felt as if there was no other news in America.

The dispute began during a Warriors practice session on December 1, 1997. The Warriors alleged that Sprewell put Coach P.J. Carlesimo in a chokehold during the practice. On the day of the conflict, after consideration and communications with the NBA's central office, the Warriors suspended Sprewell for ten games. At the time this was an extreme penalty in the sport. Two days later the club decided to terminate Sprewell's multiyear contract, and the next day the commissioner gave him a one-year suspension.

Initially the parties tried to settle the matter privately but couldn't do so, and so they asked me to arbitrate. I held hearings in Portland, Oregon, for the convenience of witnesses, including players and coaches, and in New York City. I examined the testimony and documents, examined NBA discipline precedents, and discussed the issues with six law students who helped me with research in the matter.

I then wrote a long decision, taking into account everything in the record of the proceeding. I issued my decision on March 4, 1998, and watched the media world tear into my conclusion, which called for suspending Sprewell for the rest of the season's sixty-eight games, amounting to a salary loss of $6.4 million. I restored the player's contract but ruled that, if requested by the commissioner, Sprewell was obliged to participate in an anger management program.[2]

In the section of the Sprewell decision discussing my reasons, I said as follows:

> While the violence inflicted by the Grievant on the Head Coach is to be condemned, the form of the condemnation in terms of discipline must be tempered by principles of fairness. . . . Confidence in the game of basketball is dependent not only on appropriate punishment for misconduct but also on the fairness of proceedings where that punishment is reviewed.

After a great deal of reflection and consideration, I have determined to uphold the discipline imposed by the NBA, but to limit it to the 1997/98 season. In justice and fairness the Grievant should be allowed to start the 1998/99 season with this tragic event behind him instead of having it extend into the next season. In reaching this judgment, I note that a suspension for the 1997/98 season involves the loss of 68 games and $6.4 million.

I find that a penalty of 68 games is commensurate with the severity of the misconduct, addresses the wrong done to the Head Coach, the Grievant's Team, and the NBA and conveys a message that violence in the NBA will be dealt with severely but always with due regard to principles of fairness. . . . A suspension of practically an entire season is one of great severity, to be sure, but appropriate given the fact that physical altercations with a head coach strike at the very core of a structure that provides stability for a team and an organized sport.

Having so concluded, I should note that . . . [t]he severity of the discipline, the commentary that has accompanied this matter, and the experience undergone by the Grievant may well equip him in the future years of his life to be an example of a person who can overcome adversity and be a role model. As Commissioner Stern noted at the conclusion of the testimonial portion of the hearings "[Grievant] is a gifted athlete who has done well in the NBA. . . . We want Mr. Sprewell in the NBA. We expect him to be in the NBA during the '98/'99 season."[3]

At an earlier stage of my opinion, I had discussed that terminating the player's contract, as additional discipline, was not sustainable, noting the absence of any history of joint discipline for the same conduct. I concluded: "Given the magnitude of the Warriors' earlier discipline of the Grievant [of a ten game suspension] on December 1 and the NBA having become dominant in the investigatory process after that, I am unable to sustain the termination of the Grievant's contract as meeting a standard of just cause. I also find that the conduct in question was born of anger and passion and did not constitute an act of moral turpitude, which is at the core of the Team's action."[4]

After this decision I received many comments. One was from a senior partner at the firm that represented the NBA in this proceeding. In a letter to me he said that of the entire opinion, the passage of greatest interest to him was the following: "What we have is merely a privilege offered to the jury to find the lesser degree when the suddenness of the intent, the vehemence of the passion, seems to call irresistibly for the exercise of mercy."[5] His letter, and a subsequent conversation with a class of graduate students in California, led me to suggest to students of Fordham's *Urban Law Journal* that the concept of forgiveness in the law would be a good subject for a program. In conjunction with the school's Stein Center they undertook such a program.[6]

In my remarks at that program, delivered on January 28, 2000, I said: "I lament as I see in our society the constant focus on punishment, the constant focus on retribution, and on incapacitation . . . I do not see in American society today — at least the parts I am familiar with, and that is obviously a very small part — much discussion on subjects like forgiveness and the Law."[7]

In the Sprewell case, I'd done my job as best I could.[8] Some, who had arrived at a judgment based on the media commentary, later told me that they had changed their view.

While some people described the decision as lenient in its treatment of Sprewell, Sprewell himself certainly didn't agree with this assessment, twice attacking the decision in federal court in San Francisco. He complained, among other things, that the arbitrator exceeded the scope of his authority, that the decision ran counter to California's public policy against racial discrimination, and that the parties had introduced false and doctored evidence.

In a decision filed November 7, 2000, the U.S. Court of Appeals for the Ninth Circuit affirmed the lower court's dismissal of each claim.

Eventually the matter faded into history. Nevertheless, to my surprise, in the days following the issuing of my decision, I received calls from several prominent Black lawyers to thank me for the decision, one remarking that too many people "see us as thugs." I also found a message on my telephone from someone with a Southern accent who thanked me for not responding to all the criticisms, noting that the matter had settled down. This call from a stranger was comforting.

This experience helped me to better understand the plight of judges who make decisions they believe are right but which are contrary to popular opinion. Professor Daniel Collins of New York University Law School once said to me that an arbitrator must treat every case as his last, even if this may mean not having your contract of employment as an arbitrator renewed. I have tried to act according to this principle.

Given the nature of the Sprewell case, I decided to donate my fee of $98,000 to my grammar school, an institution dedicated to supporting minority students, in memory of Mom and Pop. The school used the money to beautify the area surrounding it.

A year later I read a column in the *New York Times* by Mike Wise, headlined, "For the Knicks, a Year Has Made a Difference." "After all the testimony," Wise wrote, "Sprewell began the journey from Most Vilified Sports Figure in America . . . to Madison Square Garden Fan Favorite in less than a year."[9] Wise also noted Sprewell's ability to put his team "before himself."[10] In

2018 the Garden's James Dolan paid tribute to Sprewell after banning a player from the arena.

MIBA Versus NCAA

In 2005, I was asked to serve as mediator of controversies then pending in federal court in a suit brought by the Metropolitan Intercollegiate Basketball Association (MIBA) against the National Collegiate Athletic Association (NCAA), claiming anti-trust violations with regard to the NCAA's Division I's Men's MIBA Basketball Championship. The MIBA consisted of Fordham University, Manhattan College, New York University, Wagner College, and St. John's University. The principal spokesmen for the two organizations were John Sexton, president of New York University, and NCAA president Myles Brand.

The mediation began in early 2005, with both sides ably represented by counsel. When it became clear that the parties were far apart in their positions, I suggested that the mediation be suspended until there was a prospect of an agreement. Eventually a jury trial on the issues began in federal court, and after speaking with each party I sensed that there was a basis for bringing them together.

As the trial moved forward during the day, I facilitated nighttime communications between Sexton and Brand. When they reached a point at which they needed a full day for discussions, they asked me to call the judge hearing the case to see if she would be willing to adjourn the trial for a day. She did so, and a settlement was reached that day.

On August 17, 2005, the NCAA issued a press release announcing the settlement, which called for the NCAA to buy the rights to and operate the pre-season and post-season National Invitation Tournament (NIT). The settlement also provided for payments over ten years of $40.5 million to the NIT hosting schools and $16 million to end the litigation. Brand said of the settlement, "This is a historic day for men's college basketball. The agreement provides the NCAA with an opportunity to better define the college basketball season and build on the status of the two NIT events. We intend to grow these tournaments to showcase college basketball and the student athletes who make the game great."[11]

Brand added, "I appreciate the good will with which President Sexton and the other MIBA presidents worked to find a mutually acceptable resolution. While our interests were different, we agree on the fundamental value of college sports to higher education and the importance of moving forward as a membership committed to the future of men's college basketball."[12]

PART VII
Constitutional Endeavors

It therefore astonishes me, Sir, to find this System approaching so near to Perfection as it does; and I think it will astonish our Enemies. . . . I cannot help expressing a Wish that every Member . . . would with me . . . doubt a little of his own Infallibility.

— BENJAMIN FRANKLIN

PART VII

Constitutional Endeavors

30

Presidential Succession

The essence of statesmanship is to act in advance to eliminate
situations of potential danger.

— SENATOR ESTES KEFAUVER

When I graduated from law school in 1961, I never dreamed that I'd have the
unique opportunity to apply what I had learned about the Constitution to the
Constitution itself. I was 25 years old when it all started, likely beginning with
a newspaper item I saw in the *New York Law Journal* titled, "Constitutional
Amendment on Presidential Inability Urged."[1] The article called on President Kennedy to work for a constitutional amendment establishing a clear-cut
procedure in the event of presidential inability and described constitutional
ambiguities as to presidential inability. I mentioned the subject to my college
classmate, Louis Viola, who said he had a file of newspaper clippings that
dealt with the disabilities of President Eisenhower, who had faced major medical problems during his presidency. Upon reading the clippings, I became
fascinated by the subject and decided to research the issue and offer my ideas
as to a solution.

By early 1963, slightly more than two years after the election of President
Kennedy, I had written a long article titled "The Problem of Presidential
Inability — Will Congress Ever Solve It?" and submitted it to the *Fordham
Law Review*.[2] In its opening section, the article stated that the presence in
the White House of an "able, healthy, and young president" made it a timely
moment to consider the subject, since no observations could reflect on the
current occupant of the office.[3] I recommended a constitutional amendment
as the solution. My proposal was influenced by President Eisenhower's 1958

agreement in a letter to Vice President Nixon, which said that the president could declare his own inability, and if unable to do so, the vice president could make the decision.[4]

The article appeared in the October 1963 issue of the *Law Review*. I followed up on its publication with a letter to the *New York Times*, published on November 17, 1963, in which I wrote:

> Presidents are mortal. President Garfield's shooting, President Wilson's stroke and President Eisenhower's heart attack rendered the respective President temporarily unable to exercise the powers and duties of his office. Despite this, Congress has consistently failed the American people by not acting to eliminate the possibility of a gap in the executive because of the confusion existing over the meaning of the succession provision of the Constitution.[5]

The provision in Article 11, Section 1, Clause 6 of the Constitution left unclear the meaning of the term "inability," who determined it, and what the status of the vice president was in such a case, that is, did he become president or an acting president? To drum up support for a change in the Constitution, I sent copies of my article to people who might have an interest in the subject. But not until I began writing this chapter a few years ago did I realize that I had stored away in boxes, dating back more than fifty years, the acknowledgments I had received. Here's a sampling.

In a letter dated November 13, 1963 (less than ten days before the Kennedy assassination), Ralph Dungan, an assistant of President Kennedy, wrote: "The President has received your letter and asked me to thank you for sending him the accompanying copy of your article."[6] In a letter dated November 11, 1963, Attorney General Robert Kennedy did the same, adding: "I appreciate your bringing it to my attention as this is a subject which we have been studying here in the department for some time."

By letter dated November 5, 1963, Senator Edward Kennedy said: "I look forward to reading your discussion of this complex subject." Former Vice President Nixon said in a letter dated two days before President Kennedy's assassination:

> This is a subject in which I am most interested, but due to the heavy pressures of my legal practice at this time I would not be able to do justice to a letter commenting on the article. If my schedule should lighten up in the period ahead, I will have the article in my reading file and will try to drop you a note.

Former Vice President Henry Wallace, who had served for one term under President Franklin D. Roosevelt, had a short but interesting response, dated

November 12, 1963: "It was most kind of you to send me the article on the situation in case of the President's Inability to discharge his office. Curiously enough I gave this problem no thought while I was the Vice President." Arthur Krock, then columnist at the *New York Times*, wrote in a letter dated November 7, 1963: "I wish Congress were as much interested [in the subject] as you or I." Professor David Fellman of the University of Wisconsin, in a letter dated November 7, wrote: "[I]t may well take a constitutional amendment to solve the problem, but amendments are awfully hard to come by, and I would hope we could work something out by legislation alone."

I was touched to find among these letters one from Dean Mulligan, in which he said: "The article shows scholarship and research of the highest order. Too many of our Law Review people forget about scholarly contributions to the Review after graduation and I was therefore delighted to see your very fine piece." He added: "My only quibble with your conclusions is point 5 on page 128 giving the right to the President to declare a cessation of the inability. Query: Do you mean the Vice President or the former President. If you mean the latter, it would seem to me that problems could be created." (I had said the president.)

The dean had obviously read the article, as had Nathan Siegel, an attorney in the Office of Legal Counsel in the Department of Justice, who, in a letter dated November 19, questioned the wisdom of an impeachment remedy, as discussed in the article, in a "neglect of duty" context. By letter dated November 14, 1963, then political science professor James C. Finlay, S.J., of Fordham said: "We are always delighted at the success of our former students in this department." In a note from Nigeria, dated April 4, 1964, my college professor Father Joseph McKenna, S.J., praised the article and concluded: "The piece turned out to be timelier than you knew. Keep up the good work."

Finally, in a letter dated November 11, Lewis F. Powell Jr., president-elect of the ABA and a future U.S. Supreme Court justice, wrote: "The ABA is indeed interested in this question, and I am sure your article will be most helpful if we should be called upon again to testify. Quite obviously you have done an enormous amount of research and work in the field."[7]

The Death of President Kennedy

The focus of my writing changed dramatically on November 22, 1963 — a month after my Fordham article was published — when people around the world were shocked to learn of the assassination of President Kennedy. Like so many Americans, I took weeks to process this national tragedy. Kennedy, the grandson of Irish immigrants and the first of his faith to be elected president, was my hero. The press debated what might have happened had Kennedy lived but been disabled.

And not surprisingly, given this tragic turn of events, my article began receiving attention. On November 24, Arthur Krock cited my views in his column in the *New York Times* as part of a discussion of what would have happened had Kennedy lived but been disabled.[8] I also received a call from CBS News, asking for a copy of the article for a program it wanted to develop on presidential succession. Lowell Beck, deputy director of the ABA's Washington office, later said to me that he thought the article would be helpful for educating a group about the issue. He and other key staff urged the ABA, which already had a position on the issue, to provide renewed leadership in solving these problems.

In response, the ABA convened a two-day conference in Washington, D.C., on January 20 and 21, 1964, on the subject of presidential inability and vice presidential vacancy.[9] Twelve lawyers were invited to participate, along with several guests.[10] I was one of the twelve because of my article. I had no sense of what was to come, and, as a young associate at Skadden, I worried that involvement in this issue would divert time from my billable work at Skadden, although happily, the firm was totally supportive of this activity.

The ABA Conference and Consensus

Before the conference in Washington's celebrated Mayflower Hotel, each participant received a binder containing reading material, with my article as the first item. If nothing else, the article provided a detailed history of presidential disability from colonial America to 1963, and discussed precedents in the fifty states and foreign countries, along with the many proposals that had been made to address the problem.

The article suggested giving the president and vice president the authority to declare presidential inabilities, with the additional recommendation that, in making any determination, the vice president should secure the opinions of the heads of the executive departments — that is, the Cabinet.[11] Other material in the binder included an article by Lewis Powell; excerpts from both President Nixon's 1962 book, *Six Crises*, and the *Congressional Record*; a copy of Senate Joint Resolution 139 (S.J. Res. 139);[12] and a copy of the transcript of the June 1963 Senate hearings.

From this conference, the following consensus developed as to the possible content of a constitutional amendment addressing the issue:

> (1) [i]n the event of the inability of the President, the powers and
>   duties, but not the office, shall devolve upon the Vice President or

person next in line of succession for the duration of the inability of
the President or until expiration of his term of office;

(2) in the event of the death, resignation or removal of the President,
the Vice President or the person next in line of succession shall succeed to the office for the unexpired term;

(3) the inability of the President may be established by declaration in
writing of the President. In the event that the President does not
make known his inability, it may be established by action of the
Vice President or person next in line of succession with the concur-
rence of a majority of the Cabinet or by action of such other body
as the Congress may by law provide;

(4) the ability of the President to resume the powers and duties of
his office shall be established by his declaration in writing. In the
event that the Vice President and a majority of the Cabinet or such
other body as the Congress may by law provide shall not concur
in the declaration of the President, the continuing disability of the
President may then be determined by the vote of two-thirds of the
elected members of each House of Congress; and

(5) when a vacancy occurs in the office of Vice President the President
shall nominate a person, who, upon approval by a majority of the
elected members of Congress meeting in joint session, shall then
become Vice President for the unexpired term.[13]

I found the meetings stimulating. I was the youngest of the 12 conference committee members, but ABA president Walter E. Craig made clear
that no one was too young to participate.[14] At the meetings, I sat near Paul
Freund, longtime professor at Harvard Law School, and Senator Birch Bayh
of Indiana, a situation that offered a once-in-a-lifetime opportunity to come
to know these two distinguished figures. Freund was America's preeminent
constitutional scholar and would later write the foreword to my first book on
presidential succession;[15] Bayh would write the foreword to my book on the
amendment itself.[16]

I was impressed by the openness of the discussions, by the way people
respectfully challenged one another's points of view, and the clear desire to
reach a consensus acceptable to all. Some favored giving Congress broad
power to legislate with respect to this area, while others, including me, feared
this approach because of the possible political uses of such a power. But no
one doubted the need for substantial reform because the existing system constituted a threat to the country's safety and security.

Professor Freund, gentle and soft-spoken with an angelic quality to him,
wondered out loud whether a disability commission with a mixed composition

might be worthy of consideration. I remember commenting, shyly, that such a commission wouldn't be compatible with the principle of separation of powers because it would place the removal power outside the executive branch. (I had studied the subject of separation of powers as a Fordham College political science major.) Freund replied, without explanation, "I agree," and thereafter didn't press the idea.

Vincent Doyle of the Library of Congress, an invited guest, suggested that we combine both approaches in a constitutional amendment, granting power to determine inability to a specific body such as the Cabinet and granting Congress power to establish another body.[17] His suggestion for an alternative to the Cabinet led to the wording contained in Section 4, which allows the vice president acting with the Cabinet or "such other body as Congress may by law provide" to declare inability and its termination.[18] The "other body" expression reflected the approach of S.J. Res. 35, then pending in Congress, sponsored by New York State Senator Kenneth Keating and supported by the ABA, the New York State Bar Association, and the New York City Bar Association.

The Senate champion of the first approach was Bayh, a new young senator from Indiana, who had succeeded Senator Estes Kefauver[19] as chairman of the Subcommittee on Constitutional Amendments. Bayh's approach was reflected in a copy he had with him of S.J. Res. 139.

Unlike with the subject of presidential inability, it wasn't difficult to reach a consensus regarding how to fill a vacancy in the vice presidency. The approach of point (5) of the consensus mirrored the practice that had developed of presidential candidates selecting their running mate. The provision calling for confirmation of a vice president by both Houses of Congress was seen as a way of expressing a national consensus in support of the president's nominee for the position.

Almost as an afterthought, someone pointed out that the determination of an inability by the vice president in point (3), with the approval of the Cabinet or another body, wouldn't work if there were a vacancy in the vice presidency. A suggestion was made and accepted and placed in point (1) that the person next in line of succession should perform that role.

I recall noticing on the second day, as we were about to conclude our work, that the draft was unclear as to whether a president who had declared his own inability could be prevented from resuming his powers and duties by the vice president and the Cabinet (or another body). I suggested making it clear that there should not be a check on the president's ability to retake power in this scenario. But the conference did not accept my suggestion. Later, in a letter dated March 29, 1966, to Larry Conrad, chief counsel of the Senate's Subcommittee on Constitutional Amendments, who asked me for a chronological listing of my activities regarding the development of the amendment, I wrote:

> At the consensus sessions I strongly advocated a constitutional amendment embodying a specific method of determining inability, and spoke in favor of the determination of inability being made by the Vice President and, if another body was considered necessary, by the Cabinet.
>
> Participated in the drafting of the consensus at an informal session after the formal session on January 20, and at a breakfast conference on January 21. Emphasized at the informal session of January 20, when it was not clear whether a consensus existed, that it was incumbent upon the panel to propose a method of determining inability. At formal session of January 21 I suggested a two-thirds vote of each House to prevent the President from resuming his powers and duties.[20]

Building a National Consensus

After the ABA conference, Senator Bayh and members of Congress responded favorably to the consensus recommendations, with some exceptions. The use of a joint session of Congress for filling a vacancy in the vice presidency wasn't adopted, nor was the idea of the person next in the line of succession having authority to act with the Cabinet when there was a vice presidential vacancy.

The consensus was presented to the Senate Subcommittee on Constitutional Amendments on February 24, 1964, by Walter Craig and Lewis F. Powell.[21] I was invited to testify in my own right on February 28, as were other members of our group.[22] Present when I testified were Senators Bayh, presiding, Olin Johnston of South Carolina, Kenneth Keating of New York, and Hiram Fong of Hawaii. Below are some of the points of my testimony:

> The circumstances surrounding the death of President Kennedy should have taught us that we can no longer afford the uncertainty that presently exists regarding the critical problem of Presidential inability. . . . I am convinced that this problem can be solved. . . . To miss this opportunity and again leave unsolved one of the most serious problems ever to confront Congress would be to trifle with the security of this great nation. Therefore, we must make every human effort to agree on a workable solution.
>
> A tremendous advance in the effort at agreement was made a little over a month ago. At that time the most workable solution which I have seen to date was proposed by a group of lawyers who were called

together by the American Bar Association. . . . The very fact that 12 individuals who represented nearly as many points of view could reach such a consensus is, in my opinion, a tremendous thing. . . . I support it wholeheartedly. . . .

First, the panel agreed that a constitutional amendment is necessary to solve the problem. . . . Some members of the panel believed that Congress has no power at all to legislate on the subject—that it merely has the power to legislate on the line of succession beyond the Vice President. Most of the panel believed that the Vice President now has the constitutional power to determine inability, and therefore, this power could not be, constitutionally, taken from him by legislation. The panel further believed that if a legislative solution to the problem were enacted, it would be subject to constitutional challenge which would come very likely during a time of inability—when we could least afford it. . . .

Second, the panel recommended that an amendment make it clear that in cases of inability the powers and duties of the Presidency devolve on the Vice President for the duration of the inability, while in cases of death, resignation, and removal, the office of President devolves for the rest of the term. This would eliminate the fear that the Vice President would oust the President if he acted as President in a case of inability. It would also give constitutional recognition to the Tyler precedent . . .[23]

Third, the panel recommended that the President be able to declare his own inability in writing. There is no good reason why this should not be. . . .

Fourth, to meet the case where a President is disabled but is unwilling or actually unable to make a determination, the panel would give the decisive role to the Vice President and the Cabinet. In such a case, the Vice President with majority approval of the Cabinet could make the determination.

The panel believed that the Vice President should not have the sole power as he would be an interested party and, therefore, too reluctant to make a determination. On the other hand, it was felt that he should not be eliminated as it would be his duty to act as President and, therefore, he should have a say in determining when to act.

The Cabinet was thought to be the best possible body to assist him in making the determination. That Cabinet members are close to the President, that they would likely be aware of an inability and would know if the circumstances were such that the Vice President should act, that they are part of the executive branch, and that the public would have confidence in the rightness of their decision were reasons for the selection of this body.

A primary consideration for [this] approach was that it would involve no violation of the principle of separation of powers. It has been said that Cabinet members, out of loyalty or fear of losing their jobs, might be too hesitant to find the President disabled. This is flatly contradicted by the fact that the Garfield and Wilson Cabinet actually urged the respective Vice President to act as President.

Fifth, the panel recommended that the President should be able to resume his powers and duties upon his own declaration in writing. Because of the possibility that a President might say he was able when he was not, it was the panel's consensus that the Vice President, subject to approval by a majority of the Cabinet, should have the power to prevent him from acting in such a case.

In a case where the Vice President and a majority of the Cabinet disagrees with the President's declaration of recovery, review by Congress would be required. The Vice President would continue to act in the interim, however. It would take a two-thirds vote of both Houses of Congress to keep the President from resuming his powers and duties. A two-thirds vote was decided upon in order to weigh the provision heavily in favor of the President and also because it would conform to the two-thirds vote required by the Constitution to remove a President from office.

Sixth, the panel recommended the inclusion of a provision that Congress could change the Cabinet as the body to function with the Vice President. It was felt that this had the advantage of flexibility so that if it should become necessary to do so, Congress could, by legislation, change the procedure relatively quickly without having to resort to a constitutional amendment. (I personally did not agree with giving Congress such a power because of the potential political uses to which it might be put).

Seventh, the panel recommended that the Vice Presidency be filled at all times. It suggested that the President be allowed to nominate a new Vice President subject to confirmation by the Congress. My own examination of all the debates surrounding the various succession laws . . . suggests that the best way to solve the succession problem is by filling the Vice Presidency.[24]

The rest of my statement addressed objections that had been raised to the consensus, offered reasons for a detailed amendment, and concluded that the ABA consensus "[w]ithout further legislation . . . is complete, is practical, is consistent with the principle of separation of powers, gives the decisive role to those in whom the people would most likely have confidence, involves only persons who have been elected by the people or approved by their representatives, and embodies checks on all concerned — the President, Vice President and the Cabinet." Finally, since it would be embodied in a constitutional amendment, there would be no question about its constitutionality.[25]

I then answered questions put to me by Senators Bayh and Johnston. Senator Johnston's state of South Carolina never ratified the amendment, but I felt that I had at least addressed any concerns Johnston may have had when he told me he was "very much pleased" with my remarks.[26] I would later have other experiences testifying before Congress, but there was nothing quite like the first time.

The Post-Hearing Period

After the subcommittee hearings, I began to assist the ABA's Washington office, headed by Donald Channell and his deputy, Lowell Beck, in promoting the proposed amendment, and also Conrad, the subcommittee's chief counsel, and later Congressman Richard Poff of Virginia, a member of the House Judiciary Committee, in formulating the amendment. To become part of the Constitution, the Amendment needed approval by a two-thirds vote in each House of Congress and ratification by three-fourths of the state legislatures.

Essentially, the ABA set up a clearinghouse in its Washington office, receiving calls from members of Congress, their staffs, bar leaders, and the media regarding the proposed amendment. ABA staffers sent material to members of Congress and their staffs, called on state and local bar leaders to lobby their congressional representatives, and made regular visits to Congress and key judiciary staff members.

I was frequently on the phone with Channell and Beck, and also their assistant, Michael Spence, as the amendment worked its way through Congress in 1964 and 1965 and then through the state legislatures. I gave speeches to bar and citizen groups, explained the proposed amendment to journalists and lawyers who were assisting in the effort, wrote articles for bar journals,[27] and appeared before the New York City Bar's influential Federal Legislation Committee to advocate a change in its position.[28]

At the suggestion of my law school constitutional law professor and mentor, Leonard Manning, after I had written a second article for the *Fordham Law Review* in 1964 titled, "The Vice Presidency and the Problems of Presidential Succession and Inability,"[29] I began to write a book on the history of presidential succession. Manning's advice was to begin the book by combining my two *Law Review* articles. He also introduced me to the Fordham University Press and its head, Father Edwin Quain, S.J., who expressed an interest in publishing such a book.

Other requests came my way in 1964, including doing an analysis for the American Enterprise Institute of the pending legislative proposals on the subjects of presidential inability and vice presidential vacancy.[30] Emalie became the glue for me on this project, writing out a summary of all these proposals. In the very early years of our marriage we discussed little except presidential succession, other than our desire to have a family.

Another request I received was to serve in an advisory capacity to a prominent committee of business leaders of the Committee for Economic Development (CED), aided by several distinguished political science professors. Some of the professors favored a solution different from the one offered by the ABA, making the experience a taxing one for me. As summarized in my letter to Conrad of March of 1966:

> Some of those who worked on [a policy] statement, particularly political scientists, strenuously opposed S.J. Res. 139. I strongly supported S.J. Res. 139's approach and succeeded in getting much of it accepted by the Subcommittee [of CED]. . . . The Subcommittee, however, refused to include the Vice President in its inability solution, giving the role solely to the Cabinet.
>
> Spoke against the omission of the Vice President at the decisive meeting of the Research and Policy Committee of CED, suggesting that the Vice President should be part of any approach and emphasizing the need for consensus [referring to the ABA Consensus] at this time in history. The Research and Policy committee agreed, so that the CED recommendation which emerged was substantially the same in principle as the S.J. Res. 139 approach.[31]

As succession-related requests piled up, I spent the non-work time that I could find trying to finish my book. This would have been impossible without Emalie, who gave up her secretarial job to help me. Although pregnant with our first child in 1964, she devoted an enormous amount of time to the project, while I did what was necessary to keep my position at Skadden. Emalie researched the congressional debates surrounding the Twelfth Amendment (providing for separate electoral votes for president and vice president), drafted a chapter on the hidden inability of President Grover Cleveland (involving a secret operation for cancer on a yacht off Long Island Sound), made editing suggestions, helped compile a bibliography, and did much of the proofreading.

The result, titled *From Failing Hands: The Story of Presidential Succession*, was published in March of 1965. The book provides a detailed account of presidential succession in U.S. history, beginning with the presidential succession provision's colonial origins. It also discusses the history surrounding the provision's application, efforts to address contingencies the provision didn't address, and executive succession in state governments and in other nations.

It was thrilling to see a dozen or so copies displayed in the first-floor window of the building at 302 Broadway, a space then occupied by Fordham University Press, where I had gone to law school. A few months earlier, on December 29, 1964, our first child, Maureen Grace, was born. I recall Emalie working that month on the book's index, along with my brother Donald and my former classmate Joe Hart, and having to leave this project when Maureen was about to arrive on the scene.[32]

Some months earlier, in March of 1964, the ABA had set up a nationwide committee in its Junior Bar Conference (JBC, later called the Young Lawyers Section), which I was asked to chair. The committee was charged with obtaining grassroots support for S.J. Res. 139, the amendment that embodied much of what later would appear in the Twenty-Fifth Amendment. Another ABA committee, chaired by Herbert Brownell, was formed to buttress this effort, along with an advisory committee on which I served and for which I took on assignments.

Almost immediately, JBC committee members began reaching out to their representatives and senators in Congress to promote the passage of S.J. Res. 139. I recall Senator Bayh saying later that one Senate colleague, Harry Byrd, told him to sign him up as a supporter of S.J. Res. 139 as he'd never before heard from so many lawyers in his state. The work of young lawyers in particular was reflected in a JBC report of June of 1965, as follows:

> In the period between August, 1964, and June, 1965, the state representatives on the JBC presidential inability committee have been instrumental in getting their state and local bar associations to endorse [Senate Joint Resolution 1][33] and [House Joint Resolution 1], their newspapers to lend editorial support of these proposals, and their fellow citizens to write letters to members of the Congress urging action on them. Articles by Junior Bar leaders appeared in bar publications in Arkansas, Colorado, Georgia, Idaho, Illinois, New York, Ohio, Oklahoma, Pennsylvania, South Carolina, [and others]. Letters to the Editor by Junior Bar leaders appeared in newspapers across the country. Literally thousands of letters by citizens and organizations were sent to the members of Congress due to the leadership of junior bar leaders.

Junior bar representatives appeared on radio and television in support of prompt congressional action. . . . Speaker bureaus were set up in a number of states for the purpose of informing organizations of the problems . . . On the eve of key votes in the Senate and the House, Junior Bar leaders made telephone calls and sent letters and telegrams to their Congressmen and Senators.[34]

The report identified by name 31 state representatives who rendered "truly outstanding leadership" in this period and another 27 individuals who made substantial contributions, including Fordham graduates James Tolan and James McGough.[35]

At a meeting of Brownell's ABA committee on August 8, 1965, following the amendment's approval by both houses of Congress on July 6, 1965, Brownell stated that "no legislative effort in the history of the Association had brought more favorable attention to the ABA from members of Congress, the news media, and the public in general than the two-year program in support of the constitutional amendment."[36] Young lawyers and senior lawyers, working closely with one another and with members of Congress and their staffs, helped achieve a milestone. Now they had to turn their attention to the ratification of the amendment. Brownell urged that "it should be emphasized to state bar leaders that effective programs on the state level could likewise be of significant public relations to state and local bar associations."[37]

A January 6, 1966, report of the JBC committee, issued six months after the amendment had been proposed by Congress, said: "As of this writing, the proposed amendment has been ratified by . . . [13 states] . . . Members of this Committee played a large role in making the above ratifications possible . . . Much groundwork for ratification in the remaining states . . . is being laid by members of this committee. . . ."[38]

A year later, a JBC report issued in January of 1967 said that only six states remained for ratification, adding that "[s]ince the state legislatures are now convening, young lawyer representatives of this Committee are at work to secure the ratification of the proposed amendment. . . . Our job during the next few weeks will be to do everything in our power to accomplish this objective."[39]

Throughout this entire period, the staff of the ABA, under the leadership of Channell and Beck, were relentless, sending to bar leaders around the country packets of supporting material, including a proposed ratification model resolution and a history of the steps necessary for ratification in each state. Reprints of my articles were included, plus an effective question-and-answer handout from the May 1964 Eisenhower luncheon. Walter Craig was exceptional in his efforts, as was his successor, Lewis Powell. Craig played a key role in the ratification of the amendment in Arizona, California, and Nevada and elsewhere, while Powell brokered a key meeting between Senator Bayh and Congressman Emanuel Celler that broke a congressional impasse that could have defeated the amendment in Congress.[40]

Among the many young lawyers who made significant contributions were Mercer Tate and Franklin Kury in Pennsylvania and Richard Hansen, an ABA conference member who gave dozens of speeches throughout Nebraska in support of the amendment and had the joy of seeing his state's legislature become the first to support ratification on July 12, 1965. I didn't focus on this seminal date until I began writing this chapter, as I was probably celebrating that day the last of my birthdays (29th) in my twenties.

The late Dale Tooley of Colorado also stood out for his remarkable leadership. He took on the task of dealing with two major newspapers, the *Denver Post* and *Rocky Mountain News*, that were pitted against each other, with the latter favoring the amendment and the former opposing it. The *Post* objected to the provisions of Section 4, which involved, it said, too many interested parties. The newspaper also complained that the provision for the president nominating and Congress confirming a vice presidential nominee was undemocratic. Tooley, who would become Denver's district attorney, encouraged the Colorado state bar to adopt the cause as a high priority and the state's representatives in Congress to vote for it.

Personal Communications

By letter dated April 10, 1964, I was asked by Beck whether, under the ABA consensus, an acting president could nominate a replacement vice president if the president was disabled and the vice president had died. I expressed hesitancy about the acting president doing so in that context.

In response to Beck's request, I wrote to Conrad on May 22, 1964, and explained the ABA recommendation that the vice president should continue to act as president until Congress reached a decision in a situation where a president disagreed with an inability determination by the vice president and the heads of the executive departments, noting that the ABA's view was "premised on the thinking that Congress would act immediately to decide the issue." I reasoned that Congress would be under pressure from the people to act and that it would have a "moral and legal obligation" to do so. I suggested to Conrad the following provision:

> Whenever the President makes public announcement in writing
> that his inability has terminated, he shall resume the discharge of the
> powers and duties of his office on the *second* day after making such

announcement, or at such earlier time after such announcement as he and the Vice President may determine, except that if the Vice President, with the written approval of a majority of the heads of executive departments in office at the time of such announcement, transmits to the Congress his written declaration that in his opinion the President's inability has not terminated, the Vice President shall continue to act as President and the Congress shall immediately thereupon consider the issue.[41]

On June 2, 1964, I explained to Conrad the reasons for the ABA's recommendation of a constitutional amendment, rather than a statute, for filling a vacancy in the vice presidency:

It may be that Congress has the power to create an office of Acting Vice President . . . and to make the Acting Vice President the Officer next in line of succession after the Vice President . . . However, the Acting Vice President would not be able to preside over the Senate in that capacity, since this function is given only to the Vice President provided for in the Constitution.

By letter, dated June 5, 1964, to Robert Nordhord, a staff member of the House Office of the Legislative Counsel, I discussed the ABA's recommendation for a two-thirds vote in Congress in a case where the president disagrees with an inability determination by the vice president and Cabinet and its recommendation of a majority vote in Congress for filling a vice presidential vacancy. With respect to the disagreement scenario, I said:

[T]he Vice President would . . . act as President until Congress had decided the issue. The ABA consensus contained no specific recommendation as to how the disagreement issue might be presented to Congress . . . [T]he Vice President should be required to transmit to the Congress, in writing, a disagreement declaration within a certain period of time. If Congress were not then in session, he would be obliged to convene a special session before such period has expired. If he failed to transmit a declaration to Congress within this period, the President would thereupon resume his powers and duties . . . Congress would be required to decide the issue . . . as soon as possible. If the Congress failed to decide the issue, or delayed for an unreasonable amount of time, the Vice President would still continue to act as President under the ABA consensus.

On June 23, 1964, in a letter to Channell, I explained that the U.S. Supreme Court wasn't given a role in determining a president's inability under the consensus because of separation of powers, the views of Chief Justice Earl Warren in opposition to Justices serving on a disability commission,[42] the analogy of the impeachment process involving only Congress, and the desirability of having a body like the Cabinet that could act quickly and unanimously.

S.J. Res. 139 was approved by the Senate Subcommittee on Constitutional Amendments on May 27, 1964, with amendments, and by the full Judiciary Committee on August 4. The full committee issued a supporting report on August 13, 1964.[43] The Senate approved the amendment by voice vote on September 28, 1964 (with only nine Senators present),[44] and again the next day by a roll call vote of 65–0.[45] The Amendment was reintroduced in the 89th Congress as Senate Joint Resolution 1 (S.J. Res. 1), in a form identical to House Joint Resolution 1 (H.R.J. Res. 1), which was also introduced in January 1965.

In a letter dated January 5, 1965, to House Judiciary Committee Chair Celler, Channell noted:

> A press release will be issued tomorrow commending you for sponsoring the proposed amendment and there will be a story on the American Bar News which is sent to 118,000 members. Also, I plan to devote considerable space to this subject in the Washington Letter which is sent to all bar associations and to 6,000 bar leaders.

In a letter dated January 25, 1965, I informed Channell of a meeting I'd had with Senator Hruska's assistant, and possibly with Hruska himself briefly, hoping to persuade the Senator not to oppose S.J. Res. 1. The senator had expressed concerns about the wording of the provisions giving Congress a role in determining an inability in the event of an inability disagreement and its power to substitute a different body for the Cabinet. The senator was a supporter of the office of the president and separation of powers, and gave strong supporting testimony before Congress concerning the proposed amendment.

On January 28, 1965, President Lyndon B. Johnson sent a special message to Congress, urging adoption and ratification of S.J. Res. 1 and H.R.J. Res. 1, stating that the provisions have been "carefully considered and are the product of many of our finest constitutional and legal minds." In February of 1965, the Senate unanimously approved S.J. Res. 1, as amended.[46] Then the House Judiciary Committee began hearings on H.R.J. Res. 1 and more than thirty other proposals for dealing with the inability problem, some containing a time limitation placed on congressional action if a presidential declaration of recovery were challenged.

On February 7, 1965, I responded to a request from Congressman Poff asking for language to cover certain contingencies. I stated that I saw essentially three situations: (1) the simultaneous inabilities of the vice president and president; (2) the inability of an acting president, and (3) the inability of a president when there is no vice president. I proposed the following provisions for incorporation in H.R.J. Res. 1:

(6) The inability of the Vice President shall be determined in the same manner as that of the President except that the Vice President shall have no right to participate in such determination.

(7) In case of the death, resignation, removal or inability of the Vice President, the person next in line of succession shall act in lieu of the Vice President under Sections 4 and 5 with the heads of the Executive Departments or other body as Congress may by law provide. (Please note that the ABA consensus had a provision along these lines.)

The letter also contained suggestions for greater clarity in the legislative history regarding the wording of the then-proposed amendment. In abbreviated form, these suggestions dealt with the proposed 10-day time limit for congressional action with respect to an inability disagreement (I thought the limit was unnecessary because of the term "immediately" in the proposal); whether the vice president acts as president during the period in which Congress decides a disagreement (as recommended by the ABA consensus);[47] whether Congress would have the power to remove the vice president from an inability determination (I said it could not under the ABA consensus); the reach of the term "vacancy" for nominating a new vice president (I said that the term was limited to death, resignation, and removal); the calling of a special session by the vice president if Congress were out of session (I said it should be mandatory when a disagreement issue is raised); the need for the transmittal of an inability declaration to Congress to be spelled out in some manner (I suggested that rules were needed); the taking of the presidential oath of office by an acting president (I said this should be the case);[48] whether an acting president can preside over the Senate (not under the Constitution); and the salary for a vice president acting as president (I recommended that it be at the presidential rate).

On February 13, 1965, I wrote to Beck, as he requested, to offer comments on testimony given by Attorney General Nicholas Katzenbach that a proposed amendment should make clear that a president declaring his own inability can resume his powers and duties upon his recovery declaration without any check by the vice president and Cabinet. I recommended such clarification, which the ABA leadership accepted. As I reflected to Conrad in my letter of March 1966:

I think it is important to note that I made a motion to this effect on the second day of the Washington Conference in January 1964, and that motion was unanimously (with the exception of my vote) defeated. The panel took the position that the recovery provisions should apply whenever a disabled President sought to resume his powers and duties, regardless of how his disability had been determined. Personally, I am in favor of the clarification (though I think language is required to carry it into effect) but, for the record, it is not consistent with the consensus.

In a letter dated February 16, 1965, Poff responded: "During the course of interrogation, I have tried to write some of the legislative history you suggested."[49] As noted, the Senate approved S.J. Res. 1, as modified, on February 19, 1964, and the House Judiciary Committee approved H.R.J. Res. 1, as amended, on March 24.

On April 1, 1965, Channell wrote that substantial opposition could develop in the House of Representatives because the House Rules Committee, by a 6–4 vote, had limited debate, granting only a four-hour open rule. He said that "most members of the House of Representatives are not fully advised as to the need for this amendment."

In an April 5th letter to Poff, as a vote approached in the House, I suggested that he consider drawing on the wisdom of Benjamin Franklin from the Constitutional Convention of 1787:

> I agree to this Constitution with all its faults, if they are such; because I think a general Government necessary for us . . . I doubt too whether any other Convention we can obtain may be able to make a better Constitution. For when you assemble a number of men to have the advantage of their joint wisdom, you inevitably assemble with those men, all their prejudices, their passions, their errors of opinion, their local interests, and their selfish views. From such an assembly can a perfect production be expected?
>
> It therefore astonishes me . . . to find the system approaching so near to perfection as it does . . . Thus I consent . . . to this Constitution because I expect no better, and because I am not sure, that it is not the best . . . On the whole, Sir, I cannot help expressing a wish that every member of the Convention who may still have objections to it, would with me, on this occasion doubt a little of his own infallibility — and to make manifest our unanimity, put his name to this instrument.[50]

In his acknowledgment letter of April 7, Poff said:

> Frankly, John, looking back down the corridor of the years of labor and scholarship which have finally brought us to this point so near to success, I am a little aghast at the dimensions and weight of the

responsibility which is mine. What, if after all this struggle, we should fail to persuade two-thirds? The thought has kept me awake at night. I am sure, with so much of yourself invested in this chore, you must share the anxiety I feel.

I felt Poff's anxiety. He added that the Franklin quote was "very helpful" and that "it fits precisely into the speech I want to make while the rule is under consideration."

On April 9, 1965, I sent a letter to the editor of the *Wall Street Journal* concerning its editorial of April 5, 1965, which had opposed the amendment. I corrected errors in the editorial as I saw them. Although the letter wasn't published, the points it made were shared in discussions I had with ABA staff members and congressional staff.

Another letter of mine on April 9, 1965, to Representative Charles Mathias, after a telephone call with him, was designed to dispel his concern that the amendment might repeal Congress's line of succession authority under Article II. I assured him that there was no intention to change such authority, and therefore, there was no need for such authority to be written into the Twenty-Fifth Amendment. Despite this effort at persuasion, Mathias didn't vote for the proposed amendment, but later, as it was being reviewed for ratification by the Maryland legislature, he declined to speak against it, as he had planned to do, in the face of strong support for the amendment in that body.[51]

On April 13, 1965, the House approved its version of the amendment, 368 to 29, containing a 10-day time limit for congressional action in the event of an inability disagreement.[52] Poff sent me a letter of the same date about my participation in the cause of reform and asked that I give consideration to the matter described in a letter he sent that day to Channell. He said that on the date of the House vote the following occurred:

Late in the afternoon the Speaker came to the Republican committee table and paid me a warm personal tribute for which I was very grateful. In the course of the conversation, he asked if I would introduce the "forty-eight hour" amendment. I told him that Chairman Celler had discussed it with me and I had agreed to introduce it. As the *Congressional Record* shows, the Speaker took the floor to urge support of the amendment. The Speaker's address, eloquent and persuasive as well as dramatic, was the factor which made our margin of success possible.

Poff added that the amendment he offered was a "tactical expression" and "nothing more than that." He said that he thought it was "unneeded to accomplish what the Speaker wanted," adding that it "may be a complicating factor which might cause serious problems at a critical time." Earlier I had shared with Poff and others such a concern on my part; Section 4 of the Amendment as adopted states: "Thereupon Congress shall decide the issue, assembling within 48 hours . . . if not in session."[53] I worried about the effect of Congress not assembling until after that 48-hour period.

In a letter to Poff dated April 19, 1965, as the conference committee of the two houses was about to try to resolve their differences, I shared my views. First, the 48-hour provision, while unwise, should remain as it was, as favored by Speaker McCormack. Second, the provision for placing a 10-day time limit on congressional action in the event of a disagreement, then strongly opposed by the Senate, should have a longer time period, like 15 days. Changing my earlier view on the subject of a limit, I said it would be a "safeguard for the disabled President."

"If the Vice President and Cabinet disagreed with a presidential declaration of recovery," I reasoned, "the Congress would be obliged to decide the issue as soon as possible, giving the various parties ample opportunity to be heard." I concluded: "It would appear to me that if after a Conference you had to give up the 48-hour provision in order to retain the 10-day provision (perhaps as extended), Speaker McCormack would be pleased as the House measure would have, in the main, remained intact." I also noted as desirable the change made in the language of Section 3 that a voluntary declaration by the president gave him the ability to resume his powers and duties on his own initiative without any check.

By a letter dated April 23, Poff replied:

> Your letter . . . illustrates that you are not wholly without political
> "savvy." Why is it, John, that most people, particularly intellectuals,
> seem to derive some particular pride from a confession of political na-
> iveté? As a practical politician, I can only hope that this is a Freudian
> scream of secret admiration for things political.

He was probably right, but I was also just 28 years old, and not wanting to appear presumptuous. Poff's letter noted approvingly that I agreed with him on the use of a time limit. He indicated his flexibility on the time period itself, and asked if I knew anyone who could approach the Speaker on the 48-hour provision. Probably wisely, I left the latter issue alone.

On April 20, 1965, in response to Brownell's request for my views, I wrote him advising that the 10-day provision would not be inconsistent with the ABA consensus.

In the weeks that followed, Poff and I had other communications, mainly regarding the time limitation. On May 26, 1965, I had conversations with Beck and Conrad and learned that the "conferees had a heated discussion regarding the 10-day provision," with the House not wanting to go beyond 14 days and with Representative William McCulloch as the main line of resistance.

On May 27, 1965, I wrote Poff after learning that the two Houses were at an impasse as to whether the time limitation should be 14 or 21 days. I explained why there was not much difference between 14 and 21 days. I stated that 21 days was not "an unreasonable outside limitation for that most extraordinary situation where Congress might delay, without good cause, in deciding a disagreement issue," and suggested that since 21 days "would allow for a more complete investigation than either 10 or 14 days I would be inclined to go along with such limitation." I sent copies of my letter to Bayh, Brownell, and Beck, which concluded: "I send you these thoughts in the hope that they may have some value."

By a letter dated May 28, Poff wrote me and stated: "Since I am one of the conferees and since what I am about to say would have the effect of weakening our bargaining power, I must ask you to keep it in confidence. I would certainly accept 21 days if failure to do so would mean the loss of the amendment."[54] On June 1, I learned from Channell that Poff and McCulloch, then the ranking Republican on the Judiciary Committee, had agreed to 21 days. By a memorandum dated June 2, Channell advised that Bayh and Celler had met that day and had agreed on a time limit of 21 days but that it was "to remain confidential until each of them [could] discuss the matter with their respective conferees."[55]

As a historical note, it appears that the Senate's willingness to accept a time limit of 21 days was influenced by Senator Sam Ervin Jr. of North Carolina. He had dug in on 21 days, accepting an unprecedented limitation on Senate action. Bayh and Senate Minority Leader Everett Dirksen also agreed on this limit. In a confidential memorandum of June 14, Channell noted that all of the conferees except McCulloch had agreed to the 21-day provision. It was unclear why McCulloch was opposed to 21 days at this point, given his earlier acquiescence of 21 days and Poff's confidential letter of May 28.

In the late spring of 1965, as passage of the amendment was imminent, I was asked by the *ABA Journal* to write an article for the national bar explaining the amendment. I did so and followed up with a more detailed explanation for the *Fordham Law Review*.[56] Other troubling issues, however, surfaced at this time. One issue involved determining when the 21-day period for congressional review of an inability disagreement would begin if Congress were out of session. Would it start on the day Congress assembled or on the date the vice president and Cabinet had raised the inability issue by written declaration?

The amendment ultimately provided that Congress would have 48 hours to assemble before the 21 days would start to run.

The Senate conferees wanted the former and apparently the House wanted the latter. Channell asked me for drafting suggestions and that I call him on Sunday night, June 7, as the conferees would be meeting the following Monday or Tuesday. The language I proposed was passed along to Conrad and became part of the Section 4 drafting process. Channell noted in a letter dated June 9, 1965, that he had discussed my suggestions "with Larry Conrad and believe[d] they were very helpful to him."

The language I received to review provided:[57]

> Thereupon, Congress shall decide the issue, assembling within 48 hours for that purpose if not in session. If the Congress, *within 21 days after the receipt of the written declaration* of the Vice President and a majority of the principal officers of the executive departments or such other body as Congress may by law provide, determines by 2/3 vote of both Houses that the President is unable to discharge the powers and duties of the office, the Vice President shall continue to discharge the same as Acting President; otherwise, the President shall resume the powers and duties of his office.

The language I suggested was as follows:

> Thereupon Congress shall decide the issue, assembling within forty-eight hours for that purpose if not in session. If the Congress, *within 21 days after receipt of the said declaration, or, if not in session, within twenty-one days after such assembling,* determines by two-thirds vote of both Houses that the President is unable to discharge the powers and duties of his office, the Vice President shall continue to discharge the same as Acting President; otherwise, the President shall resume the powers and duties of his office.

The final wording was:

> Thereupon Congress shall decide the issue, assembling within forty-eight hours for that purpose if not in session. If the Congress, *within twenty-one days after receipt of the latter written declaration, or, if Congress is not in session, within twenty-one days after Congress is required to assemble,* determines by two-thirds vote of both Houses that the President is unable to discharge the powers and duties of his office, the Vice President shall continue to discharge the same as Acting

President; otherwise, the President shall resume the powers and duties of his office.

In a letter dated June 16, 1965, which followed the issuance of the joint conference committee report resolving the differences between the two Houses, I wrote a note of thanks to twenty-nine members of the JBC committee. This turned out to be premature, however. On June 25, I saw the final conference committee's version of the amendment, reprinted in a *New York Times* article,[58] and several issues jumped out at me right away. As summarized in my letter to Conrad of March 29, 1966:

> By letter to Don Channell dated June 25, 1965 (see copy attached) advised that the "either/or" language . . . was ambiguous and suggested different language. Was advised . . . that it was 'too late' for any changes and that those consulted on the point thought there was no ambiguity. On July 1, 1965[59] . . . I received a call from Don Channell . . . that Senators Gore, McCarthy and others had succeeded the previous day in postponing debate on the amendment, having argued that the "either/or" expression was ambiguous. Spoke later in the day with you and spent the next few days doing legal research in the Suffolk bar library . . . to support the use of the "either/or" expression. Results (case citations) telephoned in to you [Conrad] on Saturday, July 3 and Monday, July 5.

What I telephoned in to Conrad, based on my research, was that the use of the phrase "either/or" meant that only one body could have such power — either the Cabinet, as in the amendment, or another body created by law to replace the Cabinet. I rejected a possible construction, not intended by the ABA consensus, of two bodies being in existence at the same time, each with the power to declare a president disabled. The "either/or" language, I was told, came from an assistant to Senator Hruska, reflecting Hruska's concern that the existing language might enable Congress to remove the vice president from the process of determining a president's inability.

Finally, I remember being startled again when, at the last moment, I noticed a scrivener's error in the draft of the conference report.[60] When I reached Senator Bayh's staff by telephone to share my observation, I was told that the amendment had been approved just that day by the Senate, 68 to 5, and was on its way to the states for ratification. In other words, the amendment was beyond rescue for correction.

On July 7, 1965, I sent a letter of congratulations to Poff on the passage of the amendment, stating that the "time limitation of Section 4 can properly be referred to as the 'Poff provision.'"

On July 8, Poff wrote me a poignant letter, asking:

Why the Washington press has so studiously avoided any mention of any Republican on either side of the Capitol in connection with this project. . . . As you know, our party is so frequently and mercilessly condemned as negative that it does seem that when we assume a positive posture and make a positive contribution, we should be accorded at least minor recognition. Do you think I am unreasonable?

I subsequently responded to Poff, noting that the ABA gave credit to both political parties and that no amendment would have been possible without President Eisenhower, Attorney General Brownell, and other Republicans, especially including Poff and McCulloch. Later Poff would write a very thoughtful review of my book in which he provided important perspectives on the differences between the two Houses in the development of the amendment.[61]

A memorandum of July 9, which I sent to the Junior Bar Conference of the ABA, stated optimistically that President Lewis Powell and former Attorney General Herbert Brownell "firmly believe that your outstanding work was instrumental in the overwhelming vote in the House of Representatives and the Senate . . . The task of getting this measure ratified is largely ours."

On July 8, I attended a celebratory gathering at the Washington office of the ABA. I made a memorandum for my files of a conversation I had with Bayh, in which he stated that "problems kept occurring up to the time the amendment was voted upon which left the outcome in doubt." He mentioned an editorial in an Alabama newspaper, which noted that under the amendment, if Johnson died, Humphrey could nominate Rev. Martin Luther King Jr. for vice president.

As a result of this editorial a number of congressmen from the South apparently told Bayh that they would have to vote against the amendment. Bayh dissuaded them from doing so. He also mentioned a voting strategy of moving the amendment immediately after Senators Gore and McCarthy voiced their objections to the use of "either/or." According to Conrad, a week before the vote Bayh accused McCarthy of trying to "kill the amendment," to which McCarthy replied in the negative and said he'd vote for it, although he didn't do so on July 6.

I add a few additional communications bearing on the ratification of the Amendment:

By letter dated October 28, 1965, I responded to Senator Bayh's request for my views on amending the statutory line of succession, stating: "In order to avoid confusion I would be inclined to defer such action until the proposed Twenty-Fifth Amendment has been ratified. I think it would be appropriate, however, at that time to amend the law so to add the Secretary of Health, Education and Welfare and the Secretary of the Housing and Urban Department to the line of succession."[62] I also suggested adding a provision to compensate the vice president at the presidential rate whenever he acts as president.

A memorandum in my file of January 18, 1966, records a call from Conrad on that date for permission to distribute my 1965 *Fordham Law Review* article to members of the West Virginia Legislature because some members were confused "as to the meaning of the amendment to such an extent that ratification was in doubt." I gave permission and copies were thermofaxed for distribution in that state. Two days later the amendment was ratified in the state of West Virginia. Alabama presented a different kind of challenge, as Governor George Wallace was looking for opportunities to rally against any new congressional action, based on principles of states' rights. The Alabama State Bar, for that reason, hesitated lobbying in 1965 for Alabama to ratify the amendment. In time, however, Alabama would become the 43rd state to ratify the amendment on March 14, 1967.

The amendment, as proposed, contained a seven-year time limit for ratification, following a similar time limit established for other constitutional amendments in the twentieth century. It was ratified on February 10, 1967, when Minnesota and Nevada added their approval, giving rise to the question as to which state officially placed the Amendment in the Constitution.[63] All told, 47 states have ratified the Amendment. The three that did not were Georgia, North Dakota, and South Carolina.

Special Moments

Looking back, several moments remain vivid.

The first was meeting President Eisenhower in an anteroom of the Mayflower Hotel on May 24, 1964, just before he gave a speech in support of the proposed reform. I was overwhelmed to have an opportunity to shake his hand. He was reserved in appearance, humble, and deferential. No one was quite sure what he would say, a point that Senator Bayh discusses in *One Heartbeat Away: Presidential Disability and Succession*.[64] To everyone's pleasant surprise, Eisenhower put his enormous weight behind the drive for the amendment, describing his personal experiences with medical disabilities and his faith in the office of the vice president and the executive branch being able to deal with the issue responsibly. He did not push for a disability commission, as some believed he might.

The speech was connected to a program organized by the ABA. I contributed to a handout that was distributed at the program, which contained a descriptive history of the problem of presidential inability followed by a question-and-answer section. The questions included: Why is a constitutional amendment necessary? May the president voluntarily declare his inability? May the president be declared disabled other than by his voluntary action? Why should the office of vice president be filled at all times? Why not hold a general election for a new vice president? The handout became a useful document for the ABA to circulate to people seeking information on the amendment.

A second moment involved a communication I received in late 1965 from Stephen Lesher, press secretary to Senator Bayh, mentioning an article in the *South Carolina Law Review* by Professor George Haimbaugh Jr., titled "Vice Presidential Succession: A Criticism of the Bayh-Celler [sic] Plan." Lesher said that the article was being widely distributed among state legislators and asked if I would write a response, explaining that if left unanswered, the article "could be trouble."

Fortunately, the *South Carolina Law Review* invited me to offer a rebuttal,[65] to which Haimbaugh gave a short response. ABA members in Arkansas were also doing their part to answer the charges contained in Haimbaugh's article. They were effective in removing a block on the amendment in the state legislature and securing a favorable vote on its ratification. We did less well in South Carolina, as noted.

Another memorable moment involved a communication of February 2, 1966, that I received from Tooley, in which he noted that the ratification vote in Colorado "will be extremely close, and we are bending every effort to contact those who have indicated a willingness to reconsider their opposition to the amendment. As well as all of the others who voted 'no' on second reading. You will probably see the results of the vote in the press."[66] The next day, February 3, I was surprised to read an article in the *Rocky Mountain News*, undoubtedly the handiwork of Tooley, reporting that reprints of an article of mine were being widely distributed in the state. The article provided an analysis of every section of the amendment, concluding with this rallying cry:

Despite widespread recognition of the serious need for a method
of determining presidential inability and, despite a long search for
an acceptable method, none has ever been found and proposed by
Congress . . . It is doubtful that a better proposal could be devised,
considering the complexity of the problems involved and the great diversity of views. The proposed twenty-fifth amendment has been made

possible because of the willingness of Democrats and Republicans alike to compromise in the best interests of the Nation. It remains for the state legislators to ratify it and to make it a permanent part of the Constitution. The nature of the subject dictates that this be done with all due speed.[67]

These words reflect the strong influence of Benjamin Franklin's clarion call of September 17, 1787, and on February 3, 1966, Colorado became the eighteenth state to ratify the amendment.

As for New York State, although my letter to the Speaker of the State Assembly elicited his statement that his body would approve the amendment shortly, the chair of the Senate Judiciary Committee wrote that the group had more pressing items on its agenda. There may also have been some confusion over whether a ratification vote required a public referendum.

I passed along this letter to Brownell, who immediately wrote a letter to the chair, leading to a different result: The committee would take up the subject shortly, and it did, with the result that the amendment was ratified in New York State on March 14, 1966. Prior to its approval, I lobbied the leadership of the New York City Bar Association to adopt a resolution favoring the amendment, reflecting the position it had taken based on the work of its Federal Legislation Committee. It adopted such a resolution and sent it on to the legislature and Governor Rockefeller.

On November 15, 1966, at a meeting of the New York City Bar Association, Herbert Brownell and I received a special award from ABA president Orison Marden for our work in the development of the amendment. The award was presented in the main meeting room of the association's building on West 44th Street, a floor below where Emalie had done her research in connection with the writing of *From Failing Hands*.

The White House, February 23, 1967

When the Twenty-Fifth Amendment was ratified on February 10, 1967, it became part of the U.S. Constitution. Although the president of the United States has no role in approving an amendment, President Johnson wished to have a White House ceremony to announce its adoption and issue an accompanying proclamation. I was invited to this historic event, which was scheduled for February 23, 1967.

When I arrived at LaGuardia Airport on the designated day, I learned that all flights were delayed due to snow. I was comforted, however, when I saw Orison Marden, believing that his presence meant the bad weather was expected to clear. However, soon later, he told me he was returning to his New York City law office, believing our departure to be hopeless. I waited and waited, and then, to my surprise, I heard the announcer say that a flight to Washington would take off shortly. I jumped aboard, although when the plane arrived in Washington, the ceremony had already begun. I hailed a cab, and it sped to the White House.

Arriving at the gate with the invitation in one hand and a small attaché case in the other, I was waved through by the guard(s) and within seconds I was at the door of the White House. Upon opening it, I saw the president emerge from the East Room, where he had given remarks marking the ratification, which I later read in his official papers.[68] He rushed to the Blue Room followed by many people, including Congressman Poff, who signaled me to join him near the front of the line to greet the president. Before I could do so, security pulled me aside, took my attaché case, and asked me what I was doing there. I explained who I was and was then allowed, without the attaché case, to join Poff on the line.

The photograph I subsequently received, signed by the president, showed me shaking his hand with my eyes closed and wearing a suit badly wrinkled by the weather. But it captured the exhilaration I experienced from meeting the president. Poff subsequently wrote me a letter, saying that the picture might have had at the bottom the words, "From Failing Hands."[69]

Uses of the Amendment

Six years later, in 1973, I was stunned to see the amendment implemented, in circumstances I never expected: the resignation of an elected vice president, Spiro Agnew, followed by his replacement, under Section 2 of the amendment, allowing a president to fill a vacancy in the office of vice president; then the resignation nine months later of President Richard Nixon and the succession to the presidency of Vice President Gerald Ford, pursuant to Section 1, following which Vice President Nelson Rockefeller was chosen under Section 2, nominated by President Ford.

In connection with these uses of the amendment, Senator Bayh asked me, in the summer of 1973, to prepare a memorandum for the Judiciary Committee on the legislative history of Section 2[70] and then to testify before the Subcommittee on Constitutional Amendments on the first applications of the amendment. I did so along with Professor Paul Freund and George Reedy, the White House press secretary for President Johnson. We all supported the first implementations of the amendment. Reedy said:

When I was preparing for this hearing, I consulted a number of my friends and people who have studied the matter, and the general conclusion I came to is that the workings of the amendment are so well accepted, and the legitimacy of the present President is so well recognized, that it does not occur to anyone, except to people who do not like the current President, to challenge the workings of the Amendment.[71]

Professor Freund testified "that no persuasive case has been made for repealing or altering section 2 of the amendment."[72]

My testimony described the legislative history of the Amendment. I concurred with other witnesses who said that a succeeding vice president appointed under the Twenty-Fifth Amendment, as well as a statutory successor such as the Speaker, could nominate a successor vice president. Freund agreed, as did James Kirby, in their separate testimony. I also advanced in my testimony, on behalf of the ABA, a recommendation that in future invocations of Section 2, joint rather than separate hearings of the two Houses of Congress should occur, even though the Houses would vote separately on the issue of confirmation in order to facilitate the selection of a new Vice President and reduce the risks associated with a vacancy in that office.

Senator Strom Thurmond of South Carolina had only one question for me: "Mr. Feerick, from your statement, I conclude that the American Bar Association had an active part in the formulation of the 25th amendment; and it is the position of the American Bar Association, and your personal position too, that it has worked, and there is no need to change. Is that correct?"[73] I replied, "Yes, sir."

Reform after the Twenty-Fifth Amendment

In the 1990s, I found myself immersed in the question of the Amendment's adequacy. This came about as a result of a recommendation in 1994 by President Jimmy Carter that the American Academy of Neurology organize a forum on presidential disability. They sought greater involvement by the medical community in the determination of presidential inability. This in turn resulted in the convening of a working group on disability in U.S. presidents.

I declined to participate in its early going, believing that I was too fixed in my points of view about the adequacy of the Amendment from a conflict-of-interest perspective. As I was told when I was invited to participate, the group's organizers generally agreed that the Amendment was not adequate, almost suggesting, as I remember the conversation, that its approach should be changed to include the participation of doctors in the process. When also asked by the ABA to be its representative on the group, I instead recommended that Joel Goldstein, a professor at Saint Louis University School of Law and a scholar on the vice presidency, be its representative, as he became.

This working group subsequently organized major sessions at the Carter Center in January of 1995, Wake Forest University in November of 1995, and the White House Convention Center in Washington in December of 1996. The next year, the working group published an impressive volume entitled "Presidential Disability—Papers, Discussions and Recommendations on the Twenty-Fifth Amendment and Issues of Inability and Disability in Presidents of the United States," edited by James Toole and Robert J. Joynt.[74] I was encouraged to participate in the Wake Forest Conference's plenary session and at the Convention Center meeting where the group's final recommendations were actively considered.

The Wake Forest Conference is memorable. Senator Bayh and I participated on a plenary panel where we expressed reservations about proposals from some in the medical community to give doctors an increased role in determining presidential inability under the Twenty-Fifth Amendment. The conference was opened by President Gerald Ford who, in a friendly aside beforehand, asked Senator Bayh what to say (though the president already had his prepared remarks). Bayh, with a hand on my elbow, pointed to an article I drafted for the *Wake Forest Law Review* supporting the amendment and summarizing my comments for the panel discussion.[75]

At the White House Convention Center, I opposed some aspects of the recommendations up for discussion. One called for a separate determination by doctors of "presidential impairment" before a political judgment of "presidential inability," which caused me to join in a minority opinion as to the desirability of such a recommendation. I was joined in that opinion by both Professor Goldstein and Senator Bayh. We concluded with the statement that "decisions regarding the exercise of executive power under the Twenty-Fifth Amendment . . . should be made by accountable constitutional officials, not by doctors, attorneys, or others who have not been elected by the people or confirmed by their representatives."[76]

I have continued to be involved in areas surrounding the Amendment since its ratification.

In 1976, I published the book *The Twenty-Fifth Amendment*, which has since become a reference on the Amendment's adoption and implementation and was nominated for a Pulitzer Prize. Two subsequent editions have been published: a second in 1992 and a third in 2014. From time to time, I continue to publish articles on the subject.[77]

I also developed two presidential succession clinics at Fordham, the first in 2010, with co-Professors Dora Galacatos and Nicole Gordon, and the second in 2016, with co-Professor John Rogan, enabling students to study the procedures for handling presidential and vice presidential deaths and disabilities. I have also been a reference for others on the Amendment and circumstances justifying its implementation. The 2016 election led to dramatically increasing attention to the Amendment, as questions were raised about its application in regards to the incumbent president.[78]

Postscript

Senator Bayh died on March 14, 2019, as I was finishing this book. His death filled me with many emotions, and memory brought me back to all my experiences working with him. It was a highlight of my life to be a young lawyer watching and assisting him successfully amend the Constitution once and attempting to amend it again to abolish the Electoral College system.[79]

In 2017, as his health declined, he had called on me and his former legislative assistant, Jay Berman, to assist him in responding to media requests about the Twenty-Fifth Amendment. The day before he died, I gave Senator Bayh's beloved wife, Kitty, a message to read to him, thanking him for being a wonderful role model for me and for his example of serving the public greatly throughout his long life. I appreciated her reading it to him and her mention of me in her moving and beautiful eulogy of her husband in Indiana.[80] In October 2019, Fordham Law School held a program celebrating Senator Bayh's legacy, articles from which appear in the *Fordham Law Review* in the fall of 2020.

31
The Electoral College System

The Electoral College method of electing a President of the United States is archaic, undemocratic, complex, ambiguous, indirect and dangerous. The President should be elected directly by the people, for it is the people of the United States to whom he is responsible.

— SENATOR BIRCH BAYH

As the drive to adopt the Twenty-Fifth Amendment was moving to a successful conclusion, members of Congress asked the ABA to examine the system of electing a president and vice president. The ABA's House of Delegates, at its meeting in February of 1966, therefore authorized the creation of a special commission to study the subject, consisting of fifteen members, many of whom were not ABA members.

Appointed to chair the commission was Robert Storey Sr., the former dean of the Southern Methodist University Dedman School of Law. He was joined by other former ABA presidents, including E. Smythe Gambrell of Georgia, William Jameson of Montana, and Whitney North Seymour of New York, and a future ABA president, William Gossett of Michigan. Former ABA president Edward Kuhn of Tennessee was designated as the commission's liaison with the ABA. I was asked to serve as staff advisor to the commission.

The commission was directed to seek a nonpartisan formula for electing a president and vice president. I undertook a number of research studies on the Electoral College and proposals to change the system, engaging law students to help in this effort and undertaking for myself a study of the two-party system and the factors that led to it. The resulting studies became important resources for the commission.

The commission met several times, with the key meeting occurring in Chicago on October 7, 1966, hosted by the then Illinois governor, Otto Kerner, who was a commission member. I was asked to begin the all-day session by discussing the proposals for reform and the pros and cons of each, and, as the meeting progressed, my study of the two-party system and views on provisions that might be in any proposed amendment. These passages from the closing session of the ABA meeting of October 1966 provide a sense of one of the two most interesting learning experiences I had as a young lawyer:

Mr. Gambrell (of Georgia): Mr. Chairman, this near unanimity here today surprises me. It is almost frightening. Do you suppose that we are truly representative of the profession, or why haven't we had a fight today? [Laughter]

Chairman Storey (of Texas): Well, Smythe, you and I know that within our many battles within and without the ABA, and in the ABA, when we debate and then come to a final conclusion or consensus, we stay with that conclusion. . . .

Mr. Gambrell: I want to congratulate you on your moderation.

Chairman Storey: No, it is not in congratulation of me. We thank these men for digging out the facts, and we are grateful to you, and I think it is marvelous that we have had practically a unanimous meeting each time. The Bar and the public did a great job in this presidential succession matter, and we believe we are going to do a significant service in this. Now, Mr. Channell, is there any reason for anybody to stay here now in view of the situation at this time?

Mr. Channell: Not one bit, no, sir.

Mr. William Gossett (Michigan): Mr. Chairman, I assume that in connection with any report made, there will be comment upon such questions at the time, discussion of the problems involved in runoff elections and so on. I assume we will have that in mind.

Mr. Feerick: Yes.

Chairman Storey: You mean in connection with any release, when it is made?

Mr. William Gossett: Any final report. I simply wanted to remind the staff that I would expect that they would discuss fully in this report such questions as this time dimension policy involved.

Chairman Storey: You understand that, don't you, John?

Mr. Feerick: Yes.[1]

I was careful not to express my personal views on the ultimate question of reform as it wasn't part of my role. In the end, the commission reached a consensus on reform, and it was impressive to see people from all regions yield to others based on the arguments and reasoning advanced. It was a unique blessing to learn from these superstars of yesteryear and enjoy their friendship and respect. Their final report stated:

> The Commission discussed the subject of electoral reform in considerable detail and reached a consensus as to what it considered to be the best method of electing a President and Vice President. Although there was general agreement on the recommendations, it should be understood that not every member of the Commission subscribes to every recommendation. There was, however, unanimous agreement on the need for substantial reform in the present system.[2]

The recommendations called for the abolition of the Electoral College and its replacement by a system of direct popular election of the president and vice president. To win, a candidate needed to secure at least 40 percent of the popular vote, and if no candidate reached that number, then there would be a popular vote runoff between the candidates who received the two highest numbers of votes for each office.

These recommendations were debated at the ABA's meeting in February of 1967 in Houston, Texas—a debate enriched by the number of former ABA presidents who participated on different sides of the issue in the House of Delegates. Edward Kuhn of Tennessee, the president of the ABA when the commission was created, said at that debate: "Gentlemen, we are American first, last, and always, and this is where we strike a blow in the year 1967 for the American people and our Nation."[3] An effort to table the proposal was defeated, as was a motion to refer it to a standing committee for further consideration. Then Storey urged that the proposal be adopted by an overwhelming vote, and it was, 171 to 57.

I wrote the first draft of the commission's report, which in its final form used the introductory words to this chapter: "The Electoral College method of electing a President of the United States is archaic, undemocratic, complex, ambiguous, indirect and dangerous." These words were seized upon by the media and appeared in congressional hearings and debates and in the writings of others.

The report challenged legislators to do something about reform at a time when growing support for Alabama Governor George Wallace's third-party presidential bid in 1968 raised serious questions about the Electoral College system. Wallace, a prominent segregationist, was seeking to receive enough electoral votes to deny an Electoral College majority to the major party candidates. Had this happened, it would have thrown the election into the House of Representatives under an anachronistic one-state, one-vote formula, unless democratic and republican electors themselves took control and achieved a majority, as was suggested by some if Wallace was likely to capture sufficient electoral votes.[4] He came close to causing havoc, winning the electoral vote of five states and receiving 47 electoral votes; his challenge exposed the gaps in the system and played a critical role in the growing support for changing the Constitution.[5]

I devoted many years (1966–1979) to this reform effort, starting with a letter to the *New York Times* in January of 1967. I wrote articles,[6] served on bar committees, gave speeches, responded to press inquiries, testified before committees of both houses of Congress, prepared testimony for ABA leaders, helped congressional staff with the drafting of a proposed constitutional amendment, and responded to questions from congressional staff concerning the work of the commission and provisions of the Constitution. When a motion for closing off debate (cloture) was before the Senate, I recorded in a memorandum a day I spent in Washington with William Gossett meeting with various U.S. Senators.

The memorandum said, in part, that Senator Ted Stevens of Alaska was opposed to cutting off debate at that precise moment, stating "that debate on the issue was extremely important for a small state in view of its limited influence in Congress." The memorandum added:

> Bill Gossett and I met with Senator Robert Dole of Kansas who from the outset of our very brief discussion seemed unusually cold, if not hostile, to the fact that we were there to express our support for direct election. Dole opened this discussion by stating that we were representing the large states' point of view. We commented on the cloture petition and the fact that moments before Senator Bayh had announced on the Senate floor that he was favorably disposed towards the Tydings-Griffin plan. Dole immediately responded that Bayh's action would not win any votes. He then stated that he had to preside over the Senate and promptly left. There was no doubt from our discussion that he was unalterably opposed to the cloture petition.

The memorandum also described discussions we had with Senator John Sherman Cooper of Kentucky, Senator Norris Cotton of New Hampshire, and Senator Bayh, and a conversation between Gossett and the White House. Two interesting sentences in the memorandum read, "Speculation had it that some (on the cloture vote) were opposed because they did not want to give

Senator Bayh additional publicity. Others said that the Administration was doing absolutely nothing to support the Amendment — that if the Administration did so, the necessary votes for cloture would be present."

There were many other challenging moments for me over the rest of the decade. On April 3, 1979, I testified before the Senate Judiciary Subcommittee on the Constitution and had this exchange with Senator Strom Thurmond, an adamant opponent of abolishing the Electoral College who seemed to hurl every imaginable argument against direct election:

> Senator Thurmond: You noted last year that the concept of federalism was one tended to form the basis for the legislative branch rather than the executive branch. Is that the official position of the American Bar Association? . . .
>
> Mr. Feerick: I don't think there is a position of the American Bar Association as such on that question . . . I believe I was reflecting a point of view of my own, and that point of view would have as important features of our federal system, certainly the legislative branch, certainly our State structure. I think the States, as an entity, as well as the legislative branch of government, play a very important part in our federal system.
>
> Senator Thurmond: What is the historical evidence or source work that you relied upon in making this assertion?
>
>   . . .
>
> Mr. Feerick: My statement was . . . based on certainly my study of the debates at the constitutional convention where the framers of the Constitution spent a considerable amount of time . . . focusing on the Federal structure in terms of the legislative branch of Government. And we had a great compromise that was reached with reference to the population element in the House and the State element in the Senate. . . .
>
> Senator Thurmond: Is one-man/one vote the only principle that comes into play with respect to the executive branch?
>
> Mr. Feerick: We believe — I believe — in the context of an election to the Executive Office, that ought to be the principle . . .
>
> Senator Thurmond: Well, if the principle of American democracy, such as a simple numerical majority, should control, then I guess we have to consider changing all of our basic institutions.
>
> Mr. Feerick: Which I would oppose personally . . . any change with reference to the legislative branch of Government; the one-person/one

vote rule is the rule, as I see it, with reference to election to the House and Senate and I simply urge in my testimony a similar rule in the case of the election of the President of the United States.

Senator Thurmond: Wouldn't you have to consider the method of submitting constitutional amendments? Wouldn't you have to consider changing even the way the Senate of the United States is constituted? . . .

You don't count only numbers, because certainly in both instances there, numbers don't control. Two-thirds of both bodies submit an amendment, three-fourths of the States have to ratify. And three-fourths of the States are smaller. . . . Every State has two Senators. . .

If you are going to change this system here, about the election of the President, aren't you changing the whole structure of Government . . . ?

Mr. Feerick: The answer to your question is no. I am only here in support of the proposed constitutional amendment to provide for direct popular election of the President . . . We are talking about an election. I am simply urging the principle that applies in every other election; namely, one person, one vote . . . There is a distinction now in the sense that the electoral college does not incorporate the one-person/one vote principle. We don't accept that there should continue to be that distinction with respect to the election of the President.[7]

Neither of us persuaded the other of his position. The testimony concluded with the Senator putting in the record that the ABA, in adopting its position through a House of Delegates, didn't apply a system of one-man, one vote.

Two years earlier, I had given similar testimony in support of the direct election amendment before the Senate Judiciary Committee, which drew similar comments from Senator William L. Scott of Virginia. At that time, I accompanied Justin Stanley, president of the ABA, who testified. In an exchange with the Senator concerning voter equality and the pooling of popular votes across state lines of people of the same outlook, the Senator asked me, "Aren't you getting away from the individual, of one-man, one vote, when you are talking about grouping together the votes? You really are talking about bloc voting here, are you not?"

Mr. Feerick: No, I am not.

Senator Scott: [T]his kind of talk is going to lose my vote rather than to gain a supporter. I believe Counsel led you here a little bit.

I am going to ask that the witnesses testify rather than the Counsel testifying in the future, and address such questions as Counsel may see fit. But let's let the witnesses testify rather than the Counsel.

Counsel apologized, and the exchange continued:

Mr. Feerick: I have been accused many times in court of leading a witness. That is an area with which I am certainly familiar. The point I was simply trying to make — and I did not make it well — was this: if I believe that you should be President of the United States . . ."
Senator Scott: I am not a candidate.
Mr. Feerick (continuing): I would want to believe that my vote [for] you was equal in weight to that of any other citizen of the United States in any other area of the United States. It seems to me that if there were people like myself of a particular point of view, that we should all be entitled to cast an equal vote with reference to the expression of that point of view.[8]

Thurmond remained steadfast in his views and in his opposition to the direct popular election amendment,[9] and Bayh was unable to persuade a sufficient number of colleagues to break the impasse and vote on the merits, though he was supported by more than a simple majority of the Senate.

Subsequently, I studied the creation of legislation to govern voting contests under a system of direct election in response to criticisms of its claimed impracticality. But no matter how hard any of us tried, especially Bayh, who remained dogged on the issue, the public tired of it and the political will to push through such reform was absent. Of the many times I tried to convince others of the value of such reform, a few remain especially vivid.

Drafting a Proposed Constitutional Amendment

In January of 1967 I was asked by ABA president Orison Marden to assist, along with Paul Freund and James Kirby, in drafting a proposed constitutional amendment embodying the recommendations of the ABA on electing a president. Marden had received a request for such a draft from Senator Everett Dirksen, then minority leader of the U.S. Senate.

Kirby and I met in a hotel room in Houston at the 1967 ABA mid-year meeting. Freund was unable to attend the meeting. Kirby and I brought with us a copy of the Constitution and the language from legislative proposals. We approached the task with the thought that the language had to be simple and general, as it was for electing Representatives and Senators. We spent hours drafting an amendment and the next day ran the draft by the ABA's Special Electoral College Committee, on which Kirby and I served, and shared it with Freund. We then delivered the draft to Marden, who in turn gave it to Dirksen. This is the document we gave to Marden:

Section 1. The President and Vice President shall be elected by the people of the several States and the district constituting the seat of government of the United States.

Section 2. The electors in each State shall have the qualifications requisite for electors of Senators and Representatives in Congress from that State, except that the legislature of any State may prescribe lesser qualifications with respect to residence and Congress may establish uniform residence and age qualifications.

Section 3. The persons having the greatest number of votes for President and Vice President shall be elected, if such number be at least 40 per centum of the whole number of votes cast for such offices. If no persons have such number, a runoff election shall be held in which the choice of President and Vice President shall be made from the persons who received the two highest numbers of votes for each office.

Section 4. The times, places, and manner of holding such elections and entitlement to inclusion on the ballot shall be prescribed in each State by the legislature thereof; but the Congress may at any time by law make or alter such regulations. The Congress shall prescribe by law the time, place and manner in which the results of such elections shall be ascertained and declared.

Section 5. Each elector shall cast a single vote jointly applicable to President and Vice President. Names of candidates shall not be joined unless they have consented thereto and no candidate shall consent to his name being joined with that of more than one other person.

Section 6. The days for such elections shall be determined by Congress and shall be uniform throughout the United States.

Section 7. The Congress may by law provide for the case of the death of any candidate for President or Vice President before the day on which a President-elect or a Vice President-elect has been chosen; and for the cases of a tie in any election.[10]

The resulting draft was placed in legislative form and introduced in the Senate in 1967. It was changed in both Houses over the next two years and was then approved by the House Judiciary Committee as H.J. Res. 681 on April 29, 1969. On September 18, 1969, it was approved in the House of Representatives by a vote of 338 to 70, with twenty-one members not voting.[11] The proposal reflected, in a different textual format, the language of the draft given to Orison Marden.[12]

This was the first time a House of Congress had passed a proposed amendment calling for direct, popular election of the president and vice president. Unfortunately, as noted, a Senate minority, led by Senators Thurmond and Sam Ervin Jr., among others, was able to prevent a vote on the merits of such a reform. This was a most disappointing moment for those engaged in reform of the electoral system.

Lobbying a New York Senator

In the late 1970s, I was asked by Senator Bayh's staff to visit with New York senator Jacob Javits to again press the case for adoption of a nationwide popular vote for president and vice president. Another effort was being made to secure a Senate vote on such a reform, against the background of the three times in American history the popular vote winner lost the election — 1824, 1876, and 1888 (the popular vote winner would later lose the election in 2000 and 2016 as well). Senator Javits described how important constituencies of his were opposed to its adoption, believing that it would lessen the influence of large states in presidential elections and therefore the special interests of groups within these states. But, he said, he thought it was the right approach for electing a president.

Not long after that meeting, I received a call from an aide to Senator Bayh to inform me that the amendment had failed to achieve the requisite two-thirds vote, with 51 senators favoring the amendment, including Senator Javits, and 48 senators opposing the amendment. Since that time there has never been a vote in either House on reform of the system. I learned, however, that public servants sometimes do vote their conscience on major questions, despite opposition from important supporters.

Supporting a Non-Judicial Resolution of the 2000 Presidential Election

In the 2000 election, George W. Bush captured a majority of the electoral votes but fewer popular votes than Albert Gore. Shortly after election day, I was asked by the president of the Florida State Senate, John McKay, to serve as special counsel to the Florida Senate as it considered whether to choose a slate of presidential electors given the uncertainty of the vote count in the November election. I was asked to come to Florida to assist with legislative hearings, and I unexpectedly received a copy for comments of a brief to be filed in a court proceeding supporting Bush's position.

After consideration, I did not feel comfortable undertaking any role in so political a context when my history on reform of the system was as a nonpartisan spokesperson for the ABA. I considered the two roles in conflict and therefore, with some sadness, called Senator McKay and advised him of my decision. Before concluding the conversation, I commented that the pending litigation regarding the election made it inadvisable for the Florida Legislature to involve itself, but if it planned to do so, it should not be before December 12, 2000. My view was based on a provision in federal law that seemed to provide an avenue for legislative action if the electoral certificates were still in doubt as of December 12, with the meetings of electors nationwide scheduled for December 16.[13]

Before I withdrew from this matter in late November 2000, I had studied this statute in depth and drafted a proposed resolution for the contingency of the Florida Legislature determining to choose electors for the state. I found striking that the U.S. Supreme Court reached an important conclusion of its own on December 12, when it issued its decision to end the recount of ballots, effectively closing the door to action by the Florida Legislature and settling the 2000 election.[14]

32

Other Constitutional Opportunities

May our former President, who brought peace to millions, find it for
himself.

— PRESIDENT GERALD R. FORD

The opportunities to serve on the ABA's presidential succession group and
then as advisor to its Electoral College Commission gave me a degree of
recognition I would never have expected. It also led to other invitations to
serve on committees and commissions, in both New York State and the ABA,
dealing with law reform.

Amending the Constitution

In 1971, the ABA created a Constitutional Convention Study Committee to
analyze and study all questions of law involved in calling a national constitutional convention under Article V of the Constitution. I was appointed a
member of the committee and was asked to serve as its reporter, which meant
doing legal research and drafting memoranda and the committee's report.

The committee consisted of two federal judges, Judge Clyde Atkins from
Florida as chair of the committee and Judge Sarah Hughes from Texas; two
law school deans, Albert Sacks of Harvard and David Dow, former dean of
Nebraska Law School; two former presidents of state constitutional conven-
tions, Adrian Foley Jr. of New Jersey and Samuel Witwer of Chicago; William
Thompson, a Superior Court judge in the District of Columbia; and Warren
Christopher, a former deputy U.S. attorney general.

As with my other ABA experiences, I was struck by the effective manner in which the committee's chair went about his role. Judge Atkins was respectful and patient in his relationship with committee members. He brought no preconceived answers to the questions we were dealing with, wanting to learn from the group's research and discussions. He listened carefully to others but never lost sight of the importance of accomplishing what was requested of the committee. His humility and dignity set a benchmark for me.

It was challenging to keep up with the analytical reasoning of members in examining such issues as to whether the jurisdiction of a convention can be limited to the subject matter giving rise to its call, or whether, as a matter of law, convening such a convention opens it to multiple proposed amendments or even to the consideration of a new constitution. Different views on these issues were expressed, but by the end of this two-year effort, the committee was unanimous with respect to each of its recommendations except one, which dealt with the applicability of the "one person, one vote" rule in the selection of delegates to a national constitutional convention. On the issue of limiting the subject matter of a convention, the committee concluded that Congress had the power to establish procedures to limit it to a single subject if requested to do so by two-thirds of the state legislatures.

The committee's report, "Amendment of the Constitution by the Convention Method Under Article V (1974)," was widely circulated, but concern developed in Congress that adopting the legislation recommended, which appeared as an appendix in the report. Some members of Congress were worried about the risks associated with a constitutional convention, such as the possibility of a "run-away convention" — that is, a convention that goes beyond the subject of its mandate. The irony was that some important congressional leaders had urged the ABA to undertake the study in the first place because of the proliferation of applications from state legislatures calling for a national constitutional convention to deal with the subject of a balanced budget amendment. By the time the ABA adopted the report, the political landscape had changed, and it seemed wiser not to revive the subject by adopting legislation. It was disappointing not to see action by Congress, but I had come to accept such outcomes on matters of political importance and reform.

In November of 1979 I was invited to testify, on behalf of the ABA, in support of its recommendations before the Senate Judiciary Subcommittee on the Constitution. The hearing was chaired by Senator Orrin Hatch in the absence of its regular chair, Senator Bayh, who arrived soon after it started. I responded to questions from these two Senators and from Senator Thurmond. In a gracious comment, Senator Hatch said, "I would like to congratulate . . .

your committee for the landmark work that you have done in this particular area . . . I am deeply indebted to your committee for many of the ideas that are in this bill."[1]

On arriving at the hearing, Senator Bayh surprised me with these words: "I think the record should show that our witness (representing the ABA), John Feerick, has been a long and faithful witness before the committee for perhaps more years than either of us would like to remember. There have been a number of opportunities over a good number of years to bring his personal expertise, as well as collecting the expertise of the ABA to bear on the decisions of this committee."[2]

He added, "Particularly, the country owes him a debt of gratitude. He was one who was very instrumental for the process by which the 25th amendment was created. We are grateful for that effort, and I think the country was well served, and because of that work and the work by legislatures and others, we were prepared for the resignation of a president, and we moved to the congressional selection for the first time in history."[3]

As to the questions, Senator Hatch asked: "In the event this committee rejects the interpretation of those who believe in the concept of a limited convention, has the convention method of amendment become an effective dead letter?"[4] I said no, pointing to the possibility of a general convention. Senator Thurmond asked whether I saw anything in the Constitution that "would prohibit the States from submitting petitions" limiting the scope of a convention. I said no, as long as "two-thirds of the states concur on a particular item or items."

Senator Bayh pushed me hard on the committee's recommendation of leaving it to the convention to decide on the vote required for advancing a proposed amendment. "Why should that be a subject for the convention to decide?" Bayh asked. "If we need a broad national consensus and the Congress is setting up guidelines, why should not the Congress require a broad consensus in support of an amendment? Why should it not meet the same test as one that is adopted by the Congress itself?"[5]

My answer was influenced by the Framers' preference for an alternative to the congressional method of proposing amendments to the constitution. This alternative method required two-thirds of the states to agree on a subject for a convention to consider. If such agreement existed, a convention would be called and Congress would be required to propose for ratification any amendment on the subject that led to the calling of the convention. The amendment would become part of the Constitution if three-fourths of the states ratified it. The two-thirds and three-fourths requirements are in the Constitution, but nothing is said about the convention vote.

Although the Senate passed legislation providing for a limited subject matter convention, excluding any role for the Supreme Court, the House of Representatives took no action.[6] In July of 1985, I was again invited to testify on the subject before the subcommittee on civil and constitutional rights of the House Judiciary Committee, with Representative Charles Schumer of New York as acting chair.

I participated as part of a panel with Professor Gerald Gunther of Stanford Law School and Professor Walter Dellinger of Duke Law School. The principal issue before the committee concerned whether a convention could be limited to a specific subject specified in advance. A subsidiary but important issue was how to deal with thirty-two applications from state legislatures requesting a Convention on the issue of a balanced budget amendment. Schumer stated:

> If two more States petition Congress to call a convention, it would
> seem that we would have before us applications from two-thirds of the
> States. But are these applications valid ones? Some would argue that
> they are not, since they all seek a limited convention. Others have sug-
> gested that they are invalid because the State legislatures did not know
> what they were doing, that because some legislatures thought they
> were merely pressuring Congress to act, those applications are suspect.
> But . . . do they as a group reflect the necessary contemporaneous
> consensus that a convention be called?[7]

Schumer described the questions as thorny ones, as there were no court cases and no constitutional guidance — that is, there was "very little else to go on."

For the next few hours the three of us responded to questions from Schumer and other committee members. Disagreeing with the ABA's position, neither Gunther nor Dellinger believed that Congress could limit a convention to a specific subject. Assuming that a congressional resolution calling for a convention sought to limit it to a single subject, the committee explored with us whether Congress could refuse to submit to the states an amendment that exceeded the call and whether there was a role for the Supreme Court.

I thought that there was a role for the Court. As to whether a state application could limit a convention to voting up and down a proposed amendment, none of us thought that would be appropriate because such an action would strip the convention of its deliberative function. We were in agreement as well on the presence of the issue of timeliness of current state applications. We also agreed on the desirability that Congress should adopt legislation that provided procedures for handling state applications for a national convention.

In response to a question by Representative Robert Kastenmeier concern-

ing the desirability of Congress adopting legislation on convention procedures, I said, "Hopefully we work ourselves out of this particular period, but
the history of the last 85 or so years tells us that we are going to continue to
receive applications from state legislatures."[8]

"There may be other potential crises in the years ahead," I added. "I do
think that that argues for the Congress to consider some kind of legislation —
the problem that I see is, if we run into a situation where two more applications come in, I sense that whatever is decided with respect to the applications, there is going to be at least a feeling . . . as [to] what are the rules, if we
are going to continue this provision in the Constitution. If we don't want to
continue it . . . then we should follow the process to get rid of it. If it's in the
Constitution, what does it mean?"[9]

The Resignation and Pardon of President Richard Nixon

The experience of watching a presidency slowly erode during 1973 and 1974
affected me deeply. I was stunned by the magnitude of the wrongs committed
by Richard Nixon and members of his staff in the Watergate scandal. I felt
strongly, however, about the legal issues that arose as to the rights of a president confronted with serious charges of wrongdoing. I expressed in articles
points of view favorable to the president on his entitlement to due process.
Ironically, a series of New York Law Journal articles that I wrote in July of 1973
on presidential impeachment became relevant, abbreviating an earlier study
I had done on the impeachment provisions for the Fordham Law Review that
focused on the meaning of "high crimes and misdemeanors." In that study, I
concluded:

> To be impeachable, an act must fall within one or two categories. It
> must violate some known, established law, be of a grave nature, and
> involve consequences highly detrimental to the United States. In the
> alternative, it must involve evil, corrupt, willful, or gross conduct in
> the discharge of office to the great detriment to the United States. Acts
> which result from error of judgment or omission of duty, without the
> presence of fraud, or for the misconception of duty, without the pres-
> ence of a willful disregard are not impeachable.[10]

The study was placed in the Congressional Record by Senator Sam Ervin Jr.,[11] who in 1974 chaired the Senate's Special Impeachment Committee,
known as the Watergate Committee.

Among the articles I wrote in this period for the New York Law Journal
were: "Filling a Vacancy in the Vice Presidency" (October 11, 1973); "Pres-

ident's 'Right' in Impeachment Probe" (April 1, 1974); "The Issue of Presidential Inability" (May 15, 1974); "The Hastings Impeachment, Acquittal"
(May 28, 1974); and "Some Reflections on U.S. v. Nixon" (July 30, 1974).

In an op-ed essay in the *New York Times* published on December 13, 1973,
in which I dealt with the availability of the Twenty-Fifth Amendment to a
president responding to daily attacks of wrongdoing, I suggested that the president might be able to invoke the amendment and step aside temporarily. In
my article, I quoted Senator Bayh, who stated: "[T]he intention of this legislation is to deal with any type of inability, whether it is from traveling from one
nation to another, a breakdown of communications, capture by the enemy or
anything that is imaginable. The inability to perform the powers and duties
of the office, for any reason, is inability under the terms that we are discussing."[12] Writing helped ease the tension I felt as a citizen during the Watergate
period, as did moderating a well-attended debate between Roy Cohn and
Ira Glasser. Cohn was a staunch defender of President Nixon, and Glasser,
who later served as executive director of the New York Civil Liberties Union,
believed that the president's conduct was disgraceful and worse. Cohn began
with an audience hostile to him and ended with applause for the excellence
and passion of his advocacy.

After Nixon resigned from office on August 9, 1974, and a few weeks later
was granted a pardon by President Ford, I was asked by the ABA's board of
governors for an opinion as to the legality of the pardon in connection with
its review of the matter. After preparing an analysis, I attended a meeting of
the board in Chicago along with another consultant, Professor Norval Morris
of Chicago Law School. Although we hadn't discussed our conclusions with
each other, we both concluded that the pardon was within the president's
constitutional power.

Based on our advice, the board of governors issued a public statement supporting the legality of the pardon. Subsequently, I was invited to contribute an
article on the subject to the *New York Law Journal*.[13] The article concluded
that the pardoning power may be used at any time after commission of an of-
fense against the United States and that, once accepted, it removes the protection against self-incrimination with respect to testifying on the subject matter
unless there is a "genuine danger of prosecution under state law." I later wrote
an article with the same conclusion for the *New York State Bar Journal*.[14]

The ABA Special Advisory Committee

In 1973, I was asked by ABA president Chesterfield Smith to serve on a Special
Committee on Election Reform that he had set up as a result of the Water-

gate scandal then in progress—a scandal that implicated numerous lawyers. Talbot "Sandy" D'Alemberte was asked to chair the group, and I would follow him in that position several years later. The committee undertook studies and programs that were unprecedented in the history of the ABA, expanding its public mission to improve the American system of government and law. Its recommendations, described below, were all approved by the ABA House of Delegates.[15]

In February of 1974, the ABA reaffirmed its recommendations to abolish the Electoral College. In August of 1974, it recommended that, in filling a vacancy in the vice presidency, Congress use joint hearings of both Houses of Congress, and that Congress implement registration by mail in federal elections and provide help to state and local governments seeking to simplify electoral procedures. In 1975, the ABA recommended that the equal-time provision of the Communication Act be repealed as it applied to candidates for president and vice president, and it offered extensive recommendations involving campaign finance reform with respect to such issues as disclosure, contribution and expenditure limitations, and public financing.

In 1976 the ABA recommended that Congress reconstitute and preserve an independent Federal Elections Commission. And in February of 1977 it recommended that the office of vice president be retained with the presidential candidates recommending their running mate, but providing before the convention a tentative list of possibilities. It also recommended that the president involve the vice president productively in the work of the presidency. On the committee's recommendation, the ABA also proposed televised vice presidential debates as an integral part of a presidential candidate debating series.

In February of 1979, after a major committee study, the ABA adopted recommendations to halt the decline in voting participation, including the convening of a White House Conference and legislation to eliminate voting barriers and provide for fair redistricting.[16] The presence of the ABA in all of these areas was well received by state and local bars, which were energized to become more involved in such issues.[17]

This service for the ABA's election reform committee enhanced my sense of purpose and meaning as a lawyer and citizen. As my tenure as chair came to an end in 1979, the committee recommended that the Special Committee be disbanded and replaced by a standing committee on election reform, a recommendation that was approved by the ABA's House of Delegates. At my concluding committee meeting, I was presented with a handsome bound volume of the committee's studies and publications, now a treasured part of my personal library.

PART VIII

The World of Government Ethics

The public is entitled to expect from its servants a set of standards far above the morals of the marketplace. Those who exercise public and political power are trustees of the hopes and aspirations of all mankind. They are the trustees of a system of government in which the people must be able to place their absolute trust; for the preservation of their welfare, their safety and all they hold dear depends upon it.

— THOMAS E. DEWEY

PART VIII

The World of Government Ethics

33

The New York State Commission on Government Integrity

Let us raise a standard to which the wise and the honest can repair.
— PRESIDENT GEORGE WASHINGTON

My public service undertakings took on a different character in 1987 when I undertook, in the words of then New York Governor Mario Cuomo, to help "make this the beginning of the most exciting reform era in the State's history."

In April of that year I received a call from Cuomo's secretary and counsel, Gerald Crotty and Evan Davis, respectively, asking whether I would be willing to chair a newly created Commission on Government Integrity. The commission was to investigate corruption in the administration of government and determine the adequacy of laws, regulations, and procedures relating to government integrity. A battle between Cuomo and the legislature had resulted in the resignation of the commission's prior chair, Joseph Califano Jr. When the legislature threatened not to fund the commission, Cuomo vowed to use funds from private sources. His persistence led the legislature to agree to fund the commission, but on the condition that all commissioners be New York State residents, which Califano was not.

The commission was established during a period of heightened corruption in New York State, with almost daily revelations of wrongdoing by public officeholders. Among these scandals were allegations of illegal payoffs involving Donald Manes, the Democratic leader of Queens County, tied to his influence in the areas of parking tickets, the granting of TV cable licenses, and the making of political appointments. Amidst these allegations, Manes took his own life as the investigations were heating up. Scandals also surfaced in various other counties associated with purchasing decisions by county officials, leading to the resignation of both Stanley Simon, the borough president of the Bronx, and Stanley Friedman, the borough's former Democratic leader. In time, the commission would identify and investigate other corruption issues in the state, especially in Poughkeepsie and Westchester County.

I initially declined Davis and Crotty's request to chair the commission. Corruption investigations weren't part of my background. And the prospect of leading the commission didn't seem realistic, as I'd just finished my first five all-consuming years as dean at Fordham and was eager to do some teaching and writing on the Constitution.

But Davis, who had pressed me hard on the matter, flew down from Albany with two other members of the Governor's staff to discuss it with me further. After the meeting, as Emalie and I were discussing the matter at home that evening, I received two telephone calls from reporters asking if it were true that I would be serving as chair.

I was actually leaning in the other direction. Emalie was strongly opposed to my serving on the grounds that it would be too time-consuming and stressful. After the call, I turned to her and said, "I guess I have to do this." The commission's mission seemed noble and critical, especially at that moment in time, and it was hard for me to say no and stick with it when asked to serve my state's government.

The next few days were a whirlwind, with many reporters wanting to meet with me. I declined these requests and didn't otherwise make myself available. I felt it inappropriate to do so until I had met with the other commissioners, all of whom had been appointed by the Governor, and in addition, I had nothing much to say. I paid a small price for my lack of response to New York Times reporter Frank Lynn, who noted in an article that I was too busy reading newspaper clippings about myself to speak with him. Dean Reilly had told Lynn that I was familiarizing myself with the history of the commission, which reached back to the 1986–1987 State-City Commission on Integrity in Government, chaired by Columbia University president Michael Sovern. The commission recommended creating the Commission on Government Integrity and urged that it have strong subpoena powers.

On April 21, 1987, Governor Cuomo and Attorney General Robert Abrams introduced me at a press conference. The transcript of the event captured a rare moment of humor by me in a serious context. Asked why I had accepted this position, I replied, "Beats the hell out of me." And in response to a question by Gabe Pressmen, I said, "I have to disclose that your father was my dentist growing up."

The experience of dealing with the press, while not entirely new to me, was quite different from the way it had been for me in the past. In the 1960s and 1970s I was a frequent source of information for reporters and columnists wanting to know more about the Constitution. I gave them a great amount of time and provided them with helpful material, judging by how they used what I suggested. As the senior lawyer for a striking union, I shared information with reporters during the New York newspaper strike of 1978 and especially appreciated the thoughtful inquiries of Abe Raskin of the *New York Times* and other reporters as to the status of the negotiations.[1]

But this was different. The commission I had just agreed to chair was clothed with confidentiality obligations which meant that I couldn't be as open as I'd been in the past. The position required investigations of corruption then endemic in the state's political system. In speaking of the campaign financing of elective officials, Governor Cuomo described it as a "terrible system." He understood the system intimately, and I came to understand what he meant. *New York Times* columnist William Safire observed more generally that "a great gray area exists called unseemliness. It ain't illegal. But it just ain't right."[2]

The commission's charter dictated that its seven members were to investigate the issues and then lay out a reform agenda. In addition to me, the commissioners were Richard Emery, Patricia Hynes, James Magavern, Bernard Meyer, Bishop Emerson Moore, and Cyrus Vance Sr. We put together a splendid staff led by Peter Bienstock, Kevin O'Brien, and Thomas Schwarz as special counsel.

The executive order constituting our charter identified a number of areas for investigation: the use of public or political party position for personal gain; conflicts of interest by office holders; enforcement mechanisms relating to unethical practices; government sale or leasing of real property, sponsorship of development projects, and solicitation of government business; campaign contributions and expenditures; representation of private parties by public and political party officials before public agencies; and the process of selecting judges.

My life became chaotic in ways I never expected. Mom and Pop, who were not well at the time, would both pass away during this period of service, which ended in 1991. I thought of resigning but was buoyed by Father O'Hare, S.J., Fordham's president at the time, who urged me to keep going, explaining that he viewed this service as highly consistent with Fordham University and the Law School's emphasis on public service.

As I began this work, I received advice from two former law partners, Leslie Arps and Joseph Flom. Arps urged me to let the facts speak for themselves and not to be a loudmouth, shooting from the hip and leaking information to the press to draw attention to myself and the commission. He said he had followed these guidelines back in the 1950s as an assistant prosecutor for the New York State Crime Commission, which was charged with ferreting out corruption on the waterfront, and the public hearings that were held drew highly favorable commentary.

Flom suggested that I read *Plunkitt of Tammany Hall* by William L. Riordan,[3] without explaining why. I was curious as to his recommendation; Flom, like Arps, was astute when it came to the affairs of the world. I read the book and was stunned by what I learned of an earlier New York political culture, captured by Plunkitt's statement, "I seen my opportunities and I took 'em." This book, which was written around the turn of the last century and explored such subjects as "honest graft," the plight of reformers, and bosses seeking to preserve the nation, made for *interesting* reading. By the time I finished serving as chair of the Commission on Government Integrity, I'd found many unsettling parallels between the two worlds.

The start-up of the commission was punctuated by widespread demands that it act as a prosecutorial body. Some people took a shot at me personally, a law school dean with no background in criminal investigations. Some were upset by the corruption in the city and state surrounding the commission's creation, and rightly so. Still others felt that rather than creating the commission, government leaders should have dealt directly with the issues themselves and not foisted them off on a commission of citizen volunteers. Others urged us to take immediate and bold steps to deal with the corruption that appeared widespread in the state.

The pressure on the commission to make immediate headlines was compelling. But we weren't an established prosecution office with cases ready to proceed based on investigations of law enforcement agencies. For a while we had an office at the World Trade Center II, with a skeletal staff and no agenda, simply a mandate, with subpoena power, to probe widely at both the state and local levels in the areas within our charter.

When the commissioners met for the first time, we found that we were of one mind. Our work had to be done carefully, fairly, and thoroughly. We had to go where the facts took us and avoid witch-hunting or rushing too quickly to conclusions. By 1988, we were able to hold public hearings on campaign finance abuses in the state that drew wide press support. In time, the commission issued seven reports that presented a picture of a corrupt campaign finance system and offered a blueprint for campaign finance reform.

The commission found appalling how people who had business before the state sought to use donations to influence office holders. The titles of four of its seven reports — "The Albany Money Machine: Campaign Financing for New York Legislative Races," "The Midas Touch: Campaign Financing

Practices of Statewide Office Holders," "Evening the Odds: The Need to Restrict Unfair Incumbent Advantage," and "Poughkeepsie '85: A Case Study of Election Law Abuses" — all carefully chosen by the commission's staff, tell the story of a system riddled with flaws, gaps, and holes, along with weak enforcement that encouraged evasion, abuse, and outright corruption.

One of the more challenging investigations involved a Syracuse-based shopping mall developer called Pyramid. We detailed the company's use of the state's campaign finance system in a town board election held in Poughkeepsie in 1985 to oust a board opposed to the construction of a mall and replace it with a board in favor of the idea. When the investigation was over, Pyramid's top officer admitted, "You shouldn't be able to do what we did in Poughkeepsie." But despite our report and recommendations, the corruption within and surrounding the state's campaign finance system appears to me to be the same today.

After other investigations, the commission made recommendations to close loopholes in the state's Ethics in Government Act; abolish judicial elections for full-time trial courts; reform the laws governing how candidates get on the ballot in state primaries; limit the influence of political patronage on personnel procedures and practices; and change the way New York gives money to private drug treatment providers. In other reports, the commission laid out findings and recommendations with respect to the state's Open Meetings Law (requiring meetings of federal and state government agencies be open to the public), the need for ethics training for state and municipal employees, a new approach to municipal ethical standards, enhanced protections for whistleblowers, and a statute requiring the forfeiture of a pension for government employees convicted of a felony involving their public duties.

Each report was developed through careful investigatory research by a highly diligent staff. In its final report, the commission stated that the laws of New York State fell woefully short in guarding against political abuses in an alarming number of areas and that New York hadn't demonstrated a real commitment to government ethics reform. The report urged the state's leaders to act before new scandals emerged and to give ethics reforms the emphasis they deserved. Sadly, many of our recommendations fell on deaf ears.

All in all, the commission collected evidence from individuals and government officials by conducting twenty-five days of public hearings, questioning more than one thousand people, privately and publicly, and examining thousands of government records and documents. It exercised subpoena power 213 times and laid out its findings and recommendations for reform in more than twenty-three reports.

As part of its investigative work, the commission found evidence of possible violations of law which it transmitted to the appropriate law enforcement authorities for review. The commission also engaged in extensive litigation in state and federal courts to enforce its subpoenas and respond to efforts to hinder its investigative work. For purposes of this litigation, the law firm of commission member Cyrus Vance, Simpson Thacher & Bartlett, and especially his partner, Conrad Harper, expended an enormous number of pro bono hours in support of the commission, enabling the commission to continue its investigative work rather than devote substantial resources to litigation. The court decisions, many of which were in response to appeals, were uniformly favorable and in some instances established legal precedents.

There were also some positive responses to the commission's work. Its creation contributed to the adoption of the Ethics in Government Act of 1987. An investigation into the "housekeeping accounts" of the political parties involving secret, unidentified political contributions was ended midstream in 1988 when the New York Legislature passed a law opening such accounts to public scrutiny.[4] There was no need to seek to enforce the subpoenas the commission had issued since the investigation itself accomplished the intended reform.

Another investigation, focusing on the application of the Open Meetings Law to local government, came to a successful close on the eve of a scheduled public hearing in Rochester, just as I arrived to chair the hearing. The use of closed political party caucuses to conduct government business, I was informed, had just been abandoned, thereby making the need for a hearing moot.

Our most public investigations were in areas of campaign financing. The testimony received at these hearings suggested that excessive political gifts were more than a pure expression of American democracy at work. One witness said that he contributed "more to avoid a negative impact [on his business] than trying to incur a positive result." Some business people told commission staff members that "it would be bad business judgment to stop contributing to campaigns."[5]

Among those who testified were Donald Trump, whose political donations in 1985 exceeded $150,000.[6] In Trump's testimony, he said that he was only giving to support friends and people who would benefit the city, not trying to influence politicians to help his business interests.[7] I asked him if "a large contribution puts unnecessary pressure on a public official?" Trump responded: "I don't think the large contribution is a great thing, but I do think it's the lesser of the evils."[8] In another point of his testimony, he expressed his view that candidates would spend too much time fundraising instead of working if limits were lower.[9] While campaigning in 2016, the president said: "I was a businessman. I give to everybody. When they call, I give. And you know what, when I need something from them two years later, three years later, I call them. They are there for me. That's a broken system."[10]

Others testifying said they had no idea how much they had given; others, playing it safe, gave to opposing candidates vying for the same office. What seemed clear was that many business people saw their contributions as a cost of doing business — as advance payment for benefits they would not otherwise receive. The sad reality was, as the commission's staff noted, large gifts from those doing business with the state government did in fact bring access that average citizens did not enjoy and created an appearance of indebtedness that was damaging to public confidence in government.

Of all the commission's investigations, the most difficult one to close involved allegations of political corruption in the affairs of the judiciary. The planned public hearings in this matter would have been based on testimony from a convicted felon. After long discussion within the commission, we concluded that it wouldn't be appropriate to damage an institution and its staff members based almost entirely on such testimony.

Reporters who anticipated such hearings were disappointed, but, to their credit, they accepted the outcome of our decision-making process, in part, I think, because they trusted in our good faith. On the other hand, another investigation focusing on the extent of patronage hiring at a New York City job referral office known as Talent Bank drew enormous media attention. Mayor Edward Koch, who created the Talent Bank, and others in his administration, including the city's personnel director, testified at a series of hearings held by the commission. The city's personnel director was indicted for perjury and resigned from his position. Our report on the investigation was titled "Playing Ball with City Hall — A Case Study of Political Patronage in New York City," and we scheduled its release for Monday, August 7, 1989. Unfortunately, the commission's work was tarnished when a draft of the report leaked.

On Saturday, August 5, 1989, several newspapers printed excerpts from the draft report critical of the city administration. Mayor Koch responded angrily, claiming that I had lost control of the commission. He pointed a finger at a commission member as the source of the leak and demanded that the commission investigate the matter. Instinctively, I defended the group, but I resolved to try to get to the bottom of the leak.

For the next month or so I conducted a confidential investigation, questioning each commissioner and senior staff member under oath. It was a horrible experience for me, as I had to examine my colleagues. I discussed the results of the investigation with two senior commissioners, Vance and Bernard Meyer. Reluctantly, they accepted my recommendation to close the investigation and move on.

I gained an appreciation for the work of the many fine investigative reporters who covered the commission's work, particularly Frank Lynn of the *New York Times*, who was balanced in his reporting.

Shortly after the deaths of Pop (in 1988) and Mom (in 1989), when I was wondering how much longer I could continue with this service, the Albany *Times Union* published a Christmas Day editorial on December 25, 1989, praising the commission's work. It began with the words: "In just two years the state Commission on Government Integrity has earned a reputation for holding elected officials to the highest ethical standards — often in the face of strong opposition from those under scrutiny. Both the panel and its chairman . . . deserve the public's gratitude for what was accomplished and for pointing the way to what remains to be done."[11] The editorial gave me heart to keep going.

As the commission's work ended, Lynn asked me what it was like to serve as chair, to which I replied, "It has been good for my character development." He seemed dumbfounded by my answer. I explained that "to take on something you did not want to do or like doing, then face all kinds of criticism for the service, and then work as hard as you can at such service as required by the duty at hand, helps you grow."

Of the commission's work, the *New York Times* wrote in an editorial of October 4, 1990:

> With this indictment of New York State's "primitive" campaign and government ethics rules, the state's Commission on Government Integrity recently closed shop. So ended a valuable, if frustrating, three-and-a-half-year inquiry into the dark underside of New York politics — frustrating because no one in Albany seems embarrassed. Most of the commission's recommendations aren't new. But armed with subpoena power, the anticorruption panel . . . succeeded where previous blue-ribbon efforts failed. Its well-publicized hearings and reports documented the urgent need for reform and stirred unusual public interest. . . . Even after all the commission's work, is anybody in Albany listening?[12]

34

New York State Ethics Commission

The whole art of government consists in the art of being honest.
— PRESIDENT THOMAS JEFFERSON

In March of 2007, nearly two decades after my work with the Commission on Government Integrity, I was asked by Patricia Salkin, director of the Government Law Center of Albany Law School, to deliver the keynote remarks at the 20th anniversary celebration of the Ethics in Government Act of 1987.[1] Although I was now involved in the area of poverty law for Fordham's Center for Social Justice, I agreed to give the remarks because of my esteem for Salkin. On that occasion she introduced me to James King, chair of the temporary State Commission on Lobbying, whom she described as the "nicest person in Albany." Little did I know, King and I would soon be joined at the hip as members of a new commission on public integrity.[2]

Later that month, Governor Eliot Spitzer informed me by telephone that he wanted me to chair the New York State Ethics Commission, merge it with the State Commission on Lobbying, and then chair the newly formed group, the New York State Public Integrity Commission. Emalie, as before, said, "Don't do it." She recalled for me what I'd gone through chairing the Commission on Government Integrity and reminded me that I was now in my 70s.

By contrast, my friend Thomas Schwarz encouraged me to accept the invitation, stating that there was no reason not to do so based on anything he knew about the governor. I also spoke to Father McShane, who encouraged me to accept "so long as it does not completely disrupt your family." My work on the Commission on Government Integrity had done that when five of our six children were still living at home and Mom and Pop were not well. Now it was just me and Emalie. Even though Emalie didn't like the idea, I reluctantly agreed to serve out of a sense of obligation, encouraged by the counsel of Father McShane. I thought it would now be easier to balance the work with my commitments to the Law School, its new Center for Social Justice, and my family.

On April 16, 2007, I appeared in Albany at a press conference at which Governor Spitzer announced my appointment as chair of the State Ethics Commission and his choice of me to chair the Public Integrity Commission in September. Except for Lieutenant Governor David Paterson, most of those present seemed to be reporters and members of the governor's staff. I said at that event:

> In accepting this appointment, I continue the work of the dedicated men and women who served with distinction and great commitment as members and staff of the state commission on government integrity. . . . When that commission ended its work in September 1990, it faulted the leadership of the state for not demonstrating a commitment to the area of government ethics reform. This is what I said in a letter to the governor dated September 18, 1990: "At a time when people around the globe are looking at democracy as a model, we are not proud of New York's failure to take a strong leadership role in areas of ethics reform."

In concluding, I said, "I promise my best effort to the position. I will serve as long as my energy and health permit and that of my wife. I seek no rewards for doing this uncompensated work other than the satisfaction of doing it right, with the help of God." I dedicated my service on this committee in memory of three members of the Commission on Government Integrity with whom I served who had died in the intervening years—Cyrus Vance, Judge Bernard Meyer, and Bishop Emerson Moore.

In a question-and-answer session that followed, a reporter asked about my view as to the extent of political corruption in the state compared to earlier periods. As I began to elaborate, the governor interrupted by noting that I was a full-time law professor and that the audience shouldn't expect a brief answer. This brought laughter, although, as with my work on the previous ethics commission, there was little of that on my part for the next twenty-two months. As I was leaving the press conference, the reporter who asked the question approached me and said that corruption in the state was worse now than it had been when I left as chair of the Commission on Government Integrity. "How could that be?" I wondered to myself. Corruption had been pretty bad when I chaired the commission twenty years earlier.

Getting Started

As soon as I was appointed for this assignment, many tasks became obvious. First, I had to meet with the commissioners and staff to learn about pending matters (including investigations), and to familiarize myself with the commission's history and the new law. I drew on Fordham Law students, volunteer lawyers (including recent graduates of the school), and a part-time adjunct professor to educate me about the law and the commission's history. The group wrote scores of memoranda for me, analyzing every sentence of the statute.

It was also important for me to meet the members and staff of the lobbying commission. Its reputation, attributed in no small measure to David Grandeau, its executive director, was that of aggressiveness. Shortly after I was appointed, I met with King, who assured me that I had the lobbying commission's full support and offered its help in carrying out an effective merger.

Other tasks I had to attend to included resigning from the many boards and panels on which I served to avoid conflicts of interest and to make more time available for this new assignment.

The positions included those with such organizations as the Irish Hunger Memorial Foundation Board, the Archdiocese of New York, the American Irish Historical Society, Brooklyn Legal Services, the Committee for an Independent Public Defense Commission, New York Medical College, the Metropolitan Corporate Counsel Board of Advisors, and the *New York Law Journal Board*. I also withdrew from a few arbitration assignments and found myself unable to give my duties as an NFL arbitrator sufficient attention. I found this avoidance of conflicts of interest far more extensive than the earlier commission in 1987. Despite understanding the need to eliminate actual and even potential conflicts of interest, I was still sad that I was leaving a chunk of my life behind me.

As I prepared for my volunteer assignment, I was surprised by comments I received from friends who asked me why I would undertake this public service. One, an experienced Albany lobbyist and a college and law school classmate, said that "people up here really don't want to know you." Another person, who had served in the state legislature and as a U.S. attorney, said essentially: "Get out of there as quickly as you can. Everything is rounded in Albany." Still another experienced hand in the ways of Albany said in effect that many people were surprised that I was willing to get my hands dirty in Albany politics. I dismissed these comments because of my belief in the nobility of public service, a belief strengthened by the example of such service by the late Cyrus Vance and Herbert Brownell, with whom I had developed close professional relationships.

Choosing an Executive Director

Settling on an executive director for the newly formed Public Integrity Commission was a challenge. The task was made complicated by the views I began to hear that the legislation calling for the merger of the two commissions was driven by a desire to get rid of the executive director of the lobbying commission. As I went through the process of selecting an executive director, it was clear that there was a lot of ugliness in the realm in which I was functioning.

I first considered for the position Suzanne Dugan, who was then serving as the ethics commission's acting executive director, but she had just accepted a position in the comptroller's office to build an ethics group, at $40,000 more than her present annual salary.

I had ads run for the position and received about thirty resumes. I tried to meet with as many applicants as I could. Some who impressed me held important staff positions in the legislature, but a choice from that sector would have brought immediate hostility to the commission, given prevalent attitudes toward that branch of government. Some who expressed an interest in the job worked in the Office of the Attorney General. Others who expressed an interest were associated with existing commissions. Identifying the right person was extremely difficult, and I hectically traveled all over the state to interview candidates.

By May of 2007 I had eliminated all but two persons for the position. After conferring with James King, the chair of the lobbying commission, I decided to go with a former federal prosecutor with an outstanding background in law enforcement. If that person declined, I would offer the position to Herbert Teitelbaum, who had a superb background in the area of civil law and possessed strong management qualifications. Mayor Koch would later describe him as the epitome of integrity.

The prosecutor declined the offer, telling me later that her family and friends had advised her not to take the position because they believed that whoever accepted it would face serious attacks. How prescient they were. (I should also add that in choosing an executive director, I neither had communications with, nor received resumes from, the executive chamber, despite insinuations that Governor Spitzer had selected that person.)

Teitelbaum accepted the position and jumped into his new responsibilities with earnestness and enthusiasm. He met with the staff of the two commissions in groups and individually, developing an organizational framework for the commission and fostering a spirit of togetherness among the two staffs. I had made the judgment, with which King agreed, that the combined commissions should occupy a new space, since moving one staff into the space of another group had the potential to increase everyone's anxiety. Thanks to the incredible efforts of Commissioner John Egan of the Office of General Services, new space in Albany was found for us at 540 Broadway.

The Selection of Commission Members

Another challenge involved selecting the members of the commission. I made it clear to the governor's assistants that I wanted to have input into the governor's choices. I met several times with the governor's appointments officer, joined at times by a member of his legal group. Thirteen members were to serve on the commission, selected by different appointing authorities. My expectations were simple: The six members to be appointed by the governor had to represent the best of the State of New York, reflect some continuity with the previous ethics and lobbying commissions, and include women and members of minority groups. (Two women served as members of the ethics commission, but there were no women on the lobbying commission nor were there any members of color on either commission.) I therefore identified in my submissions members of minority groups, and I was pleased that Governor Spitzer chose all but two of the people I recommended.

The members appointed by Governor Spitzer included James King; Howard Levine, a former member of the New York Court of Appeals; Loretta Lynch and Dan Alonso, former distinguished federal prosecutors; Robert Giuffra Jr., a member of the ethics commission and a former law clerk to the chief justice of the United States; and Andrew Celli Jr., vice chairman of the lobbying commission and a friend of Governor Spitzer (who was recused from the investigation, then in progress, of the 2007 scandal involving political surveillance known as Troopergate).

When the State Ethics Commission ended its work, four of the six commissioners to be appointed to the Public Integrity Commission by other government officials were also in place: John Brickman, Daniel French, John Mitchell, and David Gruenberg. These appointments were made by the attorney general, the state comptroller, the senate majority leader, and the assembly minority leader. It was not until the commission met in October of 2007 that Richard Emery, a law partner of Andrew Celli and a former member of the Commission on Government Integrity, was added to the roster by appointment of the senate minority leader. Late in the year, Virginia Apuzzo, who had held several state and federal government positions, was also added by appointment of the assembly speaker.

Closing the Door of the State Ethics Commission

I came to learn that since its creation in 1968, the ethics commission had been a leader in New York State, if not the country, in issuing advisory opinions to guide conduct by public servants, in managing more than twenty thousand public disclosure filings, and in conducting sensitive investigations of allegations of improper conduct, including one that had led to the resignation of the then comptroller, Alan Hevesi. It also had a reputation for not leaking information as it went about its confidential work, though that history would lead to comments by reporters that the commission wasn't sufficiently aggressive. This charge wasn't true, but as a new chair I found it exasperating to read these comments. The commission's dedicated staff of public servants also found them dispiriting, although they had learned to endure such remarks.

By July of 2007, Herb Teitelbaum had left his law partnership and was in place to assist with the merger. But late that month, after the attorney general issued a report on the Troopergate scandal, which concerned "spying" by the Governor on the travel plans of the Senate majority leader, my forty-fifth year in public service changed dramatically. The report was critical of both government officials. Although it found no violations of the law, it did, however, leave questions unanswered, since those compiling the report didn't have the benefit of testimony under oath by the Governor and other top aides.

For the next few weeks, the ethics commission considered whether it had jurisdiction to investigate this matter. The staff obtained documents used by the attorney general, examined the law, and then discussed with members of the commission the question of its jurisdiction. Upon determining that we did have jurisdiction, the staff began to issue subpoenas, acquire a broader range of documents, and examine witnesses.

Another issue arose later that summer when the executive chamber expressed the view, as I saw it, that this investigation should be concluded quickly before the work of the Public Integrity Commission started. I made clear that our commission wouldn't be rushed to a conclusion and that the commission wasn't the source of the leaks appearing in the press. In September of 2007, Teitelbaum learned that my appointment as chair would be for only two years, unlike others chosen by the governor for longer terms, and expressed concern. The shorter the term, he said, the less secure my position.

Donald and me at a happy family occasion

On active duty in the United States Army in July 1962

The White House, February 23, 1967, on the proclamation of the Twenty-Fifth Amendment by President Lyndon B. Johnson; joining in the picture is Congressman Richard H. Poff

To John D. Feerick with best wishes – Lyndon B. Johnson

January 1967: Meeting of the American Bar Association Conference on Presidential Succession, with Senator Birch Bayh explaining his proposal and me (next to him) taking notes, as were others in the room

At a Twenty-Fifth Amendment forum
with Senator Birch Bayh (on my right)
and Congressman Richard H. Poff, both
principal framers of the Amendment

Testifying before Congress on a subject of the Constitution

Paying tribute to Dean Martin on the unveiling of his portrait. *From left*: Dean Diller, Dean Martin, me, and Dean Treanor

Class visit to Congress for meetings with Members, including Tom Suozzi '89, a student at Fordham when I was Dean

Bess and Louis Stein attend the presentation by Dean McLaughlin of the Stein Prize to Chief Justice Warren E. Burger

Family gathering at Rockefeller Center in 2017 when I received the American Bar Association medal

A family celebration of Uncle Pat's birthday in Lake Carmel, New York

1982: My administrative team. *From left*: Reilly, Crowley, me, and Hollister, with Moore and Hanlon behind us, and McGough at the far right

Opening of Edith Guldi Platt Atrium with faculty and administrators present for the picture

1983 Groundbreaking for law school expansion. Richard Bennet '42, E. Carter Corriston '60, me, and Father James Finlay, S.J.

1991: Breakfast in Ireland with President Mary Robinson at the left followed by Jim Gill, Nicholas Robinson, daughter Jean, and me

Leading Citizens of Northern Ireland visit Fordham for training in dispute resolution with Professor Jacqueline Nolan-Haley and Seamus Dunn, both sitting to my left

President Bill Clinton visits Fordham in 1993, with Dean Andrew Rivera in the rear behind me and Dean Vairo to the president's left

The unveiling of the portrait of Frances Berko '44 (sitting in a wheelchair), a nationally acclaimed advocate for the disabled

The opening of the School's first technology classroom under the leadership of Joel Reidenberg (*standing*), joined by Associate Dean Michael Martin and Professor Jacqueline Nolan-Haley

Alumni celebrate the honoring of Professor Katsoris, sitting with Father O'Hare. *Standing from left:* James Tolan, Eugene Souther, me, John Keenan, Paul Curran, and Michael Stanton, with Jim Gill planting the kiss

Presentation of alumni medal of achievement to Professor John Calamari with Patricia Hynes applauding at the center and joined by (*left to right*) former Deans McLaughlin and Mulligan, Father O'Hare, James Tolan, and Professor Katsoris (*at podium greeting Calamari*)

Emalie as a high school senior at the Academy of the Sacred Heart of Mary, Sag Harbor, in 1956

August 25, 1962: Our wedding day, with my parents (*right*) and Emalie's parents and Msgr. George Killeen

Emalie and me on our wedding day, sitting in her grandfather's car

Emalie and family on the birth of our first child

November 1991, outside of Mom's thatched cottage. *From left*: Donald Jr., Donald Sr., me, and my brother-in-law, Lawrence Lambe

Emalie and me with our children on our fiftieth-wedding anniversary. *From right to left*: Rosemary, Maureen, Margaret, John, Bill, and Jean

Our grandchildren when they were younger

With our grandchildren on our fiftieth-wedding anniversary. *To my right:* Ryan, Roddy, Sean, Connor, Brynn, Caitlyn, Ian, Liam, David (*upper right*), Chris, Dylan (*closest to Emalie*)

Emalie and her siblings. *Left to right:* Mary Jo, Ricky, Elinor, Jon, Harold, Bill, and Emalie

With our family and first grandchild on the occasion of our thirtieth-wedding anniversary

Right: Edith Guldi Platt atrium, now the Platt Court, at the Fordham Gabelli School of Business

Below: Justice Sandra Day O'Connor, the first woman to serve on the U.S. Supreme Court, at the opening of the expanded Law School building in 1981 (*Keith Meyers/The New York Times/Redux*)

In response to Teitelbaum's concern, I called the governor's appointments assistant to ask about the shortness of my term, and she told me that at the end of two years I could be re-appointed for another term. Teitelbaum also expressed concern about the New York State Ethics Commission's electronic system and the Public Integrity Commission's telephones being part of the state department system. There was a risk of others "listening in," he said. He felt it was essential that we be removed from that system to safeguard confidentiality. Steps were taken to accomplish his suggestion.[3]

The public's interest in our work at this time centered on the Troopergate investigation. By September 24, when the Public Integrity Commission opened its doors, as Wayne Barrett noted on October 2, 2007, in the *Village Voice*, "The only news in New York politics that's mattered for three months (and counting) is the bizarre hype surrounding the ho-hum charge that new white-knight governor Eliot Spitzer tried to plant a story about Senate Republican leader Joe Bruno's state-subsidized travel." He added, "After decades of editorial pages barking in every newspaper of the state about . . . Albany . . . it was doubtless surprising to learn that the town's biggest scandal . . . was the alleged fixing of a few paragraphs . . . in a front page story this July in . . . the *Times Union*."[4]

When I moved on to the Public Integrity Commission, I regretted that some of the outstanding members of the ethics commission, with whom I had served, would no longer be colleagues. Of course, I would have new colleagues with whom I would develop a very close relationship as well.

35

The New York State Public Integrity Commission

Tribulation is a treasure in the nature of it,
but it is not current money in the use of it,
except we get nearer and nearer our home, heaven, by it.

— JOHN DONNE, MEDITATION, XVII

At the opening of the new space of the Public Integrity Commission on September 24, 2007, I outlined the commission's vision:

> We have a vision of a model agency in terms of all its statutory missions: education, regulatory guidance to the public seeking to obey the law, investigations, enforcement, training and the like. It will take time, hard work, a dedicated group of commissioners, and a staff working together to accomplish these goals.

On October 10, the commission's first public hearing was held. I opened the session by saying, "As we start, I would like to encourage the formation of working groups of commissioners to assist the staff in looking at all aspects of the new legislation and offering suggestions that will enable the commission to discharge its responsibilities in a way that promotes public confidence." I added: "Some areas for working groups include coordinating with staff on the preparation of formal opinions to be presented to the full commission for consideration, providing inputs, as appropriate, on investigations, developing proposals for public hearings, examining the areas of procurement, lobbying and addressing recusal questions."[1]

The commission also unanimously appointed Teitelbaum as executive director and instructed him to hire a general counsel. Teitelbaum's excellent work in effectuating the merger was noted and greatly appreciated by all. A few newspapers ran a picture of the commissioners being sworn in as a group by the Secretary of State. I had suggested a swearing-in to reinforce the significance of our obligations to the people of New York State.

For the next fifteen months I would work as hard as I ever had in my life on this assignment, despite the fact that it was a volunteer undertaking, and I had to sandwich in my work at Fordham. I often left my home in Westchester at 4 in the morning and returned late at night either the same day, the next day, or the day after, depending on my schedule. No lights except street lights were on when I left my house in the morning, stopping for a cup of coffee a couple times along the way. I'd watch the sunrise as I neared my destination, arriving shortly before 7:30 a.m. How I remember those stress-filled mornings! During this period I spent nearly every other day doing commission-related work either at my home or at Fordham in New York City.

On my frequent visits to the commission's offices, I made it a practice to chat individually with staff members to get a sense of what they were doing and give them an opportunity to offer comments and suggestions. I met frequently with senior members of the legal staff and the investigative group to make sure I was kept abreast of sensitive matters they were handling.

The number of people engaged in the commission's work was small, fewer than sixty, given the limited nature of its budget. (By contrast, the Commission on Government Integrity was much bigger in both size and budget, at least in 1987.) And yet, without much fanfare or public affirmation, the group at the Public Integrity Commission had jelled. I was proud of all they accomplished under Teitelbaum's leadership, developing public training, educational, and other programs, including a new website.

The work of the staff was all-encompassing. In 2008, during its first full year of the commission's operation, its work included initiating 42 investigations of violations of the law; reviewing public disclosure forms; reviewing and auditing reports filed by lobbyists; conducting training and education programs for the more than 250,000 state employees and 6,600 registered lobbyists and their clients subject to the commission's jurisdiction; drafting more than 150 written advisory opinions that essentially became law (for example, on the use of state resources and gifts by lobbyists); monitoring more than 18,000 legislative bills; and responding to reporters who sought information on a daily basis.[2]

Despite the fullness of the commission's agenda, nothing seemed more important to the outside world than Troopergate. At times the investigation seemed to have a Watergate frenzy to it, with the major focus being whether the commission "would get Spitzer." Our group was a cauldron for a steady stream of attacks, with newspaper articles making endless references to "sources

close to the commission," "sources with knowledge of the Troopergate investigation," "sources familiar with the matter," "a source close to the scandal,"
"a source close to Spitzer," "a source close to the Senate probe," "a commission source," "GOP state senators," and on and on. Every now and then, a
comment would be made to the effect that "maybe PIC will come through
yet." Walter Ayres, the commission's spokesperson, consistently helped me
deal with the media and was extraordinary in his patience, dedication, and
decency. In trying to be as helpful as possible given the confidentiality limitations placed on him, he would hand-deliver material to the state's Legislative
Office's press room.

Setting Up Working Groups

Directly after the opening hearing of October, I turned my attention to setting
up working groups, including for the Troopergate investigation. My selection of members to serve on the Troopergate group were obvious choices:
Judge Howard Levine; Loretta Lynch, later Attorney General of the United
States; Robert Giuffra Jr., an experienced white-collar defense lawyer; and
John Mitchell, who had been appointed by the State Assembly's Republican
minority leader. I also placed myself on this working group.

On October 12, I sent all the commissioners a confidential memorandum
listing the working group assignments for both commissioners and staff, along
with correspondence related to the commission's Troopergate investigation,
including a recent letter from the governor's office. On October 15, the
Troopergate working group met for the first time and were given a summary
of testimony taken in the investigation.

After discussion, the working group commissioners decided to consult privately with the Albany County district attorney concerning the testimony, out
of respect for the rights of witnesses appearing before the commission and any
continued investigation the district attorney might plan regarding this subject.
I made contact with the district attorney, and Teitelbaum followed up.

On Saturday, October 20, Ayres received a call from a reporter at the *New
York Post* that he had information identifying the members of the working
group and had obtained the correspondence the commission had received
from the executive chamber. My sense was that someone at the commission
leaked the information to the press about my mailing to commission members.

On Monday, October 22, a highly damaging article appeared in the *Post*,
under the headline "'Tricks' Probe Is Tainted: GOP," followed a day later by
an editorial titled "Feerick's Tainted Probe." The gist of both was that I had
"approved the formation of a special subcommittee dominated by Spitzer-
appointed members to oversee the probe," and, quoting an unnamed "com-

mission source," that the group was designed to give "Spitzer total control of the investigation." The editorial concluded, "Feerick apparently caved in to Spitzer."

The article was a harbinger of things to come. It mentioned the receipt by the Public Integrity Commission of a letter from the governor's counsel, suggesting that an inappropriate communication had occurred, although that was not the case. Fortunately, no other newspapers joined the bandwagon, but the damage was done. Beyond that, I wondered who within the commission had leaked this information, first, apparently, to Republican state senators, as the article noted, and then to the press. And why? I immediately saw a connection between the leak, the working group meeting of October 15, and the resulting consultation with the district attorney. I surmised that the leaker(s) disliked this working group and wanted to destroy both its credibility and its usefulness.

It is impossible to describe the despair I felt at that moment, not unlike the pain I experienced by the leak in 1989 of the draft report of the Commission on Government Integrity. I thought about resigning, but too much was happening for me to abandon ship. The political battle then going on between the governor and the Senate majority leader was terrible, with two seasoned Albany veterans telling me they'd never seen anything like it before. I felt as if I'd entered a Byzantine world far removed from the "idyllic" life of a professor of law at a school in New York City.

November presented another challenge. Early in the month, Teitelbaum told me of a call he had gotten from the Albany district attorney, suggesting that he had information Teitelbaum had leaked to the executive branch the fact that the district attorney was continuing his Troopergate investigation. Teitelbaum denied any such communication. Nonetheless, out of deference to the district attorney's reopening of his investigation, the commission slowed down its investigation of the matter for the rest of the year, except for gathering necessary documents from anticipated witnesses who might testify before the commission when the time was right.

The month of December was a busy one for me. Teitelbaum took a brief planned personal leave, and, with no general counsel in place, I picked up the slack in his absence. As a result I spent much of the Christmas–New Year's period in Albany and on the telephone dealing with various issues. Unfortunately, Teitelbaum's absence, even though it had been approved in advance, turned out to be another subject for press attention.

The New Year

The early part of 2008 was filled with continued skirmishes over documents, contemplated litigation by the commission to gather more documents, the resumption of our examination of witnesses, and dealing with attacks on the commission from "unnamed sources," as they were often described in the press. On February 10, I met with the Albany district attorney to discuss his concerns regarding confidentiality. Two weeks later, Teitelbaum and I met with the governor's counsel to discuss ground rules for the commission's forthcoming examination of the governor.

These early months of 2008, as was the case in the fall of 2007, played havoc with my responsibilities at Fordham and on my family life. Except for my teaching days at Fordham, most of the rest of my time was spent dealing with Troopergate issues. I was absent from family occasions, and colleagues covered for me at the Law School. Close friends and family members, including my children, asked me to give up this service entirely. Emalie pleaded with me to do so. They saw and felt my exhaustion and my absence when health issues arose within the family. When a relatively new commissioner asked me in early 2008 what it was like chairing a commission like this one, I responded, "I had not had an up day yet." By that point, ten months of what seemed like almost full-time volunteer work had gone by.

The Governor's Resignation

March of 2008 was one of the many months when the commission had to deal with the unexpected, to say the least. The New York world (and beyond) was shocked beyond words by the news on March 10 of a scandal that enveloped Governor Spitzer concerning a relationship with a prostitute and the use of public funds for transportation to facilitate that relationship. (The fact that the governor had made ethics a keystone of his administration only fueled the flames.) The revelation led the governor to announce his resignation from office on March 12, just two days after the scandal was disclosed in the *New York Times*.

Over the next few days I received calls asking if I was going to resign out of disgust, having been "Uchered," as one caller said, into public service on false pretenses. Some outside the commission suggested that we should end our Troopergate investigation as quickly as possible (since as one person said, "The king is dead"), but my response was that we'd finish considering this issue carefully and fairly, taking whatever time was required. During this period, Spitzer testified before us under oath, as did other members of his administration.

Reaching a Decision

After the completion of the testimony, I asked the staff to provide the commission with a thorough report on the investigation. In late June, the commission convened to discuss the issues presented in the investigation. After a full discussion, it reached its conclusions, resulting in a unanimous vote charging four people with violations of the law — the former governor's chief of staff, his homeland security assistant, the acting chief of state police, and the governor's director of communications.

A detailed Notice of Reasonable Cause was drafted, approved, and then issued by the commission on July 24, 2008, along with all of the testimony given in the investigation and hundreds of exhibits. Such a public airing of the details of an investigation was unprecedented. We'd come a long way and had done our work diligently and fairly. We went where the evidence took us. We charged no one where the recorded evidence to support a charge was absent.

The commission's work was reported on favorably, described by some, including the *New York Times*, as the most comprehensive of the investigations of Troopergate and the only one to find any violations of law. Even reporters critical of the commission complimented its work. But not everyone was happy with the result. Some complained that Spitzer should have been charged with a violation of law, and others commented on the length of the investigation and the alleged leaking of information.

Of all the comments I received at the time, the one that touched me most came from a commission member who wasn't a lawyer. "John, I can only imagine the level of frustration and upset you've put up with over these last few months," it began. "I just wanted you to know that I believe that throughout the process you have been a superb leader. Thanks for all that it must have cost you." Teitelbaum told me that on receiving a note from his wife saying how proud her father (Morris Abram, a distinguished civil rights lawyer) would have been of his service, he broke down and cried.

To Leave or Not

A few days before the Notice of Reasonable Cause was issued, I began to give serious thought to leaving. In addition to being exhausted, I felt that the work of the commission had robbed me of my personal and academic life. Emalie urged me to leave the commission now that I had completed the bulk of the Troopergate investigation. After two days of discussions with my family at my sister Maureen's house in North Carolina, I typed out a letter of resignation, and on August 1, I called James King to read it to him. I found it unnecessary to discuss the exhaustion I felt, which was obvious to those with whom I had worked closely.

I was startled by his reaction. "Tear it up," he said, adding that my leaving would lead to the disintegration of the commission. I didn't expect this response. After further discussion with my family, I decided to rip up the letter and go forward for a while more. To revive my energy, I took a trip to Ireland with Emalie after the commission's meeting of August 5.

On the eve of the trip, however, I received a communication from the Office of the Inspector General alerting me to the opening of an investigation based on a referral from the Albany County District Attorney's Office. The office was going to investigate the allegation of the previous November that Teitelbaum had leaked information about the district attorney's reopened Troopergate investigation to the executive chamber. Upon my return from Ireland, this investigation became the bane of my existence.

The inspector general was the chief assistant in the Queens County District Attorney's Office when the Commission on Government Integrity issued its highly critical report of election-related activity in that office after public hearings in 1988. I received communications from former staff of the Commission on Government Integrity urging me to object to this new investigation on the grounds of conflict of interest. I brushed aside such expressions. I wanted all of this over with as soon as possible so that I could move on with my life.

In the fall of 2008, as all of this was going on, I informed Teitelbaum and Barry Ginsberg, the commission's general counsel, of my decision to leave as chair at the year's end, believing that the investigation would be concluded well before then. I shared my decision with King, who was now supportive. Teitelbaum and Ginsberg were upset but understanding. When Teitelbaum mentioned that he also had been thinking of leaving, I asked him to defer doing so until a new chair was in place. He agreed. It is impossible for me to describe my state of mind during these events. In brief, the entire experience, especially the issue of an internal leak or leaks, had taken its toll on me. Emalie said at the time that I was "lower than the whale tracks." It was worse than that. I had no life at all.

Moving On

I delayed my announcement for the rest of the 2008 calendar year. On January 12, 2009, I notified Governor Paterson of my decision to leave as chair, effective on Lincoln's Birthday. I also told the commission's outstanding pro bono counsel, Zachary Carter, of my decision and thanked him for his extraordinary service to the commission in dealing with the inspector general's investigation.[3]

I'll forever treasure the notes and comments I received from my fellow commissioners upon my resignation, along with the mounted and autographed coffee cup given to me by the staff as bagpipes played in the background (courtesy of a staff member's husband) at a farewell reception at the commission's office. I was reminded of the words of Justice Francis Timothy Murphy who, on leaving an institution that had meant a great deal to him, said, "It was time to walk up the avenue with a skip and a smile."[4]

Of course my feelings about the experience of chairing the Public Integrity Commission differed from Justice Murphy's as he looked back on his service as presiding justice of the Appellate Division for the First Judicial Department. When it became clear that, for political reasons, he wouldn't be recertified, he left the court and obtained a position at a leading law firm.

As I walked away from the commission, however, there was one shining moment, an unexpected dinner for me given by the leadership of Fordham University, attended by some of Fordham's most prominent graduates. They presented me with a welcome-back memento, and I responded with a speech, thanking Emalie who had supported me and endured the challenges of the past two years. Of the many expressions of support I received, none were more important than those from my children.

A Public Affirmation of the Commission

Months after I had left the Public Integrity Commission, the commission had to address the inspector general's report. With the report as his basis, Governor Paterson asked the twelve commissioners and staff leadership to resign. Counsel for the commission responded strongly to the assault, leading the governor to back off his request and later express confidence in his appointees to the commission, as did state office holders with respect to their appointees. The governor praised the then acting chair of the commission, Loretta Lynch, calling her an outstanding prosecutor who would serve well as a U.S. Attorney. Teitelbaum decided to leave, as he had planned, and Barry Ginsberg became executive director.[5] My successor as chair of the commission, Michael Cherkasky,[6] conducted his own review of the commission's Troopergate investigation and issued an extraordinary document in which he stated:

> I have learned over the years that things are not always the way they initially appear. While this statement is not in any way a presentation of findings of a formal review, I have now reviewed as much of the available information as possible and have come to a series of conclusions.
>
> First, the Commissioners acted in an unbiased and objective manner in reaching their decisions in the "troopergate" matter. There is simply no evidence that John Feerick and the other Commissioners were anything but neutral and fair. They based their decisions on

the evidence and applied the law to the facts without fear or favor. In fact, of all the agencies to have investigated the "troopergate" matter, they are the only group — not the IG, not the DA, not the Attorney General — to have charged anyone with violating the law. Further, all the decisions were unanimous, this by a Commission that represents a broad spectrum of political views, appointed by seven different people, Democrats and Republicans. . . .

Finally, I must add that while I agree with certain aspects of the IG's report, I would caution about its tone, and the use of resources necessarily devoted to such a lengthy report. We have so many serious problems to fix, in ethical governance and other areas, that we should require a greater use of discretion before we incur time and money on such an insignificant project. And when reports are issued that impact the reputations of our citizens, care must be exercised not to exaggerate.[7]

PART IX
Marriage and Family

Whatever you would wish at your dying hour to have done in health, that do now while you may.

— ST. ANGELA MERICI

36

Our Growing Family

Even though people may be well known, they hold in their hearts
the emotions of a simple person for the moments that are the most
important of those we know on earth: birth, marriage and death.

— JACQUELINE KENNEDY ONASSIS

Emalie was the second of seven children. She had a strong Catholic upbringing, inheriting her faith from her devoted parents and having it nurtured by religious sisters from grammar school through college. Her practice of the faith has been a benchmark and influence for me, as she goes to mass regularly and says the rosary daily with prayers for loved ones and friends. By all accounts, she was active in sports growing up, a "tomboy," some said, who loved to ride horses and play the piano. She excelled in school, succeeding in math early on but later deciding to major in English literature, and graduating with high honors.

When Emalie and I began our life together, we fantasized about having a dozen children, but as our children came along, we gradually reduced that number, concluding that six might be what we could manage. The firstborn was Maureen, followed by Margaret, Jean, Rosemary, John, and William. A period of twelve years, 1964 to 1976, spanned their births. We spent the first years of our marriage (1962–1968) living in Riverdale, a beautiful area in the northwest Bronx. We enjoyed taking our children to Van Cortlandt Park and watching them go sledding on the streets surrounding our apartment building at 3840 Greystone Avenue.

Other families in the building were raising small children, and we enjoyed getting to know them. One such family, the McNamaras, lived there until

2019. Their son Michael, who was a few years old when we moved in, has since become a leader of the New York Bar and a good friend, along with his wife and children.

In 1968, the idea of buying our own home became a reality. We had settled on a price we could afford, between $30,000 and $50,000. I had hoped we could stay in the Bronx, and so we looked at homes in Riverdale, but we couldn't afford the prices there. We considered buying a two-family house that was being built down the street from us to accommodate Mom and Pop, but that didn't pan out, either. It would have been a tight fit for us with three children, as well as our expected additions. While it didn't seem practical to buy that house, it was hard to move away from the Bronx and from Mom and Pop. And so we began focusing on building a house for them in Lake Carmel, New York, closer to the homes we were exploring in the suburbs.

After looking at newer homes on Long Island and in Westchester County, Emalie and I settled on a recently built two-story colonial at 41 Highridge Road in Mount Kisco. It had five bedrooms, a study downstairs that we could convert into a bedroom, and a basement we could finish, plus an acre of hilly land. The cost was $58,000.

We chose this location because of the quality of the local schools and our sense that other families with young children would be buying homes on this road, as a few already had. The house was near the Mount Kisco train station, and the fact that it was on a direct line with Grand Central Terminal, a few blocks from Skadden, where I then worked, was another advantage. I used our meager savings for the down payment, and I had to borrow $2,000 from my father-in-law to cover the closing costs. We moved in on Friday, January 29, 1969. The following Monday, a major snowstorm closed down the roads. It was our welcome to the suburbs.

For the next thirty-three years we lived in this house, raising our children to adulthood there. The house was always open to other children in the neighborhood, and many saw our home as a meeting place, where they gathered for kickball, basketball, and tricks on the swing set. In 2002, when Emalie and I moved to Larchmont, a town about forty minutes south, we left behind many of the wonderful friends we had made. We were pleased that our son John, then 29, wanted to hold on to the house. With a bank loan and a mortgage, along with hard work and sheer determination, he made it work, spurred in part by the memories of the life we shared there.

I have happy memories of attending parents' days at our children's grammar school, Roaring Brook School in Chappaqua. It was a joy to go to their concerts and to accept teachers' invitations to speak to classes on the subject of my writings (principally on the Constitution). My daughter Jean recalls a visit I made to her sixth-grade class with Mrs. Jones, who ran a "tight ship" of a classroom. When asked to introduce her father by describing his profession, Jean informed the class that he was a "labor lawyer." Mrs. Jones replied, "Well, what is that Jean?" Pause, Swallow. Pause. Jean confessed she didn't actually know what I did! Over the years, we came to know some of the teachers well as they taught multiple children of ours.

My daughter Rosemary told me that her most notable memory from these years was of Mr. Brownsword, a teacher who, she says, "brought school to life for me." She recalled a doll that hung above his desk called "Sir Laughalot." Whenever someone excelled in the classroom, Mr. Brownsword would hit it with a yardstick. Rose also attended a summer camp he ran in Maine. She described the camp as a "magical" week where she "fished for lobsters, picked wild blueberries, swam in a quarry and went canoeing." Margaret also has memories of Mr. Brownsword. She remembers with fondness his reading to the class, as well as having playdates with his daughter, Nancy, who was the same age as her. It was also while she was in Mr. Brownsword's class that Margaret performed the lead role in the school musical, *H.M.S. Pinafore.*

Jean, who would eventually go on to study English literature, recalls her fourth-grade teacher, Mrs. Gross, who had a reputation for being a hard teacher. Jean was pleasantly surprised to discover a different side to her, especially in the "wonderful hours she would spend reading the book *The Phantom Tollbooth.*" Jean recalled, "I loved her animated interpretation of that story. I also recall having my first exposure to theater in her class — she put on a version of *Hamlet.* I played Ophelia, the spurned lover of Hamlet who goes crazy. I was supposed to enter the stage midway through the play, saying some lines expressing her descent into madness, but I missed my cue altogether. That was the end of my acting career, but the start of my career as a Shakespearean."

Maureen's most memorable elementary school teachers were Mr. Applebaum and Mr. Schneller. "I had them in 5th grade," she said. "Up until their class, I had always considered myself slow academically, as I was young for my grade and a late bloomer and I learned to read later than most of my peers. However, Mr. Applebaum and Mr. Schneller recognized some math aptitude in me, which they continually reinforced, and they helped me to learn to think of myself as bright and smart. This change in perspective was hugely empowering and helped set the stage for me to excel in school in later years."

John spoke of a young second-grade teacher, Ms. Carlisle, as a favorite because she was gentle, positive, and friendly. Bill fondly remembers his pre-first-grade teacher, Ms. Costello, because "she made you feel good about yourself." He recalls ripping up a prop telephone book as part of a circus put on in his class, which made him feel "super strong." John and Bill's teachers at Fordham Prep also left an impression. John attributes Jesuit Father Lombardi for encouraging him not to be meek, while Bill points to Father William O'Malley for inspiring his interest in reading and writing, as he often read books and poems to his students.

The teenage years were difficult ones for us. Emalie often had to cope alone with the care of our large and rambunctious family, as I was seldom around because of my work at Skadden and then at Fordham. When I asked Maureen why none of our children became lawyers, she replied that it had to do with Emalie constantly exclaiming, "Where is your father!" Emalie once remarked that she was lucky to have come out of this period with her sanity intact.

Mom and Pop were very helpful to us when the children were young. They came over often to help—babysitting, tidying our home, and doing other chores to lighten the burden. At times we brought the kids to them as well.

Donald's wife, Meg, was also of enormous help. She would sometimes look after our children while Emalie and I were away. Meg was extraordinary, as she too had six children of her own to care for.

Our children grew up in an affluent community, and when I began to enjoy financial success, Emalie and I didn't change our ways in some areas, although in others we did. In my years at Skadden and at Fordham, I tried to take the family out to dinner on Friday nights, usually for pizza or Chinese food, as a way of catching up with one another. My children remember, even on these occasions, our restraint with desserts and the number of soft drinks they could have—both to promote good health and to encourage a modest lifestyle. Because of its low prices, Caldor became a preferred place to buy clothes and toys, although my children found the clothes embarrassing because so many of their peers wore designer brands.

As I turned 40, I realized how little I had done with my children, and so I turned to skiing to forge a deeper bond with them. I learned the basics, and soon I had the joy of watching them surpass my skill. Meanwhile, they laughed at my expense as I barreled down the mountain with little control, never one for good form! For several years we spent weekends together skiing at the Windham Mountain Resort in the Catskills. Many a Friday night I made the long drive with them in our station wagon, sometimes having all six in tow, while Emalie stayed behind for a breather. We relished the music in the lodge, hot chocolate by the fire, and the chaotic meals that we novices tried to assemble without Emalie's guidance. My children remember how each morning we packed peanut butter and jelly sandwiches to cut down on costs, and how they lined up on benches so I could help tighten their bulky ski boots.

For several summers we also returned to the Tyler Place in Vermont, where Emalie and I had spent part of our honeymoon decades earlier. My children fondly remember the end-of-the-week grand finales, when the staff performed skits and songs for the guests, concluding with a nostalgic version of Randy Sparks's song "Today," a family favorite that has been passed down to my grandkids.

Most summers we also spent time in Southampton. In the 1960s and early 1970s, Emalie's parents made room for us at their family resort, Horizon Hills, which overlooked Shinnecock Bay and had an uninterrupted view of the Atlantic Ocean. We also stayed at their house on Hill Street in Southampton. In 1974 Emalie and I bought a small house off Majors Path close by, where the kids would spend most of their summers as they grew. They loved our trips back to Horizon Hills to indulge in use of the pool, and they recall long bike rides to the inlet, which exhausted their little legs as they pedaled ferociously in an attempt to keep up with me.

Emalie, our "crazy glue" as our children described her, did everything imaginable when it came to raising them, taking them to music lessons, to school events, to parties at the homes of friends, to dentist and doctor's appointments, and to religious lessons at church, as well as making sure they had the clothes they needed, did their homework, and went to bed on time. Despite the demands on her time and the struggle of running the house often single-handedly, still many times, Emalie found time after the children were asleep to go over drafts of my writings and make editorial suggestions.

I usually came in late at night from work and left early. When the kids were little, they would sometimes greet me with a game of hide-and-seek, jumping out to scare me as I rounded a bend. Other times they would extract a game of octopus, for which I would lie on the ground, as they ran around me, trying to avoid being captured by my arms and legs. They described how scary it was to be seized by one of my tentacles and the effort their siblings went to try to pull them free from my tight grip. Still other times, I was called upon to discipline, asking them to account for their bad behavior and sometimes deciding that a slap to the hand was in order. Truth be told, I was not very strict with them, and the kids came to know that.

My daughter Maureen recalls one night as a teen sneaking out of the house after bedtime in her pajamas to join a friend for some mischief. A few hours later, their car crashed on ice and the only refuge they could find was a nearby bar, where they went to phone for help. Maureen's friend refused to call her parents, knowing she would be in deep trouble. So they reached out to me instead and I came right down. Maureen says I hardly looked at her or said a word on the drive home, but she was grateful for my help. Apparently, her friend still remembers the silent treatment I gave them.

A Celebration of Togetherness

Celebrating the Christmas season at the Trapp Family Lodge, another place Emalie and I had gone on our honeymoon, was a particular highlight of the year for me. The Trapp family had discovered this idyllic, enchanting mountain valley in 1942 after fleeing the political troubles in Europe at the start of World War II. In the 1980s we purchased time shares next to the lodge, and each year since we've taken advantage of all the activities the Trapp family makes available.

At Trapp, we shared meals and played sports and games, which included moments where we expressed our singing talents. I was shocked and a bit embarrassed when I saw my unedited rendition of "Climb Ev'ry Mountain" on Maureen's Facebook page. For many years, I skied downhill at Mount Mansfield, Vermont's highest mountain, but as I got older, my activities became limited to swimming in the pool and long walks, as well as our annual hikes to the cabin five miles above the Lodge. I also found myself spending more time on the computer for work purposes, setting my books aside for family games and collective meals. Emalie spent her time there relishing moments of quiet to read when the kids were out and would occasionally make trips to town with the children and grandchildren for lunch or to browse the goodies at the country store.

The Education of Our Children

Nothing was more important to us than our children's education. Beyond the wonderful elementary school they attended in Chappaqua, they spent two years at the Robert E. Bell Middle School. Emalie and I wanted our children to attend a Catholic high school, but they wanted to go to a public school. The area had an outstanding public high school, Horace Greeley, which made the decision harder.

Maureen left the public school system after two-and-a-half years at Greeley and transferred to Hackley, a private school in Tarrytown, which turned out to be a very good choice. Only Jean would end up graduating with a diploma from Greeley, where she was academically challenged and made lasting friendships. Margaret left home for high school, but after a year at Kent, in Connecticut, she returned home and attended the School of the Holy Child in Rye, as did Rosemary a few years later. Our two sons went to Fordham Preparatory School, where they had been offered scholarships.

Because our children enjoyed academic success in high school, they had the opportunity to attend strong colleges. Maureen went to Washington University in St. Louis and then transferred to Fordham's College of Business Administration, choices influenced by her then boyfriend and now husband, Lester LeBlanc. Jean, Rosemary, and Bill all went to Georgetown College, where Emalie's father and two of her brothers had gone.

Jean, who gave important service to Georgetown in reviewing its student code of conduct, graduated as valedictorian of her class;[1] Rosemary focused on social justice and related extracurricular activities and enjoyed academic success in theology, and Bill starred on the crew team and graduated with honors. Margaret attended Barnard College after having enjoyed her years at the School of the Holy Child, an all-girls school. She excelled at Barnard. John went to Williams and became a leader in community service, particularly in the areas of hunger and homelessness.

Four of our children used their college years as an opportunity to explore the cultures of other countries. Margaret went to Oxford for a semester. Jean spent part of a year in Florence at Georgetown's Villa le Balze, formerly owned by the Rockefellers. Rosemary studied at Hebrew University in Israel, and Bill spent a year at Louvain-la-Neuve in Belgium.

Jean returned from Italy with a deep love for Renaissance art and culture, nurtured by her studies there. Rosemary came back with a knowledge of Hebrew and an enhanced understanding of the Old Testament. Bill succeeded in courses that were all taught in French, returning home fluent in the language.

All six of our children extended their formal education beyond college. Maureen received a master's degree in business administration from New York University. Margaret received a master's degree in psychology from Teachers College at Columbia University and then a doctorate in developmental psychology from Cornell. Jean, as the recipient of the 1990–1992 Georgetown's Allbritton Scholarship, graduated with a master's degree in philosophy from the University of Oxford, followed by a doctorate in English from the University of Pennsylvania. Rosemary received a Master of Divinity from the Jesuit School of Theology at Berkeley. John graduated with a medical degree from New York Medical College, and Bill received a master's degree in reading and literacy from Bank Street Graduate School of Education, later earning a special education certification.

Special Occasions

Among the most precious possessions Emalie and I have are notes from our children celebrating special occasions, such as birthdays, anniversaries, and holidays. When Emalie turned 60, our children gave her a beautiful video celebrating her life, which was assembled by our daughter Jean and presented at a dinner with family and a few friends. One of our dear friends present that night, Father Joseph O'Hare, S.J., described the evening as a tribute to motherhood. Many of us, including Emalie, cried during the showing of the video. To add to the magic of that moment, another video was quietly made of her reactions throughout the presentation, which is as equally moving. A framed plaque, titled "What our mother means to us," was given to Emalie by our children and provides a glimpse of their affection for her:

Maureen said, "You are the heart and soul of our family."

Margaret, in a touching poem called "Mother," concluded with the words: "And then again the cycle begins, with new little ones she's mother again. An angel from God, a light from afar. They call her 'Nana' or sometimes 'Grandma.'"

Jean spoke of Emalie's patience, courage, strength, grace, generosity, and wisdom, ending with the observation that she was "home" for all her children.

Rosemary described the gifts she'd received from her mother: generosity "beyond the trappings of materialism," a sense of humor, a contemplative nature, an understanding of the value of children, thoughtfulness, and faith. She concluded by remarking, "Mom is clearly a master of the best and most beautiful things in life."

John wrote of his mother's unconditional love, affirmation, unconditional forgiveness, and her advocacy for her children.

Finally, Bill spoke of his bond "with the most angelic and gentle of moms" and concluded: "I speak for all of your children when I say that your love is the ink with which we write our life stories. You often say that if we'd all just light one candle, how bright the world would be. I think we all know that you far exceeded that and the kindled flames here tonight are just a few of the many you've spent your life lighting."

This summary hardly does justice to our children's words inscribed on that plaque. Patient, humble, and unassuming, Emalie goes about her life and good works quietly and prayerfully, with a total commitment to our family, immediate and extended, as well as friends, acquaintances and strangers in need of assistance.

On this special family occasion, Emalie's oldest sister spoke movingly of her as her best friend, and her youngest sister said she taught her how to be a mother. Donald spontaneously added that the verses that Emalie sent to family members celebrating holidays and special occasions were themselves worthy of a book collection because of how rich they are.

Our six children are our precious jewels. And with the arrival of their children, we have additional jewels — eleven grandchildren. Beyond our immediate family are my siblings and their spouses, ten nieces, and three nephews, as well as my children's spouses, my Irish cousins, and their children and grandchildren.

Concluding Reflections

Emalie and I celebrated our 50th wedding anniversary at a special place located on Highland Lake in Maine, following a plan carefully developed by our children. On August 18, 2012, we gathered from all over the country for a week of memorable activities, ranging from hiking trips, golf, biking excursions, motor boating, swimming races, board games, and the like. I remember Emalie and I racing in paddleboats, each assisted by one of our children (I won't say who won). It all came together at dinner one night that week, where our children and grandchildren expressed their sentiments in song, dance, piano playing, gymnastics, poetry, and a video production. My grandson Dylan, who was then 11, was the MC. The video began with a poem by Saint Theresa of Avila:

> Her heart is full of joy with love.
> For in the Lord her mind is stilled.
> She has renounced every selfish attachment.
> And draws abiding joy and strength
> from the One within.
> She lives not for herself, but lives
> To serve the Lord of Love in all.
> And swims across the sea of Life
> Brestings its rough ways joyfully.

Although Emalie and I were by that point in our 70s, the week made us feel young again.[2]

37

Deaths in the Family

Take, Lord, and receive all my liberty,
my memory, my understanding
and my entire will,
all I have and call my own.
You have given all to me.
To you, Lord, I return it.
Everything is yours; do with it what you will.
Give me only your love and your grace,
that is enough for me.

— ST. IGNATIUS LOYOLA

In the mid-1970s, Emalie and I and others in the family began to notice signs in Mom that we failed to understand. We thought she had become hard of hearing and arranged for her to be fitted with a hearing aid. When this didn't solve the problem, and fearing that her memory was failing, we arranged for her to be examined at New York University Hospital. There we learned that Mom might be experiencing effects from a mini-stroke or two that she'd had years before.

Not long after this, Pop began to call on Emalie for help. He said that Mom was becoming forgetful, and he worried that she might not find her way home if she went out by herself. Emalie, an angel as always, would drive up to Lake Carmel to care for Mom or would bring her to our house on weekends, giving Pop some quality time to enjoy his community activities in Lake Carmel. This arrangement continued for several years. The burden on Emalie was enormous, given the fact that she had six very active children to raise and did most of the raising without any help.

As the challenges regarding Mom's health became greater, Pop needed additional help caring for her on a daily basis. He arranged for a home care aide to come on weekdays, but the weekends and evenings remained uncovered. Family members who lived nearby were called on more and more, and those who lived outside New York were asked to do what they could to help as well.

Our daughter Margaret, who by 1983 could drive, would go from her high school in Rye to Lake Carmel to stay overnight so that Pop wouldn't be alone. Around the same time, Margaret was helping Uncle Pat deal with medical issues involving Aunt Catherine and often took her to doctor's appointments. This helps explain the devotion Pop and Pat had for Margaret, in particular.

Pop's health was never great because of his years of heavy smoking. Despite having a related breathing condition, chronic obstructive pulmonary disease, he did everything possible to take care of Mom. He took her to family events, to Irish functions, and to dinners with friends. Dinner at Middlebranch in Carmel was a particular favorite of theirs.

But our world of coping became more difficult in 1985 when Pop learned that he had colon cancer. His reaction was to let nature take its course, which, in essence, meant no surgery. An oncologist told me that Pop would die within six months unless he had surgery, which would likely give him three more years of life. I, along with others, insisted that he have the procedure. He finally relented and had the surgery at New York Hospital in the summer of 1985.

Joseph Crowley, my teacher and friend at Fordham, recommended his oncologist and his surgeon. Crowley had learned around the same time that he too had colon cancer, but he didn't pursue surgery and tragically died six months later. Joe's doctors were able to give Pop a gift of three more years of life, for which I remain deeply grateful.

Upon returning home from his surgery, Pop put enormous pressure on me to find a nursing home for Mom. As her health declined from what appeared to be dementia, Mom became more and more confused. This became evident in certain behaviors, such as putting a cup and saucer on the stove to make tea or putting on a bathrobe rather than an overcoat when she went out. She eventually needed help with dressing and other tasks. It was painful to see her so decline, but she never ceased being my wonderful mother, whom I loved deeply.

As Mom's condition worsened, Pop concluded that it was impossible for any of us to give Mom the total care she needed. Pop's quality of life was also being affected. I sought the counsel of Charles Fahey, S.J., a professor at Fordham University, who was wise and experienced in the area of aging. He suggested that I listen to Pop. He also recommended that I have Mom examined by the dementia center of Burke Rehabilitation Hospital in White Plains, Westchester. He also said that if we decided to place Mom in a home, we should find one that would be convenient for family members to visit.

I followed his advice, had Mom examined at Burke, and with Emalie's help, found a nursing home called Cedar Manor, located in Ossining, New York. On October 22, 1985, Mom, then 76, entered the home. Pop and Donald drove her there. I wasn't able to go with them because I found the experience of placing Mom in a nursing home heart-wrenching.

I can't describe how hard it was for me to see her institutionalized, but I was to discover how much life was left in her, even in such a restricted setting. During my weekly visits I met many endearing individuals who sang, danced, played the piano, and chatted with one another. I never knew how much Mom was aware of her surroundings, or at what point, if at all, she had ceased to know me. But she always seemed comforted by the presence of family, and her decline was gradual, occurring over more than a decade. When strangers visited us, she became agitated and nervous, but we were always friendly faces to her even if she didn't know exactly who we were. What I believe is that in some way we remained familiar to her until her death in July of 1989.

One aspect of placing a loved one in a nursing home is the financial reality. The pain experienced by a spouse, not to mention children, can be unbearable. I watched Pop liquidate his savings to the point at which Mom was eligible for Medicaid. His own pride and dignity prevented him from taking money from us. Donald told me that the fact that he'd leave no material legacy for his children and grandchildren weighed heavily on him. What Pop didn't realize was that he and Mom would leave a far greater legacy.

Between 1985 and 1989, each of us did what we could to help. Maureen came up from North Carolina, Anne came to visit from California, and Donald and his wife, Meg, were always around. Whenever Kevin came back for a visit from Holland, where he then lived, Pop, delighted by the visit, would grill him a steak. Friends and neighbors provided part-time home care for Pop and visited him often. Emalie and I visited Mom regularly, often joined by one or more of our children.

Some of my children remember walking with Mom outside Cedar Manor and her singing along with us her favorite Irish melodies, like "When Irish Eyes Are Smiling." Usually Emalie would start with the opening refrain, and Mom would take it from there. My son Bill shared this memory from his pre-teen years after reading a 2016 article on Alzheimer's:

Sunday afternoons. Johnny got shotgun and I would slip into the back seat of Dad's work car. We would take the back roads to Ossining, arrive at Grandma's nursing home, and walk those institution hallways. I didn't like that part — walking through those halls with their distinctly stale odor of hospital food, disinfectant, and decay.

We'd find Grandma in a room of chairs and wheelchairs. She wasn't the only one there with that unmistakable languid gaze. We'd take her by the arms, exit the home, and meander the grounds. On occasion, we'd serenade Grandma with a few lines of "Danny Boy," listening expectantly for when she crooned a line or two, joining in the upturn of its melody. I was a self-absorbed kid, not realizing the deep reality that this was Dad's mom. I didn't have a clue.

I didn't know Grandma before Alzheimer's disappeared so much of her. I can only imagine now the deep well of love that surrounded her that she brought to others, and that was mirrored in the slow walk of Dad and his mom on the side of a suburban road filled with the scent of freshly cut grass, crisp spring air, and the rhythm of cars passing by.

Reading this thoughtful piece brought me back to those days albeit with a different perspective. I have since learned that stored musical memory is not harmed by Alzheimer's so that in turning to music to communicate with her, we had found a real conduit to the mother we loved.

Pop's Death

In late 1987, while Mom was in Cedar Manor, Pop underwent surgery for a cancerous growth, the second such surgery during that period. When I saw him in the recovery room, he said, "Not again," meaning that we should leave him with his own way of handling his medical issues. This time I accepted his request.

However, I didn't expect his call two months later asking if Emalie and I would visit the Rosary Hill home for the terminally ill in Hawthorne, ten miles from our home in Mount Kisco, to let him know what we thought of it. We did so immediately and informed him that it was heavenly in appearance and that we'd experienced a sense of peace on the visit.

Shortly after, on May 24, 1988, Pop checked himself into the home. People rarely enter a home without medical intervention and often can only do so through a doctor's arrangements, but Pop could be convincing, and his enchanting Irish brogue was real. Apparently, he was ready for such a step, perhaps sensing that his time was short. I was taken aback by the suddenness of it all, but Pop, ever a man of understatement, was not one to add to our burdens by sharing his pain and suffering.

Before entering Rosary Hill, Pop had made it a practice to visit Mom, usually with Uncle Pat and sometimes with Aunt Catherine, who was then not well. My memories of Mom's single visit to Rosary Hill remains striking. I had brought her there from Cedar Manor. She was in a wheelchair, frail and withered, and she probably didn't know who Pop was. He hadn't seen her since he entered the home a few months prior, and his happiness in seeing her that day radiated from his face. It meant so much to me to see how deep his love was for her, even after 53 years of marriage and her then present condition.

The date of this visit was July 12, 1988, my 52nd birthday and, as it turned out, Pop's 79th. For all the years I knew him, he celebrated October 3 as his birthday, but on this day he announced that July 12 was his real birthday. I didn't believe it, but we complied and celebrated his birthday on that day at Rosary Hill. A year later after Pop died, Donald and I, along with our brother-in-law Larry Lambe, were in Ireland and sought out more information on Pop's real birthdate. You can imagine our astonishment when we found in an old book in the rectory of Ballinrobe's St. Mary's Church a reference to John Feerick being baptized on July 14, 1909 — Pop, we concluded. Perhaps he wanted to keep the focus on my birth date or hide his association with Orangemen's Day?

It appears that when Pop was born, a requirement existed that births had to be registered with the civil authorities within a certain period of time following a birth. Sometimes, parents of a newborn would miss, not know of, or forget the requirement. When they got around to complying, they would put down a date that was within the required period so as not to invoke a penalty. This likely explains two dates on Pop's Mayo records — namely, October 3 as his birth date and October 23 as the registration date. Regardless as to why he chose to celebrate October 3 as his birthday, that's the day we celebrated.

Pop had entered Rosary Hill on May 24, 1988, and died there on August 2. He enjoyed his stay, especially the kindnesses of the staff. He remarked that he could have whatever he wanted to eat (and possibly to drink) and was pleased to have a telephone credit card (his first credit card, I believe) that let him communicate daily with family and friends. He asked me when I visited to bring him his favorite ice cream from a nearby store.

Pop's death was piercing in ways I had never experienced. We were comforted by the beautiful funeral Mass celebrated by many members of the Jesuit community, including Fathers McShane and O'Hare. I recall that Father George McMahon of the Society of Jesus, the principal celebrant, said in his homily that Pop gave his children the Catholic faith and helped them nurture it. Despite such moving words, it was incredibly difficult for me to say goodbye to Pop, and it would be many weeks before I could function adequately.

Donald said in a letter to Father O'Hare, "It is very difficult to lose a loved one, especially a parent; however, we believe Pop is in our Lord's hands." I received a surprising glimpse of Pop's feeling toward me the night before he died. He pulled himself up from his bed and asked where he was, to which I replied, "Everything is O.K." He then said to me, "You are a beautiful person," a comment that stunned me. Never before had he said anything like that to me. I knew how highly he regarded my siblings, but to hear his words about me on this occasion brought tears to my eyes.

My feelings of remorse ran in many directions. I thought of times when I was fresh growing up and he made me toe the line. I thought of the summer after the fifth grade when I failed math and he kept me at home to master the essentials. I remembered his taking me to Yankee Stadium, buying me a two-wheel bicycle, and returning my jar of coins after losing a bet with him about the 1951 playoff game.

I remember him giving me pointers about how to drive a car and all the times he came to my home to paint or fix something or help cut the grass. I thought of the love he gave to Mom during her difficult times. I cried when I focused on how reticent I'd been by not letting him know how much I loved him and how much I learned from him, especially his work ethic, seriousness of purpose, and love of his family. Perhaps it's because it so resonates with my own relationship with Pop that I have played often Phil Coulter's "The Old Man," and listened carefully to the words of the song.

Mom's Death

Less than a year later, on July 16, 1989, the day the liturgical feast of Our Lady of Mount Carmel is celebrated, we experienced Mom's death, something I wasn't prepared for. I was on my first trip to Ireland, and the week before, as I made my way to the airport, I'd stopped off to see Mom to tell her I'd be visiting her birthplace. She seemed radiant that day, and, as I left, I thought that possibly her health was improving. I remember remarking on her appearance to Emalie and our children (Rosemary, John, and Bill), with whom I was traveling. The week that followed, the one I described earlier, remains my most powerful memory of Ireland.[1]

July 16 turned out to be our last full day in Mayo. In the late afternoon, Uncle John and I visited Foxford's St. Michael's Church to light candles for Mom, Pop, Pat, and Catherine. It was around 6 p.m. when we did so. The church's Angelus bell rang as we were leaving. Shortly later, we joined members of the family of Martin Boyle, Mom's younger brother, Eileen Condon, a first cousin on Pop's side, and her husband, John, at Brogan's Pub in the Pontoon region, as the next morning we were to leave for the south of Ireland. During dinner, a call came from Donald to tell me that Mom had died that day. I later realized that she had died right around the time I was lighting the candle to her.

Shocked and heartbroken, I wept uncontrollably on Martin's shoulder. His presence kept me together when I needed someone so linked to Mom. As it turned out, the news from Donald reached me, fortuitously, because Martin Boyle's son Kevin was in America with his wife, Mary, visiting Donald when he got the call from the nursing home informing him of Mom's death. Kevin and Mary knew where I was that evening. Had Mom died the next day, we wouldn't have been reachable.

Emalie, I, and our three children raced back to Gannon's Bed and Breakfast, where we were staying, to pack our suitcases and arrange a flight back to New York. We left for Shannon early in the morning. On the flight home, I wrote and rewrote a eulogy for Mom, basically using the same words each time. I also made a list of the steps that needed to be taken for her wake and funeral, including placing a newspaper notice of her death. Little did I know at the time that Donald had done all of that already, helped the previous year by Pop before his own death, who left Donald money to pay for Mom's burial. The loss of Mom and Pop within a year's time filled us with grief, but I was fortunate to have discovered more about them than I thought possible on my first visit to Ireland. The trip strengthened my sense of continued connection to them.

Mom's funeral was held at St. James Apostle Church in Carmel, New York. When it came time for me to deliver the eulogy, I couldn't bear to do it, my pain being so deep. I passed it over my shoulder to Donald and he delivered it. I wrote: "Our mother has gone home. She is now at peace, enveloped in and encircled by the love of the God she served so devotedly and selflessly during her life in this world. Although she has left our presence, and our pain is penetratingly deep, her example of goodness and love will be forever a major force in our lives." Donald would add the finishing touch to these thoughts, stating: "Your prayers and support are deeply appreciated. Mom was always there with her love and patience. Mom now has rejoined our father, which gives us peace. It's great to have a family, for you are our source of strength."

When Mom died, her sole assets were her new wheelchair and a booklet listing the names and telephone numbers of people close to her, the dates of the deaths of her mother, her sister Elizabeth, and her grandparents, and their ages. Inside the booklet was a personal identification card stating that, in case of an emergency, "Please call a priest." She lived always with a deep faith in God and belief in a life hereafter, and she surely had earned at that moment eternal life with the God of her faith.

Donald's Death

Eleven years later, in 2000, we would experience the jarring death of my brother, Donald. The loss of Mom and Pop was exceedingly difficult but predictable, as Mom had deteriorated over many years and Pop had been given a diagnosis of three years of life when he underwent surgery in 1985. What was not expected was Donald's death at age 62, caused by an inoperable esophageal cancer that was diagnosed in the summer of 1999.

Told he had six months to live, Donald beat the odds and lived out a full year. Though he knew his time was short, Donald treated his cancer as a fact of life, stating in a letter to Father O'Hare, S.J., dated April 24, 2000, "I am currently undergoing treatment for my cancer ailment in New York and in Germany. Germany offers a fourth modality of hyperthermia treatments along with chemotherapy. My good cells are not completely destroyed; so it gives me a better quality of life."

Because of that "better quality of life," he was able to set up, while bedridden, a scholarship program at Fordham. It was to be in memory of Mom and Pop, with Donald stating, "Our parents were special to us and we wish to share their love and goodness with Fordham." He then made a five-year pledge of $50,000 toward the scholarship, which was to begin in January of 2001, and concluded the letter with the words, "Thank you for all the love and prayers given to our family and to me by the Jesuit Community and yourself."

Donald also expressed the hope that he would get to attend the Fordham golf tournament, but that did not happen, as he left us on July 29, 2000, a few days after telephoning Father O'Hare about our family's decision to set up a $1 million scholarship fund in memory of Mom and Pop. Generosity and Donald were companions throughout his life. When his fraternal twins graduated from Fordham Law School in 1992, he sent Fordham a gift of $2,000 with a letter to the dean (me) giving thanks "for the Christian values and knowledge that your law school has imparted" to his children.

Donald and I grew up just two years apart. He enjoyed playing stickball and stoop ball, and he was a tough center on a neighborhood football team known as the Gaels. Although short in stature, you couldn't push him back. Shoveling snow, delivering papers, and working in supermarkets were some of the ways he earned money to go to the movies, buy candy or a soft drink, and later, as we got older, to cover educational expenses. As children we fought like the dickens and played our games with friends on separate streets of the Bronx. Though he wanted to follow me as a lawyer, his plans were cut short by the arrival of twins, followed by four other children, and we went in different directions with our careers. As adults Donald and I were the best of friends.

Donald went to All Hallows High School in the Bronx and then to Fordham College, where we overlapped for two of our four college years. After graduation, he earned a master's degree in business administration from St. John's and then went on to enjoy great success in finance. Of immense importance to him was volunteering large amounts of time to his church, St. Francis of Assisi in West Nyack, New York, Fordham, Breezy Point Cooperative in the Rockaways, and Daytop Village, a drug addiction treatment center in Rockland County.

During our adult years, the bonds of family expressed themselves in countless ways. At our weddings, we served as each other's best man, delivering the wedding toasts. My toast was, "May the love which joins your hands and hearts today grow deeper with every hour of your life together. May today's happiness be but a glimmer of the happiness you will know together. May your fondest hope be the least of your joys." As previously noted, Donald delivered for me a classic Irish toast.[2]

When Donald died, I tried to put in words what he meant to me and our family. Here, in part, is what I said at his funeral Mass, celebrated on August 1, 2000, in a eulogy entitled, "It's the little things that matter":

> Don was always there, together with his beloved Meg, like peanut butter and jelly, on all the important occasions of our lives, present with happiness and laughter. The children of his siblings remember his humor, easy-going manner, his golfing tips, his taking them to sporting events or attending their events or visiting them when they studied out of state or the country, his investment advice, his travel tips, his fashionable hats and ties, the ever-present twinkle in his eye of having one up on life, and his directness at times such as when he said to one of his nieces, "You are twenty-three, it's time to get on the ball and go to law school."
>
> Our Uncle Pat, a grand presence in Don's life, remembers Don's special caring for his wife a month before she died and for making possible Pat's return to Ireland last year to celebrate his 95th birthday (1999). Donald, after organizing that trip, wasn't able to go because of the challenge that began for him at that time.
>
> Donald was the person we could always turn to for assistance and

guidance. There wasn't an area of life he did not help us with. The stories are legion of the help he provided each of us somewhere along the line. For me, when my emotion and stress were so great that I couldn't get something done that I had the responsibility for as the senior member of the family, Donald took over and got it done, such as delivering my mother's eulogy and helping my father find institutional care for her as she dealt with the final period of her life. His strength in the most difficult of situations was incredible.

Donald was the first among all of us, a loving brother and presence — our resource, guide, cheerleader, and defender extraordinaire. Donald excelled off stage, away from the limelight. He had no peer in our family. How can I ever forget the lonely support he gave me in the aftermath of my Latrell Sprewell decision, saying to all, "My brother got it just right and time will show that."

Donald's impact on our lives is everywhere. Of all the legacies he left his siblings and our children, we will never forget the manner with which he dealt with the subject of life and death, his extraordinary courage and spirituality in dealing with his cancer. He lived his life to the fullest to the end, accepted without complaint or question the judgment of his God, kept us focused on the positive, telling us, "Everything is O.K.," and then showed us how to die gracefully. He died with a rosary in his hand, with Meg holding one hand and his daughter Margaret the other and with his children all around him as his wife sprinkled on him holy water from the shrines at Knock and Lourdes.

As Emalie put it in her last letter to Donald, a letter that meant so much to Meg and her children:

> Haven't we all been richly blessed by walking on this pilgrimage with you? No one gets to heaven alone. Everyone who arrives there brings along a host of other people. Heaven is not a "for me only" thing. It is definitely an "Us Thing." We travel the way together — hand in hand with many others. We may arrive there at different times, but those whose hands we have held on the journey either have arrived there before us or are not far behind. And we know we will all be together around that wonderful banquet table of the Lord sooner or later.

In 2005, our family learned that the Breezy Point Cooperative wanted to honor Donald for his volunteer service and for his support in its times of financial need, as well as for having helped create an annual arts festival. The community expressed its gratitude by naming a street there "Donald Feerick

Way." At the naming ceremony, I was asked to say a few words on behalf of the family. I said:

> There is a certain irony present on this occasion because Donald was someone who traveled below the radar screen. That's where he worked and that's where he excelled. He simply loved to give and help others. That you would want to honor his memory, four years after his death, speaks volumes about what is at the core of this community. . . . From this time forward, when we see the sign Donald Feerick Way, we will pause and remember a wonderful person who was so central to his family and so devoted to this community.

When in 2012, Breezy Point was devastated by Hurricane Sandy, the sign was blown away. Someone, however, had found the sign among debris. In July of 2016, it made its way back to our family and was restored to its position on the street.

38

Roses in December—Rediscovering Mom and Pop

A Man's real possession is his memory. In nothing else is he rich, in nothing else is he poor.

— ALEXANDER SMITH

God gave us memory that we might have roses in December.

— JAMES M. BARRIE

After Pop's death in August of 1988, my desire to go to Ireland began to grow. To see where he and Mom were born, to meet their siblings and their children and grandchildren, to learn more about their siblings who had died, and to talk with friends from their youth became an overriding goal of mine.

What I knew about my parents' siblings was limited. I had met Mom's brother Michael several times while growing up[1] and her brother Jim on his brief visit to the United States in the 1970s. Pop's sister Margaret had visited us in 1985, joined by her daughter Mary, Mary's husband, Bob Allen, and their son, David. But these events had occurred before my curiosity about family history had developed. It seemed to me that there would be time later to learn about my relatives and origins. How wrong I was.

Of the fifteen children born to my maternal grandparents, Maria Moran and Patrick Boyle and my paternal grandparents Ellen McDermott and David Feerick, only five would choose to live abroad. Two would settle in England, and only Mom, Pop, and Uncle Pat would choose to settle in America.

None of the fifteen had a formal education beyond grammar school. Of the fifteen, two (Robert Boyle and James Feerick)[2] died as young children. Mom's sister Elizabeth died at age 18, and Pop's sister Ellen died tragically at the age of 41, as discussed later in this chapter. Fewer than half married.

My siblings and I grew up without ever knowing any of our first cousins, making my first trip to Ireland in 1989 an emotional experience. On July 7, 1989, I climbed aboard an Aer Lingus flight to Shannon Airport, along with Emalie and our three youngest children, Rosemary, John, and Bill. It was thrilling to arrive in Ireland early the next morning. Donald and Pat had sketched out for us a long scenic route.

We spent the rest of the day following the coastal route to Mayo, which exposed us to the majestic Cliffs of Mohr and the Burren in County Clare. John slept most of the way, awakening from time to time and asking, when he saw the water, whether we were still in Galway (we were). We stopped for lunch on the coast in Roundstone, where we had the most spectacular views of the water. On and on we drove, surrounded by scenic views and sheep pastures. Finally we entered Westport, a popular tourist area, and then arrived at Gannon's Bed and Breakfast, located next to the post office in Foxford, which the Gannon family also operated. Our plan was to stay for a week.

We had mapped out an ambitious agenda. We planned to visit Mom's brother John in the nursing home in Ballina where he resided and visit Mom's brother Martin and his family. We hoped to meet with Pop's sister Margaret and her husband and family, as well as friends of Pop in Ballinrobe, if we could find any still around. And it was clear that no visit to Mayo would be complete without a trip to the Shrine of the Blessed Virgin at Knock, about twelve miles from the cottage where Mom grew up.

My goal was to collect as much information as I could that would shed light on my parents' youth. We intended to spend the first week in Foxford meeting family members and piecing together family history before venturing out to the other parts of Ireland that Mom and Pop had mentioned over the years. Our plans for the second week, however, were aborted by Mom's death.

Settling into our B&B, we found Mary Gannon a truly delightful hostess, with her husband and young children working in the kitchen and post office and maintaining the dining room and bedrooms. We fell in love with her and her family, and I have hardly ever made a trip to Mayo since without stopping in to say hello and enjoy a meal or tea and biscuits. It was with sadness on my 2012 trip that I learned of the death of her husband, Patrick, who had a long history in Irish athletics and the Republican movement. I recall the admiration they both expressed for Uncle Jim and his service in the Irish War of Independence. Mary, though older, had not changed a whit.

On July 9, Emalie and I met Uncle John Boyle at a nursing home in Ballina. He was small and seemed feeble, but his face was filled with life as he gazed at me, recognizing me from the photographs of us and our children that Mom had sent him over the years. He had given these photos pride of place by displaying them prominently on the mantle of his cottage in Culmore, along with prayer cards and other forms of religious expression.

Greeting each other for the first time in person, we embraced and tears flowed. His first words were of Mom, whom he loved dearly. He said that Mom lived in a room separated only by the thinnest of veils from heaven. "When her time comes to return to God," he said, "she will take the smallest of steps to pass from the one room to the next."

I wasn't prepared for the emotions that gripped my body at these words and was left momentarily speechless. Pulling myself together, I asked if I could take him to the Shrine at Knock. Before I knew it, he was in our car and off we went. Together we partook of the Stations of the Cross and recitations of the rosary and visited the churches and chapels located at Knock, as well as bookstores and gift shops inside and outside the Shrine area. The ninth of July, my first full day in Ireland, was a whirlwind of worship. I took part in more religious rituals that day than I ever had in my life.

That week, Uncle John and I made more visits to Knock and visited the cemeteries where my ancestors were buried. He had an encyclopedic memory of dates and events in the family's history. He could recall with exacting precision the Ireland of Mom's youth. The feebleness I observed upon first seeing him wasn't born out by the energy he exhibited at Knock and in the cemeteries. He lived with God, earning the appellation among family and friends of "the Monk."

Hearing stories of John's past was like opening a window onto the struggles and difficult choices that faced Mom and Pop as they came of age in Ireland. Born in January of 1901, he was the second oldest and lived his life in the cottage of his birth, helping his mother care for his younger siblings, including Mom, with cooking and other tasks. He also worked in the garden in front of the house and did some of the farm work.

From time to time, he worked on the farms of neighbors to earn pocket money, which he saved. Later he would give some of his savings to Uncle Pat to help restore their mother's gravesite, a project in which I later became involved. It was in this cottage of her youth that Mom stayed when she returned home in the 1960s and 1970s, then the home of her bachelor brothers, Jim and John. Jim died there in 1979, and eventually John's health made it necessary for him to enter a nursing home, thereby leaving the cottage unoccupied.

As I'd learn on my visits, Uncle Jim Boyle was an outstanding Irish patriot. He was a commander in the IRA's West Mayo brigade, leaving his country after the 1921 Peace Treaty to find work in England. I had a sense from Uncle

Pat that Jim's leaving was inevitable because he didn't accept the Irish Free State, nor did Uncle Pat for that matter. Jim was an "old IRA man," said his nephew Desmond Boyle, "who, in addition to his skills with a rifle and artillery, played the flute and always carried a tin whistle in his pocket." According to Des, Jim played the flute in the Irish pubs of Doncaster, England, and he sang and danced as well.

John and Jim were always energized by visits from Mom and other American relatives, and they shared with visitors their stories and music. Despite the lack of a formal education, both were well read and knowledgeable about Irish and world affairs. Because of his service in his country's War of Independence and for the Irish Army during World War II, Jim was revered by his community.

On their first trip to Ireland in 1985, my daughters Maureen (age 21) and Jean (17) visited John, who then lived alone, and remember his great hospitality. Upon their arrival he rushed to provide them with tea and biscuits and, upon their departure, he insisted that they not leave empty handed, entrusting them with a rusty box of Irish tea. "He was a ray of sunshine," Jean said, "in an otherwise dilapidated cottage." Maureen and Jean had to collect water from a well outside, since there was no running water in the house. The visit was so memorable to Jean that she made it the subject of her college application essay. In her first draft, she said:

> He lived alone in a seemingly ancient, thatch-roofed cottage (the one in which my grandmother was born), deeply ensconced in the hills of Ireland. Wearing soiled and shabby clothes, he welcomed us with an enormous smile, lighting up his entire face. Despite the fact that he had never met us, he knew exactly who we were, and verified this knowledge with a picture of our family hanging from his ceiling amongst many religious articles.
>
> We visited with him for several hours, amazed at both his physical and mental capacities, all the while observing the cluttered, dusty environment in which he lived. Not only was everything completely out of order, there was no running water in the entire cottage. However, we realized that although his lifestyle was quite different from that to which we were accustomed, to him it was home and quite special.
>
> It was immediately apparent that he was very lonely and longed for visitors. Our visit meant a lot to him. He lived essentially without people day to day, aside from a daily nurse who came to check up on him. It pained me to think of how long each day must be for him, and I wished I could bring him back to America with us.

The experience was an eye-opener for my daughters who had grown up in a big house in a privileged neighborhood. In looking back on the memory of her visit with John, Jean said that he reminded her of the old man in William Butler Yeats's poem "Fergus and the Druid": "Look on my thin grey hair and hollow cheek. And on these hands that may not lift the sword,/this body trembling like a wind-blown reed./No woman's loved me, no man sought my help."

Mom's oldest brother, Michael, didn't take part in the War of Independence, as he shied away from violence. He was well-built, ruddy in complexion, and very neat in appearance. He typically wore a hat, a suit, a crisp shirt, and neat trousers, and he followed political events in the United States. On his visits to America, he talked politics at our kitchen table and seemed overly worried about the atom bomb. Michael was a skilled craftsman of cabinets and a brick layer who enjoyed a reputation for excellence in both areas, as well as in painting. We had little knowledge of Michael's work in America, although it was said he worked as a doorman, collecting unemployment insurance when he was laid off. As I was finishing this account of Mom's siblings, I learned that at some point during his life, Michael had been involved in a fatal bicycle accident in Dublin. The other cyclist, who was a father, subsequently died from the accident. This event appears to have greatly affected Michael.

As our first week in Ireland progressed, I had the wonderful experience of meeting Mom's youngest brother, Martin, and his wife, Delia, along with their children and grandchildren. They were the parents of twelve children but had lost two sons at a very early age. Some of my cousins thought that I looked like both Uncle Martin and Uncle Jim and resembled them in some of my mannerisms.

Martin was easy-going, mild-mannered, and gentle. He was very well-read, a great writer, and played the accordion. He especially loved to play old Irish favorites such as "Maggie in the Woods," with a version by the Irish Volunteers proclaiming "If I had Maggie in the woods, I'd keep her there til morning." Martin had a beautiful singing voice. His rendition of "Noreen Bawn," a song my mother would also sing, brought everyone to tears. The song recounts the tale of a young woman emigrating from Ireland and then returning, frail and scarlet, to die: "There's a grey-haired woman weeping, lonely kneeling on a grave. Oh my darling she is saying, I am lonely since you've gone."

Martin spent his adult years working as a farmer in Mayo, but he traveled to England when job opportunities presented themselves. The happiness I felt in his home made evident the love he and his wife had earned from their labors in raising a large family and giving each of them a pathway in life. It was sheer joy to listen to Des play the accordion as his way of greeting us. The evenings we spent with Martin and Delia were always animated by storytelling, with sandwiches, cakes and biscuits, coffee and tea, and an abundance of Jameson Irish Whiskey. It was striking to discover that Martin and Delia's grandchildren bore a close resemblance to my own children.

Mom's younger sister, Elizabeth, died in September of 1932. In his oral history, Uncle Pat described her as "a very pretty, tall, dark-haired girl, who was very helpful with the housework." On learning of her death, Pat said, "I took a long walk to think it over. It can't interfere with your way of living, because you can't go back, you try to go forward. It wasn't easy for us to hear the bad news, especially at 18 years of age."

As I finished writing this chapter, Maureen found in an old photo album a Christmas card sent to Mom by her sister in 1928. Printed inside were the words: "May good luck never turn from you. With very happy memories of a Bygone time. I Send Season's Greetings For Auld Lang Syne." The card was signed from "Lizzie to Jane" and included the handwritten words, "wishing you a happy xmas."

That week I also traveled to Ballinrobe to learn more about Pop, but his two surviving siblings, Michael and Margaret, weren't there. I learned that Michael, the youngest in the family, lived in Birmingham, England, with his wife and two children. I made seeing him a priority on a later visit to England. Margaret lived with her husband in Galway, and I was unable to visit with her, although I did meet her daughter Eileen and her husband, John Condon.

I had met Margaret previously on a trip she made to the United States in 1985. She was incredibly kind and caring on that occasion, expressing great love for Mom, washing her, feeding her, and making sure that she found her way home whenever she left the house for a walk. Margaret's return to Ireland at that time was not easy for Pop, who so enjoyed her company. The close bond between them was obvious. Fortunately, on my future trips to Ireland I would have the opportunity to visit Margaret and her family.

Margaret's tremendous energy explained how she was able to raise nine children, three of whom belonged to her sister, Ellen Kineavy, who, at the age of 41, was hit by a van as she was taking food and beverages to men working in the fields and died. Margaret and her husband, Mick, raised Ellen's children on the farm they owned in County Meath. Not long after that tragedy, which occurred in 1956, Margaret and Mick moved to the west of Ireland, first to Roscommon and then to Salthill, Galway.

Bob Allen, Margaret's son-in-law, said that Margaret was a down-to-earth person whom he greatly respected for her acceptance of people from different religious and national backgrounds, Bob being an Englishman himself. He mentioned her sense of humor and recalled "just after I joined the family, I was driving with Mary in the front seat and Margaret in the back. She talked continually (to herself) until I eventually told her she was the only woman I had ever met that could have an argument with herself—and lose! A little later she saw a couple of men jogging along the road. She asked me 'what are they doing that for?' I replied, 'for their health.' She responded, 'get away, I'd say they have a bet down!'" Bob also shared with me that Margaret's husband Mick had a rival for Margaret's hand in marriage. He said that Mick "eventually saw the man and 'sorted it out.'" He was not sure exactly how, but noted that the rivalry "persisted all their lives and surfaced periodically at football games when they would be shouting for different counties."

Pop's youngest sibling, Michael, left Ireland when he was 17, ending up in Birmingham. He was 12 when Pop left for America, and they would never see each other again, though in later years they would speak by phone on Christmas Day, a practice Donald and I tried to continue for a while following Pop's death, as Pop's surrogates. We were unable to do so for long, however, because of Donald's health and then because Michael became ill and died on March 15, 2002. His wife, Florence Edith, was an Englishwoman, with whom he had two sons, John and Kenneth.

Michael looked like Pop's twin and was energetic and constantly in motion. He bounced all over the living room, showing us family memorabilia and serving us tea and biscuits. Jean, who visited him and his family while studying at Oxford in the early 1990s, recalls the same restless energy.

Michael's work life was spent largely in Brierley Hill at Round Oak Steel Works. His job as an "ingot weighman" involved working atop a platform as molten steel was poured into molds. The work was dangerous and required skill and attention. His sons, John and Kenneth, followed in his path of hard work—John in structural and civil engineering and Kenneth as an electrician. Pop's other brother in England, Patrick, lived alone in Leeds, England, and spent his life as a laborer. Little is known of his interests and avocations.

Despite the absence of any of Pop's relatives in Ballinrobe, on my first trip there I met a few people who remembered his family. One, a farmer named James Mannion, grew up on a farm near Pop's and recalled for me Pop's first visit back to Ireland in 1965: "There was a knock on the door," James said, "and there was your Pop inquiring whether my house was for sale." Mannion then exclaimed, "The Yank has returned!"

He said Pop had arrived in a fancy rented car and that he was a practical joker at heart, a characteristic inherited by some of my children and grandchildren. It was a thrill to see him again, Mannion said, and to enjoy a Jameson together.

For the rest of that July afternoon, Emalie and I sat in the Mannion home listening to stories of days gone by, of farm life, dances, walking and biking to school, chores on the farm, and other activities of Pop's boyhood on the Kilmaine Road. Mannion told us where to go to find the graves of my grandparents and provided information as to the lives of Pop's brothers, Michael and Patrick, noting that they had left to find work in England and never returned.

Pop's brother Martin, who had remained on the family farm with his mother until she died in January of 1964, was described by Mannion and others as tall and handsome, with a flair for dancing and singing. He was an active participant in the choir of Ballinrobe's St. Mary's Catholic Church and was highly sociable, well-read, and knowledgeable about opera because of an opera society in town. He didn't enjoy the life of a farmer and sold the house and land and moved to the town of Ballinrobe after his mother died. I had a sense that the change left a vacuum in his life and that, despite his talents, his enormous potential went unfilled. His last days appear to have been difficult ones, as reflected in an article in a local newspaper recording his death in 1985.

Mannion gave us a glimpse of his own intellectual attainments, reciting poems one after another from memory, as his wife, gentle and kind, served us sandwiches, tea, and biscuits. It was hard to say goodbye to the Mannions, as in their home, on a small family farm in Ballinrobe, I had discovered "a bit of Pop" again. I made it a regular practice on my return trips to Ireland to drop in on them, always with a bottle of cheer. It was painful to later learn of their deaths.

During my first meeting with James Mannion, he pointed us toward the farm where Pop was raised. It was a thrill to see the land despite the fact that his house was gone, replaced by a newer home, which was set back from the road as Pop's had been. Its occupants, the Keanes, had done a good job of maintaining the farm and developing their own lovely garden in front of the house, although the beautiful flower boxes that adorned the front windows when Martin lived there were gone. Emalie and I took pictures of the setting, hallowed ground for me then and ever since.

That Ballinrobe adventure ended in August of 2016 with a meeting with Patsy Walsh, a distant cousin, at the Shrine at Mayo. In a delightful conversation, he shared with me memories of growing up on the Kilmaine Road in Ballinrobe and coming to know Pop's brother Martin. Martin was conspicuous, Patsy said, because he owned a cream-colored Ford Cortina Mark II 1300 Deluxe with an automatic transmission. Another Ballinrobe neighbor confirmed this story, saying that Martin had perhaps the only automatic in Ballinrobe, if not in all of Ireland. Martin achieved a level of financial success unknown to any of my other Irish ancestors.

39

My Family: Immediate and Extended

I have a dream that my four little children will one day live in a nation where they will not be judged by the color of their skin but by the content of their character.

— THE REV. MARTIN LUTHER KING JR.

The deaths of Mom and Pop, followed by my brother Donald and Uncle Pat, created a vacuum in my life. The world has never been quite the same for me since their passing, but happily, Emalie, our children, their children, and my siblings brought another world of meaning to my life. Along with our six children, we have eleven grandchildren: David, Christopher, Liam, Ryan, Sean, Roderick, Dylan, Connor, Ian, Brynn, and Caitlyn. And of course I must mention their devoted fathers: Lester LeBlanc, William LeBlanc, Kyle Snow, and Roderick Cardamone. As for my siblings, I offer these descriptions.

Maureen

Donald is described elsewhere in this book, as is my sister Maureen. Of Maureen, my sister-in-law Meg wrote:

> Maureen and I met once before Donald and I were married in 1964. Maureen told me of her independence as the first member of the family to study outside the United States. She studied at the Sorbonne University in Paris and completed her graduate work there. Upon her return to New York City she taught French in the New York City school system. After Maureen and Larry [Lambe] married, they lived

in Suffern, New York, where she taught French in the East Ramapo school district. Since Maureen lived closer to us, she would visit often, babysit for our children and spend a lot of time with us.

The children loved Maureen and we loved the break in our routine. When Larry was transferred to North Carolina, Donald always kept in close contact with them. We would often travel to North Carolina and spend good times together. Maureen was a gracious host to all.

Maureen has a strong sense of faith and is especially proud of her Irish roots and her Catholic faith that she attributes to her family's upbringing. Throughout the years Maureen has demonstrated her faith by her active participation in church activities.

Maureen has always been involved in her community. She is a reader in the Reading for the Blind Program that is broadcast on the radio, and has also been involved with the Columbiettes, Habitat for Humanity, and the Ladies Ancient Order of Hibernians. In the 1970s Maureen and her family took part in a Northern Ireland project where a teenage boy, Dermot Murphy, spent a couple of weeks with their family to observe the American way.

Maureen takes pride in keeping herself physically fit through exercise, walking and water aerobics. She keeps her mind healthy by reading, sewing, completing word jumbles, using the computer, and pursuing her interest in politics and justice.

Maureen shows her creativity in so many ways, as she can tackle any sewing project and be determined to finish a very successful piece. She enjoys cooking and sharing recipes, and, years ago created a Manhattan cocktail for Uncle Pat with her own special strong ingredient to make him happy.

Another quality I admire about Maureen is the compassion that was shown to my family when Donald was dying.

Maureen continues to be "young at heart" and remains a strong figure in our family. She is always "interested" and is always interesting. I just love her!

Kevin

Of Kevin, I provide this portrait from the perspective of Maureen:

A great deal of noise filled our household when Kevin was brought home from the hospital on July 29, 1946. I was not too happy to have another brother and was looking forward to having a sister to play with. Our apartment was small, and a crib was set up in the bedroom shared by Mom and Pop. Kevin was a pretty baby with curly hair and a round face, and I discovered he was just the right size for my new doll carriage, plus my doll dresses fit him perfectly.

Most of my memories of Kevin's early years come from looking at pictures that were taken on the roof of 305 East 161st Street on special occasions. Being his older sister by five years, it was my responsibility to keep an eye on him when playing outdoors, and I remember one occasion having a hair pulling fight with a neighborhood youngster because she made Kevin cry. During his teenage years he accompanied our father and Uncle Pat to Lake Carmel to help build Uncle Pat's house and listened to many stories his uncle and father told about Ireland.

After graduating from St. Angela Merici in 1960, he went on to Cardinal Hayes High School and then Fordham University, where he received a Bachelor of Science in economics, a subject he himself felt very unsure about but was encouraged to take, based on his brother Donald's advice. He graduated from the university in 1964, receiving a Master of Science in counseling and psychology in 1971 and a law degree from Fordham in 1982.

Education was stressed and encouraged in our household, and Kevin excelled at school and received scholarships and grants to complete his education. His choice of work as a parole officer was a way of having a direct impact on the lives of others. He would go on to instruct FBI agents in undercover negotiation techniques, and later to become managing counselor for Mitsui Marine, an insurance agency. During his career he traveled to the Netherlands with his former wife, Betty, and their two daughters, Kelly and Maura, and while there worked as a tax counselor and marketed investment services.

These many experiences define Kevin's personality and explain his understanding of the human psyche. Throughout his life Kevin has been a comfort to his parents and others, a good listener, and someone who provided me and my siblings advice when needed. Over the years, he became an excellent cook and was often called upon to man the outdoor grill and choose the wine for the meal.

His interest in art led him to pursue a long-time interest, sculptures in wrought iron, which he sells online. Kevin also enjoys a successful law practice by handling all kinds of matters and most recently serving as a mediator and arbitrator of disputes, some of them on a pro bono basis. He is generous with his time, helping others and serving the profession of law in bar association activities and the work of the courts.

Kevin is the proud father of two daughters and two grandchildren and is happily married to Jodi Ellis living in Bloomington, Indiana.

Anne

Anne was born when I was 17 years old. However, our age difference didn't lessen the bond we shared as siblings. Anne noted in a communication to me that she received "plenty of attention from her siblings," adding, "I remember you once bringing home these huge dolls for me to play with. I was thrilled. Sometimes I would climb up on Donald's lap while he was reading a newspaper. He never seemed to mind. Kevin was a teaser and often picked on me in a playful manner. Maureen was like a young mother to me. I think she must have been a real help to Mom in raising me."

Of Anne's arrival when he was seven, Kevin said,

> She was an alien intruder and I was not prepared for her landing or existence. I had no foreboding, at age seven, that my life was to change so drastically. Mom and Pop's attention was to shift to the new arrival. Thus we began on a new journey. I came home to find a new bed in Mom and Pop's house. A crib. I had no idea where it came from and that in it was a new person, that alien called Anne Marie.
>
> I do not recall her crying or making a lot of commotion. She seemed to be watching with her eyes directed out. I recall her standing in the crib and swaying back and forth. I watched as she grew and ate. She had a hearty appetite.
>
> She started school and did well enough. She was a good student like all of us at the 161st Street ranch. I was probably moved to a new bed, but that seemed like an upgrade, so I had no complaints. She stayed in the parents' bedroom away from mine. I was with the boys (David and Donald). I had arrived, so to say. She was pleasant and cheerful and listened to what I said and told her. She did not give me any grief. She did not follow me around, so I did not have to explain her to any of my friends. She did not eclipse me at the dinner table and was a nice accompaniment to all that happened, even when we moved to Grand Avenue in the Bronx.

When Anne was 18 she gave birth to a lovely child, Elizabeth (Betty). Betty's father, Placido Lopez, was later killed in a motorcycle accident while he served as a soldier. Years later, Anne married and bore another beautiful child, Kaitlyn.

"We became close without really thinking about it," Kevin said. "She was a good mother and a hard worker and had to make up time for all the detours she engineered. But she did. She picked herself up time and again and moved on and on. I had lots of respect for her zest for life and her struggle to figure it all out. She raised two wonderful daughters and they are the better for it. That alien had come a long way. She is my little sister."

Anne pursued a career in health administration and is now a clinical research manager at a healthcare company in California.

Extended Family

My extended family is quite large. Donald and his beloved Meg gave birth to six children and they, in turn, to eighteen grandchildren, at the time of his death. Maureen and her husband, Larry, are the parents of three children, two of whom, in the aggregate, are the parents of six grandchildren. Kevin is the father of two daughters, one of whom has a son and daughter, and my sister Anne, has two daughters and two granddaughters.

Emalie is the second oldest of seven children, whose siblings are the parents of a total of sixteen children. Her siblings are Meredith (Mary Jo Joyce), William (deceased), Harold, Jonathan, Elinor (wife of Richard Hoar), and Richard. Mary Jo's husband, Thomas Joyce Jr., was also a lawyer and a graduate of New York Law School. He died on July 6, 2018, and I was privileged to deliver his eulogy. Tom Jr.'s father was also a graduate of Fordham Law School, as is Mary Jo's son, Thomas.

Emalie's Parents

Emalie's mother, Edith Guldi Platt, excelled at playing the piano and organ. Mary Jo described Edith best for me:

> I know my mother had to work for my father in his office, because times were hard after the Depression and he couldn't afford a secretary. My mother gave piano lessons to kids after school. She taught us a few pieces that we had to play at all the recitals. Mom helped bring the community concerts to Southampton. Professional musicians would come and perform in the High School auditorium. My mother used to play the organ and direct the choir at Sacred Heart Church for over forty years in Southampton. She played at Masses and at

weddings and funerals of people who belonged to all stations of life. Sometimes my mother would play music that she composed. When she was calm, the music was soft, gentle and peaceful and when she was sad the music was mournful and made you feel like crying.

Emalie's father, William Bangs Platt Jr., was a direct descendant of Richard Platt, an Englishman who helped found New Milford, Connecticut, in 1638. He was a self-described nightingale, chained to a plow as a lawyer. He loved poetry and had a flair for writing. As a lawyer, he masterfully wrote briefs and counseled clients. Still, he found a way to make his voice heard, as can be seen in the creativity of his briefs. In his eulogy, I described him as a "nightingale wearing the mask of a lawyer." His father (William Bangs Platt Sr.) grew fruits and vegetables on the old Platt farm in Southampton, located on route 27A, and sold them on a site where the Southampton Publick House is now located.

Dad-Platt served as village attorney of Southampton for twenty-three years, helping guide the village throughout the 1940s and 1950s. He served on the village's Zoning Board of Appeals, chairing it for three years, and he served as an appeals agent of the local Southampton draft board during World War II. He served also on the Southampton Hospital Board, helping to found the hospital's school of nursing, and he helped establish Southampton College, encouraging friends and clients to donate land and giving ten acres of his own property on which student accommodations were later built. One observer noted that he had contributed more than one million dollars in free legal services to the college and that without him the college would not have become a reality. For many years he also served as a trustee of his church.

As for Me

I include the following perspective I have of myself. It was delivered on January 9, 2004, on the occasion of a Twelfth Night Spoof at the City Bar Association of New York. It involved a hectic life of nonstop commitments on my part. The spoof bore the title "Fordham Flash." Here's what I said on that occasion:

> They call me the Fordham Flash. But what kind of Flash am I? I find myself having to use a prop almost all the time, as now, since I no longer can remember my lines. I ask you, upon hearing these additional facts, how can it be said that I am the Fordham Flash? I have not played in any organized sport — baseball, football, or basketball. Nor have I run track or taken part in a marathon, by running or walking.

Indeed, I saunter along with a slight limp, my right leg shorter than the left. I soon will be using my Uncle Pat's cane. My language has not changed very much from when I left the Bronx. It has been a Bronx Irish accent all the way, and a rough version at that. My haircuts cost $12 and are done by John the Barber located on Ninth Avenue and 57th Street.

My hair, of course, has turned gray over the years and has thinned, but the process has been disguised due to the creativity of John the Barber. My cars have almost always been purchased secondhand, usually with close to 100,000 miles to start. This long record was put in jeopardy this Christmas when my wife surprised me with a brand-new car, which she subsequently confessed came from our savings for old age. However, this aberration may turn out only to be temporary since she is now eyeing the car and may be using it most of the time!

My suits and ties don't change very often, nor do my shoes. The shoes I wear tonight, for example, I found in Ireland. They have become my favorite because they are wearable all the time without incurring any stain in either snow or rain. It is true that I often lose my raincoat, either leaving it in a restaurant or on a train, but thankfully my wife's blue raincoat always is there awaiting me for such an occasion, of which there have been many. I wear it tonight simply because I lost my relatively new raincoat over the holidays.

It is true as well that I lose my wallet by leaving it on top of a taxi or in a train car. But this causes no problem since I carry so little money and few credit cards. Just the other day I left some papers and checkbooks on the train in Larchmont, but no problem because the very next morning I received a call from a person from Rye who said he found the papers on his morning train ride into New York City.

And, of course, I need to add that I have been married to the same woman for almost 42 years [now 57], and a very good woman at that. Together we have raised 6 children in a house we occupied for 33 years, and now they have given us 10 grandchildren, with another soon to be added.

There was once upon a time a person known as the Fordham Flash. His name was Frankie Frisch, and he is immortalized in the Baseball Hall of Fame. He did it all — hit, throw, steal bases and slide with the best of them, and when he walked away from it all, he coached and did radio play-by-play of games. We both were born in the Bronx and attended two schools of Fordham — the Prep and College in his case, and the College and Law School in my case. We left our alma mater to make our different marks on the world but both in a Fordham way. We expressed a zest for life in all of its variety, accompanied always by a devotion to our beloved Fordham without limits.

To his memory, I dedicate the words played to the music of "I Cain't Say No," from the Broadway show *Oklahoma!*

Everyone who heard me sing that night — in my characteristic, off-key fashion, "I'm just a guy who cain't say no" — promised to keep it a secret. As one prominent member of the bar said, "I finally discovered his Achilles' heel." Emalie said that in the restroom a lady on entering said, "That fellow can't sing even a few lines." Thankfully, Father O'Hare rescued me that night with a kind, humorous perspective as I was "roasted" (as he had done in 1996 when the state bar presented me with its gold medal) by noting that if I were "John the Good" or a "saint," he would have to be a martyr!

PART X
On a Personal Note

To laugh often and much; To win the respect of intelligent people and the affection of children; To earn the appreciation of honest critics and endure the betrayal of false friends; To appreciate beauty, to find the best in others; To leave the world a bit better, whether by a healthy child, a garden patch, or a redeemed social condition; to know even one life has breathed easier because you have lived. This is to have succeeded.

— RALPH WALDO EMERSON, "TO LAUGH OFTEN AND MUCH"

40
What I Learned

Lord make me an instrument of thy peace.
Where there is hatred, let me sow love.
Where there is injury, pardon.
Where there is doubt, faith.
Where there is despair, hope.
Where there is darkness, light,
And where there is sadness, joy.

— PRAYER OF ST. FRANCIS OF ASSISI

The words by St. Francis hung on a plaque in my law school office for two decades, along with a picture of Don Quixote and a poem titled "Desiderata."[1] The poem read:

Go placidly amid the noise and haste, and remember what peace
there may be in silence.
As far as possible, without surrender, be on good terms with all
persons.
Speak your truth quietly and clearly; and listen to others,
even the dull and ignorant, they too have their story.
Avoid loud and aggressive persons,
they are vexatious to the spirit.
If you compare yourself with others,
you may become vain and bitter,
for always there will be greater and lesser persons than yourself.
Enjoy your achievements as well as your plans.

Keep interested in your own career, however humble;
it is a real possession in the changing fortunes of time. . . .
Be cheerful.
Strive to be happy.

And let me add a few tenets of my own for daily living:

(1) The importance of dreaming and striving to achieve your dreams. It's hard to have meaning and purpose without goals to motivate you, help you focus, and provide an incentive to achieve.

(2) The importance of serving others. We're challenged to acquire money and possessions. But in letting money be a controlling force, you run the risk of stripping meaning and purpose from life. All around us, opportunities exist to serve others. The obligations of humanity and citizenship demand it. And we should not forget in doing so the educational institutions that helped shape our lives. Donald, among others, was exceptional in this area, as shown by the letter he wrote to Father O'Hare shortly after Pop died. Donald said:

> I was fortunate recently to receive a significant bonus at my place of business. I had wanted to make a donation to Fordham over the last three years; however, with four in college it was difficult. It is still difficult with three at Fordham this year; however, the Lord must be looking favorably upon us. We need to support you and your staff in your efforts to educate our youth, and to give them a reason for being.

(3) The importance of following your bliss. Parents shouldn't pressure their children to follow in their footsteps when something else is speaking to them. I recall the case of a law student whose father wanted him to be a lawyer from the earliest time. The student's love of his father took him to law school where he became depressed because there was something else he wanted to do. Fortunately, the parents let go and gave their son an opportunity to pursue that interest. He did, the depression disappeared, and the parents reveled in his success in another field. I was happy to have had an opportunity to play a small role in this situation as a result of meeting with the student, sensing his challenge, and inviting his parents in for a meeting with me for a discussion.

(4) The importance of example. Without power, money, or possessions, Mom and Pop lived abundantly meaningful lives. We all have the ability to inspire others through our work, accomplishments, and

responses to challenges. One student (Merril Springer '03), among the thousands I have known, inspired me by her fortitude in dealing with an aneurysm that left her temporarily without speech and limited physical capacity. Through sheer grit and persistence, she worked through an arduous rehabilitation program, then returned to law school, and today enjoys a successful career as a lawyer.

Mayor Koch had felt wronged by me after the Commission on Government Integrity, which I chaired, investigated his administration. In 2001, he wrote me a letter to make amends, saying: "Life is too short to dwell on the past. Let's look to the future and how we can improve the lives of others." A few weeks before he died, he sent me a note of gratitude for the holiday card I sent him with a family picture and personal notes from my daughters Maureen and Jean. Maureen and Jean had met Mayor Koch at a lunch with Jim Gill, his law firm partner at Bryan Cave.

(5) The importance of the present moment. How difficult it is to stay in the present moment when we have tasks to deal with, demands on our time, and dreams to achieve. And yet, it's in these now moments that we may have our greatest opportunities for meaning and purpose.

I made a promise to Fordham graduate Kevin Toner '86, to keep alive the message of a story which captures this message. The story involves a lawyer who returned to his hometown to visit with old friends and family. The lawyer met with an old friend to play a game of tennis, and during their game, his friend's father drove up to tell his son that his wife was in the hospital. Their infant son was facing a critical medical emergency.

The friend left with his father, and the lawyer noticed that he'd left behind a set of keys. The last thing the lawyer wanted to do, in his day of many reunions, was to return his friend's keys to him at the hospital, but he had no alternative. As he stood waiting for his friend to appear from the operating room, the lawyer saw many people anxious for news of the baby's situation. The friend emerged, and everyone learned that the child had died.

As the parents were sharing their grief, they saw the lawyer standing in the corner. They came over to him, hugged him, and thanked him for being there. The lawyer subsequently said that "for the rest of that morning I sat in the hospital room and watched my friend and his wife hold the body of their infant son and say goodbye. It's the most important thing I have ever done."

I've thought many times of this story and the importance of not letting the pressure of everyday life take away our capacity to feel for one another. Nor should our plans for the tomorrows of our life rob us of the opportunities of the moment to provide assurance and support to others.

(6)The importance of the human qualities of empathy, civility, courtesy, compassion, and recognizing the dignity of every person. As His Holiness, Dalai Lama XIV, said: "Be compassionate not just with your friends but to everyone. Be compassionate. Work for peace in your heart and in the world. Work for peace and I say again Never give up. No matter what is going on around you, Never give up."

Margaret Friedberg, the niece of my college classmate Tommy Giordano, told me a story that touched me deeply and reflected this sentiment. Whenever Giordano and his brothers wanted to go to a school dance, their mother would make them promise to spend a significant part of the evening dancing with a girl who hadn't been asked to dance by anyone. Tom's mother would interrogate him and his brothers afterward to see if they had kept their promise. They did!

(7)The importance of being a bridge builder, finding ways to calm "troubled waters," to borrow an expression by the British author Mary Ann Evans (also known by her pen name, George Eliot). Reaching out and touching others have been among the most satisfying experiences of my life.

(8)The importance of making a difference, a Jesuit ideal. This is what I said to a student who interviewed me as I was leaving as dean:

A long time ago a graduation speaker at Fordham Law School, who had been a judge, urged the graduating class to be good people. What he meant by that was to do things right in terms of ethics and integrity. To try to contribute to our country, whether it be the legal system or the community, by finding things that aren't working (and you don't have to look, because they come to you each day) and involving yourself and making some difference there. And showing respect and care for others.

I'm not sure that one can ask for much more than that because each of us will decide what we want to do with our lives and part of that will depend on what opportunities come to us. But whatever that might be, whatever place you find yourself, make some difference. It doesn't have to be the deanship of a law school, which is a more public kind of position. So many of the opportunities where I feel I made some small difference were quiet moments, quiet conversations with a student or a lawyer or someone who was hurting, and I found myself able to make a suggestion, or listen, or do something that could help ease the pain.

So, opportunities are everywhere, just take advantage of some of these opportunities. Someone once said, "Do one thing that's positive every day of your life, so that at the end of the day you look back and feel there was something you did somewhere, whether it was holding the door or not rushing away from somebody who needed somebody to talk to."[2]

41

Advice to My Grandchildren

People are often unreasonable, irrational, and self-centered.
Forgive them anyway.
If you are kind, people may accuse you of selfish, ulterior motives.
Be kind anyway . . .
In the final analysis, it is between you and God.
It was never between you and them anyway.
— "DO IT ANYWAY" — A PRAYER ATTRIBUTED TO MOTHER TERESA

Letter to My Grandchildren

As you know, I've spent considerable time in the past few years writing a personal history.[1] I wanted to share with you in letter form some of what I consider important. I don't expect you to absorb at this stage of your life everything I say in this letter, but I wanted you to know at least this much about me. Much of what is here is reflected in letters I have sent you and your parents and in writings and speeches of mine, too many for you to make any sense of me. I'm really not that complicated, however, even though that's a word I use a lot.

First, I want to let you know how much I love you and wish each of you a wonderful life. It has been an amazing experience for me to be your grandfather, watching you come into this world and then begin to grow up.

With each of you, I've had some memorable experiences, reading a children's book to you, visiting your classroom to give a talk on the Constitution, or be part of an oral history project, going to a ball game with you, watching you play a sport, attending your birthday parties and other events of importance in your life, such as your First Holy Communion and Confirmation, swimming in a pool with you, breaking up a fight among some of you, chatting with you about school or some other subject, going sleigh riding with you, playing football with some of you or simply throwing a ball with you, or going out for a meal with you. Among the meaningful experiences for me were boat trips and museum visits and places we went to like Liberty Island, Rye Beach, Great Adventure, or Chinatown.

Most special each year was taking you to New York's Thanksgiving Day Parade with the youngest sitting on my shoulder. And how I recall trying to climb a tall mountain in Ireland with five of you (Croagh Patrick, which you scaled but I did not). I have especially enjoyed our times together in the Christmas period at the Trapp Family Lodge and in Southampton during the summers. So much joy and so many wonderful memories.

I had similar experiences with your parents, whom I love dearly, including camping trips and summer vacations at the Tyler Place in Vermont and skiing at Windham and wintering for a week or so at Disney World in Florida. Sooner than I would like to believe, each of you, like your parents, will be adults, part of a world that at times can be very cold and harsh, if not cruel. But don't be confused by all of this, because each of you can make it warmer and more humane by how you relate to other people. Self-interest runs very strong in the world you'll be part of; it always has from my readings of history and always will based on my experiences over the past fifty-plus years. To be self-interested is part of our nature. We can do something about checking that habit because we have a free will and intelligence and a conscience.

Many of us rush along the journey of life, focusing on our daily challenges, without pausing to see beyond the immediate. I have noticed how quickly we rush for a seat on a train or how fast we drive a car on the highway. Sometimes we do not see someone with a greater need for that seat or the reason why a person ahead of us on the highway is driving more slowly than we want.

As I've aged, I see all of this more clearly and feel embarrassed whenever I fail to yield my seat or let someone pass me on the highway or stay ahead of me in the lane I'm traveling. It takes work to deal with our own self-interest, as I've discovered. It's not important to always be first. But there is a "firstness" of sorts when you yield a personal interest to some greater good. Slowing down does not prevent you from getting to where you want to go. I have discovered that from watching your grandmother. She does not like to be rushed and, unlike me, is patient in all things and matters. She has a wonderful balance to her, always considering the interests of others in every possible setting. She is, for that reason, first in everybody's affections.

I know how important it is to be the best you can be in the undertakings of your life such as in school, in your work, and in sport competitions. God gave us what talents we have and expects us to make the most of these gifts. We fail in not doing so unless, of course, circumstances make it impossible. But as you strive for what some might describe as success, I hope you'll always do so in the framework of what is proper, ethical, and right. By this I mean avoid cheating, lying, and "stepping" on others who get in the way. Be of good cheer in dealing with others. Show respect even where you feel disrespected.

I used to say in my teaching of law students that disrespect doesn't know how to deal with respect, so keep respecting. You can substitute the words good and evil. What I mean by this is meet the evil in the world by staying with what is good. Violence shouldn't beget more violence is another way to put it.

Promote community: Do what's in the best interest of the community. This at times may mean sacrificing some of your own personal interests. A senior law school professor to whom I paid tribute at his funeral Mass, Father Charles Whelan, offered to not take a raise to which he was entitled (and would then give to the Jesuit community) so that there would be more money for younger professors.

Don't be unnecessarily harsh and critical of others. Try to find ways to help others deal with their shortcomings or to help them see that what they are doing is inappropriate. Be positive. Avoid tearing down another person to advance your own interest. Let your advancement be based on your good works and accomplishments.

See how much good you can do if you don't take credit for it. There's so much satisfaction in seeing things accomplished that lift a person or organization without having to be acknowledged for having done so. I've discovered how much you actually can accomplish by allowing others to receive the credit. It's not unlike those ice hockey and other games you played where your assist helped a teammate score the tying or winning goal and become the hero, or where your defensive play made all the difference.

You all seemed to do this intuitively. I confess, however, that, as human beings, we do need some expression of gratitude, some affirmation. A child needs to be affirmed by a parent or teacher, and so do adults in their particular settings. Never forget to express gratitude to others who extend to you an act of kindness or support. Do not assume they know it. Say thank you. There is a great power in the use of those words. We too often forget that.

As you enjoy your particular successes, be modest. There are likely to be others who made them possible. Mention them and thank them. Like the gift of life, we should not forget to reach back, where appropriate, to remember your parents (perhaps even grandparents and other loved ones), and our God. They had something to do with our successes, perhaps more than we realize.

The book is dedicated to Mom and Pop, Donald, Uncle Pat and Aunt Catherine, and your Nana. Without all of you, my loved ones, I would have had limited success in this life. Indeed, I would have had no life at all without Mom and Pop.

You grew up in somewhat affluent circumstances. Your parents worked hard to make this possible, and they in turn were assisted to some extent by their parents. It is important for family members to help each other. Some have more than others, just like people who aren't in our family. Don't be jealous of each other. Help strangers who come into your life, especially the poor, marginalized, disabled, or elderly.

The scriptures of the major religions urge that we respond to the needy, poor, and oppressed. There are more poor people in the world and more suffering than we realize. The world is a community, and each of us must do what we can to protect that community. Simply making gifts of money is not enough. We need to give time when we can to causes, organizations, and institutions. At times you will have opportunities to lead, and I hope you seize these consistent with the rest of your life. We all can lead in some way. Be loyal to institutions that contributed to your station in life.

Go about your life honestly, ethically, and morally. It's wonderful to be a role model of probity, but it's not always easy to know what to do when you see so much bad behavior around you. Sometimes you may get suffocated by it. Find a way to remove yourself from such suffocation, protect who you are, and move on with your life. Making choices is at times very difficult. Draw into such moments your loved ones and friends for their guidance, wisdom, and help.

I've been wordy because, as I said at the beginning, I love you very much and want you to know what I learned and believe as the first member of your Boyle/Feerick family to be born in America. I ask only that you read this letter and reflect on what I've said. Thank you and God bless you, America, Ireland, and the whole world.

Appendixes

We pray that people of all faiths, all races, all nations . . . will come together in a peace guaranteed by the binding force of mutual respect and love.

— PRESIDENT DWIGHT D. EISENHOWER'S FAREWELL ADDRESS, 1961

Appendixes

Appendix A: Non-Feerick Surnames Associated with My Family

As for the non-Feerick surnames associated with my family, the public information below is informative:

Public Information — Heraldry Names Ltd.

MacDermot

The surname MacDermot, with variations like McDermott, is derived from the Irish Mac Diarmada, meaning son of Dermot. The person from whom the surname is considered taken lived in the 12th century. He was a direct descendant of Maelruanaidh Mor, the brother of Conor, King of Connacht and the ancestor of the O'Connors who ruled in the 10th century. It is said that the two brothers agreed that, in return for surrendering any claim to the kingship of Connacht, Maelruanaidh and his descendants would receive the territory of Moylurg, which is located in the north of modern County Roscommon and includes the towns of Boyle and Frenchpark. The area has since been associated with the McDermotts. When virtually all of the old Gaelic aristocracy were dispossessed of their lands during Cromwellian confiscations, the Moylurg MacDermots salvaged some of their old possessions and moved to Coolavin in the 17th century beside Lough Gara in neighboring County Sligo. A number of other branches formed over the centuries, the most prominent being the MacDermot Roe ("red") located near Kilronan in County Galway and the MacDermot Gall ("foreign"), which usurped the chieftanship for a short time from their base in east Roscommon. Among the most famous of the McDer-

motts is Sean Mac Diarmada, one of the seven signers of the Proclamation of the Irish Republic, the act of which led to his execution by
the British in April 1916.

Moran

The majority of Morans are of Connacht origin, with concentrations
in Mayo, Leitrim and Roscommon. Moran is the Anglicized version
of several Irish names. O Morain, derived from "mor," meaning "big"
and roughly translated as "little big man," arose in County Mayo, near
the present day town of Ballina. Another version of the name, O Mur-
chain, from murchadha, meaning "sea-warrior," originated near the
border with County Kildare. Two Connacht families had the name
O Mughrain, another form of Moran. One was a minor branch of the
Ui Maine tribal grouping based near Criffon in County Galway. The
other was related to the O'Connors of Connacht. The presence of
these families is recorded in the names of their territories, with Ardmo-
ran and Lismoran in Mayo, Kilmoran in Galway and Rathmoran in
Fermanagh.

Boyle

The surname Boyle includes such variants as Boal and O'Boyle. In
Irish the name O Baoghill is thought to mean "pledge." The family
was powerful and respected and shared control of the north-west of
Ireland with the O'Donnells and the O'Dohertys during the Middle
Ages. Many Irish Boyles have Norman origins, but the majority are of
Gaelic origin with a significant number descended from the Scottish
Norman family of de Boyville, a name connected to the town of Beau-
ville in Normandy, France. The Boals are connected to this town. A
Welsh branch of the same Norman family, antecedents of the Boyles,
Earls of Cork and Shannon, was descended from Richard Boyle, who
arrived in Ireland from Kent in 1588 and grew extremely wealthy, tak-
ing over the Irish estates of Sir Walter Raleigh. His ancestor was a Nor-
man lord in Herefordshire known as Humphrey de Binville. Robert
Boyle (1671–91), son of the first Earl of Cork, is best known for Boyle's
Law ("the volume of a fixed quantity of gas at a constant pressure is
inversely proportional to its pressure").

My great-grandparents, Jane Pryle and James Boyle, had five children:
Patrick, Michael, Mary, Jane, and Catherine. Jane appears to have been the
oldest, born in the 1860s. She married George Hoffman and they had four

children: George, Ruth, Jane, and Mary. The second sister, Mary, was born on September 28, 1868, and married James Ryan, who died on September 1, 1909. Mary died on December 7, 1923, and is buried with her husband and other family members at Mount Carmel Cemetery in Lombard. Mary also raised four children: Bridget, Catherine, Therese, and John. The third and youngest sister, Catherine, born in 1883, married Dennis Lynch of Connecticut on October 3, 1910, and they raised four children also: Mary, Aloysius, William, and Loretta Jane. Dennis Lynch died in 1935 and Catherine in 1949, both in Chicago. Two other Boyle sisters, Bridget (married to John Tunney of Culmore) and Anne (married to "Richard" Collins), remained in Ireland. I have a sense that Mom, called Mary Jane by her friends, may have been named in honor of her Boyle aunts in Chicago but there are other possibilities given that the names of Mary and Jane appear elsewhere in her family tree, including her mother, Maria, and her paternal grandmother, Jane Pryle.

In October of 2015, I made a trip to Chicago to locate the graves of Mom's aunts: Elizabeth Sheridan Moran, Mary Boyle Ryan, and Catherine and Jane Boyle. I succeeded in locating the graves of the first two at Mount Carmel Cemetery in Lombard, Illinois, both buried in humble settings.

Appendix B: My Dean's Reports

1981–1982

My first dean's report, covering the 1981–1982 school year, contained a beautiful tribute to former Dean McLaughlin, titled "All Talents in All Seasons," and also a tribute to Professor John McAniff on his retirement after sixty years as an adjunct. The report spoke admiringly of Professor Joseph Perillo's service as acting dean in expanding the faculty, establishing a legal process course, and moving forward with the plan to double the school's space.[1] Perillo also brought to the school Professor Georgene Vairo and twenty new adjuncts, nine of whom were graduates of the Law School.

The report also introduced the new members of my administrative team: Joseph Crowley as associate dean, Gail Hollister as assistant dean of students, Robert Reilly as assistant dean of alumni initiatives, James McGough as director of financial aid, and from McLaughlin's years, Assistant Deans Robert Hanlon Jr. and William Moore.

In this school year, I issued a second dean's report with a picture on the cover of Professor Manning, who had died on January 5, 1983, noting his profound impact on the school. The cover of the report heralded the activities of the students, focusing on our three journals (the *Fordham Law Review*, the *Urban Law Journal*, and the *International Law Journal*) and their successes in moot court competitions. The changing curriculum at the school was reflected in a chart comparison of the courses in 1961 and in 1983, noting at the time sixty adjuncts and almost one hundred elective offerings.

1982–1983

This report noted that there were present at the school thirty-eight full-time faculty members, and Professor Mary Daly '72, had joined the faculty. Among the adjuncts was Raymond O'Keefe, returning to the school to teach advocacy after a long absence. The student body stood at 1,230 students, and the new class's GPA and LSAT scores placed Fordham among the top 20 law schools in the country.

The report reflected the school's sadness over the death of William White '33. It highlighted new initiatives taking place, including the Stein Institute on Law and Ethics, expanded career services for students, the beginning of a summer session for students, and the commitment to developing a robust clinical education program. Also noted was the attendance of more than one thousand graduates at the annual alumni luncheon, where Judge Lawrence Pierce '51, received the medal of achievement, and Governor Mario Cuomo was the featured speaker.

The report thanked the late Judge Robert Trainor for constituting an emergency loan fund for students and Mulligan for chairing again the annual fund committee, which reached the $300,000 mark. In the report the generosity of Leo Kissam was underscored. Father McGinley said, "To him, law was a great profession and Fordham a topflight school for the profession."

1983–1984

The dean's report for 1983–1984 honored three faculty members, Robert Byrn, Perillo, and Thomas Quinn, for forming "a foundation of excellence in the areas of Torts, Contracts, and Commercial law, respectively." Also recognized were: Barry Hawk for his internationally recognized Corporate Law Institute, Gerald McLaughlin for launching an Institute on Financial Services, Crowley for developing a program on the role of unions, Peter O'Connor for developing a program on "Bad Samaritanism," and Perillo for developing the Stein Institute of Law and Ethics and for organizing a workshop on the role of a law school in the cause of legal reform.

Professors Deborah Batts,[2] Carl Felsenfeld, and Roger Goebel joined the faculty. Stalwarts from the McLaughlin and Mulligan years were also making their mark: Professor Michael M. Martin became the moderator of the law review, and Professor Quinn, while updating his highly acclaimed *Uniform Commercial Code Commentary and Digest*, was promoting throughout the academic world a commitment of service to those in need.

Contract scholars Perillo and Calamari were co-writing a book for students titled *How to Thrive in Law School.* Yung Frank Chiang, the school's first Asian American professor, was blazing paths in the law community. Martin Fogelman was carrying the banner for the school at national meetings of the Association of American Law Schools and within the university. Professor Constantine "Gus" Katsoris was bringing distinction to the school as a public member of the Securities Industry Conference on Arbitration.[3]

My corporations professor Robert Kessler was active with articles and book supplements in the field of corporate law, and Professor Michael Lanzarone, my Law School classmate, was writing articles on labor law and urban issues. Professor Earl Phillips was publishing a well-received monthly consumer credit newsletter and truth-in-lending report. Professor Ludwik Teclaff,[4] with whom I worked in the library as a student, was finishing his seventh book, *The Economic Roots of Oppression.*

The report spoke of rising admissions to the school (there were eight hundred day students and four hundred evening students then enrolled) and the growing support of students in areas of career services. Other activities described included a school newspaper, a yearbook, a student musical production ("The Follies"), and new associations for Black, Hispanic, and Asian students. The Student Bar Association was organizing blood drives, social gatherings, orientation programs, a student directory, and a boat ride around Manhattan. Linda H. Young arrived from Skadden in the Spring of 1983 to become assistant dean of students and a beloved presence at the school, continuing the great work of Professor Hollister. Graduation in 1983 was marked by the presentation of the Eugene J. Keefe Award to Professor Andrew Sims.

The 1983–1984 report noted that Judges Kevin Duffy '58 and Irene Duffy '57 received the alumni medal of achievement, a law school first for a husband and wife team. The report also noted that the *Urban Law Journal, International Law Journal,* and moot court had started alumni groups, and alumni chapters had been established in Atlanta, Chicago, Los Angeles, and San Francisco. Dean's medals of recognition were bestowed upon four former faculty members: Joseph Doran,[5] Joseph McGovern,[6] Bernard O'Connell, and William White (awarded posthumously).

1984–1985

The 1984–1985 report highlighted the establishment of a center for European Community Law and International Anti-Trust Law and the growing emphasis on career planning, with the Career Planning Center bringing on three full-time staff members, headed by Maureen Provost.

The report noted that both Professor Edward McGonagle, "long a student favorite," and Professor Katsoris, "no one has ever accused Gus of speaking too softly," received the Bene Merenti Medal. Also honored were Archibald Murray of the Legal Aid Society with the alumni medal of achievement and Judge Edward Weinfeld with the Stein Prize.

1985–1986

The report for 1985–1986 showcased on its front cover the pictures of four outstanding faculty members in the classroom — Calamari, Maria Marcus, Vairo, and Quinn. The report, dedicated to Professor Crowley, noted with sadness his passing in December 1985.

1986–1987

The report began by marking the 25th anniversary of the school's presence at Lincoln Center and the celebration of the school's evening division, which opened in 1912, when the school was located at 140 Nassau Street. Present at the celebration was the evening division's oldest living graduate, James Fitzgerald '18, and two former evening graduates were honored on the occasion with the dean's medal of recognition: Governor Malcolm Wilson '36 and Judge Marilyn Hall Patel '63. The student body was at 1,300, of which 42 percent were women.

The school also honored David Edelstein '34 on the occasion of his 35th anniversary as a federal judge. Professor Robert Kaczorowski, a legal historian, and Professor Michael Malloy of Seton Hall Law School joined the faculty. Caroline Gentile was appointed director of the Joseph R. Crowley Institute of Labor and Employment Law, and Margorie Martin '78 joined the school to assist in clinical education and other administrative roles.

1987–1988: Thanks a Million

The report announced the arrival of future full-time faculty star Steven Thel. It also noted the presentation of the alumni medal of achievement to Judge John Keenan and the Stein Prize to Justice Lewis F. Powell Jr., as well as the selection of Maureen Provost to serve as president of the National Association for Law Placement. The report contained a special tribute to Professor Peter O'Connor, who joined the faculty in 1973. He was noted for his civility and professionalism; as his health declined, he apologized when he had to sit for the final few weeks of the term, saying it was not "the O'Connor style."

Additionally, the report mentioned a board of visitors being established with Denis McInerney as chair '51, and the naming of a lecture series in memory of Noreen McNamara '51, a distinguished Connecticut lawyer.

1988–1989

The report contained tributes to two beloved adjunct faculty, George Brooks and McAniff, who had passed away that school year. During this year, Professor Kaczorowski published an article in the *Yale Law Review* on the Civil Rights Act of 1866, argued a pro bono case before the Supreme Court, and served as a consultant on a multivolume series of articles for the bicentennial of the Bill of Rights. Barry Hawk received the Bene Merenti Medal in 1988. At its presentation, a story of Hawk humorously noted how law became his default profession: "He was destined to enter one of three professions — clergy, military, and law. . . . He was not called to the clerical life. His hopes for rapid promotion in the military were dashed when he made a wrong turn and drove his tank through Philadelphia. Only law remained." The report also thanked the leadership of Jim Gill and the generosity of the legions of alumni and friends of the Law School who "made the difference between a solid academic program and the opportunity to be a preeminent law school."

1990–1991

The report for 1990–1991, the university's sesquicentennial, noted that there were at the Law School 162 faculty, student, and alumni events. The report contained a special tribute to Professor Calamari on his retirement from the full-time faculty and welcomed the arrival of Professors Deborah Denno,[7] James Fleming, William Treanor, and the return of Professor Martin Flaherty after clerking for Justice Byron White on the U.S. Supreme Court. The report announced the unveiling of a portrait of former governor Malcom Wilson and of twenty-eight devoted past faculty members. Mulligan received the Stein Prize and Associate Dean Vairo received the student's Eugene J. Keefe Award. The report also mentioned that Judge Lawrence Pierce was the 1991 graduation speaker for a historic second time.

1991–1992

This dean's report was dedicated to Father Laurence J. McGinley, S.J.,[8] and Professor Edward Yorio, both of whom had died that school year. As a tribute to Yorio, the class of 1992 commissioned a portrait of him for the school's collection.[9] Reflecting on the previous decade, the report noted the growth of the full-time faculty from thirty to fifty-seven professors, commenting that "with the retirement or passing of some of the legendary teachers at Fordham, we have added a dozen or more new teachers and scholars who are making their marks [and] are the legends of the next generation."

Mention was made of the growing student commitment to legal and community activities focused on the poor and the general public, with the report observing, "This is the character of the Fordham lawyers of tomorrow." It mentioned that the LL.M. programs were attracting lawyers from around the world.

The report also heralded the arrival of Professors Tracy Higgins, Daniel Richman, and Ian Weinstein. It spoke of impressive faculty writings and recorded the development of a technology center within the Leo Kissam library. Lectures, colloquy, and institutes were in abundance during the school year, including conferences by the Stein Institute, then directed by Professor Daly, and a two-day conference by the Corporate Law Institute under Barry Hawk's leadership. Also active during the year was the Fordham Center on International Criminal Law, directed by Professor Abraham Abramovsky, and a faculty studies colloquy led ably by Professor Marc Arkin, which attracted scholars from Harvard and other leading law schools. The school received some five thousand applications, and the admissions office boomed with "new ideas, new technology and high morale." Professor Marcus, the faculty moderator, was quoted as saying: "All the moot court teams brought home the gold — actually the silver and bronze — and what a pleasure it was to coach and watch them."

But there were challenges that year. The report said that Fordham weathered a difficult job market because of a recession, with a drop in the number of on-campus employers. The report also noted a special law school and alumni trip to Adare, Ireland, in November of 1991, to host a breakfast on November 19 for president of Ireland Mary Robinson — a memorable contribution to the university on its 150th anniversary. The report concluded by announcing that the Law School had achieved its highest overall giving ever — $2,178,216 to the annual fund and $392,658 in endowment gifts.

1992–1993: Fordham Law Celebrates 75 Years of Women

The report was dedicated to Father Finlay, who died in December 1992. It also honored, by reprinting their bene merenti citations, Professors Michael M. Martin, Frank Chiang, and Donald Sharpe for twenty years of outstanding service and announced the arrival of new faculty, Matthew Diller, Nicholas Johnson, and Terry Smith. There were new student groups, including Older and Wiser Law Students (OWLS) and Italian and Irish American student associations.

In the spring, the school began the celebration of the 75th anniversary of the admission of women to Fordham Law School, with the unveiling of portraits of Ruth Whitehead Whaley '94, the first African American woman to be admitted into the bars of New York and North Carolina, and of Frances Berko '44, a national leader in the quest for rights for all disabled citizens. The report also noted the creation of a corporate counsel association and the establishment of the Stein Scholars Program. Judge Loretta Pieska '73 was the guest speaker at the annual alumni luncheon, applauded by the eleven hundred people in attendance for her induction as a federal judge. Judge Marilyn Hall Patel was the graduation speaker that year, and Andrew Maloney '61, a former U.S. attorney, was honored with the alumni medal of achievement.

1993–1994

This report announced the opening of the George McMahon, S.J., residence hall at Lincoln Center and the celebration of the 75th anniversary of the admission of women to Fordham Law School. The celebration was developed under the outstanding leadership of Patricia Hynes '66, and Professor Vairo '79. The year-long celebration concluded with graduation remarks by U.S. Attorney General Janet Reno. The report also noted the appointment of Nitza Escalera as assistant dean of students and the naming of Associate Dean Vairo as the Leonard F. Manning Professor of Law. The young alumni committee was established, chaired by Tim Brosnan '84.

Also in that school year, students won national moot court championships, and Chief Justice Warren Burger delivered a second Sonnett Lecture.[10] The year was distinguished by the establishment of the Brendan Moore Trial Advocacy program, made possible by the extraordinary generosity of his family. The report contains a full-page profile on Brendan Moore. The school also received a very generous gift for the Kissam library in memory of Jay Edgar Swanin '32.

1994–1995

The report opened by announcing that the Law School won the National Moot Court Championship. The students (Edward Hassi, James Bliss, and Michael Cryam finished first in a field of 230 teams from 150 law schools. The school also won the Craven Constitutional Law Moot Court Competition, finishing first in a competition of teams from 26 schools. The faculty also agreed to adopt pro bono guidelines for itself, a possible first in the country in regards to a faculty making a commitment to pro bono. More than half of the student body (700) engaged in some form of public service.

The report also announced the establishment of the William Hughes Mulligan Chair in International Legal Studies, designed to bring distinguished scholars from around the world to teach at Fordham, and the appointments of Mark Patterson, Benjamin Zipursky, and Professor Elizabeth Cooper as associate professors of law. Michael M. Martin was appointed associate dean after serving as a member of the faculty since 1972; Dean Vairo was recognized for her seven years of "exemplary, truly exceptional service" as associate dean; and Professor Katsoris was awarded the alumni medal of achievement. Behind all the school's efforts that year, the report noted, was the "incredible, selfless leadership of Michael K. Stanton '59, president of the alumni association."

1995–1996

The report featured on its cover pictures of twelve of the then untenured faculty and future leaders of the school: Professors James Cohen, Jeffrey Colon, Elizabeth Cooper, Diller, Higgins, Johnson, Nolan-Haley, Patterson, Terry Smith,[11] Vorspan, Weinstein, and Zipursky. It highlighted the establishment of the Joseph Crowley Program on International Human Rights.

The report was filled with many sad moments in the school's history, including the deaths of three giants: Dean Mulligan, Louis Stein, and Louis Lefkowitz. A centerfold highlighted the school's 90th anniversary celebration, with pictures from a gala on that occasion attended by twelve hundred graduates. Katherine Franke joined the faculty as an associate professor, bringing to the school a background in civil rights and gender and sexuality studies. Also noted were special recognitions given to E. Carter Corriston '60, B.J. Harrington '59, Robert Gaffney '69, and Frank Lucianna '51. Fundraising was stated to be at another all-time high ($3.6 million), as was the size of the graduation class (565, including 43 graduating with Master of Law degrees).

1996–1997: The Students of Today's Fordham Law School

The dean's report, dedicated to Father O'Hare, thanked him for his support of the school. The report marked the dedication of the new $54 million William D. Walsh Family Library at Rose Hill and highlighted the establishment of the Calamari Distinguished Professorship of Law and the Philip Reed Chair in Civil Justice and Dispute Resolution, noting Professor Daniel Capra's appointment to the latter. The report mentioned that the faculty had

published fifteen books and sixty-one law review articles that year and organized thirty-four major conferences. The report gave special recognition to
Michael Stanton '59. As Dean Reilly said, Stanton was "on the job (as president of the alumni) every day of his four-year tenure."

Many honors came during this year: Treanor's article on the Takings
Clause of the Constitution was recognized as the best of the year by one publication, Chantal Thomas was honored by the Black Law Students of Harvard
Law School with the Young Alumni Award, Professor Katsoris was recognized
by the Securities Industry Conference on Arbitration, Kevin Brown '97 was
honored by the New York State Bar Association for his leadership on the death
penalty defense project, and Paula Roberts '71 was recognized for her work on
child support and public benefit issues. Other graduates who were honored
by organizations at the school included Judge Robert Corcoran '57, Daniel
Scannell '40, and Eugene Murphy '59.

The school itself was recognized by the Hispanic Judges Association of
New York for its commitment to diversity and by the National Association of
Public Interest Law for its national leadership in the field of public service
activities. The annual giving pages drew attention to hundreds of other graduates, none more helpful than alumni president Bill Frank '66 and Ernest
Stempel '46, creator of the school's largest scholarship endowment. The Walter Absolon '27 memorial scholarship was established that year.

The report mentioned seven adjuncts who were honored with Bene Merenti Medals for twenty years of devoted service, including Thomas Fitzpatrick
'66, who also had served on the full-time faculty, and John Parker '59, who was
succeeded in his teaching of estate law by his daughter Kim. Page-long pro-
files of four student leaders from diverse backgrounds appeared in this report
as well: Rose Rodriguez of the Bronx; Michael Moyer of Ketchikan, Alaska;
Jeanmarie Grubert of Larchmont; H. Vern Clemons of Little Rock, Arkansas;
and Roy Richter of Brooklyn.

1997–1998: Fordham in the Wider World

The report for 1997–1998 traced Fordham's influence across the country and
the world. The Crowley Program on International Human Rights culmi-
nated in a human rights investigative mission to Turkey that involved both
law school faculty and students. The report stated that the group looked at
three main issues: practices in the State Security Courts, cases involving police torture of political prisoners, and intimidation of human rights activists
and defense attorneys.

In this school year, thanks to Professor Katsoris, a Securities Arbitration clinic to protect investors was added to the mix. There were twenty-nine faculty-organized programs, twelve special-event joint ventures with lawyers and the judiciary and bar associations, and five conferences by student groups. The report also noted that fourteen hundred J.D. and seventy-five L.L.M. students were enrolled at the school, with students coming from thirty-three states, twenty-six countries, and the U.S. Virgin Islands and Puerto Rico.

1998–1999: Our Collective Energies

The report featured page-long reflections by leaders at the school as it entered the new century: Dean Escalera on the dedication of current students to academic excellence and public service; visiting Bacon-Kilkenny Professor Jesse H. Choper, the Earl Warren Professor of Public Law at the University of California, Berkeley, on realizing our potential as research universities; Professor Matthew Diller on "Channeling Our Energy" through the rule of law and access to justice; Professor Mary Daly on "Expanding Our Orbit" on the issues involved in the international delivery of legal services; Professor James Kainen on "Building Critical Mass" through the use of technology and the possibilities presented for professors, students, and practicing lawyers; and Professor Michael W. Martin on "Maintaining Our Momentum," with a focus on how the alumni help catapult the school's public service mission.

I opened this report, stating:

> And as our reputation continues to grow, so does our vision of the future. To achieve that vision, we are taking advantage of the time to continue to enhance the intellectual life at the School, to increase our commitment to social justice, and to expand the School's profile in the international legal community as well as to marshal the resources that will allow us to accomplish this work.

Elsewhere in the report many memorable occasions were recalled, including the 50th anniversary luncheon of the alumni, attended by eleven hundred, with former Senator Bill Bradley as guest speaker, and the presentation of the school's first humanitarian award to Professor Raymond O'Keefe for his work with lawyers battling substance abuse. Concluding the report was a listing of faculty publications by forty-three faculty members, beginning with eight articles (four in the *New York Law Journal*) by Professor Abramovsky and ending with four writings by Professor Zipursky, including articles in the *Fordham* and *Pennsylvania Law Reviews*.

1999–2000

My 1999–2000 report began with a special message titled "Striking the Balance":

> In another millennium, a wise man said that the key to life is "to keep a balance [and] acknowledge the powers around us and in us." These words seem to aptly describe the way in which the School measures itself as we strive to remain in the top rank academically while also nurturing the spirit of public service which has been one of our hallmarks.

The report noted that the millennium tribute was attended at the Lincoln Center campus by more than twelve hundred graduates, with U.S. Supreme Court Justice O'Connor as the guest speaker. She was greeted with sustained applause and noted in her remarks Fordham's foresight in inviting her to the first event she participated in marking the new millennium. The report also announced the inauguration of a $10 million national merit scholarship program in honor of Francis Mulderig '52.

Throughout the report, reflections were offered by faculty and graduates. Professor Nicholas Johnson, chair of the school's self-study committee, said "What comes out clearly in the Self-Study process is how much our success depends on the individual initiative, ambition and talent of faculty and staff. . . . However, one thing we come together on is a commitment to excellence in all aspects of the institution." Thomas Kavaler '72 said that "lawyers in private practice are essential. With fewer lawyers, there would be more gunfights." Thomas Quinn observed that "the best product of a law school is not merely to train lawyers but to do so in the highest tradition of the law — in the service of others."

2000–2001

My final dean's report, dated December of 2001 and titled "Broadening Our Scope," began with a dedication to the past deans of the Law School, leaders of the alumni association, and to those whose lost loved ones on September 11, 2001, especially to the families of the Fordham Law graduates who had died.

The report added: "Fordham Law certainly looks differently today than it did ninety-five, forty, twenty-five, and even five years ago. We are bigger. We are stronger. And we are changing at a faster pace than ever before. But our reason for being is as recognizable and recallable today as it was the day of our founding. We do what we do because we believe that the law is a noble profession in the service of others and that doing good always comes before doing well. After all, how could we go on if we didn't. Why else would we continue?"

The report noted the graduation in May 2001 of more than five hundred J.D. and LL.M. students; the recognitions received during the school year by students and faculty; the activities of the school's institutes and centers; the celebration of the 12th anniversary of the LL.M. program, with an alumni trip to Italy, where a new chapter of the Fordham law alumni association was established. It also noted the beginning of the summer law program in Ireland. Of the program, Dean Perillo stated, "Our host institutions went to extraordinary lengths not only in their hospitality, but also by arranging special programs with judges, members of the bar, young lawyers, and experts on the current political situation. I have studied the workings of many summer programs, and I know of no other program that so smoothly integrated the faculty of the host institutions with the American faculty. I have never seen this level of student enthusiasm for any program."

Appendix C: Remarks on Receiving the ABA Medal

Thank you for this extraordinary honor. I am humbled by your selection of me to receive the Association's highest honor, and I thank you, President Linda Klein, and the Board of Governors for considering me worthy of being this year's recipient. And I thank those who sent nominations on my behalf, which I learned about after my selection.

I accept this medal in memory of my parents, Mary and John Feerick. They were immigrants from County Mayo, Ireland, who each traveled alone to America in the late 1920s seeking a better life for themselves and the family they would eventually have and raise. Their gentle spirit and quiet voices are with me at this moment, as are the voices of my teachers (Ursuline Sisters, Marist Brothers, priests of the Archdiocese of New York, and the Jesuits and lay teachers of Fordham University). They guided me and prepared me for life as an educated citizen, nurtured in the Catholic faith, emphasizing time and again the importance of striving to do what is right, especially for those in need.

I most especially thank my wife, Emalie. She is my moral compass, a devoted mother of our six children and grandmother of our eleven grandchildren, and the person whose wisdom and judgment I have depended on throughout my life as a lawyer. I owe no one as great a debt as I do Emalie, the anchor and love of my life.

And I thank all who came today because I was to receive this honor, including all of my children, seven of my grandchildren and other family members, siblings, and the widow of my late brother Donald and their family members, and my friends from Fordham Law School.

Permit me to speak to you for just a few moments about some of my heroes and the mentors and role models who influenced and guided me, and to conclude with a heartfelt message to my friends and colleagues at the bar.

When I became a lawyer, a veteran of World War II and a U.S. Senator emerged in my life — John F. Kennedy, for whom I cast my first presidential vote. His youth, energy, and eloquent calls to serve and give back to one's community affected me greatly in how I saw my obligations as a citizen and lawyer. I can still hear his voice challenging us:

> And so my fellow Americans: ask not what your country can do for you — ask what you can do for your country.

His tragic death on November 22, 1963, felt like the loss of a family member and in totally unexpected ways impacted much of my legal career.

My law school dean, and later second circuit court of appeals judge, William Hughes Mulligan, was another hero. He was bigger than life as a teacher encouraging us, his students, many of immigrant families, to aspire to excellence as practicing lawyers and, if we had such an inclination, as scholars in the law. He breathed life and inspiration into us when we were unsure and uncertain, making us feel confident in ourselves and our abilities. His gentle humor was renowned in New York and elsewhere. He helped us laugh and experience joy-filled moments when all around us, from Vietnam to the civil rights movement to Watergate, we witnessed serious and, at times, tumultuous events.

Upon graduating, I wanted to join a small law firm and found wonderful mentors at what was then a ten-lawyer firm: Skadden, Arps, Slate, Meagher & Flom. The first was Leslie H. Arps, a co-founder of the firm, a distinguished veteran of World War II, and an investigator of corruption on the New York waterfront as an assistant state attorney general. He urged me and other firm lawyers to do everything in an "upper-margin way," his favorite expression, which set a high ethical and moral benchmark for all of us.

Another name partner, William R. Meagher, brought me to the firm as a summer associate in 1960, and taught me that summer and for the next twenty years the importance of attention to detail, preparation, precision in language, the meaning of integrity, and pure hard work. Meagher also had been an investigator of corruption in New York State and for twenty years an esteemed part-time teacher at Fordham Law School.

Les Arps and Bill Meagher extended to everyone with whom they came in contact an attitude of civility, courtesy, and decency in the practice of the law. I learned, by watching them, how essential it is to the respect of law that each human being treat all others with respect, courtesy, decency, and dignity. I also will never forget their availability to me and other young lawyers whenever we sought assistance with personal and other matters. Their office doors were always open. They were pillars of the Skadden firm, modeling the best of lawyering as I experienced it.

I found scores of other role models when the American Bar Association invited me to participate in its effort to amend the Constitution to clarify ambiguities in the presidential succession provision and then in a more than decade-long effort to abolish the electoral college system in favor of a direct popular vote system. These role models included Senator Birch Bayh of Indiana, former attorney general Herbert Brownell, Justice Lewis Powell Jr., Professor Paul Freund of Harvard Law School, and many former ABA presidents for and with whom I served in my early years as a lawyer, from Walter Craig to Chesterfield Smith.

Later, I would serve as a member of New York State government commissions and would come to be inspired by such outstanding public servants as Cyrus Vance, the epitome of lawyerly integrity; former U.S. Marine General James King, an epitome of public service in the JAG Corps for more than thirty years; Judge Howard Levine of the New York Court of Appeals, an epitome of judicial temperament and lawyer excellence; and the incomparable Judith Kaye, the late Chief Judge of New York State, and her incomparable successor, Jonathan Lippman. They were all doers, with an incredible commitment to the rule of law and working collaboratively with others in the common interest. I continue to be inspired by their life work, all of them. Their voices are with me today.

My gratitude runs over to many others: teachers and colleagues at Fordham College and Fordham Law School, and many lawyers in the organized bar of New York with whom I served on committees who inspired me. I am grateful to Fordham graduate Louis Stein for imploring our school to lead in areas of legal ethics and to my law school mate, Archibald Murray, for expressing an incredible commitment to the poor as attorney-in-chief of the New York Legal Aid Society and then as the first African American president of the New York State Bar Association. Nor can I forget the young lawyers of the ABA who, fifty years ago, joined together across the country in a great cause — to promote the passage and ratification of the Twenty-Fifth Amendment to the Constitution. I was privileged to chair the Young Lawyers Committee on Presidential Inability and Presidential Succession from 1964 to 1967. Many of these individuals have passed from this world, and I remember especially Dale Tooley of Colorado and Mercer Tate of Pennsylvania.

In response to these influences and experiences, a few years ago as a Christmas gift for my grandchildren, I wrote down, printed, and bound a small fourteen-page book, where I tried to distill the lessons of my lifetime as a lawyer.

I spoke to my grandchildren, who sat around in a group in front of a Christmas tree, about the importance of service, and conducting themselves with old-fashioned honesty and respect for all. In one passage I read:

> Help strangers who come into your life. . . . Especially help the poor, marginalized, disabled, or elderly. There are more poor people in the world and more suffering than we realize. The world is a community, and each of us must do what we can to protect that community, not simply by gifts of money but by giving time when we can to causes, organizations, and institutions. We can make more small differences in the world than we realize. At times you will have opportunities to lead, and I hope you seize these consistent with the rest of your life. We all can lead in some way.

The people who have been beacons of light to me embodied this ethos. One of the great lawyer heroes in my life, Thurgood Marshall, a recipient of this medal, I held up each year as an exemplar of the legal profession at its best at orientations of new classes of law students when I served as dean. At a time when the law was used as a tool of social oppression throughout the country, he demonstrated how it could be used as a tool for good in the fight for equality. He won numerous court victories striking down laws, practices, and barriers that denied the blessings of liberty to people of color, impeding their development and relegating them to an ineffective role as citizens and members of society. He left the bar of this country a legacy of extending the protective net of the law wider, to include those unrepresented and disenfranchised. He gave us a vision of a more humane America.

I stand at the feet of previous medal recipients. I share in common with them the ethic of service that is at the core of being a lawyer. As Robert McKay of New York University Law School reminded us: "No calling is higher, no obligation more demanding than for each of us to serve that rigorous master whom we call justice. The path is not easy, nor is the path altogether clear. But we must all join hands in that glorious search."

We, the lawyers of America, live in a time of great challenge and opportunity, with moral imperatives to serve justice and fairness.

Consider the Justice gap report issued a month ago by the Legal Services Corporation, which contained alarming statistics:

> 86% of the civil legal problems reported by low-income Americans received inadequate or no legal help. 71% of low-income households experienced at least one civil legal problem in the past year, including 71% of households with veterans or other military personnel. Many of low income will approach LSC legal aid organizations this year for

support with an estimated 1.7 million problems and, due to under-
funding and restrictions on the services they provide, these individuals
will receive little or no help for more than half of these problems.
More than 60 million people living in the United States have family
incomes at or below 125% of the poverty level.

New York City's distinguished Citizens Committee for Children has shared
with me statistics as to the millions of children who live in poverty in the
United States or in linguistically isolated households. More than 2.5 million
children are homeless.

The bar of this country, populated with 1.4 million lawyers, active, registered, and retired, can make a dent in some of these statistics through increased volunteering and participation in programs of bar associations, courts,
government departments, law firms, corporate legal departments, and law
schools and in activities of legal aid organizations and community groups.
Here in New York, under the leadership of our chief judges, more than one
thousand senior lawyers are registered in one program as attorney emeriti,
ready to serve, with a number doing so, and scores of legal service organizations in the state are ready to receive such service. The challenge, however,
cannot be met solely through volunteering, but volunteering is contagious
and can make a difference.

The Legal Services Corporation, a national leader in providing legal assistance to the poor, deserves our full support in the war on poverty. One
distinguished former general counsel of a major corporation wrote me to
say: "We have to ask ourselves why we don't have the same sense of moral
outrage over the failure to recognize that abusive debt collection practices
and landlord-tenant issues that push a family into the street or into homeless
shelters may well result in far greater costs to society than the legal assistance
(sought by LSC)." Increasing legal assistance, he said, not only serves justice
but embodies good governance as well.

I ask my colleagues of the American legal profession: Why not find a place
to serve or create a program that can make a difference in the lives of those
disadvantaged and vulnerable? We have the instinct to serve, judging by sur-
veys of the profession, and there is no greater time to do so than now when
only 20 percent of the civil legal needs of low-income Americans are being
met. I recall, as if it were yesterday, Whitney North Seymour, a former medal
recipient, exhorting us to make sure that the concept of equal justice for all —
engraved in marble on the Supreme Court's building — was not an empty
aspiration in a lawyer's code or a meaningless phrase in the Pledge of Allegiance. He spoke often of a dedication to unenforceable ideals, engaging in

activities and efforts that serve humanity, and of adherence to high standards that are not necessarily enforceable, and yet are essential, such as decency, civility, courtesy, and respect for each other and the rule of law.

As dean I said to my students at Fordham Law School, don't leave the school without leaving a legacy behind that makes us better than you found us. Many did so. I can't think of anything more meaningful as a lawyer than being able to look back and see that you left a legacy by making a difference. As Albert Schweitzer observed: "I don't know what your destiny will be, but one thing I know. The only ones among you who will be really happy are those who have sought and found how to serve."

I have done my best and used what God gave me and the moral code and values my parents instilled in me. I hope to keep it going a while longer until I have used up every bit of myself. I will cherish this medal and will try always to honor it. God bless all of you and this blessed country of ours. May we extend its blessings for the good of all, far and wide.

Acknowledgments

I thank my siblings, Maureen, Kevin, and Anne Marie, for helping me throughout this endeavor: Maureen helped research, draft, and edit throughout the eighteen-year writing process; Kevin provided perspectives on our childhoods and family from the vantage point of someone ten years my junior; and Anne Marie, seventeen years my junior, shared stories of our family from after I moved away from home.

As I wrote this book, I received invaluable assistance from Fordham University and its law school. I express to their leaders my everlasting gratitude and debt, particularly to Father Joseph McShane, S.J., president of Fordham University, and the deans of Fordham Law School who succeeded me: William Michael Treanor, Michael M. Martin, and Matthew Diller.

I benefited greatly from family oral histories: A history of Pop by Maureen made a few days before he died and a week-long series of interviews by me of my Uncle Pat (Boyle) in March of 2002; an oral history of Uncle Pat by Enda Brogan, a grandnephew, in 1999; a summary oral history done by Donald of Pop; and an interview of Uncle Pat by Midwest Radio on the occasion of his 95th birthday celebration in County Mayo, Ireland.

I express deep gratitude for the help I received from friends in the United States and from my cousins and their spouses in Ireland.

I cannot thank enough Aiden Feerick, Patsy Walsh, Gerald Delaney, and John E. Feerick for all the help they gave me in understanding the genealogical history of the Feerick surname, and Katie Boyle of Mayo for her help regarding the Boyle and Pryle surnames.

I want to acknowledge Ann Eames for editing and Fordham University Professor Corey McEleney for content suggestions and ideas on how to organize an early draft of the manuscript.

Annie Decker read the manuscript several times, offering vital suggestions and edits. I cannot thank her enough for the assistance when I needed it most. I thank my grandson Ian and my daughter Jean for the suggestions that led to the title of this book.

In the latter stages of preparing the manuscript, my niece Jennifer Feerick and my law school colleague Professor Gail Hollister read it several times, offering valuable suggestions and encouragement. Barbara Coyne, my daughters Margaret, Jean, and Maureen, and my niece Mary Beth Benedetto helped edit the manuscript throughout the writing process. My then assistant, Derek Hackett, and Fordham's Social Justice colleagues Robert Reilly and Wilma Tamayo-Abreu provided important help.

In 2019, I received an unexpected gift — Constance Rosenblum, the author of *Boulevard of Dreams: Heady Times, Heartbreak, and Hope along the Grand Concourse in the Bronx*, was to serve as copy editor of the manuscript in its final stages. She eliminated obscure and unnecessary words and paragraphs and advanced suggestions that illuminated and made the text more explanatory, readable, and lively. My assistant Olga Tomasello built strongly on this initiative, as did those who she engaged to help, Professor John Rogan, Clementine Schillings, and William Pierotti.

Finally, I acknowledge the people who entered my life and inspired, taught, and guided me over the years. I especially appreciate the many people with whom I worked and served: my colleagues at Fordham University and from my days at Skadden, Arps, Slate, Meagher & Flom (Skadden) along with the friends and teachers of my youth. I acknowledge with gratitude the responsiveness and assistance I received from the Fordham University Law Library and its dedicated staff. I thank as well recent Fordham graduate Ellen McCormick '19 for stepping in at the last moment to help me review the page proofs, as well as Clementine Schillings. And, finally, I thank most deeply the Fordham University Press, led by Fred Nachbaur and his team, for making this book a reality. And I again thank, most lovingly, my wife, Emalie.

Notes

Introduction

Epigraph: Taken with permission from Patsy Walsh, "History of the Descendants of Patrick Feerick (c. 1815–1854) of Carrowkeel, Neale, County Mayo, Ireland" (Sligo Ireland, 2015), 6–7.

1. My daughter Margaret and grandson Dylan accomplished this in 2016.

2. A few years ago, the Boyle family placed my maternal grandfather's name, Patrick Boyle, on a tombstone in Toomore, which already bore the names of Loftus, Stephens, and Boyle.

3. See John D. Feerick, "Tribute to John M. Moran," *Fordham Law Review* (*FLR*) 70 (2002): 1117.

4. "Will Share 50,000 Dollars," *Irish Independent*, September 25, 1964.

1. What's in a Name?

1. Aiden Feerick, Consultant, Genealogy Advisory Service, National Library of Ireland, Dublin, in discussion with the author.

2. Aiden identified, as at Loggerheads with the Crown, Meiler M'Feyrick of Addergoole, Walter M'Feyrick of Downbally Co. Galway, and Peirs M'Ferrick of Adegoulebeg, Co. Galway. Aiden added "that after the 1798 rebellion, a person named Feerick (or variant) was sent to Australia." Quite clearly some of the earliest Feericks were a rebellious lot. See "Feericks Family Newsletter," edited by Maureen Sargent, for information about Feerick's who served their country. On file with author.

3. See Appendix A for the non-Feerick surnames associated with my family.

4. Robert E. Matheson, *Special Report on Surnames in Ireland 1894* (Dublin, Ireland: Alexander Thom & Co. Ltd., 1894), 9. See also Heraldry Names Ltd. and

Birdie Mulloy, *Itchy Feet and Thirsty Work: A Guide to the History and Folklore of Ballinrobe* (Lough Mask and Lough Carra Tourist Development Association 1991).

2. Mom's and Pop's Origins

Epigraph: Jean and Ollie Boyle, my first cousins, shared these words in memory of their son Martin, who died tragically at an early age.

1. Bernard O'Hara, *Michael Davitt Remembered* (Co. Mayo, Ireland: Michael Davitt Memorial Association, 1984), 1.

2. I was honored to be present in Straide on August 7, 2016, and invited to speak at the 100th anniversary of the Penal Church, which is now used as a museum and exhibits relics regarding the Irish National Land League and the life of Michael Davitt.

3. Seumas MacManus, *The Story of the Irish Race: A Popular History of Ireland*, Rev. ed. (Old Greenwich, Conn.: Devin-Adair Company, 1966), 666.

4. James Laffey, *Foxford: Through the Arches of Time*, produced by Michael Staunton, and Kitty Turnbull (Ireland, self-published, 2003), 8–12. *Foxford: Through the Lens of Time*, a picture book story that followed the publication of *Foxford: Through the Arches of Time*, includes a picture of my cousin Kevin Boyle on a horse-drawn mowing machine in the 1960s. *Foxford: Through the Lens of Time* (Galway, Ireland: Castle Print, 2010), 114.

5. Ibid., 8 (quoting Samuel Lewis, *Topographical Dictionary of Ireland* (London: S. Lewis and Co., 1837).

6. J. A. Fox, *Reports on the Condition of the Peasantry of the County of Mayo During the Famine Crisis of 1880 (Dubl. Mansion House Comm. for the Relief of Distress in Irel.)* (Browne and Nolan, 1880), 32.

7. Ibid., 33.

8. See Bridie Mulloy, *Itchy Feet and Thirsty Work: A Guide to the History and Folklore of Ballinrobe* (Lough Mask and Lough Carra Tourist Development Association, 1991).

9. The Right Rev. Monsignor D'Alton, *A Short History of BallinRobe Parish* (Dublin, Ireland, 1931), 7.

10. The acreage reported for each was: James Feerick, 11 acres, 2 roods, and 10 perches of 1st-class land and 11 acres of 6th-class land; David Feerick, 4 acres of 1st-class land and 2 acres, 2 roods, and 10 perches of 2nd class land; and Patrick Feerick, 2 acres of 2nd-class land and 13 acres, 2 roods, and 10 perches of 5th-class land. A statute acre contained 4,840 square yards, a rood was one-fourth of an acre of 1,210 square yards, and a perch was one-fortieth of a rood containing 30 square yards. While all three ancestors were Roman Catholics, they were required to pay Tithes, an assessment on agricultural land, for the support of the established Protestant church at the time. It was disestablished in 1871.

11. He likely was tied to one of the eleven Feerick families living in Ballinrobe Parish in the 1780s.

12. Taken with permission from Patsy Walsh, "History of the Descendants of Patrick Feerick (c. 1815–1854) of Carrowkeel, Neale, County Mayo, Ireland" (Sligo Ireland, 2015), 6–7.

13. Ibid.

14. Ibid.

15. Griffith, "General Valuation of the Union of Ballinrobe" (Dublin, 1856), 65.

16. Joseph Stock, *A Narrative of What Passed at Killalla, in the County of Mayo, and the Parts Adjacent, During the French Invasion in the Summer of 1798 by an Eye-Witness* (T. Baylis, 1800), 3–8. For a fictional depiction of this historical event, see Thomas Flanagan, *The Year of the French* (New York: NYRB Classics, October 31, 2004).

17. The children of the Pryles live in California, but my contact with them has been limited. They are Edward (in San Francisco), James (in Oakland), and Kevin Pryle.

18. See Appendix A: Boyle notes.

19. Robert and Mary Moran, 2010.

20. The 1878 eviction notice is on file with author.

21. Although the Civil Birth Record reflects April 13, 1879, as Ellen McDermott's birth date, it is recorded that her baptism was February 12 of that year. For a possible explanation, see Chapter 38.

22. Patrick Boyle, "Pat Boyle in Knock," interview by Enda Brogan, tape-recording (July 1999); transcript on file with author.

3. Mom's and Pop's Childhood

Epigraph: These words were pulled from one of two handwritten letters Mom left behind.

1. Mom's home was considered for depiction in the Irish Hunger Memorial at Battery City Park in New York City.

2. Oral History by Enda Brogan, on file with author.

3. When Desmond Boyle died in 2015, almost a thousand people came to his funeral services in Foxford, Mayo. Of his cemetery prayer service, Father Padraig Costello said that he had never seen such thundering rain but "it was eclipsed by the playing of an accordionist" sitting on a chair under a makeshift canopy. Mary and Kevin Boyle said the accordionist's rendition of "Boolavogue" was heavenly. Desmond's tombstone at Toomore has a depiction of an accordion as well as the Celtic Cross.

4. An American Odyssey

Epigraph: Cormac MacConnell was a columnist at the *Irish Voice* for almost thirty years. *Irish Voice*, August 19, 2009.

1. Mom was joined by her cousin Della Clarke on this trip because she was then having memory lapses, and we thought Della could help her cope. Returning to Ireland always rejuvenated Mom.

2. Before being scrapped in 1932, his ship had a proud history. In 1913 it rescued passengers from a burning British liner, and the following year it helped sink an armed German liner.

3. See Appendix A.

4. See Adam Fifield, "The Underground Men," *New York Times*, January 12, 2003, https://www.nytimes.com/2003/01/12/nyregion/the-underground-men.html?mtrref =undefined.

5. Pop worked in the north of Greenland in an arctic climate, possibly at Thule Air Base, the U.S. Air Force's northernmost installation.

6. A "shape up" was an assembled group of workers from which crews were chosen for projects. A designated person would yell out the positions that needed filling, and those interested in the job would raise their hands.

7. Dan Kurzman, *No Greater Glory: The Four Immortal Chaplains and the Sinking of the Dorchester in World War II* (New York: Random House 2004). Dan skillfully incorporates firsthand accounts, gives the reader a glimpse of the horrific night, and shines light on the heroism on its maximum. I quote James Doyle's son.

8. Kevin Barry was an 18-year-old Irish patriot who participated in the Irish Volunteer Forces. He was court-martialed for murder and sentenced to execution by hanging for killing a British soldier. His youth, service, and courage left an indelible mark on his country. Mom, then 12, carried through her life the death of Kevin Barry. See Seán Cronin, *The Story of Kevin Barry* (Cork, Ireland: National Publications Committee, 1965).

9. See my tribute in John D. Feerick, "Theodore W. Kheel: An Exemplar for Alternative Dispute Resolution and a Pioneer in Environmental Interest Disputes," *Pace Env. L. Rev.* 27 (2009–10): 1.

10. "Patrick Boyle," *Irish Echo*, April 17–23, 2002. "Irish Patriot, Family Historian Patrick Boyle," *Irish Echo*, May 1–7, 2002. See the tribute I gave to Uncle Pat and my parents on the occasion of the presentation to me of the gold medal of the American Irish Historical Society (AIHS) *Newsletter*, Vol. 5, No. 1 (Jan. 2000). Uncle Pat and Donald insisted on taking a table at the dinner because of their recognition of our family. Donald died eight months later and Pat less than two years later.

5. Settling in the Bronx

1. The building has since been torn down and replaced by a Montefiore health care center, a hospital in which doctors later saved Mom's life.

2. See Robert Weintraub, *The House That Ruth Built: A New Stadium, the First Yankees Championship, and the Redemption of 1923* (New York: Little, Brown and Company, 2011.)

3. Lloyd Ultan and Gary Hermalyn, *The Bronx: It Was Only Yesterday: 1935–1965* (New York: Bronx County Historical Society, 1992). Another lovely book, Constance Rosenblum's *Boulevard of Dreams*, traces a magical history of the Grand Concourse,

a wide expanse of eight lanes and tree-lined medians that opened in 1909. Constance Rosenblum, *Boulevard of Dreams* (New York: New York University Press, 2009), 220–21.

6. Growing Up in an Irish Immigrant Family

1. I grew up being called David by my family and friends. When I went to high school, people began calling me by my first name, John. See Chapter 2, under Pop's Ancestors.

2. Sigel was a patriot in both Germany and the United States (a major general in the Union Army). According to the New York City Parks website, "Franz Sigel Park also figures in early Bronx history. The west slope of the park (Walton Avenue) was once part of a path used by local Indians. During the Revolutionary War, George Washington, Count de Rochambeau, and their respective American and French military staffs, used a high rocky ridge at the site to monitor the movements of British troops camped alongside the Harlem River." "Franz Sigel Park," NYC Parks, last visited April 20, 2019, http://www.nycgovparks.org/parks/franzsigelpark/history.

7. Uncle Pat, Our Life-Long Companion

1. "Drawing the turf" is a phrase referencing a centuries-old tradition of removing sections of earth from the bog lands in Ireland, consisting of many layers of leaves, herbs, and roots, which turned into peat over thousands of years. The turf, or peat, is removed with a spade called a *sleán* and is spread out to dry in the sun. Later, the dried turf is used to build fires that provide heat and light.

2. See "Mayo Profile: Patrick Boyle," *Dance Journal of the Mayo Society of New York* (*DJMSNY*), March 1997.

3. For a longer discussion, see Chapter 38.

4. Patrick Boyle, "Pat Boyle in Knock," interview, tape 5.

5. I delivered Pat's eulogy and told the story of his life as he gave it to me in his last week. Later, in a speech I gave at the Friendly Sons of Saint Patrick of Putnam County's annual dinner, I spoke about the people in our lives who personified a family's Irish heritage. Pat was that person for me. I repeated the essence of the speech at the annual St. Patrick's Day dinner of the Friendly Sons of St. Patrick in Rockland County in 2012.

6. "Mayo Profile," *DJMSNY*.

8. Memories of the Nearby House That Ruth Built

1. Derek Jeter, "Jeter's Full Speech Text from Derek Jeter Day at Yankee Stadium," speech, New York, September 7, 2014, Fox Sports, https://www.foxsports.com/mlb/story/derek-jeter-speech-from-jeter-day-at-yankee-stadium-090714.

2. Jon Kelly, "Boy of Summer," *New York Times Magazine*, September 21, 2014, 43.

9. St. Angela Merici Grammar School, 1942–1950

1. Pamphlet written by Graceann McKeon, on file with the author and St. Angela Merici.

2. Ibid.

3. Ibid.

4. Years later, when I first noticed the plaque, I suggested that it be brought to the attention of Cardinal Edward Egan, which led to a subsequent visit by members of Babe Ruth's family, including his youngest living granddaughter, Linda Ruth Tosetti. She was moved to tears, saying, "I am speechless and touched, I had no idea. . . . He never forgot his roots and where he started." *Catholic New York*, May 10, 2007, 2.

5. My graduation from St. Angela Merici took place at the school on June 25, 1950, with the Rt. Rev. Msgr. Joseph Foley presiding. There were thirty-two girls and thirty-eight boys in the class. The program included "O mira caritas" from an ancient manuscript; Beethoven's "The Heavens Resound"; R. Ramondi's "O sacrum convivium," preceded by a "Solemn Benediction"; and "The Star-Spangled Banner."

10. Bishop Dubois High School, 1950–1954

Epigraph: Dubois 1951 Yearbook, page 9, on file with author.

1. This was a unique trip in that I had the opportunity to pass both Yankee Stadium and the Polo Grounds at a time when Mickey Mantle and Willie Mays were early in their Hall of Fame careers. On one occasion I glimpsed my personal hero, Joe DiMaggio, walking by himself on the bridge separating the two stadiums. Peering into the Polo Grounds from the bridge provided, at times, a glimpse of the New York Giants baseball team as well.

2. In 2010, to honor his memory, I would attend the dedication of the old St. Patrick's Cathedral as a minor basilica in Lower Manhattan, where his remains are buried. It is located on Mulberry Street between Prince and Houston Street, New York City. See John Loughery, *Dagger John: Archbishop John Hughes and the Making of Irish America* (Ithaca, NY: Cornell University Press, 2018), 89.

3. In reflecting on Jim's life of courage, I recalled his advocacy for migrant workers seeking a fair wage and his chairmanship of the Joint Commission on Integrity in the New York City Public Schools. Jim pushed hard for necessary reforms despite political opposition.

11. Fordham College, 1954–1958

1. University catalogue of 1904–1905.

2. Thomas C. Hennessy ed., *Fordham: The Early Years: A Commemoration of the Jesuits' Arrival in 1846* (New York: Something More Publications, 1998), 59.

3. See Thomas J. Shelley, *Fordham, A History of the Jesuit University of New York: 1841–2003* (New York: Fordham University Press, 2016), 228–50.

4. Jack Coffey was a 1910 graduate of Fordham University whose name is on a playing field at the school for soccer and football. Some consider him the father of Fordham athletics.

5. His softball team won the senior division's championship, defeating the team I pitched for, 6–2. The school newspaper reported it this way: "Senior A's John Feerick was hurling a fine ball game until the fifth frame. In that inning, singles by Bob Knoebel and Tom Defosse, a couple of walks, and Jack Haggerty's triple, sent four runs across the plate" to give Tom's team the title. *Dateline '58.*

6. He passed away on October 1, 1983, at the age of 47. Congressman Mario Biaggi gave a beautiful tribute to him on the floor of the House of Representatives, stating: "While at PS 205, Tom was able to influence the lives of many young children. He always had time for their problems and their needs, no problem was too small and to Tom every child was special." Mario Biaggi, "Tribute to Thomas C. Giordano," *Congressional Record* 130: 42 (April 3, 1984).

12. Fordham Law School, 1958–1961

1. See Joseph A. O'Hare, S.J., "A Dean for All Seasons," *FLR* 70 (2002): 2185–87.

2. *Mulligan's Law: The Wit and Wisdom of William Hughes Mulligan,* ed. William Hughes Mulligan Jr. (New York: Fordham University Press, 1997).

3. These remarks appear in *Mulligan's Law.* Ibid., xiii–xvii, 1–4.

4. Robert J. Kaczorowski, *Fordham University School of Law: A History* (New York: Fordham University Press, 2012), 189.

5. Ibid.

6. See *Fordham Law Downtown Days and Nights: Alumni Recollections of the Woolworth Building and 302 Broadway* (New York City: Fordham University).

7. Ibid.

8. The 1959–1960 Fordham University School of Law "Bulletin of Information" reads, "Design of the School is to give a practical and scientific professional education in law." It further stated, "The school believes in the principle of Natural Law that all men are endowed by their Creator with inalienable rights and that certain legal implications flow therefrom." "Bulletin of Information 1959–1960," *Flash: The Fordham Law Archive of Scholarship and History,* January 1, 1959, 9–10.

9. "Though approved by the city in 1955, Fordham's relocation of its professional schools to the two Lincoln Square blocks was challenged in a lawsuit charging 'that the university's land purchase constituted a state subsidy of religion and violated the constitutional separation of church and state.' Fordham prevailed in the lawsuit in the spring of 1958." John L. Puckett and Mark Frazier Lloyd, *Becoming Penn: The Pragmatic American University, 1950–2000* (Philadelphia: University of Pennsylvania Press, 2015), 349.

10. John D. Feerick, "In Memoriam: Leonard F. Manning," *FLR* 51, no. 4 (1983): xiii–xiv.

11. See John D. Feerick, "To John D. Calamari — In Appreciation and with

Affection," *FLR* 63 (1995): 929–31. Six other tributes to Calamari appear in this volume, including a tribute from Michael Stanton, the president of the alumni association.

12. He was one of five graduates I identified in the school's centennial graduation address of 2006 as personifying in their different ways the values of the Law School. The others were: Ruth Whitehead Whaley, Class of 1924; Frances Berko, Class of 1944; Denis McInerney, Class of 1951; and Archibald Murray, Class of 1960.

13. Years later, I would present Justice Stewart with the Louis Stein Prize and befriend his classmate from the Yale class of 1941, Harold Segall, who would help me build the Philip Reed Endowments at Fordham.

14. Malachy became the first dean of Hofstra Law School, leaving a full-time faculty appointment at Fordham to do so.

15. Eugene J. Morris, "The Role of Administrative Agencies in Urban Renewal," *FLR* 29 (1961): 707.

13. Meeting the Love of My Life: Emalie

Epigraph: Donald, my best man, shared these words in his toast to me and Emalie on our wedding day.

1. See Chapter 39, section "Emalie's Parents."

2. Fifty years later, after a weeklong celebration of our marriage in Maine hosted by our children and grandchildren, we returned home near midnight to discover in our Larchmont home rose petals from the door of our house right into the nearby kitchen where there were two bottles of champagne on the kitchen table surrounded by boxes of chocolates and vases with beautiful flowers. We were overcome by this finale to our celebration and would later discover that this was our son Bill's gift to us.

14. Learning in Part-Time Jobs

1. Constance Rosenblum, *Boulevard of Dreams*, 53.

2. The boy's facility became known as Spofford Youth House in 1957, then later as Spofford Juvenile Center.

3. Gerald Posner, *Case Closed: Lee Harvey Oswald and the Assassination of JFK* (Open Road Media, 1993), 11–12. Don Delillo, a classmate of mine at Fordham College, references the Youth House in his book *Libra*.

4. Arizona v. California, 373 U.S. 546 (1963); Argued January 8–11, 1962. Restored to calendar for re-argument June 4, 1962. Reargued November 13–14, 1962. Decided June 3, 1963.

15. Joining a Small Law Firm — Skadden, Arps, Slate, Meagher & Flom

1. See *The Skadden Story: An Autobiography* (U.S.: Skadden, Arps, Slate, Meagher & Flom, 2014) and my comments, 20–22, 93–95. See also Jim Freund, "Dinner Tribute to Joe Flom," *University of Miami Law Review* 54, no. 4 (July 2000): 853–57.

2. See generally, George A. Kubler, A *Short History of Stereotyping* (New York: Brooklyn Eagle Commercial Printing Dept., 1927), and Kubler, *Historical Treatises, Abstracts and Papers on Stereotyping* (New York: J.J. Little and Ives Company, 1936).

3. See, for example, "Law Firms and NLRB," *New York Law Journal* (NYLJ), January 2, 1981; "NLRB Bargaining Orders Absent a Showing of Majority Status," *NYLJ*, April 3, 1981; "Solicitation, Distribution Rules," *NYLJ*, October 2, 1981; and "Wildcat Strikes — Recent Developments in Damage Recovery," *NYLJ*, April 2, 1982.

4. See, for example, "The United States without New York City? Its Resources Vital to Nation's Welfare," *NYLJ*, November 17, 1975; "The Polygraph," *NYLJ*, June 4, 1976; "Labor Movement to Face Challenges with Changing Economy in Future," *NYLJ*, January 30, 1984; and "Women Lawyers Struggle Against Many Barriers," *NYLJ*, May 3, 1993.

5. In 1978 I was asked to write an article on the Supreme Court's Bakke decision. I left a Skadden partner's meeting the day of the decision to take a call from the *Journal*, asking if I could do an article for the next day. I dictated a column over the telephone with the help of Baer and Arfa, and a week later wrote a more analytical account. Writing for the *NYLJ* became a special part of my life as a lawyer.

6. I also gratefully acknowledge the contributions made by Ron Siegal, Ruth Raisfeld, and Bruce Gitlin, who provided invaluable research assistance, as well as Carl Rifino, Pearl Zuchewski, and Gary Brown.

7. Gridley v. Lever Bros. Co, 411 N.Y.S.2d 248 (N.Y. App. Div. 1st Dep't 1978).

8. Aeronaves De Mexico, S.A. v. Triangle Aviation Services, Inc., 515 F.2d 504 (2d Cir.1975).

9. Judge Kaufman's widow asked me to pay tribute to her husband at a special session of the Second Circuit on June 2, 1992. See 972 F.2d cxvi (2d Cir.1992).

10. John D. Feerick, "Judicial Independence and the Impartial Administration of Justice," *Record of the Association of the Bar of the City of New York* 51, no. 3 (April 1996): 233–45.

11. Observations compiled by the NYSBA Special Committee on Judicial Independence entitled "Independence of the Judiciary: The Right of a Free People."

16. Leaving Skadden

1. Gossett's father-in-law, Charles Evans Hughes, who was governor of New York and a former chief justice of the United States, served as a speaker at Fordham Law School's inaugural graduation in 1908.

2. Hawk later informed me that Crowley wanted such a program and asked him to come to a lunch with an outline, which became our program.

3. These graduates included Tom Kavaler, Ray Sanservino, Joseph Reimer, Gail Hollister, Pam Chepiga, Elizabeth Clancy, and Patricia Whelan.

4. John D. Feerick, "Judge Denny Chin: A Student of the Law," *FLR* 79 (2011): 1494. He also received my highest grade.

5. They included Daniel Fusaro and Edward Guardaro, who served in important

positions on the administrative side of the Second Circuit; Marion Guilfoyle, who would later serve as Grand Marshal of the St. Patrick's Day Parade in Manhattan; and three prominent practicing lawyers, Robert Clerkin, Loretta Conway, and Evelyn King. They all worked in coordination with Frances Blake.

17. Becoming a Law School Dean: An Overview

1. See generally Thomas J. Shelley, *Fordham, A History*, 225–31.

2. See Mulligan, *Mulligan's Law*, 166–67

3. Emalie had noted my disappointment at not having secured a major challenge grant that Father Finlay and I had been seeking from the Kresge Foundation in the hope that it would jump-start the school's capital campaign.

4. For a brief overview of my dean's reports, please refer to Appendix B.

5. For many graduates imbued with the Jesuit tradition, his institute was a major, positive development at the school.

6. See the tributes to him in John D. Feerick, "Tribute: Charles M. Whelan: A Life in the Service of Others," *FLR* 75 (2007): 2835.

7. Capra promised, when I began as dean, to make the school proud, and he did so as a scholar and servant of judicial commissions and bar committees.

8. See tributes to Professor Sweeney in: *Fordham International Law Journal* (*FILJ*) 37, no. 1 (2013): i–viii; and *FILJ* 32 (2008): 1133–34.

9. See John D. Feerick, "George Bundy Smith — A Good Lawyer," *Albany Law Review* 68 (2005): 207.

10. See my tribute, "Judge Denny Chin: A Student of the Law," among others, in *FLR* 79, no. 4 (2011): 1491–96.

11. William Lifland served, as a lawyer at Cahill Gordon, as antitrust counsel to many companies and trade groups. He was a luminary in his field and author of two books on antitrust law.

12. John D. Feerick, "William J. Moore," *Fordham Urban Law Journal* 29, no. 1 (2001): 7–8.

13. Her successors included Linda Young, Robert Reilly '75, Andrew Rivera '88, and Nitza Escalera. Dean Escalera would serve inspiringly and longer than anyone else in the school's history in that position.

14. On her retirement, she was honored with the dean's medal of recognition at the 2015 annual luncheon of the alumni association, attesting to her unique role in the history of the school.

15. Wypyski left Fordham when he was invited to become a charter member of the Hofstra Law School faculty as the law librarian.

18. Commitments, Challenges, and Special Moments

1. See also "The Relevance of Religion to a Lawyer's Work: An Interfaith Conference," *FLR* 66 (1998): 1075; "Rediscovering the Role of Religion in the Lives

of Lawyers and Those They Represent," *Fordham Urban Law Journal* 26 (1999): 1041 (a program for which I gave introductory remarks along with Professor Pearce, Jennifer Mone, and Rabbi Ismar Schorsch).

2. For the remarks at this program, see "Inauguration of the Catholic Lawyers' Program of the Institute on Religion, Law and Lawyer's Work," *Fordham Urban Law Journal* 30 (2002): 277.

3. It was led ably up to August 2011 by Amy Uelmen, who took her magical ways to Washington, D.C., and Georgetown Law School.

4. See John D. Feerick, "Tribute: Charles M. Whelan; A Life in the Service of Others," *FLR* 75 (2007): 2835. He spent more than half of his life at Fordham and was a marvelous human being.

5. Solomon Amendment, 10 U.S.C. § 983 (2012).

6. With some encouragement by Peter Mullen, calling on behalf of the Cardinal, I withdrew to avoid controversy as the next recipient of the Cardinal's Thomas More Medal. A few years later, I was presented with the medal by John Cardinal O'Connor thanks to the advocacy of James Gill.

7. See "A Millennium Dedication to the Fordham Law Faculty, Past and Present," *FLR* 68 (1999): Supplement, reprinting twenty-two tributes since the *Review*'s beginning.

8. Kaczorowski, *Fordham University School of Law*, 350.

9. Ibid., 351.

10. Robert J. Kaczorowski, "Fordham University School of Law: A Case Study of Legal Education in Twentieth-Century America," *FLR* 87 (2018): 877. At the same time, the Law School was recruiting students with the highest GPA and LSAT scores in its history and was placing among the top 20 law schools for scholarly publications. Ibid.

11. The night was a most moving experience for my family and me. The comments delivered that night by Dean Michael Martin, former dean William Treanor, Professor Gail Hollister, and Dean Robert Reilly are recorded in a video, so I need say no more other than to thank those who spoke for the legacy they left for my loved ones.

19. The Many Hats a Dean Wears

1. I was honored to develop a close working relationship with James White and the legal education section. He described our relationship in a tribute in *Fordham Law Review*. See James P. White, "John D. Feerick: A Man for All Seasons," *FLR* 70 (2002): 2197.

2. See Mary C. Daly, "Teaching Integrity in the Professional Responsibility Curriculum: A Modest Proposal for Change," *FLR* 72 (2003): 265.

3. See Kaczorowski, *Fordham University School of Law*, 870–75.

4. Ibid., 264–367.

5. Complaint, *United States v. American Bar Association*, No. 95-CV-1211 (D.D.C.

June 27, 1995), https://www.justice.gov/atr/case-document/accreditation-practices
-law-schools-complaint.

6. Commission to Review the Substance and Process of the American Bar
Association's Accreditation of American Law Schools, *Report* (ABA, 1995), 20.

7. In 1991, Denis McInerney was recognized with an honorary degree for
personifying the best of the Law School.

8. See James F. Gill, *Rambling with Gill* (New York: Zagat Publishing, 2011).

9. In 1982, he helped facilitate the largest gift in the school's history at that time
from the corpus of a trust established by Leo Kissam.

10. The founders included E. Carter Corriston, Denis Cronin, Thomas Curnin,
James Gill, Edward Greason, Thomas Kavaler, Denis McInerney, Mathias Mone,
Hon. Loretta Preska, Eugene Souther, Michael Stanton, James Tolan, John
Vaughan, and me.

11. Following his death on October 4, 2009, a tribute to Meacham was given in
the House of Representatives. Charles B. Rangel, "Celebrating the Life of Harlem's
Beloved Thornton J. Meacham, Jr., Esq.: A Trailblazer for African-Americans,
Lawyers and Legal Professionals," *Congressional Record* 155, no. 149 (October 15,
2009): E2549–E2550.

20. Fordham Law Goes to Ireland

Epigraphs: The Nobel Peace Prize 1998 was awarded jointly to John Hume and
David Trimble for their efforts to find a peaceful solution to the conflict in Northern
Ireland. Both quotes appear in a historic issue of the *Fordham International Law
Journal* in April of 1999, which captured reflections by twenty-eight individuals and
included as an appendix the Northern Ireland peace agreement of April 10, 1998.
In a sense this issue was a culmination of multiple involvements by the school in
Northern Ireland. *Fordham International Law Journal* 22, no. 4 (1999): 1136–1905.

1. See *The John F. Sonnett Memorial Lectures at Fordham University School of
Law: A Half-Century of Advocacy and Judicial Perspectives*, ed. Dennis J. Kenny and
Joel E. Davidson (New York: Fordham University Press, 2018).

2. John Burger, "Model for Ireland — Fordham-Ulster project introduces conflict
resolution to community leaders." *Catholic New York*, Vol. XV, No. 41, July 4, 1996

3. Clyde Haberman, "NYC; Here, Too, A Terrible Beauty." *New York Times*,
July 2, 1996.

4. Ibid.

5. Ibid.

6. John Burger, "Model for Ireland — Fordham-Ulster project introduces conflict
resolution to community leaders." *Catholic New York*, Vol. XV, No. 41, July 4, 1996

7. Ibid.

8. The early success of the first summer abroad program is attributable to the
pioneering work and teaching of many Fordham professors and the organizing work
of Professor Perillo, Ken Pokrowski, and Liza Palmer (and later, Orla O'Malley).

Nolan-Haley took over the leadership of the program from Perillo, followed by Professor Kainen and then Professor Michael W. Martin. The subsequent development of a student internship program under Martin's exceptional leadership with organizations and institutions in the North and South of Ireland has given a distinctive academic brand to the program and enlarged considerably the reputation of the school in Ireland.

9. The briefing book also detailed the menus that would be available to us, as for example in Belfast: Breakfast — Assorted Muffins, Banana, Yogurt Variety, Orange Juice, Coffee, Tea; Lunch — Chicken Diane, Wild Rice, Steamed Carrots, Caesar's Salad, Dinner Roll with butter; Upside Down Cheesecake with Blueberry Sauce, Iced Tea; and Snack — Assorted Muffins, Fruit, Orange Juice, Coffee And Tea. On Friday, December 1, dinner consisted of beef stroganoff with egg noodles, steamed broccoli, mixed green salad with tomato-basil vinaigrette, dinner roll with butter, German's chocolate cake, iced tea/punch, and wine.

10. Ian Paisley was a Protestant pastor in Northern Ireland who subsequently became politically involved. While he initially opposed the peace process, he subsequently formed a power sharing government with Sinn Féin and governed amicably with Martin McGuiness as deputy first minister. *Encyclopædia Britannica Online*, s.v. "Paisley, Ian," last updated April 2, 2019, https://www.britannica.com /biography/Ian-Paisley.

11. Hon. Liam Hamilton, "Matters of Life and Death," in *The John F. Sonnett Memorial Lectures at Fordham University School of Law: A Half-Century of Advocacy and Judicial Perspectives*, ed. Dennis J. Kenny and Joel E. Davidson (New York: Fordham University Press, 2018).

12. Remarks at a State Dinner Honoring President Mary Robinson of Ireland, 1 Pub. Papers 917–18 (June 13, 1996).

13. See Laura Blumenfeld and Roxanne Roberts, "Dublin Their Pleasure," *Washington Post*, June 14, 1996, https://www.washingtonpost.com/archive/lifestyle /1996/06/14/dublin-their-pleasure/f882e692-45f2-4b7f-b83b-5a7b786ee886/?noredirect =on&utm_term=.ecb8e3026a7a.

14. The Montana Freemen were an anti-government militia that engaged in an eighty-one-day armed standoff with the FBI.

21. Leaving the Deanship

1. Kaczorowski highlighted the insufficient physical space at the Law School during this period in *Fordham University School of Law: A History*: "The 1994 ABA visitation report identified the Law School's physical plant as the school's most serious problem: 'too many people . . . for the limited amount of space.' The ABA visitors concluded that 'without additional space and faculty,' the Law School would 'not be able to continue [its] high student enrollments and maintain the quality of its program.'" Kaczorowski, *Fordham University School of Law*, 320.

2. A self-study is a school's assessment and evaluation of itself.

3. They were received from John Costantino, Margaret Hill, George D'Amato, Thomas Moore and Judith Livingston, the estate of George Meehan, James Leitner, Carol Zabar, Dennis Kenny, and others.

4. See the introduction to this book.

5. See a later conversation I moderated between Justice Sandra Day O'Connor and Judge Judith Kaye. "The Robert L. Levine Distinguished Lecture," *FLR* 81 (2012): 1149–67.

22. Becoming a Classroom Teacher

Epigraph: My teacher, Father David Cronin, S.J., would often use this quote to motivate his students.

1. *FLR* 79 (2010): 1160. The transcript of the program contains rich history likely to be drawn on by scholars and historians in future years.

2. *FLR* 79 (2011): 907–49.

3. John D. Feerick, "Response to Akhil Reed Amar's Address on Applications and Implications of the Twenty-Fifth Amendment," *Houston Law Review* 47 (2010): 41–66. This article, and the 2010 Fordham article, would not have been possible without the assistance of Brandon Gershowitz.

4. Akhil Reed Amar, "Applications and Implication of the Twenty-Fifth Amendment," *Faculty Scholarship Series* 786 (2010).

5. Fordham Law School Clinic on Presidential Succession, "Ensuring the Stability of Presidential Succession in the Modern Era: Report of the Fordham University School of Law Clinic on Presidential Succession" *FLR* 81 (2012) Reports, 3: 1–175.

6. Earlier, I co-taught a seminar on alternative dispute resolution with former general counsel of the American Arbitration Association F. Marisa Peterson, Joel Davidson '75, and Eric Tuchmann, general counsel of the American Arbitration Association (AAA).

7. See Chapter 27: The Catholic Church.

8. Other recipients of this award include Father O'Hare, Professor Katsoris, and former New York Chief Judge Jonathan Lippman, former judges Irene and Kevin Duffy, Robert J. Reilly, and Mutual of America and its former chairs, Thomas Moran and William Flynn.

9. Kaczorowski, *Fordham University School of Law*, 318–19.

23. Serving Others

1. My earliest venture was ten years before in making a political donation of a few dollars to a classmate, Jack Haggerty, when he ran for Congress. Though not successful, he went on to enjoy a distinguished career, serving as principal assistant to the New York State Senate majority leader, Warren Anderson.

2. The *Fordham Law Review* dedicated the 2017 presidential succession

symposium, Continuity in the Presidency: Gaps and Solutions, to Senator Bayh, and I wrote the dedication. John D. Feerick, "Dedication to Senator Birch E. Bayh," *FLR* 86, no. 3 (2017): 907–9.

3. See Jim Freund, "Dinner Tribute to Joe Flom," *University of Miami Law Review* 54, no. 4 (July 2000): 853–57.

4. John D. Feerick and Michael Sweeney, "Building Public Trust through Judicial Selection Reform," *Government Law and Policy Journal* 10, no. 2 (2008): 46–50.

5. See "Getting to the Heart of the Corporation: Effective Pro Bono Strategies," in *Pro Bono Service by In-House Counsel: Strategies and Perspectives*, ed. David P. Hackett (New York City: Practicing Law Institute, 2010), 9–19.

6. See his extensive case history in Matter of Wiesner, 943 N.Y.S.2d 410 (N.Y. App. Div. 1st Dep't 2012).

7. Ibid., 425.

8. Ibid., 417.

24. The Voluntary Bar

1. See Arthur Liman, *Lawyer: A Life of Counsel and Controversy* (New York: Public Affairs, 1998); and Floyd Abrams, *Speaking Freely: Trials of the First Amendment* (New York: Penguin Group, 2005)

2. The two chairs I served under, Sheldon Elsen and Martin Richman, were outstanding.

3. Overwhelmed by the need of senior lawyers seeking employment assistance, I earlier made a speech to the leaders of the City Bar Association advocating an assistance program.

4. Special Commission of the Association of the Bar of the City of New York, *Dollars and Democracy: A Blueprint for Campaign Finance Reform* (New York: Fordham University Press, 2000), xi.

5. The committee called on Congress to reject measures that would allow for removal of federal judges by means other than impeachment. See, for example, Ruth Hochberger, "Bar Panel Hits Bill on Removal of U.S. Judges," *NYLJ*, May 13, 1977.

6. John D. Feerick, "President's Column: A Public Profession — If We Can Keep It," *44th Street Notes* (The Association of the Bar of the City of New York), March 1994, 9(3): 1–2.

7. For a tribute I gave in memory of Bob McKay, see "Memorial for Robert B. McKay," *NYCBA Rec.* 45, no. 8 (1990): 911–23.

8. See Kostya Kennedy, *56: Joe DiMaggio and the Last Magic Number in Sports* (New York: Sports Illustrated Books, 2011), 94.

9. I was helped in their drafting and fact development by two Fordham law students, Jennifer Mone and Thomas McGrath.

10. First Session on the Nomination of Ruth Bader Ginsburg, to be Associate

Justice of the Supreme Court of the United States, Hearings Before the S. Comm. on the Judiciary, 103d Cong. 561 (1993).

11. For a Transcript of the Trial, see NYCBA Rec. 50, no.4 (1995): 430.

12. Michael J. Powell, *From Patrician to Professional Elite: The Transformation of the New York City Bar Association* (New York: Russell Sage Foundation, 1988).

13. For my grandchildren most especially, I happily refer you to the Record of the Association of the Bar of the City of New York for information of my presidency, Vol. 49, No. 8 (1994, my concluding remarks); Vol. 48, No. 5, 525 (1993, my interim report); and Vol. 47, No. 6 (1992, my inaugural remarks); and see a book about the Association from 1970–1995 written by Professor Jeffrey Brandon Morris: "*Making Sure We Are True to Our Founders*": *The Association of the Bar of the City of New York 1970–95* (New York: Fordham University Press, 1997): 157–76.

25. Public Service: From Carey to Koch to Cuomo to Bloomberg to Kaye

1. A former Chair, Carolyn Gentile, described it on the occasion of its 50th Anniversary as the "oldest continuous law reform agency in the common-law world." Carolyn Gentile, "Speech Given at the Fordham University School of Law on the Occasion of the Celebration of the Law Revision Commission's 50th Anniversary December 14, 1984," *Fordham Urban Law Journal* 14 (1986): 103.

2. Report of New York State Committee, *An Open Courtroom: Cameras in New York Courts*; *New York State Committee to Review Audio-Visual Coverage of Court Proceedings* (New York: Fordham University Press, 1997), xvi.

3. Ibid., xix.

4. New York City Family Homelessness Special Master Panel, *Family Homelessness Prevention Report* (2003); New York City Family Homelessness Special Master Panel, *Report on the Emergency Assistance Unit and Shelter Eligibility Determination* (2004).

5. "'I stayed up all night crying, terrified that one of my children might fall out the window,'" *Mitchell-Lama Residents Coalition*, Vol. 16, Issue 4 (2001): 3, www .mitchell-lama .org/newsletters/MLRC_Newsletter_Dec2011.pdf.

6. New York City Family Homelessness Special Master Panel, *Final Report* (2005): 1.

7. New York State Commission to Promote Public Confidence in Judicial Elections, *Interim Report to the Chief Judge* (2003); idem., *Report of June 29, 2004* (2004); and idem., *Final Report* (2006).

8. Judith S. Kaye, *The State of the Judiciary 2006* (2006): 4–6.

9. 556 U.S. 868 (2009). The decision concerned the importance of judges recusing themselves when there is an actual or probability of bias or if there is an economic interest in the case that they have to decide.

10. N.Y. R. Chief Admin. § 151.1.

11. Campaign for Fiscal Equity, Inc. v. State, 86 N.Y.2d, 316 (1995).

12. Campaign for Fiscal Equity, Inc. v. State, 100 N.Y.2d 893 (2003).

13. Campaign for Fiscal Equity, Inc. v. State, 8 N.Y.3d 14, 35 (2006).

14. Chief Judge Kaye (agreeing with our panel) wrote that the court majority "does not resolve the inadequate funding of the New York City public schools and reaches a result that is well below what the governmental actors themselves had concluded was required." Ibid., 34 (Chief Judge Kaye concurring in part and dissenting in part). She added, "[F]or more than 200 years . . . it has been the province and duty of the judicial branch to enforce compliance with constitutional norms, including (when necessary) as against the other branches of government. Defendants' continued failure to cure the violation properly obligated the courts to determine the extent of non-compliance and to direct a remedy." Ibid., 35.

15. See the Judicial Referee's report, as adopted by the New York Supreme Court: Fiscal Equity Campaign v. NYS. 719 N.Y.S.2d 475 (NY.2001).

16. See Michael B. Rebell, "CFE v. State of New York: Past, Present and Future," *NYSBA Government, Law and Policy Journal*, Vol. 13 (2011): 24, reviewing court decisions and offering perspectives.

26. Boards of Not-for-Profit, Charitable, and Public Institutions

1. Robert M. Kaufman later wrote a wonderful memoir titled *Paying Back—A Refugee Kid's Thank You to America* (Amherst, MA: Modern Memoirs Inc., 2013).

2. I have many happy memories of the people with whom I served at Sentinel. Among them was Bob Mathias, a two-time Olympic gold medalist and sports hero of mine when I was a teenager because of his athletic accomplishments at Stanford and his performance in the Olympics. He was the youngest man ever to win the Olympics decathlon gold medal and he won it twice. Indeed his picture, I thought, was often found on cereal boxes on Mom's kitchen table. He corrected me at one board meeting, stating that it was the picture of another extraordinary pole-vaulter, Bob Richards. Among my treasures is an inscribed copy of Mathias's autobiography, "The Bob Mathias Story; An American Odyssey," which he gave me at his last Sentinel meeting. In it, he described the joy he received from his Sentinel service and the car trips he made with his wife, Gwen, to the board meetings. The inscription reads: "To John. All the best. Will miss all of you on the Board." We certainly missed him. He died on September 2, 2006.

27. The Catholic Church

Epigraph: Vatican Council, "Chapter IV: The Laity," in *Dogmatic Constitution of the Church: Lumen Gentium, Solemnly Promulgated by His Holiness, Pope Paul VI on November 21, 1964* (Boston: Pauline Books and Media), 51.

1. Jacob Lupfer, "Conscience vs. Authority at Pope Francis' Synod on the Family (ANALYSIS)," *Washington Post*, October 14, 2014, https://www.washingtonpost.com /national/religion/conscience-vs-authority-at-pope-francis-synod-on-the-family-analysis /2014/10/14/8f126b96-53c3-11e4-b86d184ac281388d_story.html?utm_term=.5d6bf277d0f3.

2. Cindy Wooden, "Synod's Final Report Calls for 'Accompaniment' Tailored to Family Situations," *Catholic Herald*, October 24, 2015, https://catholicherald.co.uk /news/2015/10/24/synod-report-calls-for-accompaniment-tailored-to-family-situations/.

3. See "2017–2018 New York Archdiocese at a Glance," Michael J. Deegan, accessed April 24, 2019, https://catholicschoolsny.org/about-us/.

4. See "Facts and Numbers," Inner-City Scholarship Fund, accessed April 24, 2019, http://www.innercityscholarshipfund.org/about_facts.cfm.

5. Cardinal Timothy Dolan, "Dying . . . and Rising," *Catholic New York*, October 30, 2014, http://www.cny.org/stories/dying and rising,11715?

6. St. Vito — Most Holy Trinity Parish Mass program for September 20, 2015.

28. Learning the Art of Conflict Resolution

1. See a tribute to him by Benjamin Weiser in "After Nearly 44 Years, and 3 Major Terrorism Trials, a Judge Leaves the Bench," *New York Times*, October 10, 2016, https://www.nytimes.com/2016/10/11/nyregion/after-nearly-44-years-and-3-major -terrorism-trials-a-judge-leaves-the-bench.html.

2. A volume with all of them can be found on a shelf in my home.

3. For that I thank my then assistant, Joseph DeGiuseppe, who helped provide supporting citations to the transcripts for almost every statement written in the opinion accompanying my awards. He is now a distinguished member of the bar.

4. See Chapter 29.

5. Mike Wise, "Pro Basketball; N.B.A. Owners Needn't Pay Locked-Out Players," *New York Times*, October 20, 1998, https://www.nytimes.com/1998/10/20/sports/pro -basketball-nba-owners-needn-t-pay-locked-out-players.html.

6. Since this award, the subject of a player lockout in various sports — football, basketball, and ice hockey most particularly — has recurred, and the existence of the award, I was informed, has promoted stability in the sports field.

7. Sprewell v. Golden State Warriors, 266 F.3d 979 (9th Cir.), opinion amended on denial of reh'g, 275 F.3d 1187 (9th Cir. 2001).

8. Steve McNair and the National Football League Players Association v. the Tennesse Titans and the National Football League Management Council, May 16, 2006. On file with author.

9. For where I expressed views on handling conflicts, see John D. Feerick, "The Peace-Making Role of a Mediator," *Ohio State Journal on Dispute Resolution* 19 (2007). See also "Theodore W. Kheel: An Exemplar for Alternative Dispute Resolution and a Pioneer in Environmental Interest Disputes," *Pace Environmental Law Review* 27, no. 1 (2009–10).

29. Conflicts in the Public Eye

1. I'll always appreciate both the article in the *Daily News* by Mitch Lawrence, reminding everyone that I wasn't a criminal court judge but a labor arbitrator, and the

reporting of Mike Wise of the *New York Times*, who followed the proceeding closely and commented on the challenge of reaching a decision in such a difficult matter.

2. For the decision, see Howard L. Ganz, *Understanding Business and Legal Aspects of the Sports Industry*, vol. 1 (New York: PLI, 1999): 429–536.

3. Ibid., 533–35.

4. Ibid., 530–31.

5. Benjamin N. Cardozo, *Law and Literature* (New York: Harcourt, Brace and Co., 1931), 100–101.

6. See "The Role of Forgiveness in the Law," *Fordham Urban Law Journal* 27 (2000): 1349, and also my explanatory remarks on pages 1351–52.

7. See Pope Francis, *The Church of Mercy* (Chicago: Loyola Press, 2014). See also Harold Baer Jr., *Rehabilitation and Incarceration: In Search of Fairer and More Productive Sentencing*, ed. Robert C. Meade Jr. (Chicago: American Bar Association, 2019).

8. See release, dated March 17, 1998, of the American Arbitration Association, entitled "Don't Fault Arbitrator in Sprewell Case," stating: "In conclusion, the process of arbitration worked. A very divisive dispute was resolved in a formal, civilized proceeding. An issue concerning violence was resolved in a non-violent fashion. From beginning to conclusion, this case was resolved within weeks by a neutral arbitrator who allowed both parties to fully present their cases."

9. Mike Wise, "On Basketball; For the Knicks, a Year Has Made a Difference," *New York Times*, March 27, 2000.

10. Ibid.

11. "NCAA, MIBA End Litigation; NIT Tournaments Purchased," *NCAA News Release*, August 17, 2005.

12. Ibid.

30. Presidential Succession

1. New York State Bar Association, "Constitutional Amendment on Presidential Inability Urged," *NYLJ*, September 11, 1961.

2. See John D. Feerick, "The Problem of Presidential Inability — Will Congress Ever Solve It?" *FLR* 32 (1963): 73.

3. Ibid., 76.

4. Ibid., 112–13, 126–28.

5. John D. Feerick, letter to the editor, "Fixing Presidential Succession," *New York Times*, November 17, 1963, E8.

6. Many of the letters quoted throughout this chapter can be found on the Fordham Law Library's online Twenty-Fifth Amendment Archive at https://ir.lawnet.fordham.edu/twentyfifth_amendment_archive/.

7. On file with author.

8. See, for example, Arthur Krock, "Kennedy's Death Points Up Orderly Progression in U.S. Government," *New York Times*, November 23, 1963, at 9E.

9. Lowell R. Beck's book, *I Found My Niche, a Lifetime Journey of Lobbying and Association Leadership* (Sarasota, Florida: Peppertree Press, 2016), 80–105, gives an excellent account of the ABA's engagement with the field of presidential inability and the creation of its Conference.

10. The members were former attorney general Herbert Brownell; Walter Craig, president of the ABA and chair of the meetings; Professor Paul Freund of Harvard Law School; Jonathan Gibson of Chicago, chair of the ABA committee on jurisprudence and the law; Richard Hansen of Nebraska, author of "The Year We Had No President"; James Kirby Jr., former general counsel of the Senate Subcommittee on Constitutional Amendments; Ross Malone, general counsel of General Motors and a former U.S. deputy attorney general; Dean Charles Nutting of the George Washington Law Center; Lewis Powell Jr.; Martin Taylor of New York, chair of the state bar committee on the Constitution; and Edward Wright of Arkansas, chair of the ABA House of Delegates. See John D. Feerick, *From Failing Hands: The Story of Presidential Succession* (New York: Fordham University Press, 1965), 244.

11. The heads of the executive departments are referred to as the Cabinet, but other individuals might be invited by a president to be part of his Cabinet, such as ambassadors to the United Nations.

12. S.J. Res. 139 provided explicitly for the president, vice president, and Cabinet (i.e., heads of Executive Departments) to handle a case of presidential inability. S.J. Res. 139, 88th Cong. § 6 (1963). S.J. Res. 35 left it to Congress to determine the method by statute. S.J. Res. 35, 88th Cong. (1963).

13. See Feerick, *From Failing Hands*, 244; see also James C. Kirby, Jr., "A Breakthrough on Presidential Inability: The ABA Conference Consensus," *Vanderbilt Law Review* 17 (1964): 463.

14. See discussions in Feerick, *From Failing Hands*, 244–54.

15. Ibid.

16. See John D. Feerick, *The Twenty-Fifth Amendment: Its Complete History and Applications*, 3rd ed. (New York: Fordham University Press, 1976, 1992, and 2014 editions).

17. For Doyle's views more generally, see transcript on file with author of a meeting in 1964 of the Committee for Business Leaders for Economic Development.

18. U.S. Const. amend. XXV, § 4.

19. Senator Kefauver passed away in the summer of 1963.

20. The views the ABA expressed were reflected in the proposed amendment in 1965.

21. See Presidential Inability and Vacancies in the Office of Vice President: Hearings Relating to the Problem of Presidential Inability and Filling of Vacancies in the Office of the Vice President before the Subcomm. on Constitutional Amendments of the S. Comm. on the Judiciary, 88th Cong. 84 (1964) (statement of Walter Craig, President, American Bar Association).

22. Ibid., 149–58.

23. Following President William Harrison's death in 1841, Vice President John

Tyler declared that he was president, instead of merely assuming the powers and duties of the presidency.

24. Ibid., 150–52 (my statement).

25. Ibid., 153.

26. Ibid., 154.

27. See John D. Feerick, "The Problem of Presidential Inability — It Must be Solved Now," *New York State Bar Journal* (NYSBJ) 36 (1964): 181; and John D. Feerick, "A Solution for Presidential Inability," *American Bar Association Journal* 50, no. 4 (April 1964): 321–24. I was required by the State Bar's Journal to remove my point of view from the article because it was not consistent with the State Bar's position. I had stated that "[the ABA solution] is a workable solution" — "it is imperative that a workable solution be agreed upon now." See John D. Feerick, letter to Eugene Gerherdt, February 27, 1964.

28. In December of 1963 Representative Emanuel Celler of the House Judiciary Committee addressed the Legislation Committee, encouraging it to study the problem of presidential inability and succession. The committee began its review by creating a subcommittee and obtaining copies of my 1963 Fordham article, brought to their attention by my law firm colleague, Barry Garfinkel. I was asked to address the bar subcommittee and strongly urged, at its meeting of early February 1964, that it change the committee's existing position and adopt the ABA consensus. The full committee eventually did so, with suggested modifications, in its report of May 1, 1964, and the change was approved by the City Bar at its annual meeting of May 12, 1964.

29. See generally John D. Feerick, "The Vice-Presidency and the Problems of Presidential Succession and Inability," *FLR* 32, no. 3 (1964): 457.

30. See *Presidential Inability and Vice Presidential Vacancies*, Cong. Q. Almanac, http://library.cqpress.com/cqalmanac/cqal641304708.

31. One exception was the recommendation that the ending of a determination of presidential inability be made "by majority vote of the Cabinet, the President concurring." John D. Feerick, letter to Larry A. Conrad, March 29, 1966.

32. The collaboration Emalie and I developed in the field of presidential succession led us to co-author a book for high school students on the vice presidents of the United States. Emalie P. Feerick and John D. Feerick, *The Vice Presidents of the United States* (New York: Franklin Watts Inc., 1967). It was published as part of the Grolier Publishing Company's First Book series in 1967, and it was dedicated to Maureen Grace, a baby during the time we wrote it. I dedicated subsequent writings to our other children, to family members, and to Professor Leonard Manning.

33. S.J. Res. 1, 89th Cong. (1965). S.J. Resolution 1 is the successor to S.J. Res. 139.

34. Memorandum from Junior Bar Conference, Am. Bar Ass'n, 1964–1965, "Final Report of the Junior Bar Conference Committee on Presidential Inability and the Vice-Presidential Vacancy," June 15, 1965 (on file with author).

35. Ibid.

36. On file with author.

37. On file with author.

38. Memorandum from Young Lawyers Section, Am. Bar Ass'n, Mid-Year (1965–1966), "Report of Committee on Presidential Inability and Vice-Presidential Vacancy," January 6, 1966 (on file with author).

39. John D. Feerick, letter to Stanley H. Burdick, January 19, 1967 (on file with author) (enclosing a report of the Young Lawyers Committee on Presidential Inability and Vice-Presidential Vacancy).

40. See Birch Bayh, *One Heartbeat Away: Presidential Disability and Succession* (Indianapolis: Bobbs-Merrill, 1968), 302–4.

41. Some of this language is reflected in Section 5 of S.J. Res. 1, as it appeared when passed by the Senate in 1965. See S.J. Res. 1, 89th Cong. (1965).

42. See Feerick, *From Failing Hands*, 248.

43. S. Rep. No. 88–1382, at 14 (1964).

44. 110 Cong. Rec. 23,002 (1964).

45. Ibid., 23,061.

46. 111 Cong. Rec. 3286 (1965).

47. My letter of February 7 also stated that Section 5 of the proposed amendment was unclear as to "who is entitled to exercise presidential power after the President declares his ability and before the Vice President brings the matter before Congress. The Vice President is intended to act in that period, I am sure, but the . . . language does not and will not permit him to do so. Since Section 5 is designed to meet an extraordinary case such as that of an insane President, it would be extremely dangerous to leave a gap here as such a President might declare himself able and immediately discharge the heads of the Executive Departments, thus preventing the Vice President from taking the necessary steps to get the matter before Congress."

48. I subsequently came to a different view of that issue — namely, of an oath not being required. See Feerick, *The Twenty-Fifth Amendment*, 114.

49. See the House hearings of February 1965, where some of my suggestions were reflected in the questioning by Representative Poff. *Presidential Inability: Hearings Before the Committee on the Judiciary*, 89th Cong. (1965).

50. Max Farrand, ed., *The Records of the Federal Convention of 1787*, vol. 2 (New Haven: Yale University Press, 1911), 642–43.

51. In writing this book, I discovered in the National Archives a reference to my 1965 Fordham article being helpful in explaining the amendment to state legislators in Maryland.

52. 111 Cong. Rec. 7968 (1965).

53. U.S. Const. amend. XXV, § 4.

54. Richard H. Poff, U.S. Representative, letter to author, May 28, 1965 (on file with author).

55. Donald E. Channell, Dir., D.C. Office, Am. Bar Ass'n, letter to author, June 2, 1965 (on file with author).

56. See John D. Feerick, "Proposed Amendment on Presidential Inability and

Vice-Presidential Vacancy," *American Bar Association Journal* 51 (October 1965): 915; John D. Feerick, "The Proposed Twenty-Fifth Amendment to the Constitution," *FLR* 34 (December 1965): 173.

57. Italics added to highlight the language changes surrounding the 21-day provision.

58. E. W. Kenworthy, "Conferees Back Succession Plan," *New York Times*, June 25, 1965, at 1, 16.

59. The House approved the amendment by voice vote on June 30, after explanation by Poff.

60. It should have used "executive departments" twice in Section 4 instead of "executive departments" and "executive department," the latter expression creating an ambiguity. See William Safire, "Desecration," *New York Times*, July 31, 2005 (he referred to it as "the Ineradicable Typo").

61. Richard H. Poff, review of *From Failing Hands: The Story of Presidential Succession*, by John D. Feerick," *Columbia Law Review* 67 (Feb. 1967): 401–2. In addition, he said of the book "that it was an important background study for the 89th Congress in its successful attempt to write a constitutional amendment nearly two years after an assassin's bullet again demonstrated the importance of continuity in Executive power." Ibid., 400.

62. S.J. Res. 139 originally dealt with the line of succession, but the Subcommittee on Constitutional Amendments in May 1964 eliminated the provision for a cabinet line of succession after the vice president.

63. See discussion of this subject in Feerick, *The Twenty-Fifth Amendment*, 107.

64. See Bayh, *One Heartbeat Away*, 119–24.

65. John D. Feerick, "Vice Presidential Succession: In Support of the Bayh-Celler Plan," *South Caroline Law Review* 18 (1966): 226.

66. See John D. Feerick, *The Twenty-Fifth Amendment*, 106.

67. See Feerick, "The Proposed Twenty-Fifth Amendment," 203.

68. He began by quoting John Dickinson from the Constitutional Convention and concluding, after singling out many individuals and organizations and "particularly the leaders of the American Bar Association," with the statement that "they have further perfected the oldest written constitution in the world. They have earned the lasting thanks of the American people, for whom it has so long secured the blessings of liberty." Lyndon B. Johnson, "Remarks at Ceremony Marking the Ratification of the Presidential Inability (25th) Amendment to the Constitution," February 23, 1967, https://www.presidency.ucsb.edu/node/237706.

69. The words, which would later become the title of my book, come from John McCrea's 1915 poem "In Flanders Field," inspired by the death of a friend in World War I. It was suggested to me by my father-in-law.

70. See, for example, S. Doc. No. 93–42, at 279–300 (1973).

71. Examination of the First Implementation of Section Two of the Twenty-Fifth Amendment: Hearing on S.J. Res. 26 Before the Subcomm. on Constitutional Amendments of the S. Comm. on the Judiciary, 94th Cong. 134 (1975).

72. Ibid., 136.

73. Ibid., 147.

74. For a summary of their recommendations, see the recent edition of my book, Feerick, *The Twenty-Fifth Amendment*, 3rd ed. (New York: Fordham University Press, 2014), 232–36.

75. See John, D. Feerick, "The Twenty-Fifth Amendment: An Explanation and Defense," *Wake Forest Law Review* 30 (1995): 481.

76. John D. Feerick, Joel K. Goldstein, and Senator Birch Bayh, "Minority Opinion Regarding Recommendation 4," in *Presidential Disability. Papers, Discussions, and Recommendations on the Twenty-Fifth Amendment and Issues of Inability and Disability in Presidents of the United States* (Rochester: University of Rochester Press, 2001), 538.

77. See "Response to Akhil Reed Amar," 41; "Presidential Succession and Inability," 907; "Presidential Inability: Filling in the Gaps," *Politics and the Life Sciences* 33 (2014): 11; "The Twenty-Fifth Amendment: A Personal Remembrance," *FLR* 86 (2017): 1075; "Remarks: Presidential Succession and Impeachment: Historical Precedents, from Indiana and Beyond," *Indiana Law Review* 52 (2019): 43; and "The Twenty-Fifth Amendment: Its Crafting and Drafting Process," *ConLawNOW* (2018–2019), http://ideaexchange.uakron.edu/conlawnow/.

78. See Rebecca Harrington, "A Loophole in the 25th Amendment lets 14 People Remove a Sitting President from Office," *Business Insider*, March 15, 2017; Jerry Goldfeder, "President Trump and the 25th Amendment," *NYLJ*, April 27, 2017, 1; Evan Osnos, "Trump Could Get Fired," *New Yorker*, May 8, 2017; Matt Taibbi, "The Madness of Donald Trump," *Rolling Stone*, September 19, 2017; Jon Meacham, "Could the 25th Amendment Be Trump's Downfall? Here's How it Works," *Time*, January 11, 2018; Alan Blinder, "How the 25th Amendment Came to Be, by the People Behind It," *New York Times*, September 7, 2018; Meagan Flynn, "How 'The Caine Mutiny' and the Paranoid Capt. Queeg Influenced the 25th Amendment's Drafters, Making It Harder to Sideline a President," *Washington Post*, September 10, 2018; Matthew Kahn, interview with John D. Feerick, "A Real, Live Framer of the Constitution," the *Lawfare Podcast*, September 17, 2018. I gave many interviews during this period, including with National Public Radio, Irish Radio Network USA, and the *New York Daily News* (along with writing an op-ed column), as well as delivered speeches, led class discussions with students, gave talks to lawyer groups and other audiences, including a senior citizen center in Westchester (the Osborne) where enormous interest in the subject existed.

79. "A Modern Father of Our Constitution: An Interview with Former Senator Birch Bayh," *FLR* 79, no. 3 (2010): 781–822.

80. See my tribute to Senator Bayh, in John D. Feerick, "Senator Birch Bayh's Death Spurs Memories of the 25th Amendment's Origins," *NYLJ*, May 15, 2019, https://www.law.com/newyorklawjournal/2019/05/15/senator-birch-bayhs-death-spurs-memories-of-the-25th-amendments-origins/.

31. The Electoral College System

Epigraph: American Bar Association Commission on Electoral College Reform, *Electing the President* (Chicago: American Bar Association, 1967).

1. Transcript on file with author (Transcript, pages 232–33). Not reflected is the quality of the discussion that day from Professor Paul Freund of Harvard Law School, Senator and Judge Kenneth Keating of New York, Professor and Dean James Kirby Jr., former congressman Ed Gossett of Texas (who had advocated in Congress a constitutional amendment embodying a district vote plan vote), President James Nabrit Jr. of Howard University, Professor G. Herman Pritchett (a former president of the American Political Science Association), Chief Counsel Stephen Schlossberg of the United Auto Workers Union (representing Walter Reuther, the union's president), Governor Henry Bellmon of Oklahoma (later U.S. Senator), Herman Phleger of California and former legal adviser to the State Department.

2. American Bar Association Commission on Electoral College Reform, *Electing the President*, viii–ix.

3. "Proceedings of the House of Delegates: Houston, Texas, February 13–14, 1967," *American Bar Association Journal*, vol. 53 (April 1967): 379.

4. Wallace won 46 electoral votes, Humphrey 191 electoral votes, and Nixon 301 electoral votes.

5. See James A. Michener, *Presidential Lottery: The Reckless Gamble in our Electoral System* (New York: The Daily Press, 2016), 3–29.

6. See, for example, "The Electoral College: Why It Was Created," *ABAJ* 54 (1968); "The Electoral College — Why It Ought to Be Abolished," *FLR* 37 (1968): 1; "The Electoral College — Its Defects and Dangers," *NYSBJ* 40 (1968): 317.

7. Direct Popular Election of the President and Vice President of the United States, Hearings Before the Subcomm. on the Constitution of the S. Comm. on the Judiciary, 96th Cong. 241–43 (1979) (testimony of John D. Feerick).

8. The Electoral College and Direct Election of the President and Vice President, Hearings on S.J. Res. 1, 8, and 18 Before the S. Comm. on the Judiciary, 95th Congress 232–33 (1977) (testimony of John D. Feerick).

9. Years later, in a report of the Senate Judiciary Committee supporting the amendment, Thurmond, while not agreeing with the recommendation, would offer the opinion that the system needed to be changed to eliminate the office of elector, the contingent election of one vote for each state in the House, and the winner-take-all system of awarding electoral votes. See S. Rep. No. 96-11, at 71–72 (1979).

10. See comments by Senator Dirksen in submitting this language to the Senate on April 14, 1967, as an amendment to Senate Joint Resolution 2, 113 Cong. Rec. S9613-15 (1967).

11. 115 Cong. Rec. 26007 (1969).

12. In the period from 1967 to 1969, I had communications with Congressional

staff in the House and members of Congress concerning the content of the amendment and from Congressman Poff with respect to succession contingencies.

13. See 3 U.S.C. §5 (2012), providing that electoral vote controversy determinations made under state law at least six days before the meeting of the electors "shall be conclusive, and shall govern in the counting of the electoral votes as provided in the Constitution. . . ."

14. See Bush v. Gore, 531 U.S. 98, 1060 (2000).

32. Other Constitutional Opportunities

Epigraph: This quote comes from President Ford's speech upon taking office following President Nixon's resignation, August 9, 1974.

1. Bills to Provide Procedures for Calling Constitutional Conventions for Proposing Amendments to the Constitution of the United States, on Application of the Legislatures of Two-Thirds of the States, Pursuant to Article V of the Constitution, Hearing on S. 3, s. 520, and S. 1710 Before the Subcomm. on the Constitution of the Comm. on the Judiciary, 96th Cong. 52–55 (1979), 52.

2. Ibid, 54–55.

3. Ibid.

4. Ibid., 55.

5. Ibid., 57.

6. The ABA Special Committee believed that circumstances might arise justifying judicial intervention if Congress inappropriately rejected a state application or declined to submit a convention proposal to the states for ratification. Not to allow intervention could have the effect of allowing Congress to "bury" the amending alternative intended by the framers.

7. See Constitutional Convention Procedures, Hearings Before the Subcomm. on Civil and Constitutional Rights of the Comm. on the Judiciary, 99th Cong. 4 (1985).

8. Ibid., 75.

9. Ibid., 77.

10. John D. Feerick, "Impeaching Federal Judges: A Study of the Constitutional Provisions," FLR 39 (1970): 1, 54–58. The president's brief before the House Judiciary Committee drew on the article.

11. The Senator was most thoughtful in a letter, dated April 23, 1971, sent to Barry Garfinkel, concerning the article, stating: "I was honored to place in the Congressional Record the excellent law review article written by your partner, John Feerick. I have never seen a piece of work in this area which displayed the scholarly research and painstaking analysis as does the article by Mr. Feerick." The article reflected the depth of research done for me by Edward Yodowitz, a Skadden lawyer, and Robert Quinn of the Fordham Law Review. My indebtedness to them was acknowledged in the article and is reaffirmed here.

12. John D. Feerick, "The Way of the 25th," New York Times, December 13, 1973.

13. "President's Power to Pardon Before Conviction," *NYLJ*, September 27, 1974, 1.

14. John D. Feerick, "The Pardoning Power of Article II of the Constitution," *NYSBJ* 47 (1975): 7.

15. I asked my good friend Tom Schwarz to undertake for the committee a study of public financing of elections, which was cited in Buckley v. Valeo, 424 U.S. 1 (1976).

16. The committee issued its report in 1978. American Bar Association, Special Committee on Election Reform, *The Disappearance of the American Voter* (Chicago: American Bar Association, 1978).

17. Craig H. Baab, Joanne Prolman, Steven Uhlfelder, and others of the ABA's staff provided invaluable staff assistance.

33. The New York State Commission on Government Integrity

1. Newspaper strike of 1978, see Chapter 29: Conflicts in the Public Eye.

2. State of New York, Commission on Government Integrity, *Restoring the Public Trust: A Blueprint for Government Integrity*, vol. 1 (1988), 18.

3. William L. Riordan, *Plunkitt of Tammany Hall* (New York: McClure, Phillips and Company, 1905).

4. See N.Y. Elec. Law, §14–124 (effective May 9, 1988).

5. State of New York, Commission on Government Integrity, *Restoring the Public Trust: A Blueprint for Government Integrity*, vol. 1 (1988), 7.

6. State of New York Commission of Government Integrity, "Hearing on Campaign Finance Practices of Citywide and Statewide Officials," March 14, 1988 (New York County Trial Lawyers Association), 251.

7. Ibid., 263.

8. Ibid., 261.

9. Ibid., 257.

10. Andrew Belonsky, "What Donald Trump's Political Donations Reveal About Him," *Rolling Stone*, April 26, 2016.

11. "Mr. Feerick's Legacy," *Times Union*, December 25, 1989, A18.

12. "New York's Enduring Ethics Scandal," *New York Times*, October 4, 1990, A28. The *New York Times*, in an editorial of November 30, 2009, described the Commission on Government Integrity as "widely respected" and the commission's ethics reform agenda for New York State as a model for Albany to consider. "It's All About the Money: Failed State," *New York Times*, November 30, 2009, A30. The 2016 New York Legislative session reflected some of these recommendations in the passage of government ethics reforms. The reforms were introduced by Governor Andrew Cuomo two weeks earlier in an address at Fordham Law School where he praised the work of the commission. In November of 2017, the voters of New York approved a proposed constitutional amendment to establish a pension forfeiture law for public officials guilty of corruption, a recommendation that was part of the commission's agenda.

34. New York State Ethics Commission

1. John D. Feerick, "Restoring Public Trust in Government" (keynote, 20th Anniversary of the Ethics in Government Act: Revisiting Sweeping Reforms and Redefining Public Integrity, Albany, NY, March 2007).

2. James King passed away three years later, on June 11, 2010. I was honored to deliver his eulogy at Westminster Presbyterian Church in Albany.

3. In the commission's annual report for 2008, the commission stated: "Consistent with its efforts to maintain its independence, the Commission became operationally independent of the New York Department of State, which had provided personnel, purchasing and information technology support in the past." New York State Commission on Public Integrity, 2008 Annual Report, (2008), 1.

4. Wayne Barrett, "The Truth Behind Troopergate," Village Voice, September 25, 2007, https://www.villagevoice.com/2007/09/25/the-truth-behind-troopergate/.

35. The New York State Public Integrity Commission

1. On file with author.

2. See New York State Commission on Public Integrity, 2008 Annual Report, (2008), 1–15.

3. I didn't expect any expression of gratitude for my service and was surprised to receive an acknowledgment from Governor Paterson, who said, "I want to thank John for his extraordinary service to the people of New York, especially in his most recent role as Chairman of the New York State Commission on Public Integrity. I wish him enormous continued success at Fordham Law School and good health for many years to come."

4. Francis T. Murphy, "Remarks by Hon. Francis T. Murphy," New York State Bar Journal 70, no. 3 (March/April, 1998): 12–13

5. My successor as chair said of Teitelbaum that the information he was said to have provided to the governor's office "may have been improper" but was of "a de minimis nature." He minced no words when it came to the commission's talented counsel, Barry Ginsberg. He praised Ginsberg's sense of professionalism, stressing that "he was properly doing his job as a lawyer for the commission and as a public servant, serving with 'honesty and integrity.'"

6. Cherkasky was appointed by Paterson the same day as the IG released his report, the governor stating, "'Today I am pleased to appoint a person of exemplary experience and unquestioned integrity' as the new chairman." Judy Silberstein, "Governor Taps Cherkasky to Restore Integrity Commission," Larchmont Gazette, May 14, 2009, http://www.larchmontgazette.com/news/governor-taps-cherkasky-to-restore-integrity-commission/.

7. "New York State Commission on Public Integrity Statement by Chairman Michael G. Cherkasky," June 11, 2009. On file with the New York State Commission.

36. Our Growing Family

Epigraph: St. Angela Merici was the first woman to establish a religious order for women (Order of St. Ursula, November 25, 1535), and was canonized as a saint by Pope Pius VII on January 24, 1807; Feast Day, May 31.

1. My daughter Maureen would also graduate as valedictorian of her class at Fordham's College of Business Administration.

2. On August 25, 2017, we celebrated our 55th anniversary with a small family gathering at the Elks Club in Southampton, where we danced and feasted and celebrated the many blessings of our life together. Earlier in the day we received a special blessing at the Basilica of the Sacred Hearts of Jesus and Mary by Msgr. William Gill.

37. Deaths in the Family

1. See the introduction.

2. See the epigraph at Chapter 13.

38. Roses in December—Rediscovering Mom and Pop

1. An immigration card of his described him as admitted as an immigrant on March 19, 1957, with his date of birth given as December 21, 1899. It is unclear when he finally returned to Ireland.

2. Robert was born in 1907, and James in 1913.

40. What I Learned

1. "Desiderata" is copyrighted by lawyer Max Ehrmann.

2. Taken from an article a student wrote in April of 2002 for a publication at the school called "Capital Forum."

41. Advice to My Grandchildren

1. In 2012, I began to doubt my capacity to complete this book and mentioned to my daughters that they would most likely need to finish it for me. I told them that I had a message in the last chapter to my grandchildren. My daughters urged me to at least finish that chapter of the book, which we later published. This chapter is what appears in that book.

Appendix B. My Dean's Reports

1. In the year before he retired, *Fordham Law Review* published many tributes to him. See *FLR* 71 (2002): 623–25.

2. Professor Batts joined the faculty after a clerkship with Judge Lawrence Pierce on the Second Circuit and several years as an Assistant U.S. Attorney. She would leave Fordham in 1994 to become a federal judge in the Southern District of New York, on the recommendation of Senator Patrick Moynihan.

3. A full-time faculty member for almost sixty years, Katsoris has cared deeply for students and graduates. He was a looming presence inside and outside my office throughout my deanship, reminding me always of the Jesuit heritage of the School and its obligation to serve others. As stated by him in his classic history of the Law School, "This commitment to service has been with Fordham since its first classes at the Rose Hill campus in the Bronx and has remained a guiding light in the halls of each new building from lower Manhattan to Lincoln Center." Constantine N. Katsoris, "In the Service of Others: From Rose Hill to Lincoln Center," *FLR* 82, no. 4 (2014): 1536.

4. This dean's report paid tribute to Teclaff with a profile of his life, describing his government service to Poland, and his arrival in the United States with his wife, Eileen, in 1952.

5. See Joseph W. McGovern, "Dedication Joseph A. Doran — Professor Extraordinaire," *FLR* 69 (2001): 1231.

6. See John D. Feerick, "A Tribute to Joseph W. McGovern," *FLR* 70 (2002): 1535–42.

7. Denno came to Fordham Law with a background in sociology and would render outstanding contributions in the area of appropriate criminal justice punishment.

8. See Shelley, *Fordham, A History*, 349–53, as to McGinley's towering leadership of Fordham, including the Lincoln Center campus.

9. See John D. Feerick, "Dedication to Professor Edward Yorio," *FLR* 60 (1992): 803–13.

10. See Warren E. Burger, "The Special Skills of Advocacy: Are Specialized Training and Certification of Advocates Essential to Our System of Justice?," and "The Decline of Professionalism," in *The John F. Sonnett Memorial Lectures at Fordham University School of Law: A Half-Century of Advocacy and Judicial Perspectives*, ed. Dennis J. Kenny and Joel E. Davidson (New York: Fordham University Press, 2018), 53–67, 68–76.

11. Professor Smith, following my tenure as dean, joined the faculty of DePaul University College of Law.

Index

JOHN FEERICK is a professor of law at Fordham Law School and the occupant of the Sidney C. Norris Chair of Law in Public Service. He teaches and writes in areas of the Constitution, legal ethics, and conflict resolution. His books include the third edition of *The Twenty-Fifth Amendment: Its Complete History and Applications*, and *From Failing Hands: The Story of Presidential Succession*, which was helpful to the framers of the Constitution's Twenty-Fifth Amendment.

MONSIGNOR THOMAS J. SHELLEY, a priest of the Archdiocese of New York, is Emeritus Professor of Church History at Fordham University. His publications include *The Bicentennial History of the Archdiocese of New York: 1808–2008* and *Fordham, A History of the Jesuit University of New York: 1841–2003* (Fordham).

Printed and bound by CPI Group (UK) Ltd, Croydon, CR0 4YY

13/04/2025

14656496-0001